Charles Wilkes and
the Exploration of
Inland Washington Waters

ALSO EDITED BY RICHARD W. BLUMENTHAL
AND FROM MCFARLAND

*With Vancouver in Inland Washington Waters:
Journals of 12 Crewmen, April–June 1792* (2007)

*The Early Exploration of Inland Washington Waters:
Journals and Logs from Six Expeditions, 1786–1792* (2004)

Charles Wilkes and the Exploration of Inland Washington Waters

Journals from the Expedition of 1841

Edited by
RICHARD W. BLUMENTHAL

McFarland & Company, Inc., Publishers
Jefferson, North Carolina, and London

LIBRARY OF CONGRESS CATALOGUING-IN-PUBLICATION DATA

Charles Wilkes and the exploration of inland Washington waters : journals from the expedition of 1841 / edited by Richard W. Blumenthal.
    p.   cm.
Includes bibliographical references and index.

ISBN 978-0-7864-4316-1
softcover : 50# alkaline paper ∞

1. United States Exploring Expedition (1838–1842)
2. Scientific expeditions — History — 19th century.
3. Ethnological expeditions — History — 19th century.
4. Voyages around the world — History — 19th century.
5. Wilkes, Charles, 1798–1877 — Diaries. 6. Explorers — United States — Diaries. 7. Sailors — United States — Diaries.
8. Seafaring life. I. Blumenthal, Richard W., 1946–
Q115.C74   2009   917.97'7042 — dc22   2009017943

British Library cataloguing data are available

©2009 Richard W. Blumenthal. All rights reserved

No part of this book may be reproduced or transmitted in any form or by any means, electronic or mechanical, including photocopying or recording, or by any information storage and retrieval system, without permission in writing from the publisher.

On the cover: American naval officer and explorer Charles Wilkes; chart of Elliott Bay; map background ©2009 PicturesNow

Manufactured in the United States of America

McFarland & Company, Inc., Publishers
  Box 611, Jefferson, North Carolina 28640
    www.mcfarlandpub.com

Table of Contents

Preface	1
1. Wilkes' Narrative	3
2. Charles Wilkes' United States Exploration Expedition: Instruments and Methods	51
3. Oregon Territory, Strait of Juan de Fuca	70
4. Volume XXIII Charts	112
5. The Journal of Augustus L. Case	131
6. George Colvocoresses: Four Years	156
7. The Journal of Acting Master George T. Sinclair	167
8. The Journal of Joseph Perry Sanford	197
9. The Journal of James Alden	215
10. The Journal of Samuel B. Elliott	225
11. The Narrative of Joseph B. Clark	242
12. The Journal of Purser R. P. Robinson	250
13. Private Notes of J. W. W. Dyes	263
14. The Journal of Charles Erskine	268
Appendix: List of Officers and Men Attached to the United States Exploring Expedition	275
Bibliography	303
Index	305

Nothing can exceed the beauty of these waters, and their safety: not a shoal exists within the Straits of Juan de Fuca, Admiralty Inlet, Puget Sound, or Hood's Canal, that can in any way interrupt their navigation by a seventy-four gun ship. I venture nothing in saying there is no country in the world that possesses waters equal to these.

—*Charles Wilkes*

Preface

This text is a natural follow-up to *The Early Exploration of Inland Washington Waters: Journals and Logs from Six Expeditions, 1786–1792* (2004), and *With Vancouver in Inland Washington Waters: Journals of 12 Crewmen, April–June 1792* (2007). The first book traced the exploration of John Meares, the Spanish and George Vancouver from 1786 to 1792 and included their journals. The second presented the journals of Vancouver's men. This text is about the next major exploration to inland Washington waters, that of Charles Wilkes and the U.S. Exploring Expedition in 1841.

I began collecting journals of the expedition shortly after completing the first two books, spending many weeks attempting to decipher the microfilm copies at the National Archives in Seattle. I followed this activity with a week in the National Archives in Washington, D.C., where the curators provided me access to the original journals. Just handling these historical documents with their stained and water-marked pages rendering the handwriting unintelligible in places, the nearly rotten bindings that were cracked and worn from age, and the musty smell created a sense of awe. I could almost envision the officers and crew retiring to their scant accommodations on board or in a tent each evening to jot a few lines.

As was the case with the journals published in the first two books, each journal posed questions, sometimes answered by reviewing another, sometimes not. The exploration of Admiralty Inlet south into Puget Sound is generally clear. That is, usually, it is easy to determine the location of the explorers. That is not the case with the San Juan Islands where documentation of the exploration is wanting. Much of it was accomplished late in Wilkes' visit to the waters of inland Washington. For whatever reason, details are unfortunately missing from the journals.

As in the first book, I have concentrated on the origination of place names. When a location was formally named, I included this "cite" in bold small caps. As will be seen, Wilkes named many locations which were later changed by the British explorer Captain Henry Kellett aboard H.M.S. *Herald*. Kellett surveyed the islands in 1846, five short years after Wilkes. While it appears that Kellett ignored Wilkes' names, in fact, Wilkes' chart of the San Juan Islands was not available to the British Admiralty until Kellett's charts were ready for publication. Thus, Kellett had no reference and provided his own names, generally honoring the earlier Spanish explorers. The first American survey after Wilkes was performed by James Alden in 1853, an original member of the Wilkes Expedition. Alden adopted most of Kellett's names, restored or provided additional Spanish names, and included some of Wilkes' on his charts. Additional British exploration from 1858 to 1865, a period where there was virtually no American exploration in the area, added more names, particularly to the channels and harbors. Similarly, these names were generally adopted by the Americans.

I would appreciate receiving comments, criticisms, corrections, and so on, and may be reached through the publisher.

Richard W. Blumenthal
Bellevue, Washington
July 2009

1

Wilkes' Narrative

Charles Wilkes was born April 3, 1798, in New York City. He was the youngest of three sons and one daughter born to John Deponthieu Wilkes and Mary Seton. Upon the death of his mother in 1801, Wilkes was cared for by various female relatives and friends among which was his aunt, Elizabeth Seton, canonized by Pope Paul VI in 1975 as the first Roman Catholic American saint and for whom Seton Hall University was named. Educated at various boarding schools, Wilkes entered the merchant service in 1815 and over the course of the next few years saw service on several ships. On January 1, 1818, he received an appointment as a midshipman in the U.S. Navy and was assigned to the *Independence* in Boston commanded by Captain William Bainbridge. He then saw duty on the *Guerriere* (1818–1819), *Franklin* (1821–1822), *Waterwitch* (1822–1823), and *O'Cain* (1823). Returning to New York, he prepared for his lieutenant's examination and was promoted on April 28, 1826. Just two days earlier, he married Jane Renwick, a childhood friend. For the next several years, he continued his studies, mostly in hydrography. At one time, he was tutored by Ferdinand Hassler, the first superintendent of the U.S. Coast Survey. Later, he studied with Nathaniel Bowditch, author of the *New American Practical Navigator*.

The United States Exploring Expedition of 1838–1842 was authorized by an Act of Congress in 1828. The resolution allowed the president to send a public ship to explore the Pacific coast, islands, harbors, shoals and reefs. However, a special appropriation was not included. Wilkes volunteered for duty with the expedition and drew up a list of required instruments. Unfortunately, due to a lack of funding, interest waned.

Wilkes was next assigned to the *Boston* (1830), transferred to the *Fairfield* (1830–1831) and then placed on leave awaiting orders, a typical event in the peacetime navy. He renewed his academic interests and in 1833 took charge of the Depot of Charts and Instruments in Washington, D.C., the predecessor to the Navy Hydrographic Office and today's Navy Oceanographic Office.

On May 14, 1836, Congress passed an appropriation to the Naval Appropriation Bill authorizing the president, then Andrew Jackson, to "send out a surveying and exploring expedition to the Pacific Ocean and South Seas." The Honorable Mahlon Dickerson, Secretary of the Navy, was responsible for outfitting the Expedition. He requested that Wilkes prepare an equipment list and arrange for the purchase in Europe of items that were needed. Wilkes left in August 1836 and returned the following January to find the preparations for the Expedition in disarray. Although hoping for an assignment, he decided to distance himself from the chaos, and spent the next year in survey activities along the east coast.

Wilkes was not the first choice for command. Thomas Ap Catesby Jones resigned in disgust over delays from the Secretary of the Navy. The command was then offered to Commodore Shubrick who declined. Next it was offered to captains Kearney and Gregory who also declined. On March 20, 1838, Secretary of War Joel R. Poinsett offered command of the Expedition to Wilkes. President Van Buren approved the selection on April 20. Needless to say, there were a considerable number of protests with the command assigned to such a junior officer in the Navy. Of Wilkes' approximately 40 counterparts, 38 had more sea experience. However, because this was intended to be an exploration as opposed to a military expedition, some of the resentment declined. Wilkes immediately set out to select his officers, crew and scientists, and to outfit the ships.

J. K. Paulding, the new Secretary of the Navy, identified the objectives in a letter dated August 11, 1838: "...purpose of exploring and surveying the sea, as well to determine the existence of all doubtful islands and shoals, as to discover and accurately fix the position of those which lie in or near the track of our vessels in that quarter, and may have escaped the observation of scientific navigators."[1]

Wilkes had at his disposal the sloops of war *Vincennes* and *Peacock* and the brig *Porpoise*. *Vincennes*, launched in 1826, drew 700 tons and was 127 feet in length, and *Peacock* drew 559 tons, was 118 feet in length and originally constructed in 1828. *Porpoise*, launched in 1836, drew 224 tons and 88 feet. *Peacock* was lost in 1841 off the Columbia bar, but all hands were saved. As a replacement, Wilkes purchased the merchant brig *Oregon* (250 tons and 85 feet in length). In addition, the store ship *Relief* (468 tons, 109 feet), and the tenders *Sea Gull* (110 tons, 73.5 feet) and *Flying Fish* (96 tons, 70.25 feet in length) were subsequently added. *Sea Gull* was lost with all hands off the Chilean coast in mid–1839.

The squadron departed the east coast Saturday, August 18, 1838. The ships sailed to South America and surveyed the coast. In late February 1839,

---

[1]Wilkes' Narrative, Vol. 1, p. xxv.

they departed for the first Antarctic expedition. By July, the fleet headed for the western Pacific where a survey commenced, followed by a second Antarctic expedition early the next year. By March 1840, the ships began exploration of Australia and New Zealand, followed by Fiji in May, and Hawaii in September. Departing Hawaii on April 5, 1841, the *Vincennes* and *Porpoise* arrived at Cape Flattery on April 29, surveyed Puget Sound and departed Washington waters in early August. The fall was occupied by surveys of the Columbia River and San Francisco Bay. By mid–November, Wilkes returned to Hawaii but departed ten days later for west Pacific surveys.

Wilkes returned to the east coast on June 10, 1842, with a wealth of data and scientific information including geological, botanical, zoological, anthropological and other materials. Even with the accomplishments, the return was anticlimactic. The Congressional attitude was unfriendly, the public, indifferent. Further complicating the situation were charges and counter charges between Wilkes and his officers regarding the treatment of the men. A court martial was convened, and Wilkes was found guilty of a single charge — ordering punishment more harsh than what was legal. Although reprimanded, on August 1, 1843, he was placed in charge of the extensive collections and made responsible for documenting the findings. The collections were initially displayed in the Patent Office in Washington, D.C., construction of which was completed in 1840, and moved to the Smithsonian in 1857. During the intervening years, Wilkes published his Narrative in early 1844 in five folio volumes and an atlas, but spent the next seventeen years supervising the publication of fifteen additional volumes and nine atlases devoted to specimens collected by scientists, and information from his crew.

Wilkes was promoted to Commander on July 13, 1843, and to Captain on September 14, 1855. Wilkes' wife died in 1848. In 1854, he married Mary Lynch Bolton. He returned to active duty in 1861 during the Civil War. In command of the *San Jacinto*, Wilkes intercepted the British mail steamer *Trent* and took prisoner two Confederate commissioners, en route to England. While American reaction was euphoric, the English were outraged. To avoid war with Great Britain, President Lincoln released the prisoners. On September 8, 1862, Wilkes received an acting appointment to rear admiral. During the following two years, he continued to alienate his superiors. Again court martialed, he was found guilty on April 26, 1864, of disobedience of orders, insubordinate conduct, disrespectful language, disobedience to a general order or regulation, and conduct unbecoming an officer. He was given a three-year suspension and a public reprimand. However, late that year, President Lincoln reduced the penalties. In August 1866, Wilkes was promoted to rear admiral and placed on the retired list.

In 1865, Wilkes purchased property in North Carolina and established an iron works. Despite his frantic attempts, the endeavor was unsuccessful and he was forced to sell in 1874. During the early 1870s, he became involved again with the Navy to finish the volumes on hydrography and physics, the latter of which was never published. Discouraged and in poor health, Wilkes died in his home in Washington, D.C., on February 7, 1877. He is interred at Arlington National Cemetery.

Wilkes' Narrative is based upon his handwritten journal as well as those of his officers and crew. In some instances, notes from his personal journal provide additional information not contained in the Narrative, and vice versa. Although the text below is primarily from the Narrative, a few notes from the journal are also included (journal entries are separately identified).

[Narrative, Vol. 4, p. 294] During the night I took into consideration the loss of time that must arise from awaiting an opportunity to cross the bar,[2] and after due reflection came to the conclusion that it would be better to proceed at once to the Straits of Juan de Fuca, and there begin my work on this coast. At daylight, therefore, (bearings of the cape had been taken the night previously and our position carefully calculated, and a course steered to run along the coast), I spoke the *Porpoise*, and immediately bore away to the northward. Signal was then made to her to follow. Both vessels then proceeded at the rate of eight or ten miles an hour.

The weather was very thick, and the wind south-southwest. At ten o'clock the *Porpoise* was close under our lee-quarter. I was myself below, when I was informed by the officer of the deck that we had entered disturbed water. A number of birds were around the vessels, and a cast of the lead gave fifteen fathoms. By the time I reached the deck, land was seen through the haze, close aboard. [p. 295] The ship was at once brought by the wind and all the studding-sails taken in.

The same discovery was made on board the *Porpoise*, and she was in the act of communicating it by signal. Neither of the vessels now had much water under their keels, and both were in imminent danger. We owed our safety to the good qualities of the vessels, which were on this occasion very evident, and to the conduct of the officers and crew, whose promptness and attention to the execution of the orders deserve my highest praise, and reflect great credit on their discipline.

Our situation caused me much anxiety for a short time; and this was one of the many hair-breadth escapes from wreck, incident to this cruise. The difficulty of our position was enhanced by the heavy sea we had to encounter, into which the vessels plunged so heavily as to endanger our spars. The same cause had prevented us from bending the chain cables, so

---

[2]Originally Wilkes intended to first visit the Columbia River.

that we had no means of anchoring until after we had passed the most dangerous points.

We had several casts of the lead in five, six, seven, eight, and nine fathoms.

In examining into the cause of our being found so unexpectedly in this position, I am led to believe that there is a current that sets upon the coast: and in this I was confirmed by trials made afterwards.

Soon after we were out of danger, it cleared up sufficiently to give us a view of the land, which proved to be Point Grenville of Vancouver, and Destruction Isle. The latter is easily known by some remarkable perforations through a rock near it.

Near Point Grenville, several accidents have happened, both to English and Russian vessels; and a boat's crew belonging to one of the latter, was inhumanly massacred by the Indians.[3]

It was also near this spot, that the very remarkable occurrence of the wreck of a Japanese junk happened in the year 1833. The officers of the Hudson Bay Company became aware of this disaster in a singular manner. They received a drawing on a piece of China-paper, in which were depicted three shipwrecked persons, with the junk on the rocks, and the Indians engaged in plundering. This was sufficient to induce them to make inquiries; and Captain M'Niel was dispatched to Cape Flattery to obtain further information, and afford relief, should it be needed.

He had the satisfaction to find the three Japanese, whom he rescued from slavery; and the Hudson Bay Company with the characteristic liberality, sent them to England. Thence they took passage to China, where I understand they still remain, in consequence of their being unable to obtain a passage to Japan.[4]

[p. 296] As a memorial of this extraordinary incident, porcelain of Japanese manufacture, which was purchased from the Indians who plun-

---

[3]Wilkes referenced massacres to Spanish and English vessels near Destruction Island. On July 14, 1775, Spanish Captain Juan Francisco de la Bodega y Quadra aboard the *Sonora* dispatched crew ashore for wood. All were killed by local Indians. Quadra named the island Isla de Dolores or Island of Sorrows. Captain Charles W. Barkley of the *Imperial Eagle* had a similar experience. He sent a crew ashore to explore the Hoh River. All six were killed. Barkley named the river Destruction River. Eventually, it was renamed for the Indians living at its mouth and the name Destruction was moved to the island.

[4]Wilkes' information is slightly incorrect due to misrepresentations of the actual events. The *Hogun-maru* departed the Japanese port of Toba on October 11, 1832, but was disabled by a typhoon. Its crew of fourteen drifted in the currents across the Pacific and landed near Point Grenville sometime between February and May of 1834. By that time, there were only three survivors who were taken captive by the Indians. Captain McNeil aboard the *Llama* rescued two in late May or early June. Arrangements were later made for the third.

dered the junk, was seen in possession of Mr. Burnie, the agent of the Hudson Bay Company, at Astoria.

On the 29th and part of the 30th, [April 1841] we had light airs and calms, so that we made little or no progress. In the afternoon of the 30th, the breeze freshened and carried us briskly to our destination. While thus proceeding, a large canoe, containing about twenty Indians, endeavoured to board us; but I was too anxious to reach an anchorage to regard their desires.

I was in hopes that the wind would continue fair, and enable us to have reached NEAH HARBOUR ere night; but as we approached Cape Flattery and opened the Straits of Fuca, it became contrary. We were therefore compelled to pass the night, which proved dark and rainy, under way. We had but little knowledge of the dangers that might surround us; but our frequent tacks throughout the night showed us that but few existed at the mouth of the straits.

The coast of Oregon, to the south of Cape Flattery, is rocky, much broken, and affords no harbours, except for very small vessels. It may therefore be considered as extremely dangerous, and particularly on account of its outlying rocks. The soundings on this coast, however, I afterwards discovered, may serve as a sure indication by which danger may be avoided, and safety may be insured by not approaching the coast into soundings of less than seventy fathoms.

On the morning of the 1st of May, we found ourselves well into the straits; and as I proposed to defer the survey of this part of them until my return, we hastened to reach Port Discovery, where we anchored at half-past 6 P. M. on the 2nd of May; just forty-nine years after Vancouver, pursuing the track of De Fuca, had visited the same harbour.

The Straits of Juan de Fuca may be safely navigated. The wind will for the greater part of the year be found to blow directly through them, and generally outwards: this wind is at times very violent. The shores of the strait are bold, and anchorage is to be found in but few places. We could not obtain bottom in some places with sixty fathoms of line, even within a boat's length of the shore.

The south shore is composed of perpendicular sandy cliffs, that run back into high and rugged peaks, and is covered with a forest of various species of pines, that rises almost to the highest points of the range of mountains. The highest points themselves are covered with snow; and among them Mount Olympus was conspicuous, rising to an altitude of eight thousand one hundred and thirty-eight feet.[5]

---

[5]Actual height is 7,965 feet according to the National Park Service. It is the highest peak in Washington's Olympic range.

[p. 297] The north shore is rocky, and composed, as far as we could examine it of conglomerate, and in some few places of a reddish granite.

In the morning we were boarded by a large canoe, with Indians who spoke a few words of English; and we had occasion to notice the wide difference between them and the Polynesians, both in language and appearance. No contrast can be more striking than this. They seemed to have scarcely any idea of decency, and to be little less elevated in their moral qualities than the Fuegians.

The principal man of the party was dressed in a coarse coat of red cloth, with the Hudson Bay Company's buttons, and corduroy trousers. He had neither shirt, shoes, nor hat, although the rain was falling fast. The others were habited in blankets or skins, and wore conical grass hats, resembling in shape those of the Chinese.

The first inquiry was, whether we were Boston or King George's ships, by which terms they distinguish Americans and English.

They brought with them for sale some fish and a few furs. On the latter they appeared to set a high value, and were not a little disappointed when they learned that we had no desire to purchase them. They readily parted with their fine fish for a few fish-hooks and a little tobacco.

These Indians were short, thick-set, bow-legged, muscular, and seemed capable of enduring great fatigue. The most obvious peculiarity was the shape of their heads, which appeared to have been compressed, both before and behind, so as to give them the form of a wedge. Their cheek-bones were high, and their eyes, which were fine, were set wide apart: their colour was a light copper. The oblique eye of the Chinese was not uncommon, and they had long flowing hair: aquiline or Roman noses were prevalent. Their countenances wore an expression of wildness, and they had, in the opinion of some of us, a melancholy cast of features.

It was amusing to us, who had no very exalted opinion of the Feejeeans, to observe the contempt our prisoner Vendovi[6] entertained for these Indians, which was such that he would hardly deign to look at them.

They manifested little curiosity, which was not excited even by the appearance of a ship so much larger than any they could have before seen, armed and manned in a manner so superior to what is usual in the vessels that visit them for traffic.

They wore but few ornaments, and that on which they seemed to set the greatest value was a small silver tube stuck through the cartilage of the nose. A few of them had small brass bells suspended around the rim of their ears.

---

[6]Vendovi was a native chief of Fiji. Wilkes took him prisoner because of his activities associated with the massacre of crew members while visiting that island.

[p. 298] Their language was one of the most disagreeable we had yet heard full of gutturals, and the sounds *klick*, *kluck*, and *tsck*.

Late in the afternoon, we reached and weathered the low sand-point, called by Vancouver New Dungeness, and stood over for his Protection Island. We passed within less than a quarter of a mile of the point,[7] where we had three and a half fathoms water.

After passing that island, an extensive bay opened, on whose shores we saw the long poles mentioned by Vancouver, and represented in his book. The use of these he was unable to discover, but the Indians informed us that they were for the purpose of suspending nets for taking the wild-fowl that frequent these shores in great numbers. On these poles the nets are set up at night, at which time the geese search these grounds for food: fires are then lighted, which alarm the birds, and cause them to fly against the nets, by which they are thrown upon the ground, where, before they have time to recover themselves, they are caught and killed.

The description of Vancouver is so exactly applicable to the present state of this port, that it was difficult to believe that almost half a century had elapsed since it was written. The beautiful woods and lawns of Protection Island, in particular, exist unchanged. The lawns still produce the same beautiful flowers and shrubs, and although closely surrounded by dense woods, do not seem to have been encroached upon by their luxuriant growth, although there is no apparent reason why it should not long ere this have overrun them.

Our anchorage in Port Discovery was close to the shore, in twenty-seven fathoms water. It is a well-protected harbour, and very convenient of access, but the depth of water and the high precipitous banks, would almost preclude its being made the seat of a settlement.

The name of Port Discovery was given by Vancouver. It is eight miles long, two miles in average width, and its points, which terminate in low sandy projections, interlock each other. The shores are supplied with large quantities of shell-fish. Protection Island covers it completely to the north, and would render it easily defensive against the most formidable attack. The only objection to it as a harbour is that already spoken of, the great depth of the water, which in the middle is no where less than forty or fifty fathoms, and is often as much as sixteen fathoms close to the shore.

The Indians whom we found dwelling here are of the Clalam tribe. They occupy a few miserable lodges on one of the points, and are a most filthy race, so much so indeed that to enter their lodges is absolutely disgusting. They are no more than a few rudely-cut slabs, covered in part by coarse mats.

---

[7]Kanem Point.

[p. 299] There is no permanent settlement of Indians at Port Discovery, and during our stay we had visitors from the various neighbouring tribes. The two sexes of all who visited us were dressed almost alike, and can hardly be distinguished in external appearance from each other: both wear their hair long, and both are equally dirty. All the adults have their heads much flattened, which appears to be performed as it is among the more southern tribes, by compressing the frontal and occipital bones by several thicknesses of bark, until they become set, and the head takes a permanent shape.

Their children seem to give them but little trouble: in their infancy they are tied to a piece of bark, which is hung to a tree or pole, where it is kept in motion by a string fastened to the toe of the mother, as is represented in the wood-cut at the end of the chapter.

These Indians appear to have but few of the comforts, and barely the necessaries of life. They live principally on fish, shell-fish, the cammass-root, and potatoes. They have muskets and bows and arrows: the bows are short and small, but possess great strength, and are made of yew: their arrows are pointed with iron or bone.

They also possess large sheath-knives, which they procure from the Hudson Bay Company, in exchange for furs, and from the same source they obtain blankets. For these articles the Company has a regular tariff of prices, which however, is not adhered to when a Boston ship arrives. The natives are sufficiently alive to the advantages they derive from competition, and boasted that in such cases they frequently obtained four or five blankets for articles that usually bring them only one. It was the hope of so advantageous a traffic that caused so much satisfaction when we arrived, and the failure of this hope produced, as we have seen, no little disappointment.

They are not, however, wholly dependent on this trade for their clothing, for some of the tribes manufacture a sort of blanket from dogs' hair, which is substantially woven.

During our stay at Port Discovery, they supplied us plentifully with venison, ducks, geese, salmon, a large species of cod, flounders, herrings, and crabs. They also brought shell-fish, among which were the common clam, (the quahog of the Eastern States,) mussels, and small oysters.

Besides the ornaments we saw among our first visitors, some wampum-belts and strings of dentalium-shells were observed. They have a great passion for carved pipes for which they cultivate small quantities of a species of tobacco. They also smoke the leaves of the dwarf Arbutus mixed with their tobacco: these are powerful astringents, and are also frequently chewed.

[p. 300] The colour of the younger natives is almost white, so much so as to show the blush on the cheek; and some of the women would with difficulty be distinguished in colour from those of European race. The women are to be seen weaving mats, after the Chinese fashion, of bulrushes (Scirpus lacustris), which they place side by side and fasten together at intervals. These are used, as has been stated, to cover the framework of their lodges.

Instead of the silver tube which has been spoken of, the women have a white bone stuck through the cartilage of their noses. This is kept bright, and may be said to be the only clean thing about their persons. The whole burden of domestic occupation is thrown upon them, for the men are to be seen lounging about the whole day in the sun, and spend their nights in gambling.

The canoes of this region differ from any thing we have seen on the voyage. They are made from a single trunk, and have a shape that may be considered elegant, and which is preserved from change by stretching or warping by means of thwarts. The sides are exceedingly thin, seldom exceeding three-fourths of an inch, and they are preserved with great care, being never suffered to lie exposed to the sun, for fear of rents and cracks. When these do occur, the canoe is mended in a very ingenious manner; holes are made in the sides, through which withes are passed and pegged in such a way that the strain will draw it tighter; the withe is then crossed, and the end secured in the same manner. When the tying is finished, the whole is pitched with the gum of the pine. This is neatly done, and answers the purpose well.

Although the natives we saw at Port Discovery appeared to be a peaceable race, the neighbouring tribes are frequently at war, and spoke of scalping, and other exploits, as practiced by our own aborigines.

Apprehensive that difficulties similar to those we met with in the Feejee Group might possibly occur with these Indians, I deemed it expedient to issue the following order.

[p. 301] GENERAL ORDER

The undersigned informs the officers and crews under his command, that the duties upon which they are about to enter will necessarily bring them in contact at times with the savage and treacherous inhabitants of this coast; and he therefore feels it his duty to enjoin upon them the necessity of unceasing caution, and a restrictive and mild system in all their intercourse with them.

In my General Order of July 13th, 1839, my views are expressed fully respecting our intercourse with savages, and I expect that the injunctions therein contained will be strictly regarded.

With a knowledge that many of the misfortunes that have befallen previous voyagers on this coast, have arisen from an unrestrained and unguarded intercourse with the natives, he deems it important to order officers in charge of boats, and those having men under their direction, to make it their especial duty to govern them so as to avoid any disputes or maltreatment of the Indians, and that force is never to be resorted to but in cases of self-defence.

No officer or man will be allowed to visit the shore without arms; and boats' crews, when surveying or on other duty, will be furnished with such as are necessary for their protection.

CHARLES WILKES,
Commanding Exploring Expedition

U.S. Ship *Vincennes,*
May 1st, 1840

We remained at Port Discovery until 6th May, during which time we were employed in surveying the harbour and exploring the country. Our botanists had a large and interesting field opened to them, and there are few places where the variety and beauty of the flora are so great as they are here. Dodecatheon, Viola, Trifolium, Leptosiphon, Scilla (the cammass of the natives), Collinsia, Claytonia, Stellaria, &c., vied with each other in beauty, and were in such profusion, as to excite both admiration and astonishment. According to Mr. Brackenridge, the soil on which the plants grow consists of a light-brown loam, but the general character of the soil around Port Discovery is a thin, black, vegetable mould, with a substratum of sand and gravel.

The trees grow so closely that in some places the woods are almost impenetrable. The timber consists principally of pine, fir, and spruce. Of the latter there are two species, one of which resembles the hemlock-spruce of the United States: it has a very tall growth, and puts out but few, and those small, lateral branches. Some maple-trees [p. 302] grow in the open grounds and on the banks, but they are too small to be of any service to the settler. Several trees which we cut down to make spars for the *Vincennes,* proved, although healthy in appearance before they were felled, to be more or less defective: the wood was sound and compact on one side only, while on the other it was open-grained and fibrous.

Several of the officers made excursions into the woods after game. In these they found much difficulty, in consequence of the quantity of fallen trees, that lay crossing each other in every direction. No large game, however, was seen. Of birds, crows, robins, &c., were in abundance; and some beautiful specimens of land-shells (Helices) were obtained.

Soon after our arrival at Port Discovery, I dispatched an Indian with a letter to the fort of the Hudson Bay Company at Nisqually, at the upper end of Puget Sound, to request that a pilot might be sent me. My interview with the native whom I employed for this purpose was amusing. He appeared of a gay and lively disposition: the first thing he did, when brought into the cabin, was to show me a cross and repeat his ave, which he did with great readiness and apparent devotion; but he burst into loud laughter as soon as he had finished repeating it. He and I made many efforts to understand each other, but without much success, except so far as the transmission of the letter to Fort Nisqually, and the reward he was to receive on his return.

In the excursions of the officers, several burial-places were met with. The corpses are not interred; but are wrapped in mats and placed upon the ground in a sitting posture, and surrounded with stakes and pieces of plank to protect them from the weather and wild beasts.

On the 5th of May, the officers were all engaged in surveying, while I occupied one of the points as a station, where I made astronomical and magnetic observations. I found the latitude 48° 02' 58" N.: the longitude 123° 02' 07.5" W.[8]; the variation was 20° 40' E.

The temperature in the shade, was 55°.

[Journal Vol. 3, p. 57] 5th. May. I have been employed this day in making observations for Lat.—And Long., Variation, Dip, and Intensity on the Point near the Ship which I call CARR'S PT.[9] The rest of the officers of this Ship & *Porpoise* including her commander have been engaged completing the Survey of this Harbr. The weather uncommonly fine with a light Breeze from the N^d & W^d temperature 55° in shade. Many Indians about us lazy lounging & filthy combined with their gutteral language is enough to disgust any one without their fishy smell. They seem all well disposed & desirous of cultivating our good will.

Fish we have in abundance. Salmon, Cod, flounders, Clams, Crabs, oysters (small) duck, geese, Venison. The water to be had easily and plentifully at Carr's Point.

The number of natives resident in this Bay is quite large. I had them counted in their canoes at the time of meals & the numbers were [Wilkes failed to enter the number]. The women have a miner piece of bone stuck through the Septum of the nose about an inch long though peculiar in its appearance it has not that disgusting appearance that I had imagined it would have from the accounts I have read of it & appears the only clean article about their persons.

[p. 302] On the 6th of May, finding that the messenger whom I had despatched to Fort Nisqually did not return, I determined to proceed

---

[8] The latitude and longitude of Contractors Point is 48° 02' 48" and 122° 52' 22". Wilkes' position placed him on the western shore of Sequim Bay, equidistant between Blyn and Pitship Point or about 6½ miles to the west. The accuracy of his latitude is remarkable: about 600 feet!

[9] Named in honor of Lieutenant Overton Carr. The local name of Contractors Point endured.

towards that place without further delay. We therefore got under way at half-past ten, and beat out of Port Discovery: when then stood towards Point Wilson (of Vancouver), which forms one side of the entrance into Admiralty Inlet. Turning the point, we entered the inlet, and soon anchored in Port Townsend, on its northern side, in ten fathoms water.

[Journal p. 58] 6 May. An extremely fine day. At 10.30 got under weigh and beat out of Port Discovery and rounded the Point called by Vancouver Point Wilson and went in and anchored. Roads in 10 fathoms water sandy bottom. this is a beautiful Bay and has a long level beach with a Pond of Freshwater backing it and a run into the Bay where vessels may be supplied — the Point a low sandy one called HUDSON'S POINT[10] is bold to and may be passed about a ¼ of a mile in 10 fathoms from our anchorage Mount Baker shows over Hudson Point — a large Fleet might anchor and maneuver here, there is a Bluff that joins the beach abreast the ship the top of which slopes to the water and is a beautiful lawn here and there with groups of trees and to the N^d and W^d a fine copse of pine trees-upwards of 1000 acres all ready for the plough. The soil is a lighter sandy loam and exceedingly productive. the grass was several inches high & covered with flowers & wild strawberry plants in blossoms. We anchored at 5.30 having had very light winds. The distance from our anchorage in Discovery Port is not over 10 miles I think. At night made preparations for the survey of it.

[p. 302] Port Townsend is a fine sheet of water, three miles and a quarter [p. 303] in length, by one mile and three quarters in width. Opposite to our anchorage is an extensive table-land, free from wood, and which would afford a good site for a town.

The bay is free from dangers and is well protected from the quarters whence stormy winds blow. It has anchorage of a convenient depth; and there is abundance of fresh water to be had.

In the afternoon, we landed and examined the table-land. The next day we were engaged in surveying the bay, which we commenced at an early hour. Our base was measured on a straight and level beach, nearly a mile in length, upon the north shore. At the extreme west end of the bay, we found a lodge or two of Indians. In each of these, there were apparently three or four families; and they had a patch of potatoes growing.

The soil in this place is a light sandy loam, and appears to be very productive: it was covered with wild flowers, and strawberry plants in blossom.

From this point, Mount Baker is distinctly seen to the northeast, and forms a fine sight when its conical peak is illuminated by the setting sun.

---

[10]Named for crew member Lieutenant William L. Hudson.

On the 7th, we had completed the survey; but the wind coming up from the southward and eastward, which was contrary to our intended course, we determined to remain. At noon, there was a favourable change, when both vessels moved up about eight miles, and anchored in what I called PORT LAWRENCE.[11] This is just at the entrance of Hood's Canal, and gave us a view both of it and Admiralty Inlet. The weather was unpleasant, and the only duty that could be performed was that of dredging. Several new and interesting specimens were thus taken. The natives brought us fish and venison in plenty, besides geese and ducks.

On the morning of the 8th, we made the survey of Port Lawrence, beginning at daylight. This being completed, I took advantage of the tide making to get under way with a fresh breeze, and passed with both vessels as far as a small cove on the west side of the inlet opposite to the south end of Whidby's Island. Here we anchored before sunset, and I named it PILOT'S COVE[12] from the circumstance of having been here joined by the first officer of the Hudson Bay Company's steamer, commanded by Captain M'Niel, who on hearing of our arrival, kindly sent him down to pilot up the ship.

We were under way soon after daylight, taking advantage of the tide, and continued beating as long as it lasted. This was about two hours, by which time we reached another small cove. This was named APPLE-TREE COVE,[13] from the numbers of that tree which were in [p. 304] blossom around its shores. This cove answers well all the purposes of a temporary anchorage. Before the tide began to make in our favour, we had finished the survey of the cove. We again sailed, and at dark anchored under the west shore, near a fine bay; which the next day was surveyed, and named PORT MADISON.[14] This is an excellent harbour, affording every possible convenience for shipping.

The scenery of this portion of Admiralty Inlet resembles strongly parts of the Hudson river, particularly those about Poughkeepsie and above that place. The distant highlands, though much more lofty, reminded us of the Kaatskills. There were but few lodges of Indians seen on our way up; and the whole line of shore has the appearance of never having been disturbed by man.

The wind proved fair the same afternoon, and we passed up the inlet,

---

[11] Named in honor of James Lawrence, USN, famous for his battle cry: "Don't give up the ship!" Vancouver previously named this Oak Bay.

[12] The name Pilot Point survives. Named for meeting with the first officer of the *Beaver* in May 1841, who guided Wilkes to Fort Nisqually.

[13] Named for the crab apple trees which lined the bay.

[14] In honor of the president.

1. Wilkes' Narrative

taking the passage to the right of Vashon's Island, and finally, towards evening, anchored just below THE NARROWS[15] leading into Puget Sound, within a few yards of the shore and under a high perpendicular bank, in sixteen fathoms.

The shores of all these inlets and bays are remarkably bold; so much so, that in many places a ship's sides would strike the shore before the keel would touch the ground.

On the 11th of May, the morning proved calm, of which I took advantage to survey this part of the sound, which we accomplished before the afternoon, when the tide served us. At 3 P.M. we again weighed our anchors, but had great difficulty in getting beyond the reach of the eddy winds occasioned by the high banks. The scenery about this pass becomes very fine: on all sides are high projecting bluffs of sandstone, rising almost perpendicularly from the water, with a great variety of shrubs along their base. The tide, which runs through the narrows with great velocity, causes many eddies and whirlpools, through which a ship is carried with extraordinary rapidity, while the danger seems to be imminent. The *Porpoise* succeeded in entering the narrows first, and in a few minutes was lost sight of; the *Vincennes* entered, and seemed at first to be hurrying to destruction, with her sails quite aback. We were carried onward wholly by the force of the tide, and had backed and filled only once before we found ourselves in as spacious a sound as the one we had just left. This narrow pass seems as if intended by its natural facilities to afford every means for its perfect defense.

Twelve miles more brought us to the anchorage off Nisqually,[16] where both vessels dropped their anchors about eight o'clock. Here we found an English steamer undergoing repairs. Soon after we anchored, I had the pleasure of a visit from Mr. Anderson, who is in [p. 305] charge of the fort, and Captain M'Niel. They gave me a warm welcome, and offered every assistance in their power to aid me in my operations.

Nothing can exceed the beauty of these waters, and their safety: not a shoal exists within the Straits of Juan de Fuca, Admiralty Inlet, Puget Sound, or Hood's Canal, that can in any way interrupt their navigation by a seventy-four gun ship. I venture nothing in saying there is no country in the world that possesses waters equal to these.

The anchorage off Nisqually is very contracted, in consequence of the

---

[15]While this Narrative does not use a capital "N," Wilkes' journal (p. 60) of the expedition clearly reflects it as such.

[16]The British Hudson's Bay Company dispatched John Work and a company of 40 men to explore Puget Sound. In December 1824, they reached the Nisqually River. Fort Nisqually was built in 1833 by the Company.

rapid shelving of the bank, that soon drops off into deep water. The shore rises abruptly, to a height of about two hundred feet, and on the top of the ascent is an extended plain, covered with pine, oak, and ash trees, scattered here and there so as to form a park-like scene. The hill-side is mounted by a well-constructed road, of easy ascent. From the summit of the road, the view is beautiful, over the sound and its many islands, with Mount Olympus covered with snow for a background. Fort Nisqually, with its out-buildings and enclosure, stands back about half a mile from the edge of the table-land.

In the morning I found that the ship lay opposite to a small run of water, and finding the situation an agreeable one, the *Vincennes* was safely moored there, and the boats hoisted out.

Having arranged my plans, I proceeded forthwith to put so much of them as lay within my own means into execution: the *Porpoise* and boats were prepared for surveying, and the land parties organized. Other parts of my proposed plans depended on the co-operation of the *Peacock*. My instructions, for this purpose, to Captain Hudson had been prepared previous to our arrival. I had, also, been informed that the *Peacock* and *Flying Fish* had reached the Columbia river in safety; and this news, although it turned out to be untrue, was for the moment a source of congratulation.

The *Porpoise*, with two of the *Vincennes'* boats, under Lieutenant-Commandant Ringgold, were directed to take up the survey of Admiralty Inlet. The launch, first cutter and two boats of the *Vincennes* were placed under the command of Lieutenant Case, to survey Hood's Canal.* The land party intended to explore the interior, was placed under the command of Lieutenant Johnson of the *Porpoise*. With him were associated Dr. Pickering, Mr. T. W. Waldron of the *Porpoise*, Mr. Brackenridge, Sergeant Sterns, and two men. Eighty days were allowed for the operations of this party, which it was intended should cross the Cascade range of mountains, towards the [p. 306] Columbia, proceed thence to Fort Colville, thence south to Lapwai, the mission station on the Kooskooskee river, thence to Wallawalla, and returning by the way of the Yakima river, repass the mountains to Nisqually. (The orders are given in Appendix XII.[17])

The other party consisted of Messrs. Drayton and Waldron of the *Vincennes*, myself, and two servants. Our intended route lay across the country to the Columbia river. First, I proposed to visit Astoria, then Fort Vancouver, and the Willamette settlement, and to proceed up the river as

*For orders, see Appendix XI.

---

[17]This parenthetical in Wilkes' Narrative is correct but conflicts with his own footnote.

far as Wallawalla. From Astoria I proposed to send parties from the *Peacock* into the interior, and to set on foot the survey of the Columbia river, by means of her boats.

The establishment of an observatory also claimed my attention: a suitable site was found on the top of the hill, within hail of the ship. Here the instruments and clocks were landed, and put up in a small clearing, whence the trees had been cut in order to supply the steamer with fuel.

All these preparations occupied us until the 15th, when the brig was reported as ready, and sailed the same day. During the above interval I had the pleasure of visits from Dr. Richmond and Mr. Wilson, of the Methodist Mission, stationed at this place.

In returning the visits of Mr. Anderson and Captain M'Niel, I had an opportunity of seeing the so-called fort. It is constructed of pickets, enclosing a space about two hundred feet square, with four corner bastions. Within this enclosure are the agents' stores, and about half a dozen houses, built of logs, and roofed with bark. This fort was considered quite large when it was first established, but since it has become an agricultural post as well as a trading one, it is found to be too small. Its locality is also ill chosen, on account of the difficulty of obtaining water, which has to be brought from a distance of nearly a mile. I was informed that there was now little necessity for any sort of protection against the Indians, who are but few in number, and very peaceably disposed.

Mr. Anderson and Captain M'Niel both reside in the fort with their families: both are married to half-breeds, and have several fine children. After spending some time in conversing about my plans, Mr. Anderson was kind enough to show me his garden, which is in an enclosure just without the pickets. Here I saw peas a foot high, strawberries and gooseberries in full bloom, and some of the former nearly ripe, with salad that had gone to seed, three feet high, very large and thrifty.

Near by were to be seen fine fields of grain, large barns and sheep-folds, agricultural implements, and workmen with cattle engaged in the various employments of husbandry.

[p. 307] I also visited Dr. Richmond, who had been settled here for some months, and occupies a nice log house, built on the borders of one of the beautiful prairies. Here I found Mrs. Richmond and Mrs. Wilson, with four fine, rosy, and fat children, whose appearance spoke volumes for the health of the climate. This mission has but recently been established: so far as respects its prospects, they are not very flattering. I shall have occasion hereafter to allude to the operations of the missions, and shall therefore defer any farther remarks at present. The location of the mission-house, on the borders of an extensive and beautiful prairie, can scarcely be surpassed, and would be admirably adapted for a large settlement, if the soil was in any respect equal to its appearance. This is composed of a light-brown earth, intermixed with a large proportion of gravel and stones: it requires an abundance of rain to bring any crop to perfection, and this rarely falls during the summer months. At the season when we arrived, nothing could be more beautiful, or to appearance more luxuriant than the plains, which were covered with flowers of every colour and kind: among these were to be seen Ranunculus, Scilla, Lupines, Collinsia, and Balsamoriza (a small sunflower peculiar to Oregon); but the soil is quite thin, and barely sufficient for these in many places. The best land occurs where the prairies are intersected or broken by belts of woods, that have a dense undergrowth, consisting of Hazel, Spiræa, Cornus, and Prunus. On the borders of these belts are scattered oaks and some ash, arbutus, birch, and poplars, and in some places the yew is to be found; but the predominant character of the vegetation is of the tribe of Coniferæ, which seem to occupy large ranges of the country, and among which the cedar is found to attain a large size.

In connection with the Company's establishment at Nisqually, they have a large dairy, several hundred head of cattle, and among them seventy milch cows, which yield a large supply of butter and cheese: they have also large crops of wheat, peas, and oats, and were preparing the ground for potatoes. These operations are conducted by a farmer and dairyman, brought from England expressly to superintend these affairs. A few Indians are engaged in attending the flocks, and the Company's servants are almost exclusively employed as labourers.

I have mentioned these agricultural establishments as connected with the Hudson Bay Company, and they are in reality so; but as their charter precludes their engaging in these operations, another company has been organized, under the title of the "Puget Sound Company," the shares of which are held by the officers, agents, and servants of the Hudson Bay Company, and its officers are exclusively chosen from among them. Dr. M'Laughlin, for instance, chief officer [p. 308] and governor of Fort Vancouver, on the part of the Hudson Bay Company, is also a director of the Puget Sound Company, and has the entire management of its concerns: his salary is five hundred pounds.

The capital of the Puget Sound Company is five hundred thousand pounds, divided into shares of one hundred pounds each: only two hundred thousand pounds of this have been paid in. The operations of this Company are in consequence large: they began by making large importations of stock from California, and some of the best breeds of cattle from England; they have also entered into farming on an extensive scale, using as labourers the servants of the Hudson Bay Company, who are bound by their contracts to do all manner of service that may be required of them, even to the bearing of arms.

This Company have the supplying of all the forts and stations of the Hudson Bay Company on the west side of the American continent, and also furnish the Russian ports with grain, butter, and cheese: of the former article the Russians take about fifteen thousand bushels. It is also their intention, when they shall have succeeded in breeding a sufficient stock of cattle and sheep, to export hides, horns, tallow, and wool, to England, in the return ships, which now go home comparatively empty, as the furs occupy only a small portion of the capacity of the ship. In this way it may readily be perceived that they will be enabled to drive a profitable trade, particularly when it is considered how little care the cattle require in this territory, in consequence of the grass and natural hay which the soil affords at all seasons. It is the prospect of the advantageous results to be derived from these operations, that has induced the Hudson Bay Company to change their trading establishments into large agricultural ones. For some years previous to our arrival, they had not been able to meet their own wants, and at the same time fulfil their contracts with the Russians. They were therefore obliged to purchase from the settlers in the territory, as well as send to California, to procure the requisite quantity of agricultural products. A demand was consequently created for wheat, and all that could be raised in the Willamette settlements was bought for six shillings (seventy-five cents) a bushel, and paid for in drafts on their stores in goods, at fifty per cent advance on the first London cost. This gave an encouragement to the small farmers, that was fated to meet with grievous disappointment the next season; for the Company was able not only to meet their engagements, and their own wants, but had, besides, a surplus. The prices consequently would be merely nominal, unless raised by the influx of new settlers. Whether the latter cause had any effect in creating a market, I know not; but I [p. 309] understand that in 1842 some of the settlers fed their horses upon their finest wheat.

The scenery around Nisqually is very much enhanced in beauty by the splendid appearance of Mount Rainier, which lies nearly east of it; and from some of the open prairies there are three of these magnificent snowy peaks in sight. They are all nearly regular cones, with cleft tops, as though they had a terminal crater on their summit. I was exceeding anxious to make the ascent of one of these, Mount Hood; but owing to the non-arrival and loss of the *Peacock*, I found it impossible to do so.

On the 13th of May, Mr. Anderson was kind enough to present me with two bullocks for the crews, and a quantity of vegetables, for which we felt ourselves much indebted. A large supply of milk was also sent to us daily from the dairy, and many other little kindnesses and attentions were manifested.

To return Captain M'Niel's visit, I went on board the steamer, which is called the *Beaver*.[18] She is of one hundred and twenty tons burden, and fitted with a low-pressure engine, similar to those in use in the English boats. She was now very much out of repair, having been some years on this station. Her employment was to ply between the northern posts with supplies, and bring back the returns of the season's trade; at the same time trading at the different points with the Indians. Captain M'Niel is a native of Boston, and was extensively engaged in the northwest trade. He proved to be a serious competitor with the Hudson Bay Company in their business, and was in consequence bought off. He is now a trader in the Company's service, owning stock, and receiving a share of the dividends; to qualify him for which, it became necessary for him to become a naturalized British subject.

The steamer is ill adapted to the services on which she is employed for she consumes a large quantity of fuel, and has not sufficient capacity to carry as much as is necessary for her entire voyage. She is therefore obliged to stop at intermediate places to obtain a supply of wood, which must be cut by her own crew. She is fitted with a suitable armament, barricades, and boarding-nettings, which are deemed very essential on the northern coast, where the savage tribes are both hostile and numerous.

On the 17th, the boats left the ship under Lieutenant Case, Messrs. Totten, Colvocoressis, and May. I had by this time succeeded in establishing the observatory, and had ordered a log house to be built to perform the pendulum experiments, and another for the purposes of drawing, &c. These I purposed to use on my return from the [p. 310] Columbia river trip. Lieutenant Carr, with Lieutenant Budd and Mr. Eld, were left in charge of the duty connected with the observatory, as well as of the ship.

Knowing how much time is lost on boat expeditions by the use of grog, and the accidents that are liable to occur when a strict watch cannot be kept over it, I decided not to send any spirits with the party. I am fully persuaded myself, that that portion of the ration is unnecessary; but in order not to deprive any of the sailors of it who might deem it essential, I had the boats' crews called aft, and found that nearly all were in the regular habit of drawing their grog. I then offered to any who might wish to continue the use of that part of their ration, the option of remaining with the ship, and having their places in the boats supplied by others. There was no hesitation on the part of any of them: all wished to go; and all were willing to give up their spirit ration. I take this occasion to say, that all the

---

[18]The *Beaver* was built in England in 1835. She sailed around the Horn to the west coast where her engines were installed. She saw service for the Hudson's Bay Company until sold in 1874. She was converted into a tow boat and met her demise on the rocks in Burrard Inlet in 1889.

most laborious and exposed duty of the Expedition, was performed without the spirit ration, and I am well satisfied that it may be dispensed with without injury to any one, and indeed greatly to the benefit of the naval service.*

The land expedition, under Lieutenant Johnson, was finally ready. Few can imagine the chafferings, delays, and vexations, attendant upon the equipment of a land party in this region: the buying of horses from the Indians; the non-arrival of guides; the various equipments necessary for loading the horses, securing the loads to prevent injury to the horses' backs, and the loss of them, all consume much time, and need continual foresight. Through all these difficulties and perplexities, which were of a kind that most tries the patience, Lieutenant Johnson struggled. An Indian is not slow in perceiving your wants, and views the dilemmas in which you may be placed with a becoming sang-froid. Mr. Anderson's kindness had obviated many of these obstacles; but it was impossible to proceed without the aid of the Indians, who were always prone to recede from their bargains, under a feeling that they had not received enough. After the bargain was completed, and the price agreed upon, under the form of "potlatch," or "gift," the equivalent was always to be again treated for, and thus the price of the article or service was often very much enhanced. In dealing with these Indians, it was always necessary to feign a great indifference of manner, in order to obtain the article, and also in closing the bargain after the preliminaries are settled. [p. 311] They readily close when they think their customers indifferent, for fear of a competitor among themselves, and are not in the habit of forming a combination, as they show little or no confidence in each other, and are rather disposed to rivalry. As far as our observations went, the chiefs have little authority among them.

Having seen the other parties all off, or ready to start, our party for the Columbia river also set out. It was a strange cavalcade, for most of us were but sorry horsemen, and we had every variety of accoutrements, from the saddle and bridle to the bare back and halter. We were eight in number: Messrs. Drayton, Waldron, and myself, two servants, two Indians, and a Canadian guide, with four pack-horses. All the horses and the guide were kindly furnished us by the gentlemen at the fort, to carry us as far as Cowlitz Farms, about sixty miles distant, where we intended taking canoes.

*Since our return, Congress has reduced the spirit ration one-half: this is a good step, but its total abolishment would be a better one.

From the Cowlitz Farms, Wilkes took canoes down the Cowlitz River to the Columbia, then on to Astoria. His description of this expedition occupies more than one hundred pages in his Narrative. Upon his return to

Nisqually on June 23, Wilkes learned that surveys under the command of Ringgold and Case were progressing rapidly.

[p. 409] On my return to Nisqually, my first care had reference to our provision of bread. This I found to be so far expended as to make it necessary to economize it by every means in my power, if I wished to avoid its falling short. I therefore determined to attempt to have fresh bread baked. With this view I had an oven built upon a plan borrowed from the steam-holes of the Indians. The bottom of the oven was formed upon a stage of plank, and the shape of the superstructure was given by bending twigs of hazel. These were covered with a plastic clay, which was found in abundance in the neighbourhood. A dough-trough was hollowed out of the trunk of a large tree. When the oven and trough were ready, another difficulty was to be overcome, for we had no bakers. This was remedied, however, by the assistance of our stewards and cooks; and two sailors instructed by them were appointed to take charge of the bakery. We now began to bake daily, and succeeded so well after a day or two, that the whole ship's company was daily supplied with full rations of soft bread, causing an important saving in our store of sea-biscuit.

I learned, immediately upon my return, that the surveys under Lieutenant-Commandant Ringgold and Lieutenant Case, were making rapid progress. The former, with the force under him, had completed a large portion of Admiralty Inlet; the latter had finished Hood's Canal, and had returned to take up the survey of Puget Sound. A report having been made to me, that one of the eye-pieces of the theodolite had been lost in Hood's Canal, Lieutenant Budd was ordered to relieve Lieutenant Case, and the latter was despatched to search for it. Lieutenant Case proceeded in a boat well armed, and visited all [p. 410] the stations he had before occupied, and became well satisfied that it had been stolen. While looking for it, a canoe with three Toandos joined him, and on learning what he was looking for, they said it was among the Scocomish tribe, and gave a full account of its having been picked up by a woman who was sitting near when the box was opened. Lieutenant Case took one of the men with him up the canal, to point out the place; on reaching which, they proceeded to the chief's house, who was absent, but soon returned. Lieutenant Case asked him for the missing article; the possession of which being denied, he took the chief's gun, telling him it would be kept until the eye-piece was restored. After several fruitless attempts, it could not be obtained; for the woman, it was said, had taken it down the canal. The chief, however, promised to follow her, which he did the next day. The next morning Lieutenant Case was threatened with an attack by eight canoes, which he avoided by making sail down the canal, when they desisted from following him. During the day he met the chief returning. He had been to the Scocomish village, having heard that a girl there had something resembling it, as he said, but it proved to be a cologne-bottle.

Lieutenant Case, finding that his party was too small to attempt force, restored the chief his gun. He was afterwards informed that the chief's object in visiting the villages on the canal, had been to collect his warriors. After leaving the chief, they were followed by a canoe containing five of the largest and most muscular men he had seen; all of whom were armed, and apparently disposed for some mischief. Although satisfied that the eyepiece was among them, Lieutenant Case deemed it prudent not to risk an encounter with such unequal odds, and returned to the ship. He was desirous of being furnished with a larger force, in order to return and obtain the eye-piece; but believing that a message would be equally effective, Mr. Anderson, at the fort, was obliging enough to dispatch a warmessenger, to inform the tribe, that if it were not brought back, I would punish them.

Lieutenant Case's survey of Hood's Canal was very satisfactory. Its banks, as far as TSKUTSKA POINT,[19] do not exceed one hundred feet in height, and are formed of stratified clay, with a light gravelly soil above it, thickly covered with different species of pines. This is also the character of the eastern shore, for the whole extent of the canal; but the west and north shores above this point become more bold and rocky, with a deeper and richer soil, formed by the alluvial deposits from the Mount Olympus Range.

On entering the canal, they encamped near some Suquamish Indians, [p. 411] who had received as visitors a party of fifty Clalams, by appointment to gamble for blankets: They continued their games throughout the night.

At Tskutska Point, the canal divides in two branches; one taking a northerly direction, while the other pursues its course to the southwest. After leaving the Suquamish, they met the Toandos, a small tribe inhabiting the mountains; who, from their own account, are able to muster one hundred and fifty warriors.

Lieutenant Case reports them as the best-looking men they had met with. After passing further down the canal, they found the Scocomish tribe, who inhabit its southern end. These resemble in appearance the Toandos, with whom they are in close alliance, and have one hundred and fifty fighting men.

The canal was not found to terminate at the place where the examina-

---

[19]Spelled TSKUTSKO on Wilkes' chart. It is located on the southwest tip of the Toandos Peninsula; the name has endured.

tion of Vancouver ended; but, taking a short turn to the northward and eastward for ten miles, it approaches the waters of Puget Sound within a distance of two and a half miles. The intervening country is rough and hilly. From this point, Lieutenant Case had communication with the ship; and a supply of bread, of which he was in want, was sent to him.

At the southern extremity of Hood's Canal, there is a large inlet, called BLACK CREEK, by which the Indians communicate with the Chickeelees and Columbia rivers.

Before reaching the southern end of the canal, the rocky shore of the west side, near Mount Olympus, had gradually sloped into low land, with a thickly-wooded and good soil.

At the extreme end of the canal, there was also a wide creek, which had an extensive mud-flat at its mouth. This is the case with all the creeks that empty into these waters. The water in the centre of the sound is too deep for anchorage; but there are several good harbours, all of which surveys were made. They will be found in the Hydrographical Atlas.

There is plenty of water in the small harbours; and some few of them have water enough running into them to turn mills. There is no very great extent of country for cultivation, and the climate is very similar to that experienced at Nisqually. The survey being completed, the boats returned to the ship on the 3d of July [1841].

During this time we had been steadily employed at the observatory, and by the 4th I had completed the pendulum and astronomical observations.

Wishing to give the crew a holiday on the anniversary of the Declaration of our Independence, and to allow them to have a full day's [p. 412] frolic and pleasure, they were allowed to barbecue an ox, which the Company's agent had obligingly sold me. They were permitted to make their own arrangements for the celebration, which they conducted in the following manner.

The place chosen for the purpose was a corner of the Mission Prairie, before spoken of. Here they slaughtered their ox, and spitted him on a sapling supported over the fire, which was made in a trench. The carcass could thus be readily turned, and a committee of the crew was appointed to cook him. Others were engaged in arranging the amusements, &c. All was activity and bustle on the morning of the 5th, as the 4th fell upon a Sunday. Before nine o'clock all the men were mustered on board in clean white frocks and trousers, and all, including the marines and music, were landed shortly after, to march to the scene of festivity, about a mile distant. The procession was formed at the observatory, whence we all marched off with flags flying and music playing. Vendovi and the master-at-arms bringing up the rear. Vendovi was dressed out after the Feejee fashion. It was truly gratifying to me to see them all in such good health and spirits, not a man sick, and their cloths as white as snow, with happy and contented faces.

Had it not been for the want of news from the *Peacock*, and the consequent apprehensions in relation to her fate, I should have felt and enjoyed the scene much more than I did. But the continual feeling that the ship might have been lost on some coral reef, and the idea of the sufferings her officers and crew would, in such case, undergo, tended to repress all other thoughts. This anxiety was not only felt by myself, but the officers and crew partook of it in a great degree. It was impossible to conjecture her fate, yet her continued absence and detention beyond the time of her anticipated arrival, naturally excited many fears and surmises, which, as the time passed on, made each one more certain that some disaster had befallen them.

Two brass howitzers were also carried to the prairie to fire the usual salutes. When the procession reached Fort Nisqually, they stopped, gave three chears, and waited, sailor-like, until it was returned. This was done by only a few voices, a circumstance which did not fail to produce many jokes among the seamen. On reaching the ground, various games occupied the crew, while the officers also amused themselves in like manner. At the usual hour, dinner was piped, when all repaired to partake of the barbecue. By this time, the Indians had gathered from all quarters, and were silently looking on at the novel sight, and wistfully regarding the feast which they saw going on before them. At this time the salute was fired, when one of the men, by the name of Whitehorn, had his arm most dreadfully [p. 413] lacerated from the sudden explosion of the gun. This accident put a momentary stop to the hilarity of the occasion. Dr. Fox, who was on the ground, thought that amputation of the arm above the elbow would be necessary, but it was deemed better to delay it for a time. The wound was dressed as well as it could be, and a litter was made, on which he was at once sent, under charge of his messmates, to the ship. Men-of-war's men are somewhat familiar with such scenes, and, although this accident threw a temporary gloom over the party, the impression did not last long, and the amusements of the morning were now exchanged for the excitement of horse-racing, steeds having been hired for the purpose from the Indians.[20] This sport is always a favourite with sailors on shore, and in pursuit of it they had not a few tumbles, but fortunately none were seriously hurt. At sunset, they all returned on board, in the same good order they had landed.

All the officers, together with Mr. Anderson, Captain M'Niel, and Dr.

---

[20]Whitehorn survived but never recovered the use of his hand. He was discharged on a pension when the *Vincennes* returned home.

Richmond, dined with me at the observatory, and we were in hopes of having the company of Dr. M'Laughlin; but, owing to his having lost his way, he did not arrive until the following morning. He was gladly welcomed, and it gave us all great pleasure to acknowledge the attentions that had been heaped upon us by his order, and the kindness of the officers of the fort.

He paid me a visit on board, and felt greatly pleased with the ship, which was the first man-of-war he had ever been on board of. On his leaving the vessel, the yards were manned, and three hearty cheers given him by the crew, who were aware of his kindness in ordering them a supply of fresh provisions. He dined with us, and the next morning returned to the Cowlitz Farm, on his way back to Vancouver.

After the rejoicing were ended, the surveying party was again despatched to complete the survey of Puget Sound.

The height of Mount Rainier was obtained by measuring a base line on the prairies, in which operation I was assisted by Lieutenant Case, and the triangulation gave for its height, twelve thousand three hundred and thirty feet.[21]

While engaged in these duties, I noticed from a point of the prairie, the white cones of both Mount St. Helen's and Mount Hood very distinctly. These mountains all resemble each other closely, and appear in some points of view as perfect cones. They give great interest and grandeur to the scenery. Mount Rainier is at all times a very striking object from the prairies about Nisqually, rising as it does almost imperceptibly from the plain, with a gradual slope, until the snow-line is reached, when the ascent becomes more precipitous.

[p. 414] The ascent of these mountains has never been effected, but it was my intention to attempt it, if my other duties had permitted, as I was very anxious to get a view of their terminal craters. The absence of the *Peacock*, however, and the great amount of work necessarily devolving on the rest of the squadron, made it impossible for me to undertake this additional labour.

Around Nisqually there are many beautiful rides, and if there were any vehicles, they would be equally favourable as drives; for the country admits of a carriage being driven in almost any direction, within many miles of the fort.

The Company have as yet few fields enclosed, nor is it necessary that they should have, so long as the cattle are watched and penned in at night. The practice of penning is adopted, not only to protect the animals from the wolves, but to save the manure and apply it to a useful purpose. These

---

[21] The U.S. National Park Service reflects 14,410 as the correct height.

pens are about half an acre in size, and are enclosed with our Virginia fence, made of pine rails. They are moved once a week, which, in the course of the year, gives a fertilizing effect to a large piece of ground; and all those portions of it that have been poor and barren are thus brought readily, and at little expense or labour, under good cultivation.

On this farm there were about two hundred acres under cultivation, which I was informed would yield fifteen bushels of wheat to the acre, and it is intended to convert it into a grazing farm, for which purpose a stock of cattle was on its way from California, during the year of our visit.

It is estimated that three thousand sheep, fifteen hundred head of cattle, and about four hundred horses, may be maintained at this place. Mr. Anderson, a clerk of the Company, whom I have mentioned as being in charge of the post, receives no more than one hundred pounds for his superintendence.

The observatory duties being completed, I set out, with Lieutenant Budd and Mr. Eld, in three boats, to join the surveying party under Lieutenant Case.[22] Mr. Anderson accompanied us, on a visit to the Shute's River Falls, where we intended to take horses, to ride to the Bute Prairie, with some men, to open several of the mounds, to discover their contents, if they had any.

By the stupidity of the Indian guide, we took the wrong arm of the sound, and did not discover our error until we reached its extreme limit, where, as night overtook us, we were forced to encamp.

The next day, however, we reached the falls, which were insignificant, both in height and volume of water. This arm, which I have called BUDD'S,[23] is a fine harbour, nine miles in depth, and about half a mile wide.

[p. 415] After forming our encampment near by (which was surrounded by Seringias in full blossom), and giving Lieutenant Budd and Mr. Eld orders, Mr. Anderson and myself, with six men, set off for the Bute Prairie, with shovels and picks. We reached the place about five o'clock, through a rain which had wet the bushes and undergrowth so much, that in passing through the Indian trails, we were completely drenched. These bushes consisted principally of Rubus and Alder. On our route we passed several beautiful and secluded prairies, of excellent soil, and covered with many flowers. The men began their digging early in the morning. These mounds have been formed by scraping the surface earth together in a heap. The soil, therefore, is very rich, and they have a rank growth of vegetation

---

[22] At this point, Lieutenant Case completed the survey of Hood Canal and was assisting the survey of Puget Sound.

[23] Named for crew member Thomas A. Budd.

on them. Much of this rich earth or mould must have been brought from a distance. The regularity of their construction and shape, as well as the space over which they are scattered, are surprising. Although I could obtain no direct information respecting them, I was one day told that the medicine-man gathered his herbs from them, to make the decoctions with which he effects his cures.

Although all tradition concerning them may be lost, yet the custom of these medicine-men may have survived, and taking into consideration the influence they have had and still have over the tribes, it is possible that their predecessors might have had something to do with the formation of these monuments. They certainly are not places of burial. They bear the marks of savage labour, and are such an undertaking as would have required the united efforts of a whole tribe.

The hole, which was dug directly in the centre, was about four feet in diameter. At a depth of about six feet was found a kind of pavement of round stones, laid on the subsoil of red gravel. No articles of any description were discovered in the mounds, which seemed to be grouped in fives, as in the figure annexed.[24] Although there is a general resemblance among them, they evidently have been constructed successively, and at intervals of several years. I heard it suggested that they had been formed by watercourses, but this I view as impossible, for they are situated on a level prairie, and are at least a thousand in number.[25]

Observations for latitude and longitude were obtained here, but the weather did not permit me to get angles on Mount Rainier, as I was desirous of doing. The next day I parted with my friend, Mr. Anderson, who desired to return to Nisqually, while we returned to the falls. The ride was more disagreeable than we had before found it, and I felt heartily glad to get back to the surveying parties.

[p. 416] On the 12th [July 1841], at seven o'clock, we began our surveying operations, and after a hard day's work, joined Lieutenant Case's party, when I took charge of the whole. My force, which now consisted

---

[24] The thumbnail-sized sketch appears like the face of the five die, but with lines radiating from each die spot.

[25] The mounds, called Mima from the Indian name meaning "a little further along," originally occupied an area of twenty square miles. Because of development and agriculture, they have been reduced to 637 acres in Mima Mounds Natural Area Preserve, about twelve miles south of Olympia. The circular or elliptical mounds rise up to eight feet with a diameter of up to thirty feet. What caused them is still unknown. Some scientists theorize that they were created by the tunneling of northwestern Pocket Gophers. Some believe they were the result of seismic activities. Others think they formed from glacier thawing, refreezing and meltwater channels. Still others suggest they were created by Paul Bunyon!

of seven boats and their crews, was sufficiently strong to make rapid progress: the putting up of signals, the triangulation, and soundings, were all carried on at the same time. When we reached our encampment at night, the rough draft of our day's work was completed. We continued thus employed until the 17th, when we reached the ships, having completed the surveys of all the numerous branches of this sound: those all afford safe navigation for large vessels. The land is low, and well covered with various kinds of trees, among which the pine predominates: the other trees, consisting of spruces, oaks, arbutus, alders, and great quantities of seringias in full blossom, reminded me of our gardens at home. The perfume of the flowers scented the air for a long distance around. Some of the seringia-bushes were from twelve to fifteen feet high.

The soil is in some places good, but in others it is quite light and sandy. At the head of all the branches, there are extensive mud-flats, and some small patches of salt meadow. We did not meet with many natives: those who inhabit this region were probably employed in taking fish, and they seldom remain in any place beyond the time necessary for this purpose.

On my return to the ship, I found that Lieutenant Johnson had returned, with the party of which he had charge. I shall therefore give in this place an account of their journey, and the country through which they passed, referring the reader to my orders to Lieutenant Johnson, in Appendix XII., for the route intended to be passed over, and the duties to be performed. But before leaving Nisqually, I have a few words to say about its position, and the Indian tribe of that name.

The situation of Nisqually is badly chosen for trade, for the anchorage is of small extent, and only a few vessels can be accommodated within a reasonable distance of the shore. It would also be much exposed to the southwest winds, and the hill is an insuperable objection to its becoming a place of deposit for merchandise, as it would very much increase the labour and expense of transportation. The Nisqually fort or post was chosen, as I have been informed, before the Company had an idea of transporting any articles by water. It has, however, one great recommendation, in the ease with which water may be obtained from the stream that flows in abreast of the anchorage. Much better places than Nisqually could be found in this vicinity, for the locations of a town. There is one, in particular, just within KITRON'S [p. 417] ISLAND,[26] about a mile and half to the north of Nisqually anchorage, where the shore has a considerable indentation. There, although the water is deep, vessels would be proteted from the winds which blow most violently, from the southwest, southeast, and northwest,

---

[26] Named for William Kittson of Hudson's Bay Company. Wilkes spelled it Ketron in Volume 23.

and also from any sea, while Nisqually is not: this place is equally well supplied with water, and the hill is by no means so precipitous.

The spring tides were found to be eighteen feet, those of the neaps twelve feet. High water, at the full and change, at $6^h\ 10^m$, P.M. During the whole of our stay there was found to be a great discrepancy between the day and night tides, the latter not rising as high as the former by two feet.

The country in this vicinity is thought to be remarkably healthy, and on all these salt-water inlets, the winter is represented to be mild, and but of short duration. The mean temperature, six feet under ground, during our stay at the observatory, from the 20th of May till the 14th of July, was found to be 58.5°. I was not fully satisfied that this record gave correct results for the mean temperature of the climate, although frosts do not penetrate the ground, for by the same manner of trying it, and under almost the same circumstances, at Astoria, we obtained only 54°, although that place is a degree to the south of Nisqually.

The geographical position of Nisqually will be found in the tables. The greatest range of temperature was found to be 55°, the lowest 37°; and the mean, during the same period, 63–87°: the barometer standing at 29.970 in.

The Indians around Nisqually are few in number, and the whole tribe does not amount to two hundred, including men, women, and children. They belong to the tribes who flatten their heads, and are represented as vicious and exceedingly lazy, sleeping all day, and sitting up all night to gamble. So strong is the latter propensity among all these tribes, that it is said, that after parting with all their movable property, they will go so far as to stake their wives and children, and lastly even themselves for years of slavery.

Their clothing seldom consists of more than a blanket, a pair of skin breeches, and moccasins. Little or no distinction of rank seems to exist among them: the authority of the chiefs is no longer recognised, and each individual is left to govern himself.

They are addicted to stealing, and will run some risk to effect their object: thus, several blankets were stolen from the hammocks of our men while asleep in their tents, although a sailor was known to be on guard with loaded arms, only a few paces from the spot. Mr. Anderson informed me that he had employed several of them to till the land, [p. 418] but he found them disinclined to work, although he admitted they were more apt than he had anticipated. This tribe, so far as respects the ability of committing depredations on the whites, is quite harmless, and is rapidly thinning off through diseases contracted by a change of habits. They are all of a wandering character, and change their residences in search of their food, which consists principally of fish, particularly shell-fish. Clams are seen in great quantities among them, strung on sticks, upon which they have been preserved by drying and smoking. They also store up pounded salmon, and the cammass-root. In the fall and winter they are supplied with an abundance of game and wild-fowl, on which they then live; but they are not upon the whole well fed, as they are little disposed to exert themselves to procure a supply of food, when they are not in actual want. In the winter several families live together in their large board lodges: when the spring comes on they again break up, and resort in small parties to those places where they can obtain their food most easily. This tribe, as is the case with most of those in the territory, speak a peculiar language among themselves, but in communication with others they use the Chinook language.

As the spring is opening, small parties of these Indians may be frequently seen on their way, with their goods and chattels tied on their horse's back, or in small canoes, to the different cammass and fishing grounds.

During the salmon-fishery, vast shoals of young herring are seen, which the Indians take with a kind of rake attached to the paddle. The herring are used for bait for the salmon. Their hooks are made in an ingenious manner of the yew tree, and are strong and capable of catching the large fish. They are chiefly employed in trailing for fish. A species of rock cod is also abundant, some of which exceed fifty pounds in weight. Flounders are also to be had in great quantities.

Wilkes spent sixty pages describing the inland expedition of Lieutenant Johnson, which is not reproduced here.

[p. 477] When Lieutenant Johnson returned with his party, I was still engaged with the boats in completing the surveys of the remaining arms of Puget Sound. Orders had been left with Lieutenant Carr, to have the ships prepared for sea against the return of the surveying party; and on the evening of the 16th of July, when we reached the *Vincennes*, we found every thing ready for our departure.

Lieutenant Johnson was again ordered to fit out a party to proceed across the country to Chickeeles river, descend that river to its mouth, and make a survey of Gray's Harbour. The party, besides Lieutenant Johnson, was to consist of Passed Midshipman Eld, Mr. Brackenridge, Sergeant Stearns, three sailors, and two Indian guides. I had understood that the proposed route was practicable, although difficult and somewhat dangerous.

On the 17th, in the morning, we were prepared to sail; but the party of which Lieutenant Johnson was to take charge was not ready, that officer at the last moment declining to obey the orders, (on account of my directing the officer associated with him, Passed Midshipman Eld, to be consulted as to the propriety of abandoning public property, should it become necessary,) caused his arrest. These orders have been inserted in Appendix XIV., that all may be able to judge of their tenor. Passed Midshipman Eld was then ordered to take charge of the party, and Passed Midshipman Colvocoressis to accompany him.

We had already taken leave of Mr. Anderson and Captain M'Niel, and I have here to acknowledge the obligations we were under to them for many attentions, and particularly for the facilities they [p. 478] afforded us in the equipment of the land-parties, and the hospitalities they extended to both officers and crew.

The breeze sprung up at two o'clock, when the anchor was hove up and sail made. The change in the organization of the land-party delayed us for a short time, but the gentlemen whom I had appointed to it were ready in a few minutes, and left the ship, upon which we immediately bore away to the Narrows.

It is no more than justice to Messrs. Eld and Colvocoressis, to acknowledge the promptness and good spirit with which they undertook the duty thus unexpectedly assigned them, and I take the same occasion to state that the manner in which they performed their task, and overcame the many difficulties which impeded its execution, merit my warmest thanks.

It would be difficult to give the reader an idea of the anxieties that beset me at this juncture. Day after day had passed in the anxious expectation of receiving news of the *Peacock* and *Flying Fish*, until a conviction became general, with both officers and crew, that some serious accident had occurred to one or both of them, among the dangerous coral reefs and islands they had been sent to explore. They were now three months later than the time appointed for their arrival at the Columbia river.

For my own part, after reviewing the whole of the duties assigned to Captain Hudson in my instructions, and again estimating the time necessary to fulfil them, I could not but apprehend, from the length to which his voyage was protracted, that disaster had occurred. In this state of feeling, the officers of the *Vincennes* showed a highly commendable spirit, and aware that additional labours were thus to be thrown upon them, strained every nerve to avoid any further loss of time. The officers of the *Porpoise*, as I was informed by Lieutenant-Commandant Ringgold, manifested an equally praiseworthy spirit.

With the aid of both wind and tide, we succeeded in getting through the pass at the Narrows before dark, and when this was effected, I anchored under Vashon's Island for the night.

The next day we made but little progress, owing to light winds, and a strong tide against us.

On the 19th [July 1841], we anchored off Port Lawrence, and near the entrance to Hood's Canal, and on the 20th came to anchor in New Dungeness Roads, which I had assigned for a rendezvous with the *Porpoise*, which vessel joined us on the same day.

I shall now revert for a short time to the surveying operations, performed under instructions embraced in my orders of the 11th of May, which will be found in Appendix XI.

[p. 479] On the 15th of May, the *Porpoise* left Nisqually, and anchored the first night near the point where the surveys were to begin, but outside of the Narrows.

The first bay at the bottom of Admiralty Sound was termed COMMENCEMENT BAY.[27] Into this, the PUYALLUP,[28] a small river, which, it will be recollected, was passed by Lieutenant Johnson, ten or twelve miles from Nisqually, falls. Commencement Bay affords anchorage, and a supply of wood and water may be obtained. The Puyallup forms a delta, and none of the branches into which it is divided are large enough for the entrance of a boat. The Indians were at this season of the year to be found on almost all the points, and were the same filthy creatures that have been before described.

The *Porpoise* was engaged until the 20th in surveying Admiralty Sound to the end of Vashon's Island, and on the afternoon of that day, anchored in the Port Orchard of Vancouver.

Port Orchard is one of the most beautiful of the many fine harbours on these inland waters, and is perfectly protected from the winds. The only danger is a reef of rocks, which is nearly in the middle of the entrance. The sheet of water is very extensive, and is surrounded by a large growth of trees, with here and there a small prairie covered by a verdant greensward, and with its honeysuckles and roses just in bloom, resembling a well-kept lawn. The soil is superior to that of most places around the sound, and is capable of yielding almost any kind of production. The woods seemed alive with squirrels, while tracks on the shore and through the forest showed that the larger class of animals also were in the habit of frequenting them.

The next nine days were employed in surveying Port Orchard, which consists of two inner and an outer harbours. The former, although the entrance is by a strait not more than two hundred yards wide, is from two to six miles in width, and extends for a distance of fifteen miles. The water was found deep enough for the largest class of vessels, with a bold shore and good anchorage. Lieutenant-Commandant Ringgold made a set of magnetic observations here.

---

[27]Named as the starting point for the survey of Admiralty Inlet.
[28]Wilkes spelled this Pugallop in Volume 4 of his Narrative.

Near the anchorage were seen three canoes, propped on trees, containing the bodies of Indians. These were visited by Dr. Holmes, who procured a flathead skull. The bodies were found wrapped firmly in matting, beneath which was a white blanket, closely fastened round the body, and under this a covering of blue cotton. Near by, on stages, were boxes about three feet square, supposed to contain the articles which are deposited by the Indians near the bodies of the dead, and which were not disturbed.

[p. 480] Many Indians, who were all cheerful and well disposed, visited the port during the continuance of the survey.

Port Orchard was found to communicate, on the north, with Port Madison, which we had surveyed on our way up the sound. Lieutenant Maury, with the boats, surveyed this passage, and found that it had a depth of four and a half fathoms water at low tide.

Near this passage is a place where the Roman Catholic missionaries have established a station for teaching the surrounding tribes. A large cross is erected, and a building one hundred and seventy-two feet long by seventy-two wide, which was found to contain many rude images. Many of the natives are capable of saying their prayers and telling their beads, and some were met with who could sing some Catholic hymns in their own language.[29]

The Indians frequenting this port called themselves of the Je-ach-tac tribe.

On the 31st, the same meteor that was observed by the other surveying parties was seen. Its first appearance was at an altitude of sixty degrees. Its course was not directly downward, but zigzag, and it disappeared at an elevation of twenty degrees. Its track continued luminous for half an hour, and gradually changed its shape, becoming wider and less elongated. There was no explosion heard by any of the parties.

The next point visited and surveyed was Penn's Cove, between Whidby's Island and the main. This island contains many small villages, and appears to be more thickly peopled than other parts of the sound. It is in possession of the Sachet tribe, who have here a permanent settlement, consisting of large and well-built lodges of timber and planks, similar to those already described on the Columbia and elsewhere. The chief possessed a chest of valuables, carefully preserved in a corner, the contents

---

[29] Called "Old Man House," the structure was estimated by some sources to be 1,000 feet long by 60 feet in width. Wilkes' estimate of size is likely to be more accurate. It was located just north of the Agate Pass Bridge in Suquamish. Home of Chief Seattle and his sub-chief, Kitsap, the building housed several hundred people. Completed in 1815, it stood until 1870 when the government ordered it destroyed for health reasons. Chief Seattle died June 7, 1866, and is buried in the Saint Peter's Mission Cemetery of the Catholic Church in Suquamish.

of which were shown by him with no small pride, and consisted of a long roll of paper, on which were many representations of European houses and churches, together with rude sketches of the heavenly bodies, and a map of America. These had been given to him and explained by the Roman Catholic priest, and he seemed to understand the explanation. This whole tribe are Catholics, and have much affection and reverence for their instructors.

The priests of the Catholic mission made half-yearly visits, baptizing and leaving tokens among these Indians, and have done much good in promoting a good feeling among them. They were constructing a large building for a church, near which was erected a large cross.

[p. 481] Besides inculcating good morals and peace, the priests are inducing the Indians to cultivate the soil, and there was an enclosure of some three or four acres, in which potatoes and beans were growing. The Indians were also cultivating large quantities of potatoes, in a soil fertile and capable of producing every thing. Wild flowers were in abundance, and with strawberry-vines covered the whole surface. The fruit of the latter was large and of fine flavour.

The Sachet tribe are obliged to provide for their defence against the more northern tribes, by whom they are frequently attacked, for the purpose of carrying them off as slaves. For protection against these attacks they have large enclosures, four hundred feet long, and capable of containing many families, which are constructed of pickets made of thick planks, about thirty feet high. The pickets are firmly fixed into the ground, the spaces between them being only sufficient to point a musket through. The appearance of one of these enclosures is formidable, and they may be termed impregnable to any Indian force: for, in the opinion of the officers, it would have required artillery to make a breach in them. The interior of the enclosure is divided into lodges, and has all the aspects of a fortress.

Upon the whole, the tribe inhabiting Penn's Cove are more advanced than any others in civilization.

The only spring found here was one of a mineral character, forming a deposition on every thing around.

On the main, there is much good land.

Near the harbour of Port Gardner, a fine stream[30] empties itself into Possession Sound, by four mouths. The water was not found to be sufficiently deep in any of these to admit boats at low water, in consequence of a bar or flat extending across the mouths.

Here they were surrounded by many canoes, containing Indians from the various tribes to the southward, whom they had before seen. The dress

---

[30]Snohomish River.

of the Sachet does not vary much from that of the other tribes, and generally consists of a single blanket, fastened with a wooden pin around the neck and shoulders. Those who are not able to purchase blankets wear leathern hunting-shirts, fringed in part with beads or shells, and very few are seen with leggins. The women ornament themselves with small brass bells, or other trinkets. The cartilage of the nose is also perforated, and pieces of polished bone or wood passed through it. Although the dress of these natives would seem to offer some concealment to the body, few are seen that wear it with any kind of decency. Their persons are usually very filthy, and they may be said to be at all times coated with dirt. They are fond of wearing brass rings on their wrists and fingers, and a few are seen to be tattooed [p. 482] who have some lines upon the arms and face. They disfigure their bodies by the manner in which they daub themselves with red ochre, mixed with salmon-oil, which, besides being disgusting in appearance, is extremely so in smell.

Dr. Holmes, of the *Porpoise*, had an opportunity of examining some of their maladies. Pulmonary complaints are very common, and occasion great suffering. The diseases most often met with are bronchitis, and tubercular consumption. Rheumatic affections are also of frequent occurrence. Their treatment does not differ materially from that of the tribes in the interior, already described in speaking of their medicine-men. Cures are sometimes attempted by making use of hot and cold bathing in every case, and without discrimination. Dr. Holmes saw an old man in the last stage of consumption, shivering from the effects of a cold bath at the temperature of 40° Fahrenheit. A favourite remedy in pulmonary consumption is to tie a rope tightly around the thorax, so as to force the diaphragm to perform respiration without the aid of the thoracic muscles.

Intermittents are also common, from which they suffer much. Hot baths are invariably used for this disease, after which that patient plunges immediately into cold water, where he remains until chilled. A thorough shampooing then succeeds, and a few howls and incantations complete the treatment.

Notwithstanding they hold their medicine-men in great repute, both the patients and their friends were very grateful for any aid rendered by Dr. Holmes, and readily took every thing offered them.

The brig moved, on the 18th of June, to the northern outlet of Possession Sound, through Deception Passage. This was not believed by Vancouver to afford a passage for vessels; but, although narrow, it is feasible for those of small size. The tides rush with velocity through it, and there are some rocks in the passage. The Indians had moved from their village to temporary huts on the beach, where they seemed to enjoy themselves.

Lieutenant-Commandant Ringgold, being informed by the Indians

1. Wilkes' Narrative

that a passage[31] existed to the north into Bellingham Bay, boats were sent to explore it. The information proved to be correct; but the water was so shoal, that it is, at lowest point, almost a mud-flat; and the channel, besides, is tortuous. This duty being completed, the *Porpoise*, on the 26th, was moved through the passage, and anchored under one of the small isles at the entrance.

The Indians from various parts of Admiralty Inlet, were constantly around the brig, endeavouring to derive some advantage in the way of trade. They were found to occupy various points, each tribe [p. 483] keeping distinct. Their names were, the Scocomish, Suquamish, Clalams, and Sachets, who live in harmony with each other, although they do not scruple to call one another "peshac," or bad; but this epithet is invariably given to those of a different tribe by all the Oregon Indians. The term, however, is applied with greater force to the more northern tribes, who frequently undertake incursions on them, in strong marauding parties, for the purpose of obtaining slaves: they are, in consequence, held in great dread. During the stay of the brig, an alarm occurred, which produced much consternation among them. Many sought shelter in the woods; others went off to their strongholds, and some women sought shelter alongside the brig in their canoes.

These Indians suffer little inconvenience in their changes of residence; for, having but few chattels, they can remove at a few moments' notice; and after landing at an entirely strange place, they are at home the moment their fires are lighted.

The 4th of July was spent near Point Roberts; and on the 5th, the brig reached the mouth of Fraser's river, which is about a mile wide, with a serpentine channel, leading through an extensive mud-flat. Fort Langley, of the Hudson Bay Company, is situated about twenty miles from the mouth. The country immediately around is low, and has a rich alluvial soil. It is inhabited by the Nanitch tribe, who accompanied the brig thither from Birch Bay. The mouth of Fraser's river was found to be six miles north of latitude 49° N.

Lieutenant-Commandant Ringgold, on the 20th, received further instructions from me to push the survey to the north; but being short of bread, he had sent Passed Midshipman Sandford to obtain a supply, which was at once despatched in the launch, although I expected to meet the brig at New Dungeness in a few days.

On the 20th, as before mentioned, the brig joined the *Vincennes* at New Dungeness.

I had been in hopes that, after the severe tour of surveying duty for

---

[31]Swinomish Channel.

the last three months, I should be able to give the crews some relaxation; but I found this impossible, for the duties were necessarilly much increased by the absence of the *Peacock* and *Flying Fish*, and the necessity of finishing as much of the northern survey as possible, as well as obtaining accurate information in relation to the positions, &c. I deemed it of too much importance to allow a day to go by unimproved. Orders were therefore given to the boats under Lieutenant Case to proceed to Port Townsend, to fill up the surveys and connect them with Hood's Canal and those of Whidby's Island.

[p. 484] Another division of boats, with those of the *Porpoise*, were employed in surveying New Dungeness Bay, and connecting it with Protection Island, while I was occupied in getting a series of observations for latitude and longitude, dip and intensity, at the low sand point which forms the bay. Orders were also prepared for the *Porpoise* to proceed to Port Townsend; thence to Fraser's river, visiting Fort Langley; and then through Johnson's Straits,[32] and round the north end of Vancouver's Island, to Nootka Sound.

A large boat expedition was also fitted out, of which I took charge in person, to proceed across the Straits of De Fuca, to complete the survey of the Canal de Arro, with the adjacent bays and harbours, and thence to the mouth of Fraser's river, where I anticipated falling in with the *Porpoise* again.

On the morning of the 25th [July], the brig parted company, and in the afternoon I set out, with seven boats, to cross the strait. The wind had been blowing strong, but I did not anticipate much sea or danger. It proved otherwise, however, for the tide was found to be running strong ebb against the wind, producing a very high sea, which made the passage at times perilous. We, however, crossed this distance of twenty miles without any other accident than the loss of a mast belonging to one of the boats, and reached the opposite shore in safety, though completely wet from the quantity of water we had shipped. The boats all behaved uncommonly well; and many, who had believed them unsafe, were now satisfied that they were admirably adapted for all weathers. Large fires and dry clothes soon restored the men to their wonted good spirits.

On the 26th, we began the survey of this labyrinth of islands, which was continued the next day, 27th, on the afternoon of which I was joined by Passed Midshipman May, with letters from the ship and despatches from Nisqually, informing me of the loss of the *Peacock*, on the bar of the Columbia, but that all hands were saved. This news, although bad, was a great relief to me; for I had feared not only the loss of the vessels, but had

---

[32]Wilkes meant Johnstone Strait, named by Vancouver.

serious apprehensions for the lives of the persons on board. A heavy load that had long hung over my mind was removed.

All my plans for the employment of the squadron were now at once to be changed; for it became necessary for me to proceed without delay to afford relief to our shipwrecked companions. I therefore immediately sent orders to the *Porpoise*, countermanding her previous instructions, and ordering her to repair forthwith to join the *Vincennes* at New Dungeness. On the 28th, the duties of our surveys were again [p. 485] resumed, and a finish made of those on the Canal de Arro. This was effected through the strenuous exertions of both officers and men, and the same night we reached the *Vincennes*.

Although we had completed all that was essential for the navigation of the Canal de Arro, I regretted that I had been deprived of the opportunity of examining the southeast end of Vancouver Island, which I have reason to believe offers many fine harbours. Three days more would have enabled me to accomplish this portion to my satisfaction.

On the 29th, the brig again joined us, and Mr. T. W. Waldron was at once sent with despatches to Nisqually, to pass across the country to the Cowlitz, and thence down the Columbia to Astoria. Among the despatches was an order to all the ward-room officers of the *Peacock*, to report to me in writing the circumstances that led to the loss of that ship. These will be found published in Document No. 427, House of Representatives, 28th Congress, 1st Session, dated 10th April 1844.

On the 31st, towards noon, the wind and tide permitting, we got under way, and stood down the Straits of De Fuca; but, owing to the light winds, we made little progress. Of the northern side of these straits, it had been my intention to make a very particular examination, after completing the survey of the Canal de Arro. I have understood that there is a fine harbour near the eastern end of the island, where a post has been lately established by the Hudson Bay Company; that of San Juan, near the mouth of the straits, the *Porpoise* was ordered to survey on the 2d of August, while the *Vincennes* was engaged in the survey of Neah Harbour,[33] lying on the south side of the straits, just within Cape Flattery. Port San Juan was found to afford little shelter, being exposed to the southwest winds, and the heavy swell of the ocean; and is reported as being unsafe, except for temporary anchorage.

Neah Harbour is but a small indentation in the coast, which is partly

---

[33]From Wilkes' journal, p. 106, he noted for August 2: "At noon of this day I anchored in PORT SCARBOROUGH named after the master of a Sch^r in the Employ of the H.B.C. [Hudson's Bay Company] services who has been greatly desirous of affording me the information that lay in his power."

sheltered on the northeast by NEAH ISLAND.³⁴ It is the position where the Spaniards attempted to establish themselves in 1972 [sic], and which they called Port Nunez Gaona. The remains of an old fort are still to be perceived, and some bricks were found that were supposed to have belonged to it. Water is to be obtained here in some quantity, and a small vessel would have no difficulty in getting enough. It offers a tolerably safe anchorage, though somewhat exposed to the northwest gales; yet by anchoring well in, which a small vessel may do, protection even from these gales might be had.

Wilkes journal offered a different description of Neah Bay:

[Journal p. 108] 3rd August. Finished the survey of Port Scarborough it being calm. got off about 1500 galls of water. The water is here good and sufficient for a supply for any vessel. There is some little difficulty in getting it, the brook is small and enters the Bay on a sandy beach which is shallow. with our water bags however, we found no difficulty in procuring as much as we could take in during the morning a report watering with casks more find more difficulty and it would occupy more time but a supply always be depended on. I observed the Latitude here again today & I found it (The Point of Neah Island) in 48° 24' 40" which agrees with that of Cape Flattery by Vancouver. The anchorage is very good shelter with a S. E. or S. W. wind but from the N. W. the sea in a gale would roll in heavy. to anchor here, stand into the Bay until you see the SAIL ROCK³⁵ between Neah Island & the main. You will then have 10½ to 11 fathˢ, sandy bottom and a smooth birth. I anchored rather nearer [p. 107a] to the Cape Flattery Point (POINT KILCOME³⁶) of the chart; in a N. W. Wind. I would advise anchoring to the Eastward of the Neah Island as it protects you from the sea of that Quarter 10 to 12 fathˢ·

On the night of the 2d [August], we had an eclipse of the moon.

[p. 486] The ship, on anchoring, was surrounded by many canoes of the Classet Indians, who inhabit the country around Cape Flattery. They were well disposed to trade, and were greatly surprised that so large a ship should want no furs, which were of several kinds: the sea-otter was that most prized, and held at very exorbitant prices, more than they could be

---

³⁴Originally named by Wilkes, it was changed a few years later by Captain Henry Kellett to Wyadda Island which makes use of the Makah Indian name. Ultimately, the spelling became WAADAH ISLAND.

³⁵Named for its sail-like shape.

³⁶Probably Koitlah Point based upon the Makah name of Quo-eet-la. Wilkes spelled it "Hilcome" in his atlas.

bought for in the United States. George, the chief of the Tatouche tribe, as he terms himself, was on board all day. He speaks a few words of English, and is a fine-looking man. It was difficult to make him or any of his people understand the use of a man-of-war, the number of people on board, and the care that was taken to keep them from coming on board. He showed it by continually asking, "What for so big ship?" "What for so many mans?"—all probably proceeding from his disappointment in not being able to sell his skins. I succeeded in getting his likeness with the camera lucida, with which he was much pleased; and although at first silent, and apparently surly, he finally became quite talkative.

On my remarking a scar on the bridge of his nose, and others in the tribe who had the same mark, he told me it was the custom with them to cut the nose when they had taken a whale, which they considered a great exploit. The fishing season is in August and September. Their mode of capturing a whale is with buoys, made of seal-skin, which are blown up after the fashion of bladders, and form a large oblong float: these are four feet long, by eighteen inches or two feet in diameter, and are attached by a rope to the harpoon or spear, which is thrown at the whale, and becoming fastened to him, prevents his diving down to any great depth; after having a number of these attached to him, he [p. 487] is unable to quit the surface, and is finally captured. All those whose seal-skins are attached, now divide the booty: those who are entitled to a share are easily known, for each float has a different pattern painted upon it. The number of whales taken is reported at about twenty during the season, and a quantity of oil is obtained from them by the *Cadborough*, a schooner belonging to the Hudson Bay Company, in exchange for articles of little value.

The Classet tribe of Indians is one of the most numerous on the coast that I had an opportunity of seeing, and seems the most intelligent. These Indians wore small pieces of an iridescent mussel-shell, attached to the cartilage of their nose, which was, in some, of the size of a ten cents piece, and triangular in shape. It is generally kept in motion by their breathing. They had seldom any clothing excepting a blanket; but a few who have contrived to make friends with the visitors, have obtained some old clothes: while others seem to be in the pay of the Hudson Bay Company. The principal articles of trade are tobacco, powder ("paulalee"), and leaden balls. These are preferred to most other merchandise, although more can be obtained for spirits than for any other article. This shows very conclusively, to my mind, the sort of trade that was carried on when the Boston ships entered into rivalry with the Northwest Company for the purchase of furs.

At the period of our visit, the Classet were at peace with the other tribe.

I deem this a good position for a missionary, for these Indians appear to be quite ignorant of any religious notions. I was informed, while at Vancouver, by one of the Catholic priests, that it was their intention to make a visit to them the next year, for the purpose of establishing their religion among them.

On the 3d, we were engaged in the survey of the harbour, besides obtaining fifteen hundred gallons of water. Its position (the north point of Neah Island) was found to be in latitude 48° 24' 40" N., longitude 124° 36' 46" W.; variation 21° 08' 14" easterly.

We had as many as forty canoes alongside on the 3d, with various articles for sale, including fish, venison, &c. Some of the canoes had as many as twenty persons in them. They were generally a stout, athletic race; and it was observed that the women were much better looking than those of the other tribes. Some of them, indeed, had quite fair complexions and rosy cheeks. They are not as much exposed to the weather as those we had previously seen, being provided with a conical hut, made of grass, and plaited so tight as to be impervious to water, which both protects them from the rain and sun.

It is said that this tribe can muster one thousand warriors, and they [p. 488] have the reputation of being treacherous and warlike. Many of them were fantastically painted, that is, besmeared with oil, soot, and red paint. Their dress consists of a native blanket, made of dog's hair interspersed with feathers: this is much more highly valued than the bought ones, but is rarely to be obtained. The clamour made by our numerous visitors alongside was very great, and their offers of articles were without much regard to the priority of rank, station, or any thing else.

The practice of flattening the head is prevalent here, but perhaps not so universal as amoung the other tribes we have seen. George, or King George, invited me to visit him at Tatouche, his village, about half a mile nearer to Cape Flattery than the place where the ship lay; but I had no time to spare. He informed me they had fifty lodges, made of planks, similar to those already described. His tribe live principally upon fish, of which they catch large quantities; and when a whale is taken, they literally gorge themselves with the blubber.

It was reported to me, late in the afternoon, that a ball had been fired at some of the sailors engaged in surveying; but it did not do any damage, striking the beach some little distance from them. I did not think it worth while to make any inquiry or disturbance about this matter, and only mention the fact to caution those who may hereafter visit this port that it is necessary to be upon their guard.

At 2 P.M. we got under way, with the *Porpoise* in company, and succeeded in making an offing before the fog enveloped us. These fogs are one of the greatest annoyances to vessels arriving on this coast; for, in fine weather, they are experienced almost daily, coming up with the sea-breeze, continuing through the night, and until the sun has sufficient power the next day to dissipate them.

In leaving De Fuca's Straits I anxiously watched for De Fuca's Pillar, and soon obtained a sketch of it, which is represented in the wood-cut at the end of this chapter.

XI
[Wilkes' orders to Lieutenant-Commandant Ringgold]
[p.522] U.S. Ship *Vincennes*,
Nisqually Harbour, May 13th, 1841

SIR,-

You will proceed from this anchorage, and take up the survey of Admiralty Inlet, below the Narrows, passing into the channel on the east side of Vashon's Island; thence north, examining and surveying all islets, and the shores of both sides of the straits, particularly all those bays, &c., that afford shelter for vessels, not only as harbours, but for temporary anchorage.

Off the north end of Vashon's Island you will be joined by the launch and first cutter and two boats of this ship, under Lieutenant Case.

If you should have reached this point before the boats, you will place up a signal, to indicate that you have passed it, and to which they may join their work of the channel on the west side of Vashon's Island. I shall direct Lieutenant Case to place a similar mark, if he should reach it before you, in order that neither party may be delayed.

Lieutenant Case will be ordered to continue with you in the work if you should meet there; but if he should reach it before you, he will be ordered to proceed at once to Hood's Canal; and you will then continue the survey down the inlet to the northward. On reaching Whidby's Island, you will pass into and survey Possession Sound to its extreme end, and all its inlets, &c.

If you cannot pass out of the Deception Passage, you will order a party to pass out in boats, and to carry the survey to the southward, along its western shore, whilst you sail back to its southern end, when you will take up the survey and continue it until you meet your boat party, connecting it with Wilson and Hudson Points, which form Port Townsend. You will not however, go in here, except for temporary [p. 523] anchorage, but proceed at once to the northward along Bellingham Bay and through the group of islands, pass into Birch Bay and Fraser's river, still continuing the survey as far as the entrance to Johnston's Straits. You will then return to the southward, along the eastern shore of Quadra's and Vancouver's Islands, until you arrive again at the Straits of Juan de Fuca, which will be looked for about the first week in July, when you will anchor in New Dungeness Harbour. After reaching it, you will despatch my two boats, with sufficient provisions, to make for this anchorage, ordering them to keep a look-out on the different points for information from me, which I shall leave, in case I shall have passed down Admiralty Inlet.

The following instructions will be observed for carrying into effect the surveying duty, &c.

Whenever practicable, the bases will be measured by chain, and the true direction of the base-line formed.

Astronomical observations will be particularly attended to, for latitude and longitude, by circummeridian and equal altitudes, daily, if possible, and from those points or the hills or bluffs near by, observations will be made with the theodolite on all distant points or mountain ranges, with a view to ascertain the actual position of peaks, their extent and height, and to form a connexion with your work. For this purpose, I recommend large trees to be barked or whitewashed, which will be found the most convenient signal, and easily distinguished on each side of the straits. An old piece of canvass, whitewashed and placed against a dark ground, or cut into a triangular form, and tied between bushes or trees, forms a mark easily distinguished, and be left standing.

It is extremely desirable that the points astronomically ascertained should be brought directly into connexion with each other, by triangulation, and no opportunity of getting the bearing of points in transit should be neglected.

The bays, harbours, &c., will be on the scale of four inches to the mile, but the general chart you will plot on the scale of two inches, which will include all distant points.

The officers will be particular in sketching in the shores and tracing the topography.

It is expected that the soundings will be full, and no part omitted, and that every part of the harbours that are surveyed will be attended to in this respect, as few things give so unsightly an appearance to a survey as an irregularity of soundings. In order, therefore, to have a full view of your work done, it is necessary that it should be plotted immediately, and the work kept up daily. The number of officers [p. 524] now attached to the brig will leave no excuse why it should not be done, and it will be expected by me that this part of your duty will meet with the greatest attention.

Variation will be often taken; also your dip and intensity observations should be frequently repeated.

You will endeavour to obtain all the information that may lay in your power, relative to the geological formation, and capabilities of the soil for agriculture, near and about the parts surveyed, also all minerals. The east sides of Quadra's and Vancouver's Islands are known to contain coal, which the Indians get from the surface. It would be desirable to view the locality and get some specimens, &c. All water-courses and brooks that may afford water for shipping, will be particularly noticed.

You will also pay great attention to the tides, their height and fall; set of currents, and the time of high and low water at full and change: this may be done in a few hours, by marking a staff, stuck in the water a few feet from shore, and an hour or two before high and low water, noting the time by the watch at the same time, and again when the water rises to the same point: the mean will give you the high and low water on that day, which, applied to the age of the moon, will give it on full and change.

I am desirous, also, that your dredge should be much used at all anchorages: there are many times when it can be done very successfully in deep water, and the results would be more rare and valuable.

As respects your astronomical observations, those by the north star I should much prefer to the sun for your latitude, and the time by a star I consider fully as good as by the sun; and, after a little practice, observations on stars with the artificial horizon will be found easy and convenient, interfering but little with your surveying duties during the day. The accuracy of the survey depends so much on these observations, that a few hours taken from sleep will be amply repaid.

Let all your work on paper bear date, scale, and name. The names of the Indian tribes, numbers, and extent of the districts belonging to them, it is desirable to get; all curiosities, &c., you will of course preserve.

Referring you to my General Order of May 1st, and wishing you success in the execution of these instructions,

I am, &c.

CHARLES WILKES,
Commanding Exploring Expedition

Lieut. Com. C. Ringgold,
    U.S. Brig *Porpoise.*

[Wilkes' orders to Lieutenant Case]

[p.525] U.S. Ship *Vincennes,*
Nisqually Harbour, May 13th, 1841

SIR,-

You will proceed with the launch, first cutter, *Ariel,* and *Pilot,* accompanied by Acting-Master Totten, Passed Midshipmen May and Colvocoressis, to the point in the passage west of Vashon's Island, below the Narrows (where Mr. Colvocoressis's signal was placed), from which you will begin the survey of the passage, proceeding northward until you reach the north end of Vashon's Island, where you will connect your work with the *Porpoise* on a staff erected there by that vessel. If you should find none, you will erect a large pole-signal, somewhat similar to those we have observed in the different bays; and also one on the small island opposite, which I have named BAINBRIDGE ISLAND,[37] leaving a note of your having done so for Lieutenant-Commandant Ringgold, to which he will connect his work.

You will from thence proceed (not meeting the *Porpoise*) direct for Port Lawrence, the place in which we once anchored, at the mouth of Hood's Canal, which you will proceed to survey, and endeavour to find a passage through the head of it, into Puget Sound, by some outlet or channel that may possibly exist: if one should be found, you will continue your survey through it, and into the waters of Puget Sound; if not, after completing the survey of Hood's Canal, you will return by its entrance to Admiralty Inlet, and thence toward the ship.

On your arrival at the Narrows, you will again take up the survey, connecting it with Mr. Totten's No. 1, and Mr. Eld's No. 8, and from thence into Puget Sound, taking its northern side, and islands near it in your progress

---

[37]Named for Captain William Bainbridge who commanded the *Constitution* in the battle with *Java* during the War of 1812.

to the southward and westward. From this point you will despatch one of your boats to me, with information of your progress.

The signals you put upon these islands must be well marked, so as to be distinctly seen and recognised.

You will continue up the arms and inlets, until you reach the head of the sound, and all its branches, after which you will continue the survey toward the ship at Nisqually.

In case of your falling in with the *Porpoise*, Lieutenant-Commandant Ringgold has orders to retain you in company until he reaches the mouth of Hood's Canal, when you will separate from him.

The following instructions will guide you in your surveys.

Whenever practicable, your bases will be measured by chain, and the true direction of the line found.

Astronomical observations will be particularly attended to, for latitude [p. 526] and longitude, by circummeridian and equal altitudes, daily if possible, and from those points or the hills or bluffs near by, observations will be made with the theodolite, on all distant points or mountain ranges, with a view to ascertain the actual position of peaks, their extent and height, and to form a connexion with your work.

For this purpose, I recommend large trees to be barked or whitewashed, which will be found the most convenient signal, and easily distinguished on each side of the straits. An old piece of canvass, whitewashed and placed against a dark ground, or cut into a triangular form, and tied between branches of trees, forms a mark easily distinguished, and be left standing.

It is extremely desirable that the points astronomically ascertained should be brought directly into connexion with each other by triangulation, and no opportunity of getting the bearing of points in transit should be neglected.

The bays, harbours, &c., will be on the scale of four inches to the mile, but the general chart you will plot on the scale of two inches, which will include all distant points.

The officers will be particular in sketching in the shores and tracing the topography. It is expected that the soundings will be full, and no part omitted, and that every part of the harbours that are surveyed will be attended to in this respect, as few things give so unsightly an appearance to a survey as an irregularity of sounding.

In order, therefore, to have a full view of your work done, it is necessary that it should be plotted immediately, and the work kept up daily.

The number of officers under your command will leave no excuse why it should not be done, and it will be expected by me that this part of your duty will be attended to with the greatest attention.

You will endeavour to obtain all the information that may lay in your power relative to the geological formation, and capabilities of the soil for agriculture, near and about the parts surveyed; also all the minerals; and water-courses or brooks affording water for shipping, will be particularly noticed.

You will likewise pay great attention to the tides, their height and fall; set of currents, and the time of high and low water at full and change. This may be done in a few hours, by marking a staff, stuck in the water a few feet from the shore, and an hour or two before high and low water, noting the time by the watch at the same time, and again when the water rises to the same point: the mean will give you the high and low water on that day, which, applied to the age of the moon, will give it on full and change.

[p. 527] I am desirous also that your dredge should be much used at all anchorages: there are many times when it can be done successfully in deep water, and the results would be more rare and valuable.

As respects your astronomical observations, those by the north star I should much prefer to the sun for your latitude, and the time by a star I consider fully as good as by the sun. After a little practice, observations on stars with the artificial horizon will be found easy and convenient, interfering but little with your surveying duties during the day.

The accuracy of the survey depends so much on these observations, that a few hours taken from sleep will be amply repaid.

Let all your work bear date, scale, and name. The names of the Indian tribes, numbers, and extent of the district belonging to them, it is desirable to get. All curiosities you will of course preserve.

Some articles are placed under your charge for presents and trade; you will be very economical in their use, and with your report you will give me an account of their distribution.

Of your ammunition you will take particular care, suffering no discharge to be wasted, either by your own boat's crew, or those under your command.

No grog is allowed. Your meals will be taken in time to get to your surveying duties by seven o'clock in the morning, and you will continue them until 5 P.M., when you will land and prepare the men's supper. No trading must be allowed during the time allotted for surveying duties, as it would call off the attention, and prevent the promotion of the work.

On Saturday afternoon, you will always select a suitable place for your stay until Monday morning. Neither officers nor men are to be allowed to leave the boats on excursions. When in camp, you will be particular in having a strict watch kept, under charge of an officer.

The provisions are under your charge, and you will see that no waste takes place. If you obtain sufficient fresh provisions, you will serve them out in lieu of the salt ration.

My General Orders relative to the intercourse with the natives, must be strictly observed. Any infraction of them, you may rely upon it, will be duly noticed. Your men are furnished with three suits of clothes each. They must never be suffered to remain in wet clothes at night; and you will see that they shave and keep themselves clean.

They will have ample time to wash on Saturday afternoons, and the Sunday's rest will render them able to encounter the fatigues of the week.

I shall expect from you a very particular report of all circumstances that occur.

[p. 528] A theodolite, chain, dredge, the eprouvette, and a howitzer, are furnished you for measurements of base, &c.

You will supply yourself with the signals required for surveying service, and see that each of your officers is furnished with the signal book and answering pendants.

Referring you to my General Order of May 1st, and wishing you success in the execution of these instructions,

I am, &c.
CHARLES WILKES,
Commanding Exploring Expedition

Lieutenant A. L. Case,,
   U.S. Ship *Vincennes.*

2

Charles Wilkes' United States Exploration Expedition: Instruments and Methods

Volume XXIII, Hydrography, is 514 pages in length. This is followed by the atlas (also part of Volume XXIII), published in two volumes, which includes 105 charts. The first several chapters of the text of Volume XXIII are included here, not because it pertains to Washington waters or place names, but because of its general interest in terms of the history as well as navigational issues faced by the crew. Regarding the instruments, it is important to note that many were used for land-based observations and thus have minimal uses aboard ship. For example, during Wilkes' inland explorations, artificial horizons were extensively used since the actual horizon was seldom visible due to trees, mountains, etc. As footnotes, I include a short explanation of the various instruments.

[p. 1] CHAPTER I.
INSTRUMENTS.

The manufacture of astronomical instruments at the time the Expedition was fitted out, had not attained that perfection that it had in Europe, and that it since has in this country. Confidence in our mechanics was wanting, as well as encouragement sufficient for them to compete with those of Europe, both in constructing and keeping for sale, those that were required for its use; of necessity, therefore, the instruments which were furnished the Expedition, were mostly procured from the best makers in Europe. For this purpose it was deemed necessary by the Government to send an officer to Europe, at the time the Expedition was organizing under Commodore Jones, to obtain such instruments as could not be had on this side of the Atlantic, and as would suffice for the results in the department of science which the Expedition was intended to investigate. I was requested to submit a list, and subsequently directed to proceed to Europe, with positive instructions to return in six months, or by the end of January 1837; this left me but about one hundred days to effect the object in: consequently, I could not expect to have any instruments constructed, and little time left to complete any that might be found unfinished. On my arrival, I found that all the principal instrument makers were fully occupied, and very unwilling to lay aside any of their engagements, and it was only by representing the great objects of the Expedition, and their becoming interested in them, that they were induced to furnish those I was in search of. Messrs. Troughton and Simms, Dolland, Jones of [p. 2] Charing Cross, the Messrs. Moolyneux, Parkinson and Frodsham, the Messrs. Dents, Charles Frodsham, Lloyd, and others, of England; Gambey and Chevalier, of Paris; and the Messrs. Ertel, Meyer and Fraunhofer, of Munich, all took a most lively interest in executing the orders; indeed, this interest was equally participated in by many gentlemen, who, although they had been a long time waiting for instruments which were then constructing, came forward, and desired that their orders might be postponed or laid aside until the instruments required for the Expedition should be completed. It was under these circumstances that I was enabled to execute the duties assigned me to the satisfaction of the Government, and which enabled the Expedition to go forth sufficiently well provided for the duties that devolved upon it.

The following is a list of the instruments procured, designating those in the several departments, as well as the names of those in whose establishments they were constructed, vix.: —

ASTRONOMICAL AND SURVEYING INSTRUMENTS.

1 Three and a half feet transit, iron stand, &c., Dolland.
1 Altitude and azimuth circle[1] (eighteen inch) two feet telescope, with microscope readings, by Dolland.
1 Repeating circle, twelve inch, by Ertel.[2]

---

[1]An azimuth circle was an adjustable ring designed to fit on the outside of a compass. Generally, the device included a pair of sighting vanes attached to the ring and a mirror to reflect compass graduations into the line of sight. When a distant object was sighted through the two vanes, its bearing could be determined by observing the relationship of the circle to the compass.

[2]In the mid–1700s, the German astronomer Johann Tobias Mayer (1723–1762) invented the repeating circle to measure angles more accurately than existing equipment. In 1787, Chevalier de Borda (1733–1799) perfected its design and Edward Troughton

1 Five feet refracting telescope, six inch aperture, with micrometers, &c., by Meyer and Fraunhofer.[3]
1 Three and a half feet refractor. Three inch ap., by Troughton.
2 Six inch repeating reflecting circles. Ertel.
1 Twelve inch repeating reflecting circle, by Gambey, with depression mirror.
1 Variation transit.[4] Dolland.
6 Sextants. Troughton and Simms.
2 Levels, staffs, &c. Troughton and Simms.
3 Plane tables.[5]
6 Box sextants.[6]
6 Schmalcalder's prismatic compasses.[7]

(1753–1835) improved it further. Both repeating and reflecting (which used mirrors) circles were used for navigational and surveying purposes. One such repeating circle was in the form of two circles, capable of independent rotation, one inside the other, and two telescopes, one of which rotated on the inner circle, the second rotated on the outer. The inner circle telescope was used to site the zero point while the outer circle telescope was rotated and used to measure an angle. Some instruments were accurate within 1 second of arc.

[3]There are three general types of telescopes: refracting, reflecting and Schmidt (used for astronomical photography). Reflecting telescopes used mirrors to produce images, refracting telescopes used lenses. Binoculars are simply two refracting telescopes mounted side by side.

[4]Magnetic variation is the difference between true north, i.e., the northerly direction along a geographic meridian, and magnetic north. Actually, there is no "single" magnetic north or south pole. Because the earth's magnetic field is the effect of complex convection currents in the magma, there are numerous magnetic poles, each with a different intensity and orientation. The compass points to the sum of the effects of these poles at a particular location. As these currents change, variation changes over time. Since first explored in 1831, the north magnetic pole has "wandered" more than 600 miles. Its current rate is about 15 miles annually. Variation is generally measured in degrees east or west of true north. Throughout the world, variation "varies." For example, along the west coast of North America, variation ranges from 15°E (Southern California) to 25°E (Vancouver Island). Along the east coast, it ranges from zero (west coast of Florida) to 30°W (Gulf of St. Lawrence). One of Wilkes' scientific experiments was to measure variation for which he used the variation transit. This instrument included a telescope mounted over a compass. The telescope was rotated to sight the north star; variation was read off the compass.

[5]A device for sketching topography in the field.

[6]The box sextant was invented in 1803 by instrument maker William Jones according to one source. Another credited its invention to Edward Troughton. It was essentially a miniature sextant; because of its size it was highly portable and useful for land-based surveying activities.

[7]This compass has a small prism mounted above the compass. The prism allowed the viewing of a distant object and simultaneously viewing its magnetic bearing.

2 Dip sectors.[8]
6 Mercurial horizons.[9]
1 Glass horizon.
2 Massey's patent logs.[10]
6 [p. 3] Surveying chains.[11]
6 Barlow's compensating plates.
1 Amici collamator.[12]

MAGNETIC INSTRUMENTS.

1 Variation apparatus, by Gambey.
1 Variation apparatus, by Dolland.
1 Gauss's diurnal variation.[13] Troughton and Simms.

---

[8]Development was credited to Edward Troughton in 1796. The instrument was used to measure the dip of the horizon. Dip, or "height of eye correction" is the angle between the visible horizon and the horizontal at the eye of the observer. If the observer's eye is at sea level, dip is zero. However, navigators were generally on deck, or at some height above the level of the water. Dip is an important correction to astronomical observations.

[9]Measuring the altitude of celestial objects required a horizontal reference. When not available (for example, under cloudy conditions along the horizon, or when land was present in front of the object to be measured), an artificial horizon was used. Frequently this was a pan of mercury, heavy oil, or molasses, covered by plate glass to shelter it from the wind. To use, a navigator sat or stood in front of the artificial horizon so that the distant object was in view as well as its reflection in the artificial horizon. A sextant was used to measure the angle between the object and this reflection. The artificial horizon was used primarily on land where the ocean horizon was not in view.

[10]A patent log was a device for measuring speed. The English instrument maker, Humphry Cole, developed it in 1688. It consisted of a vaned rotor, which spun in the water, connected to a register which counted its rotations. Improvements were made by Edward Massey in 1802 and provided for greater accuracy due to a more sensitive rotor. Speed and hence distance measurements with any accuracy were difficult for ancient mariners. In early times, a "Dutch log" or a light object was tossed overboard at the bow by the pilot, who then paced it to the stern as the ship sailed past. The method was later improved with timing devices (e.g., a watch or sand glass) and marks along the rail which enable the pilot to directly convert to leagues or miles per hour. Next, a log-and-line known as a "ship's log" or "chip log" was developed (perhaps in the 1500s). A log or chunk of wood tied to a line was tossed overboard at the stern and the length of line passing out over a given period of time was measured and converted to speed.

[11]Chains were used for surveying purposes on land. Over time, the length and number of links varied. However, the earlier, so called Gunter's chain (after Edmund Gunter, English mathematician and instrument maker, 1581–1626) consisted of 100 links and was 66 feet in length. One mile is equal to 80 chains.

[12]A collamator was a small telescope fixed to another larger telescope and was used to adjust the line of sight.

[13]Diurnal means daily. It is unclear if this apparatus was used to track daily cycles of celestial bodies, magnetic variation or tides.

1 Diurnal variation. Gambey.
1 Diurnal variation. Dolland.
2 Dipping needles,[14] six inches, by Robinson.
3 Dipping needles, twelve inches, by Gambey.
2 Dipping needles, six inches. Dolland.
3 Intensity needles. Gambey.
2 Intensity needles. Dolland.

METOROLOGICAL AND PHYSICAL INSTRUMENTS.

3 Standard barometers. Troughton and Simms.
6 Mountain barometers, with extra tubes.[15]
1 Iron cistern. Jones.
2 Sympiesometers. Adie.[16]
6 Daniell's hygrometers.[17]
3 Pouillet's hygrometers, à capsule.
9 Standard thermometers, by Simms, Jones, and Dolland.

---

[14]Similar to a compass, but the needle was mounted such that it would rotate vertically rather than horizontally. A dipping needle measured magnetic dip (also called inclination). This is the vertical angle between the horizontal and the line of magnetic force through the earth at a given point. Near the magnetic poles, dip approaches 90° (actually, at the magnetic south pole, the needle points straight up). At the magnetic equator or aclinic line (which wanders ±10° from the earth's equator), dip is zero. Early on, it was hoped that magnetic dip would help solve the problem with determining longitude in that each location would have a unique value. However, in the late 1800s, scientists determined that the earth's magnetic field changed over time, thus dip was of no value with respect to the determination of longitude.

[15]These barometers, built for their portability, were used for determining altitudes since atmospheric pressure decreases at a known rate with increases in altitude.

[16]The barometer, invented by Torricelli in Florence in 1643, was made by filling a graduated glass tube, approximately 34 inches in length, with mercury and inverting it in a cup of mercury. The column of mercury in the tube rose and fell based upon atmospheric pressure. In 1818, the Scottish instrument maker Alexander Adie invented and patented an improved air barometer known as a sympiesometer. The sympiesometer used no mercury. Instead, it consisted of a glass bulb filled with hydrogen connected with a second filled with oil. The instrument also contained a thermometer which was used to adjust the barometric reading.

[17]The hygrometer measured relative humidity or moisture content of the air. Daniell's hygrometer consisted of a bent glass tube which terminated in two bulbs. One was covered with muslin, the other of black glass, and contained ether and a thermometer. Ether was poured on the muslin, the black ball was cooled by the evaporation of the ether and became covered with dew. At this moment, the enclosed thermometer yields the dewpoint, and when compared with the reading of one in the air, determines the humidity. The device was invented by John Daniell (1790–1845), the British chemist and meteorologist, in 1820.

16 Six's self-registering thermometers, with copper cylinders for deep sea soundings.[18]
2 Scopeloscopes.
3 Pluviometers.[19]
1 Brass convertible axis experimental pendulum, by Jones.
1 Iron convertible axis experimental pendulum, by Jones.
1 Eight day astronomical clock, mercurial pendulum. Molyneux.
1 Eight day clock, steel bar pendulum, for pendulum experiments. Molyneux.
1 Journeyman clock. Molyneux.
Iron frame to support the agate planes and its fixtures; also clock frames and stands. Molyneux.

[p. 4] Telescopes for observing coincidences, &c., &c. Jones.
Two weekly chronometers, Nos. 1567 and 1503. Charles Frodsham.
One Siderial chronometer, No. 1615. Charles Frodsham.
Twenty-five 56hrs. Chronometers, viz.: — Nos. 2075, 2085, 2203, 1839, 2204, 2066, 2093, 2095, 1964, 2105, 2052, 2083, 2096, 2037, by Parkinson and Frodsham; Nos. 2088, 3001, 1826, 2067, 2042, 2057, by Molyneux; Nos. 972, 766, by Arnold and Dent; Nos. 169, 170, by Chas. Young; No. 850, by James Murray; and four Pocket chronometers, viz.: Nos. 2124, 733, by Parkinson and Frodsham; No. 22, by Molyneux, and No. 786, by Cotterel and Co.

We were likewise provided with suitable libraries for each of the larger vessels, and duplicate instruments of those which were liable to be broken or become injured. For the repairs, there was attached to the Expedition a competent instrument maker. Besides those above enumerated, each officer was required to furnish himself with a sextant, watch, &c. It will thus be seen that we were well provided for the performance of our duties. There were some instruments I regretted not being able to procure, and among them was Fox's magnetic dipping apparatus.

Convenient portable houses and tents, for the protection and use of the instruments, were also provided, which rendered us entirely independent of external circumstance or local aid, so much so, that if we had been obliged to occupy a bare sandbank, we should have wanted for nothing; and I trust that the labors performed will exhibit abundant proof that the opportunities enjoyed were improved with the utmost industry and all the energy we possessed.

---

[18] Self-registering thermometers measure maximum and minimum temperatures reached between the times in which they are reset.

[19] A rain gauge.

The reliance to be placed on Hydrographical labors depends upon the accuracy of the modes employed in obtaining the results. It therefore seems necessary to give a statement of these, and to explain the combinations by which the positions that have been astronomically determined are brought to prove and bear upon each other, thereby affording strong evidence of the credit the combined results are entitled to, and the confidence that ought to be placed in the surveys and charts resulting from our labors.

[p. 5] SURVEYS.

The surveys made by the Expedition were numerous, amounting to 234, during the four years of our absence from the United States. It will readily be seen, that in order to accomplish this amount of work, that some expeditious method of surveying the numerous coral islands had to be adopted; indeed, it may almost seem incredible, situated so far asunder as the surveys were, for even a much larger force than was placed at my disposal to execute them; but as the mode of conducting them will be shown, I trust that all will be satisfied that it was quite possible not only to execute the work, but to do it with accuracy.

In surveying operations it is all-important that an easy and perspicuous method should be adopted, as well in taking the observations as in recording them, particularly where it would be impossible to regain an opportunity that might, from inattention or neglect, be suffered to escape; and any one who may have the direction of such duties, should be careful that the rough charts be at once drawn from the note-books, and that these latter should be kept in so clear a manner, and in a formula so well understood, as not to require explanations. In order to effect this object, I deemed it necessary that all the officers should have a thorough knowledge of the operations by which I intended to carry on the surveying duties, and for this purpose I prepared a shore syllabus, to render them familiar with the operations, and to avoid the defects existing in all treatises on surveying that I have hitherto seen, which appear to me to omit the first and most essential explanation of the principles. Many things appear to be taken for granted which the learner does not know, nor where to look for information, and he is consequently apt to neglect their importance. In other words, he must acquire much practical experience before he can understand the performance of duties which they pretend to teach. This omission is a serious one, and prevents the works on surveying from being as useful as they ought to the learner.

I gave (in Appendix xli, vol. I) the manner of executing our surveys, by the squadron, under sail: it had not been practised before, although the method of measuring bases by sound has been extensively used. As it more properly belongs to this place, I shall transcribe [p. 6] it here, so as to bring the method into notice, as well as to explain it more fully.

METHOD OF SURVEYING THE CORAL ISLANDS.

The basis of the method rested on the measure of distances by sound. For this we had ready means, by firing guns alternately from the different vessels, any three of which being stationary, the distances and positions of objects could be determined from them by direct angles, giving a double result, or by the angles between them, taken from the shore, or from boats, furnishing data for the problem of "the three points." When both methods can be applied at the same time, it is evident that the utmost accuracy may be obtained. Upon the land, by employing many observers, and occupying all the points of a trigonometric survey simultaneously, the whole work might evidently be completed in a very short space of time; and in like manner upon the water, creating by means of vessels and boats a number of artificial stations around an island, measuring angles simultaneously at them all, and base lines by sound, the rapidity with which a survey can be performed is equally great.

By means of the system of signals prepared by me for the Exploring Expedition, I could direct the vessels to assume any position I might select as most fit for our purpose. When these were reached, general but minute instructions directed the observations that were to be taken at each, in doing which there was no difficulty. These observations were entered upon a deck-board, for which the following form was prescribed:

FORM OF DECK-BOARD

DATE.	POSITION.	TIME.	AZIMUTH OF m	LEFT-HAND OBJECT.	CENTRE OBJECT.	RIGHT-HAND OBJECT.	REMARKS.

On approaching the island to be surveyed, signal was made to prepare for surveying duty; if boats were to be used, the number of them and the vessels whence they were to be despatched was next indicated; [p. 7] and finally, the position of each vessel was to occupy was shown. The vessels having reached their assigned places hove-to, and the boats having been previously despatched, would about the same time have anchored in their assigned stations, at the points of reefs, and hoisted their appropriate signals. The vessel that is first to fire a gun then hoists an ensign at the foremast-head, which is answered by all, and the flag is in like manner displayed previous to each successive fire. The firing then goes on in quick succession from all the vessels; and at the time, all the officers being on

2. Charles Wilkes' United States Exploration Expedition 59

deck for the purpose, angles are measured between the other vessels and objects on the shore, each by a different observer, as directed and indicated by the senior officer present; these angles, together with those made by the visual tangents to the shore, have always been found sufficient to plot from. During this operation the ensign is kept hoisted at the peak, so that all the angles may be taken simultaneously; and at the same time, the altitude and azimuth of the masts of the ships is observed from the boats, for the purpose of determining their position more accurately. Altitudes of the sun for time, and angles whence to calculate the azimuth of some one of the objects, are also taken immediately before or after the horizontal angles.

When the duties at the first station have been finished the vessels and boats change positions alternately, and at each change the same operations are repeated.

To illustrate still further the mode in which the whole squadron was made to concur in obtaining unity of action, a detail of a survey and a plot of the work are given on Plate 1, Fig. 1.[20]

By these alternate changes in the stations of the several vessels and boats, continued until a circuit of the island has been made, the work is finished, and when it joins, it is proved by the last distance determined by azimuthal angles and base by sound, as for a base of verification. The deck-boards are then sent on board the flag-ship, where the work is calculated and plotted.

The survey of the island thus represented, which is about seven miles in length, was performed in three hours and thirty-five minutes. It began, as noted on the deck-boards, at 1.18 P.M., and the observations closed at 4.53 P.M.

The facility with which the operations are made can scarcely be conceived until they are witnessed, and I may add the accuracy, not less so when the proper steps are taken to carry all parts into operation. [p. 8] the measurement of the bases being all taken within a short time of each other, and the observations made by many officers at all the angles of the triangles, it leaves little correction even for personal error or inaccuracy in measuring the distance by sound, and as the angles are simultaneously measured, there can be but little variation from the truth. The objects are generally so well defined as to make their selection an easy task to even the most uninitiated.

It may be thought that the movements of the vessels would be too

---

[20]The figure showed a representative island, ship locations offshore, land locations manned and an extensive series of lines connecting the various points for triangulation purposes.

great; but this is not of any great amount, indeed is very small during the actual time engaged. There can be no doubt of the first positions being occupied, when the original angles are "kept on;" besides, the proof of the whole work by the bases of verification, fully assures one of its accuracy as well as efficiency. Indeed, I do not know what is more to be desired or obtained, except it be the rise and fall of the tides, which the short time occupied does not admit. Having fully tested and satisfied myself of the accuracy of the method, and the celerity of execution, even by ships of any squadron, not expressly fitted for surveying operations, I cannot too strongly recommend its adoption whenever an opportunity offers, believing there are few things that would add more to our knowledge of the changes going on in the islands and shores, than the results would bring to light.

Although we had recourse to sound, in many cases, to obtain our bases on land, or rather the sides of the triangles, yet these were frequently proven by a measurement base for verification, or one obtained by the subtension of a staff at a distance, where the ground did not admit of its being actually measured.

Wilkes continued with a more detailed explanation of charting the "Feejee" Islands as well as the Columbia River. The text relating to general measurements continues on page 13.

SOUND.

[p. 13] Sound has been referred to as the medium through which was obtained, oftentimes, bases for the surveys. In order to test the accuracy of this mode of measurement, I determined to make the experiment on an extended scale, by measuring the distance from Cape Frio to Rio de Janeiro; the ascertainment of the position of the former having been made a part of my instructions. This was a distance of about 76 miles. The diagram of this measurement, and its accuracy, as compared with the meridian distance taken by chronometers from the observatory, will be found in Appendix XXIII, Vol. I, although it more properly belongs to this treatise on Hydrography. The two methods, though very dissimilar, approximate closely in results; proving the accuracy of the method by sound, and the reliance that can be placed upon its employment for extended bases. Notwithstanding this apparent confirmation, I was not satisfied that the velocity of sound had been truly ascertained by experiment. The difference between that deduced by theory and experiment, respectively, equal to one-sixth, was, in my opinion, too great; and in looking for the reason of the discrepancy, I concluded it might arise from the [p. 14] measurement of the time not being sufficiently minute, and this together with the personal error in observation would, most probably, be found the cause, rather than that assigned for it, viz., the evolvement of the latent heat by its wave-like motion. On this account I became desirous of repeating the experiments under the most favorable circumstances. An opportunity was afforded by the erection of the Fire Alarm Apparatus recently in Boston, which gave me the opportunity of recording the time on a cylinder, making the second of time equal to about five inches in length, and therefore giving the time with a degree of accuracy that had never been heretofore obtained. The close agreement of the many distinguished experimenters on sound, had led me to believe that I should but verify the conclusions arrived at, yet I hoped so to vary the experiments as to enable full reliance to be placed in the results: these I have embodied in Appendix I, where I have placed them by the approbation of the Joint Committee of the Library of Congress, — in whose name I applied to the Mayor of Boston, the Hon. Benjamin Seaver, for permission to use the apparatus, which was readily and obligingly placed at my disposal.

The State House at Boston was occupied as the central position, and at other distant stations guns were placed; while the steeples in which the bells were situated were connected by triangles with the State House, all radiating from it in various directions. The distances were kindly furnished me by Mr. Boutelle, an able assistant on the Coast Survey, from the surveys in progress. After we had arranged this part, it became important that the record of the firing should be made, if possible, by the concussion, or by the same impulse which was given to the air by the discharge of the cannon, so that no personal error might affect the observation, except in the record of hearing the sound. In the case of the bells in the steeples, the magnetic circuit was broken by the hammer the moment it struck the bell; the personal error then was only to be looked for in the last record to be made, the differences between the two marks on the time-cylinder of course giving the time in seconds and parts of seconds, in lineal measurement, the sound had occupied in passing over the distance. The experiments were numerous, — in the greater distances by the report of cannons, and the lesser ones by the bells of the several churches connected with the Fire Alarm Apparatus, both marked by striking the magnetic key. The lines on which the sounds passed radiated in [p. 15] all directions, and thus afforded the means of obtaining satisfactory results, in a measure independent of atmospheric influences. The state of the atmosphere, as to pressure, temperature, moisture, and wind, was carefully noted, and duly recorded during the continuance of the experiments.

Mr. W. C. Bond, and his son, Mr. George Bond, the distinguished astronomers of Harvard University, kindly offered their aid, and recorded the observations upon the time-cylinder connected with the observatory clock at Cambridge. To these gentlemen, and to Mr. Moses G. Farmer, Telegraphic Engineer, and his assistants, I feel greatly indebted for the aid they rendered me in operating with the Telegraphs. I would also make mention of the obliging manner in which the different Telegraph Companies placed their wires and apparatus at my disposal.

LATITUDES.

The latitudes of all the principal stations have been obtained by circummerdian observations of the sun and stars, with the repeating circle; at the minor stations generally by equal altitudes with the sextant and artificial horizon. The headlands, capes, &c., which have not been observed at, are deduced by triangulation from two or more stations where observations were made: these different determinations are distinguished by appropriate marks in the tables.

LONGITUDES.

The longitudes of the principal stations have been determined by a series of observations of moon-culminating stars, east and west of the moon. In order to carry out these views, application was made to the Hon. Secretary of the Navy, to appoint Wm. Cranch Bond, Esq.,* at Dorchester, near Boston, to make a regular series of observations on the moon-culminating stars, at his private observatory, during the absence of the Expedition. Directions were also given to Lieut. James M. Gillis, of the Navy, who succeeded me at the Naval Depot, to observe a similar series at Washington. From these arrangements, the Expedition derived most important aid in the determinations of the absolute longitudes where the observatories were established. Very [p. 16] many corresponding observations were obtained of moon-culminating stars with each of these places. The duties of these gentlemen continued through the period of four years, or during the absence of the Expedition, and from their untiring assiduity, perseverance, and attention, many comparative results were also obtained in magnetism and meteorology.

At some points they have been more numerous than at others, in consequence of the weather being more favorable. These points have been connected by meridian distances measured by chronometers, and a net of triangles, if I may so express it, has thus been spread over both the North and South Pacific, which include positions whose longitudes have been ascertained by others as well as by ourselves. In many cases the meridian distances have been measured several times. In this way I have not only

---

*Since the Astronomer of Harvard University.

been able to satisfy myself of the performance of our chronometers, but of the accuracy of the positions assigned these points, which in turn aided to prove those of the islands, reefs, and shoals, which were encountered on the route from one point to another. The correctness of the determinations of the meridian distances we have had frequent opportunities of proving, by different chronometers and observations, entirely independent of each other, increasing the dependence that may be placed on them.

Although we were well provided with instruments, but few opportunities offered for the observation of occultations, or the eclipses of Jupiter's satellites. A single eclipse of the sun was observed, and only the end, owing to the first contact being lost by obscuration. This gave the position of *Peacock* or [sic] Ahii Island (south side), within a few minutes of the chronometric measurement. As respects chronometric distances, I have preferred to place greater reliance upon the determinations of short intervals, confining each to its own limit, and not to allow, by an extension of the series, the accumulation of error by any change that the comparison of chronometers may have shown in longer periods. I have invariably preferred adopting the determinations by a chronometer whose rate had proved most uniform during our passage from port to port, instead of taking the mean of the whole. The reductions of meridian distances have been computed for all intermediate points, by the supposition of a gradual increase or decrease of rate; and for any intermediate point, where a rate was obtained, the correction has been applied by the usual formula, according to the time that had elapsed when the observations were made. The weekly rates of [p. 17] the chronometers during the entire cruise are given in the table, which will show their performance and what confidence is to be placed in them.[21]

---

[21]Table III in Volume XXIII contains a listing of geographical positions. To determine the accuracy of Wilkes' observations of latitude and longitude, I selected a number of locations. Because it is impossible to determine precisely where Wilkes' observations were taken, I attempted to select well defined points as opposed to say, an island or bay. Wilkes' values, the actual value and difference in nautical miles is reflected in the following table:

Location	Wilkes		Actual		Difference
	Latitude	Longitude	Latitude	Longitude	
Bird Rocks	48° 29' 10"	122° 43' 50"	48° 29' 07"	122° 45' 43"	1.3 nm
Duncan Rocks	48° 26' 40"	124° 43' 30"	48° 24' 28"	124° 44' 31"	2.3 nm
Gig Harbor	47° 19' 50"	122° 33' 00"	47° 19' 36"	122° 34' 29"	1.0 nm
Green's Point	47° 17' 00"	122° 40' 00"	47° 16' 54"	122° 41' 43"	1.2 nm

(continued on page 64)

MAGNETIC OBSERVATIONS.

At an early period of the cruise, Barlow's plates were adapted to the azimuth compasses, and the position kept throughout. These azimuth compasses were after Kater's construction, with prismatic eye-pieces. The greatest amount of local attraction, in high latitudes, observed on board the *Vincennes*, was but 5°; in lower latitudes it was not perceptible. The situation of the compass was about half way between the mizzen-mast and taffrail amidship, and the stand was of sufficient height to enable an observation to be taken at all times without difficulty. The variation was observed at sea, when the chronometric sights were taken, both morning and evening. The result of the mean of ten observations is given. At the observatories, during the time they were established, once every day, with the variation transit. The results are embodied in tables under the proper heading. The dip and intensity were observed frequently throughout the cruise, at sea, but at times it was found impossible to obviate the motion so as to get any results that I deemed worth of record, even by means of swinging-tables and other contrivances which were resorted to with the intensity needles. The Expedition was not furnished with the apparatus of Fox. The dipping-needles were used with more success at sea, and by noting the vibrations of the needle, and taking the mean, the result could be depended upon. I resorted to the plan of always putting the ship's head north or south during the time of making the observation: this brought the line of local attraction in the plane of the magnetic meridian, and obviated the necessity of any reductions for the effect on the needle caused by the local attractions on the various rhumbs of the compass, — an element constantly undergoing changes with the latitude, and also affected by any alterations of the iron in the vessel.

Location	Wilkes		Actual		Difference
	Latitude	Longitude	Latitude	Longitude	
Sentinel Rocks	48° 38' 40"	123° 07' 00"	48° 38' 24"	123° 09' 27"	1.6 nm
Skip Jack Island	48° 44' 30"	123° 00' 00"	48° 43' 57"	123° 02' 08"	1.5 nm
Southworth Point	47° 30' 40"	122° 28' 10"	48° 30' 37"	122° 29' 41"	1.1 nm
Tala Point	47° 56' 00"	122° 38' 40"	47° 55' 55"	122° 39' 32"	0.6 nm
Viti Rocks	48° 38' 00"	122° 35' 00"	48° 37' 51"	122° 37' 15"	1.5 nm
Wilson Point	48° 08' 39"	122° 44' 43"	48° 08' 40"	122° 45' 21"	0.4 nm

In all cases, Wilkes' observations placed him consistently to the east and slightly north of the actual location. With respect to the accuracy of latitude, Wilkes was frequently within several hundred feet. With respect to longitude, 1 minute of arc is equivalent to a clock error of 4 seconds. The average error above is about 1½ minutes of arc indicating his clocks (corrected by astronomical observations) were very accurate.

Although I experimented by changing the poles of the needles, I cannot but believe that it increases the liability to errors more than it obviates them. The manner of changing the poles should always be uniform, and, if possible, by the same person. Great care is necessary to avoid scratching the needles; and in order to prevent this, [p. 18] they should be covered with paper. They are liable to be much injured by sand if this is neglected; and when scratched are soon liable to become corroded, permanent injury being the consequence. The magnets used to change the poles, if this course is adopted, should be sufficiently powerful to effect it with a small number of manipulations. It appears to me that the result of experiments with magnetic needles would be more satisfactory if this were omitted. Careful observations made on returning to the same points, would give the state of the needle, and although all the results would be rendered comparative, yet, with the changes known, they could be calculated, and must be of less amount and uncertainty than the usual mode of procuring the direct determination by changing the poles, in order to obviate the errors likely to arise from a defective axis.

TIDES.

Observations on the tides in connection with the surveys were made. Our attention was also directed to the flow of the tidal wave throughout the great Pacific, for the purpose of examining into the anomalies that it is said to exhibit. On arrival in port a station was established as soon as practicable, a position being chosen where the free action of the tide could be felt, and the tide-staffs erected, consisting of two stout poles, 3 inches square, with ratchets to receive the springs of a float 8 inches square, which caused the tide to register itself. One of these floats indicated the rise, the other the fall, — the feet, inches, and fractional parts being legibly marked on the staffs. It was noted hourly both night and day, and recorded. Floats were anchored in the stream, which gave the direction, and there the velocity of the tide was ascertained. These have been embodied in the charts and the general hydrographical information. On several islands, 60 to 80 miles apart, simultaneous observations were made, in order to mark more particularly the flow of the tidal wave. The tidal observations have been projected in the usual form in curves of ordinates, as well as the results given in tabular form, which will enable them to be readily understood and the anomalies to be perceived. I have to regret that, in some of the most interesting localities, particularly in the South Pacific, — where so great an interest has been manifested, for some years, relative to the apparent [p. 19] anomaly from the Newtonian theory, — our time for observation was often too limited for full series; but this was unavoidable, as the duties required of the Expedition did not admit of longer delays. Notwithstanding, I hope our observations will tend to throw some satisfactory light upon the subject. They are given in the chapter on Tidal Observations.

HEIGHTS.

Heights, as connected with the surveying duties, were obtained by triangulation as well as by actual levelling, observations with the barometer, sympiesometer, and the thermometer, as marking the boiling-point. They are given in a column with the tables of latitudes and longitudes.

CURRENTS.

The velocity of the current experienced by the vessels, I have inserted in a column of the table of Magnetic Variations. The difference between the *true* place and that by Dead Reckoning may be the effect of current on the ship, or the result of local attraction, oftentimes entirely unsuspected. Though included in the variation, but without knowledge of its amount, half a point or even a few degrees of local attraction would be imputed to the effect of current. It is true, there is no great danger likely to arise from this omission, or want of knowledge, on a continuous route, when observations are made from day to day, as it is generally allowed for in giving the course to be steered, yet many serious accidents have happened to vessels from ignorance of this subject. This is the reason I consider currents so intimately connected with the magnetic variation to be allowed by all navigators, and why I have joined the tables. I am satisfied, that one of the causes why our American merchant fleet are generally so successfully navigated, is owing to the absence of local attraction to our ships.

[p. 20] CHAPTER II.

RATES OF CHRONOMETERS.

In giving the rates of the Chronometers of the Expedition in the table hereto annexed, I have adopted the true rates, as derived from the observations from time to time during the cruise. These have been established through a daily comparison with one chosen as a standard, and on which the astronomical time was immediately brought from the observatory. Although this chronometer, No. 1567, was selected for this purpose principally for its loud and distinct beat, as well as its being a weekly one, and therefore not liable to the daily winding which those of 56 hours require, yet throughout the voyage it proved itself admirably adapted, not only for the uses it had been selected for, but, as will be seen, maintained a very uniform rate. It was wound every third day, as I felt satisfied its motive power would exert a more uniform motion if confined within the limits of its greatest activity. The chronometers were compared daily on board all the vessels, and every *third* day, when the squadron was in company, through their standards, with that of the *Vincennes*, which was entered in the recording books for reference and future use. These were all reduced weekly to mean Greenwich time, from their established rate and errors, and the result of their performances tabulated, thus exhibiting at a glance any deviations which might have taken place. The standard has itself been farther corrected by the variation it underwent in each week, after it had become known, on the supposition that its rate had been uniformly increasing or decreasing between any two observations or establishments of rate. The *true* rate thus established has been compared with that of the others, as shown at the weekly comparison, from which has resulted their *true* rates given in the table, bringing them all to the same test as the [p. 21] standard; the rates, which are given for each chronometer to the closest figure deemed necessary, being arranged in vertical columns, all discrepancies are easily seen, and show the reliance that is to be placed on their performance, and in our determination of longitudes through them.

By referring to the numbers in Chapter I, it will be seen by whom the instruments were made, and which have performed the best.

After such proofs, it might seem invidious were I to designate any particular instruments; yet I cannot deny, that greater confidence was felt in some, when navigating through the devious routes followed during the course of the Expedition, than in others. I must give the assurance, however, that all the chronometers were uniformly attended to with great care.

In the tables, I am aware that many discrepancies appear that cannot well be imputed to the instruments themselves; these may possibly have arisen with ourselves, but it is now beyond my power to determine: such the record books give, and they must stand. All those who are conversant with the use of chronometers well know the liability of error of a few seconds in the comparisons, and will make allowance therefore in places in which it is apparent that such may have been the case.

As the Table of Rates fully explains itself, I deem it unnecessary to offer any further explanatory remarks. It shows the changes and transfers of the chronometers, and their periods of absence from the ships; when they were returned, the comparisons and rates were again taken up, as before.

The capital letter of the name of the vessel on board of which the chronometer was placed over the head of the column, and when transferred to other vessels, is then noted in the column of remarks.

It is necessary to remark here, in reference to the *Peacock's* instruments, that the daily record of comparisons, for a part of her cruise, was

68   Charles Wilkes and the Exploration of Inland Washington Waters

lost at the time of her wreck; but I have endeavored to supply this, by the weekly and monthly returns which Captain Hudson made of their performance during the period.

Sixteen pages of tables follow this section of the Wilkes Narrative in the sample format shown below:

RATES OF CHRONOMETERS.

UNITED STATES EXPLORING EXPEDITION.

Date.	CHRONOMETER RATES.								Remarks
	V. 1567	V. 972	V. 2037	V. 2088	V. 766	V. 169	V. 3001	V. 2201	
1838.									
Aug. 10,	+1.4	-1.06	+4.24	+2.20	+0.22	+1.65	-0.95	-3.46	Rate by
" 24	+1.39	-0.09	+5.20	+5.72	+1.66	+2.13	+0.34	-2.01	Observations
" 31	+1.39	-0.24	+4.61	+8.61	+1.83	+1.23	-0.78	-2.31	At Norfolk.
Sept., 7	+1.38	+0.26	+5.19	+4.64	+2.11	+1.47	-0.31	-2.17	
" 14	+1.38	+0.71	+4.97	+0.61	+2.40	+1.19	-0.31	-2.31	

In Chapter III, PASSAGES, Wilkes noted information relating to the Company's travels from point-to-point and included such things as how the ships handled, duration of each leg of the journey, course sailed, weather, and any other general notes relating to time at sea. This is followed, as reflected below, by individual chapters relating to specific areas of exploration.

Chapter IV.   Paumotu Group.
Chapter V.   Society Islands.
Chapter VI.   Phœnix Group.
Chapter VII.   Union Group.
Chapter VIII.   Samoan Group.
Chapter IX.   Tonga Isles.
Chapter X.   Viti Group, or Feejee Islands.
Chapter XI.   South Pacific Islands.
Chapter XII.   Ellice's Group.
Chapter XIII.   Tarawan, or Kingsmill Group.
Chapter XIV.   North Pacific Islands.
Chapter XV.   Hawaiian or Sandwich Islands.
Chapter XVI.   Oregon Territory.

Chapter XVII.   Coast of Oregon and California.
Chapter XVIII. Manilla and Sooloo Sea.
Chapter XIX.   Winds.
Chapter XX.   Geographical Positions.

3

Oregon Territory, Strait of Juan de Fuca

Wilkes' Narrative (Volume IV) provides limited information regarding his observations of the territory and the naming of places. Considerably more detail is included in this Volume XXIII, Chapter XVI, Hydrography. Here, Wilkes methodically takes the reader on an imaginary voyage through Washington inland waters. However, he does not include in this text all of the place names that are identified on his charts. To adequately honor his accomplishments, I have added a postscript in italics to each section, to differentiate from his actual text, the identification and a description of the remaining place names in the same manner as if Wilkes himself described those locations.

CHAPTER XVI

OREGON TERRITORY

STRAIT OF JUAN DE FUCA.

[p. 303] In approaching this strait, I have elsewhere mentioned that the coast, to the southward of Cape Flattery, is a dangerous one, on account of the numerous outlying rocks, and the prevalence of the almost daily fogs, which prove of serious difficulty and anxiety to all navigators. Many of these rocks are isolated, lie at the distance of several miles from the coast, and surrounded by water of the depth of 10 to 15 fathoms. The coast is high and iron-bound. On account of the currents, it is desirable to avoid this part of the coast, as they set for the most part on it from the northwest. I therefore deem it preferable, for vessels bound into the Strait of Juan de Fuca, to make the land of Vancouver's Island to the northward, which is visible a long distance to seaward, and can be perceived before that of the mainland to the southward of Cape Flattery. Having attained

3. Oregon Territory, Strait of Juan de Fuca

the latitude of 48° 30' north, a due east course will lead a vessel to the centre of the Strait, into the fair channel-way, with the highland visible on both sides. Off Cape Flattery lies Tatooch Island, and the Duncan Rock. Between these there is a safe passage. We passed through it in the *Vincennes*. It is well, however, not to attempt it unless with a favorable tide and a commanding breeze. Duncan Rock is a few feet above the water: when the sea is high it breaks entirely over it. To the north of the Duncan there is a small shoal, with three fathoms on it.[1] When the tide is strong, it shows the position by whirls. From Tatooch Island, at the distance of five miles east-southeast (true), lies Scarborough Harbor,[2] formed by a small bay and Neah Island,[3] which lies off its eastern point. This harbor is protected from all but north and northwest winds, to which it is entirely exposed. It affords temporary anchorage for vessels bound in or out. [p. 304] Water may be procured in small quantities. For large vessels, the anchorage to the eastward of Neah Island, between it and SAIL ROCK POINT,[4] is to be preferred; it is more easily reached than the harbor, where the flow and reflow of the tide is regular. Whilst lying within or at the mouth of the harbor, a vessel is liable to foul her anchors unless moored.[5] The set of the tides outside is parallel with the shore. During the summer months fogs prevail after midday, which prevent or rather shut out the sight of the land from seaward; but if the latitude has been obtained, there is no need of apprehension: a vessel may stand on without fear. The wind is generally from the westward in the strait, but dies away a short time after sunset. The nights are calm. The fogs are indicated by a heavy bank of clouds to the westward, which, as the afternoon advances, gradually rises, and is driven in by the westerly breeze; they continue, or it remains hazy throughout the night. On the north shore of the strait, at its mouth, is the harbor of St. Juan. It is nearly opposite to Scarborough Harbor, and is exposed to the southwest winds; it is 1 mile wide by 3½ deep. Off QUADRA[6] and MAKOMEK POINTS[7] lie clusters

---

[1] Duntze Rock.

[2] Neah Bay, named for Captain James Scarborough, Hudson's Bay Company, who helped Wilkes. In Wilkes' journal, p. 108, this is referred to as Port Scarborough. For whatever reason, he changed the name in his Narrative, p. 485, as well as his chart, but not in this Volume XXIII.

[3] Waadah Island.

[4] Klachopis Point.

[5] The act of "mooring" involves the use of two anchors laid out in opposite directions. The anchor rodes or lines formed the shape of a "V" with the ship which rides between them, always pulling on an individual anchor from the same direction.

[6] San Juan Point.

[7] Owen Point.

of rocks, the KASET and the MUSH ROCKS.[8] The depth of water to anchor in is 9 fathoms. The holding-ground is good. Wood and water may be obtained at the head of the harbor, from a creek, near SIKI POINT.[9]

In entering the Strait of Fuca, it must be borne in mind that the prevailing winds are either up or down the strait. If they happen to be in the eastern quarter, they will become more easterly, and the same if in the western quarter. The cause of this is, the high lands which traverse the length of Vancouver Island, on the north, and the Olympic Range, on the south. They attain the height of several thousand feet, and act as a funnel, through which the wind draws either way.

The direct course up the Strait of Juan de Fuca is east-by-south (true). It will lead to New Dungeness Point, which is 80 miles distant.

The Strait of Juan de Fuca is 95 miles in length, and has an average width of 11 miles. At the entrance, abreast of Duncan Rock, it is 8 miles wide. The Vancouver's Island shore is rocky, everywhere composed of a conglomerate and a reddish granite, containing several fine harbors, which have been lately surveyed by officers of the English government.

It was not in our power to survey either the north or south shore of this Strait, between Scarborough Harbor and New Dungeness. All [p. 305] that we had time to do, was to make recognizance of the points, and to connect them. For the outline of the shore we are indebted to the Spanish surveys. There is a small harbor within POINT ANGELES, but its mouth is barred by a sandspit, which does not permit any but a vessel of small draft of water to pass in. The shores of the strait on the south is composed of perpendicular sand-cliffs, which rise gradually into high land, covered with forests of various species of pine. Mount Olympus is conspicuous to the south, rising to the altitude of 8138 feet, and is capped with snow.

The navigation of the strait by night is perfectly safe. The shores are bold; a vessel would almost strike her spars before her keel could touch. It is better to navigate on the south shore than on the north. The tides are more regular, and may be taken advantage of. They flow in a direction with the course of the strait; seldom with much velocity until they reach its eastern terminus, where they divide, a part running towards and through the Canal de Arro, and another to the south into Admiralty Inlet. A strong westerly wind on the ebb produces a heavy cross sea.

Inside Scarborough Harbor, POINT NEWELL[10] *is found on the southwestern point of the Bay. Anchorage is possible to the northeast between Point*

---

[8]Cerantes Rocks.

[9]Northeast of Port Renfrew, the San Juan River.

[10]Unnamed on current charts but located at the western terminus of the current breakwater.

Newell and POINT LEWHOUGH[11] *on the southeastern shore in 3 fathoms within 2 cables from shore. However, this area is exposed to north and northwest winds. Water is available to the east along the beach from Point Newell. Beyond Point Lewhough is* VILLAGE POINT[12] *off which the depth increases to 5 fathoms.* SEAL *and Sail Rocks lie to the south of Sail Rock Point 2 miles. Within a ¼ mile from shore, bottom was found to be between 10 and 20 fathoms from Scarborough Harbor to New Dungeness Roads.*

NEW DUNGENESS ROADS.

New Dungeness Roads is the first safe anchorage on the south shore. The point is low and sandy, extending from the high bluff, in the form of a sickle, to the eastward, between 3 and 4 miles. This sandpoint forms the protection to New Dungeness Roads on the northwest, and vessels desiring to anchor there, must double around it, from a quarter to half a mile distant, standing into the roads from 1, 2, and 3 miles, and anchor in from 10 to 15 fathoms, 1 to 1½ miles from the shore. Should it be the intention to proceed at once into Admiralty Inlet, stand on for Point Wilson, the high land of which will be visible to the east, on the starboard bow. A direct course may be steered for it, if the wind will permit. But if seeking some of the harbors to the northward through RINGGOLD'S CHANNEL,[13] steer for WATMAUGH HEAD,[14] which lies northeast, which course will lead clear of BLUNTS ISLAND.[15] Should night overtake, it would be advisable and is deemed more prudent to seek anchorage in ARGUS BAY[16] and await daylight, than attempt to pass through Ringgold's Channel at night, where the tides are strong and set in various [p. 306] directions through openings between the different islands. If this be decided on, then stand for MOUNT ERIE,[17] on PERRY'S ISLAND,[18] which will lead directly into that bay. The only dangers lying off are the WILLIAMSON ROCKS.[19] Wood and water may be obtained at an Indian settlement in the bay, and some provisions.

---

[11]Unnamed on current charts.

[12]Baadah Point, named after an Indian village at that location.

[13]Rosario Strait, named for crew member Cadwalader Ringgold.

[14]Now spelled Watmough, named for John Goddard Watmough, a lieutenant in the U.S. Army, wounded at Fort Erie in the War of 1812.

[15]Smith Island, named for crew member Simon F. Blunt.

[16]Burrows Bay.

[17]Named for Oliver Hazard Perry's victory over a British flotilla in the Battle of Lake Erie during the War of 1812.

[18]Fidalgo Island, named for U.S.N. Commodore Oliver Hazard Perry who fought in the Battle of Lake Erie during the War of 1812.

[19]Named for crew member John G. Williamson.

NAVY ARCHIPELAGO.

NAVY ARCHIPELAGO[20] is a collection of 25 islands, having the Straits of Fuca on the south, the Gulf of Georgia on the north, the Canal de Arro on the west, and Ringgold's Channel on the east. They have been named from distinguished officers late of the U. S. naval service, viz., RODGERS,[21] CHAUNCEY,[22] HULL,[23] SHAW,[24] DECATUR,[25] JONES,[26] BLAKELEY,[27] Perry, SINCLAIR,[28] LAWRENCE,[29] GORDON,[30] PERCIVAL,[31] and others. Most of them are of moderate elevation. MOUNT CONSTITUTION,[32] on Hull's Island, rises to the height of 2356 feet. Hull's Island is the largest; it is indented by two deep bays, one of which has been called IRONSIDES,[33] the other GUERRIERE BAY.[34] It is composed of reddish granite and conglomerate; in some places the granite is seen to crop out. Both Rodgers and Chauncey Islands partake of the same character. On the north of Rodgers Island, and between it and Hull's, is PRESIDENT'S PASSAGE,[35] 8 miles in length, by 1 to 2 in width. This

---

[20]The San Juan Islands, named for the United States Navy.

[21]San Juan Island, named for U.S.N. Commodore John Rodgers who commanded the *President* in its battle with the *Little Belt* in 1811.

[22]Lopez Island, named for Captain Isaac Chauncey, commander of the *Washington* in 1815 at the battle of Algiers.

[23]Orcas Island, named for Commodore Isaac Hull, commander of the *Constitution* during the war of 1812.

[24]Named for Captain John D. Shaw who saw service in the Wars of 1812 and 1815 against Algiers.

[25]Named for Stephen Decatur, U.S.N., who served during the War of 1812.

[26]Named for Captain Jacob Jones, master commandant of the *Wasp* who captured the *Frolic* in 1812.

[27]Named for Captain Johnston Blakeley, captain of the *Wasp* during the War of 1812.

[28]Named for Captain Arthur Sinclair, Sr., who commanded the *General Pike* at the beginning of the War of 1812 and later the *Argus*.

[29]Guemes Island, named for Captain James Lawrence who died during the battle between the *Chesapeake* and the *Shannon* during the War of 1812.

[30]This is a nonexistent feature. Based upon Wilkes' chart, it was located on the northwest side of Orcas, along with its nearby eastern partner, Adolphus Island, also nonexistent. Their inclusion on the chart is attributed to a disgruntled William May.

[31]Sucia Island, named for Captain John Percival, U.S.N.

[32]Named for the United States frigate *Constitution*.

[33]Eastsound, named for *Old Ironsides*, the nickname of the *Constitution*.

[34]Westsound, named for the British frigate *Guerriere*, captured by the *Constitution* during the War of 1812.

[35]This reference is to San Juan Channel. President's Passage (President Channel) has been relocated to the northwest side of Orcas. The channel was named for the *President* commanded by Commodore John Rodgers.

passes into ONTARIO ROADS,[36] between Rodgers and Chauncey Islands, and again communicates on the south with De Fuca Strait, by the LITTLE BELT PASSAGE[37]; on the north, the waters flow through FROLIC STRAITS,[38] into Ironsides Bay, and around the MACEDONIAN CRESCENT[39] between Blakeley and OBSTRUCTION, Decatur and Blakeley Islands, again into Ringgold Channel. The soundings throughout these waters are very deep, seldom less than 30 fathoms.

Navy Archipelago is also comprised of hundreds of smaller islands and rocks. On the north side of Hulls Island is POINT THOMPSON.[40] Depths of 30 to 40 fathoms were found within ½ mile from shore. Doubling Point Thompson, depths decrease to 5 to 10 fathoms inside PARKERS ROCK[41] which is in a direct line with Point Thompson to Mount Constitution. POINT DOUGHTY[42] lies to the west 3 miles and is the most northwest point on Hull Island. To the south is FREEMANS ISLAND,[43] a cable length from shore. Five miles to the southwest is FRITZ POINT[44] on Hulls Island. Depths between this and Jones Island are 10 to 15 fathoms.

To the west of this area and south of Spieden Island is a narrow channel, not more than ½ mile in width. Currents run up to 4 knots in the direction of the channel. The entire southerly portion of Spieden is barren of growth; the top and northern portion contains trees to the shore, making it look in appearance, very unusual. The shore line is steep. On the north side of the channel is SENTINEL ROCKS, 100 feet in height. At the southwestern head of the channel is MORSES ISLAND[45] with rocks between that and the shore. On the south side is PEARL ISLAND, less than ½ mile in length, very narrow and low to the water, which shelters a bay. The south portion of this bay is protected by GULL ROCK[46] beyond which is a shallow winding channel 1½ miles in length. This bay, while sheltered in all directions with Rodgers Island to the east and Henry Island to the west, is not easily accessed by larger ships.

---

[36]Griffin Bay and part of San Juan Channel, named for Lake Ontario.

[37]Middle Channel, named for the *Little Belt*, a British ship.

[38]This is a combination of Upright and Harney channels and was named for the ship.

[39]Lopez Sound and Thatcher Pass, named for the *Macedonian*, a British ship captured by Captain Decatur during the War of 1812.

[40]Named for crew member Matthew Thompson.

[41]Named for crew member George Parker.

[42]Named for crew member John Doughty.

[43]Named for crew member J. D. Freeman.

[44]Unnamed on current charts. According to Wilkes' chart, it is located on Orcas to the northeast of Jones Island.

[45]Battleship Island, named for crew member William H. Morse.

[46]Pole Island at the north end of Mosquito Pass.

O'NEAL ISLAND,[47] *lies in Presidents Passage less than ½ mile from the shore of Rodgers. To the east are the* WASP ISLETS[48] *with a clear channel behind and along the south of Hulls Island. South of O'Neal 5 miles is* BROWNS ISLAND[49] *which protects a bay on the east side of Rodgers. Doubling* POINT SALSBURY[50] *and 5 miles further are the* GEESE ISLETS[51] *which protect the southerly entrance to Presidents Passage. The northeastern shore of Rodgers Island is generally steep with depths of 50 fathoms or more within ¼ mile; the shore south of Point Salsbury shoals to 10 fathoms within ½ mile and is very rocky. Currents in the southerly portion of Presidents Passage can run up to 5 knots.*

The northern point of Chauncy Island is POINT LLOYD[52] *in the Frolic Straits. It is high and woody. Continuing north into Ironsides Inlet,* MORSES COVE[53] *lies at the head which shoals to 10 fathoms within ¼ mile of shore. Depths, even close to shore, run from 10 to 15 fathoms in the Inlet. Southeast of Point Lloyd, 5 miles, is the southern point of Blakeley Island with* FROST ISLAND[54] *nearby. The eastern side of Frost is steep; depths of 25 fathoms were found close to shore. Continuing east around the southern portion of Blakeley, double* THE POINTERS[55] *by at least ½ mile due to rocks southeast of them.*

RINGGOLD CHANNEL.

Ringgold Channel leads from the head of the Strait of Juan de Fuca to the Gulf of Georgia. It is 19 miles in length, by from 1 to 3 miles wide. On the east it is bounded by MCLAUGHLIN,[56] Sinclair, Cypress, and Perry Islands; while on the west it has Hull, Blakeley, Decatur, and Chauncey. This channel trends nearly north and [p. 307] south; a north-by-east course from off Point Watmaugh will pass clear of JAMES'S ISLAND.[57] The

---

[47] Named for an 1812 naval hero.

[48] Named for the *Wasp*, commanded by Commodore Jacob Jones during the War of 1812.

[49] Named for crew member John G. Brown.

[50] Turn Island, named for crew member Francis Salsbury.

[51] Represents the islands in the southern channel including Whale Rocks, Long Island, Buck Island, and Mummy Rocks.

[52] Upright Head.

[53] Fishing Bay.

[54] Named for crew member John Frost.

[55] Based upon Wilkes' chart, this is Armitage Island. The name was ultimately moved northeast ½ mile to its present location.

[56] Lummi Island, named for Dr. John McLaughlin who assisted Wilkes.

[57] Named for Reuben James, an American sailor who saved the life of Stephen Decatur in Tripoli.

water is deep. There are but two dangerous reefs, the BIRD[58] and the PEA-POD ROCKS,[59] which lie near midchannel; the first about 1½ miles south-southeast of James's Island; the former, between Hull's and Sinclair Islands.

Along the eastern shore of Hull's Island, a course may be set for POINT LAWRENCE[60] watching for shoals along the way. Northwest from Point Lawrence 2 miles, the SISTERS lie on the south end of CLARK ISLAND[61] with BARNES ISLAND[62] immediately to the west. There is beach on the southeast side of Clark as well as the entire west side; the northeast portion is high bluff. Depths of 50 fathoms were found ¼ mile off shore. Between Clark and Barnes Islands which are separated by ¼ mile, depths of 10 to 15 fathoms were found with 50 fathoms on the west side of Barnes ¼ mile from shore. Both islands are well wooded.

CANAL DE ARRO.

The Canal de Arro lies between the Archipelago of Arro and the east end of Vancouver's Island; it is the shortest and most direct route into the Gulf of Georgia, from the Strait of De Fuca. The distance from Point Gonzalo,[63] the southeastern extremity of Vancouver Island, to JAVA HEAD, the northeast point of the same island,[64] is 22 miles. HENRY,[65] STUART,[66] SPIEDEN,[67] JOHN'S,[68] WALDRON,[69] and GOURD[70] Islands, lie near to and on the east side of the channel course, which is north half west: this passes to the west of Stuart Island, and between it and NOON ISLAND[71]; thence north 60° east, 9 miles, brings abreast of Java Head; then steer for Gourd Island,

---

[58]Named for the numerous seabirds nesting on the rocks.

[59]Named for their shape.

[60]Named for Captain James Lawrence of the *Chesapeake* during the War of 1812.

[61]Named for John Clark killed during the War of 1812 in the Battle of Lake Erie.

[62]Named for an American naval hero during the War of 1812.

[63]Now Gonzales Point.

[64]This location is East Point on Saturna Island. Not charged with exploring north and west of the Haro Strait, Wilkes mistakenly thought the land was all part of Vancouver Island.

[65]Named for crew member Wilkes Henry, a nephew of Charles Wilkes, who was killed by natives in Fiji on July 24, 1840.

[66]Named for crew member Fredrick D. Stuart.

[67]Named for crew member William Spieden.

[68]Origin of name unknown. Although there were numerous crew aboard with the first name John, none were found with that last name.

[69]Named for crew members Thomas W. Waldron.

[70]Patos Island.

[71]Perhaps Gooch Island.

and stand over to the east for Point Roberts, on the mainland, to anchor in DRAYTON[72] or Birch Bay. Point Roberts is 7 miles south of the boundary line. The Canal de Arro is free from dangers. The tides set very much in the channel course above indicated, which may be called the Fairway. The prevailing winds permit vessels to steer this course through it both ways. Should the wind be ahead, there is ample room for beating, and no dangers unless close to the shores of the islands. There are few places where an anchor can be let go, on account of the depth of water and the rocky bottom; but anchorage need not be resorted to, unless in case of absolute necessity, and those places indicated on the chart are the best.

If heading north, pass DOUGLAS ISLAND[73] *and double* EAST POINT *taking caution off the lee shores of* TUMBO ISLAND *and* BELLS CHAIN; *there is much shoaling.*

Passage is also possible north of Presidents Channel by sailing east of FLAT TOP ISLAND[74] *and to the east of Waldron Island staying midchannel.* POINT DISNEY[75] *on the south and* POINT HAMMOND[76] *on the north of Waldron are passed. Care should be taken north and slightly east of Flattop Island for shoals. The passage is a mile in width on either side of these shoals. Channel depths could not be reached with 50 fathoms of line. To the northeast of Point Hammond lies* SKIP JACK ISLAND;[77] *½ mile east of that is a rock, barren in appearance; to the east of that is Gordon Island;* ADOLPHUS ISLAND[78] *lies east another 2 miles. All of these islands shoal within ¼ mile of shore. Beyond that, depths above 50 fathoms are common. Steer either side of Adolphus Island and pass between the Percival and* EDMUND GROUP[79] *for Drayton Bay. Anchorage is possible on the southeastern bay of the Percival Group in 5 to 10 fathoms but this area is open to southerly winds.*

DRAYTON AND BIRCH BAYS.

Drayton Bay lies east of Point Roberts, and has an irregular outline; its northern part is filled with mud, bounded by a low marsh, through

---

[72]On Wilkes' chart, this is actually a combination of Semiahmoo Bay as well as Drayton Harbor, the small cove inside Semiahmoo Bay. Named for crew member Joseph Drayton.

[73]Blunden Island.

[74]The name is descriptive of its shape.

[75]Named for crew member Solomon Disney.

[76]Named for crew member Henry Hammond.

[77]This and Bare Island were originally named by Wilkes Ship Jack Islands, after a local fish referred to as a shipjack.

[78]This island appears on Wilkes' charts on the north side of Orcas to the east of Parker Reef. It is a non-existant feature.

[79]Matia and Puffin Islands.

which one of the branches of Frazer's River formerly discharged. There is a cove on the east side, a snug harbor for small vessels. A small peninsula divides Drayton from Birch Bay. The [p. 308] latter may be said to be included in Drayton Bay, which embraces the waters between Point Roberts and POINT WHITEHORN[80]; the distance between them is 10 miles. The anchorage in all parts of Drayton Bay is safe, though somewhat exposed to the southwesterly winds. I prefer to anchor in the south part of it or Birch Bay.

Birch Bay forms a part of Drayton Bay; the water in it is not deep, ranging from 5 to 10 fathoms. The shores are low, and in places marshy. Water and wood may be procured here.

The eastern cove of Drayton Bay is separated from the main by TONGUE POINT, *a long spit of sand, wooded in the centre. From here to* RED BLUFF,[81] *3 miles to the southwest, depths of 5 to 10 fathoms were found within a mile from shore. The area around Red Bluff to* KUWO POINT[82] *is very foul with rocks.*

SANDY POINT.

The coast trends southeast. From Point Whitehorn to SANDY POINT lies POINT MIGLY,[83] the north end of M'Laughlin's Island, which is separated from the main by HALE'S PASSAGE.[84]

HALE'S PASSAGE.

Hale's Passage is 6 miles in length by three-quarters of a mile wide; it leads into Bellingham Bay. The depth of water through it, ranges from 4 to 12 fathoms, and the current sets through it northwest and southeast.

M'LAUGHLIN ISLAND.

M'Laughlin Island is 8 miles in length by 1 in width; it is elevated, with abrupt shores. On the west side it is bounded by Ringgold's Channel. The VITI ROCKS[85] lie off POINT CARTER,[86] its southern end; these rocks are visible at all times of tide. The water is deep close to the shore, which may be approached with safety.

---

[80]Named for crew member Daniel Whitehorn.

[81]Birch Point.

[82]Unnamed on current charts but just south of Birch Point.

[83]Now Migley, named for crew member William Migley.

[84]Named for crew member Horatio Hale whose mother, Sarah, wrote "Mary Had a Little Lamb" in 1830.

[85]Named for the Fiji Islands.

[86]Named for crew member William Carter.

BELLINGHAM BAY.

Bellingham Bay is 12 miles in length, northwest and southeast, and 4½ miles in width. Point Francis and Point William,[87] which embrace the bay, are but 7 miles asunder. There is good anchorage in Bellingham Bay, in from 4 to 20 fathoms water. At its northern and southern ends are extensive mud-flats. The shores surrounding [p. 309] these are low and marshy; but towards the centre the land rises and forms a bluff. Point Francis projects from the north shore in the form of an oval-shaped peninsula. Point William, the south point of the bay, is elevated; a tongue of land joins it to the main land, and separates it from PENGUIN HARBOR.[88] Near the centre of this bay, and between the two points, lies ELIZA ISLAND,[89] triangular in form, one mile in length, by half a mile wide; it is separated from the south end of M'Laughlin's Island one mile. The entrance to Bellingham Bay is between Point Carter and Point William. VENDOVI ISLAND,[90] three-quarters of a mile in diameter, nearly circular in form, lies between the two; either side of it may be taken. The Viti Rocks lie in the passage, but there is ample room to sail on either side.

PENGUIN HARBOR.

Penguin Harbor lies southwest of Bellingham Bay; it is formed by Point William and Vendovi Islands on the north and east; Lawrence Island bounds it on the south and west, and Sinclair Island covers it on the northwest; it is nearly 3 miles square. JACK'S ISLAND lies near the centre of it. The anchorage is convenient and safe, with a depth of water not exceeding 20 fathoms.

CYPRESS ISLAND.

Cypress Island lies on the west of Lawrence; its length is 4 miles and greatest breadth 2 miles; its surface is much broken, and rises higher than those in its immediate neighborhood. On its west side is Strawberry Bay, protected by HAUTBOY ISLET,[91] and contiguous to Ringgold Channel. It is a

---

[87]Both points were named and charted by Vancouver, Point William in honor of William Bellingham.

[88]According to Wilkes' description, this is the "channel" between Vendovi Island and Point William on the northeast, and Guemes to the southwest. It was named for the British ship *Penguin* captured by Captain James Lawrence of the *Hornet* during the War of 1812.

[89]Named for Lieutenant Juan Francisco de Eliza who explored the area in 1791.

[90]Named for Vendovi, a chief from Fiji, taken prisoner by Wilkes.

[91]Renamed Strawberry Island after the common name of "Fragaria elatior," a species of strawberry.

convenient stopping-place for a tide. Good water and wood may be procured there. Leading north, between Cypress and Lawrence Islands, is a safe and deep passage through to Bellingham Bay. On the north end a conical hill rises to the elevation of 780 feet,[92] and off its north point there is a small islet and rocks, half a mile from the shore.

East of Hautboy is SALSBURY POINT[93] *on the north end of the bay.*

SINCLAIR ISLAND.

Sinclair Island is also high, and separated from Cypress about three quarters of a mile; it bounds Ringgold's Channel on the east. Between Sinclair, Cypress, and Lawrence Islands, are the CONE ISLETS.[94]

[p. 310] HORNET HARBOR.

HORNET HARBOR[95] affords good anchorage; it has Perry Island on the south and Lawrence Island on the north; is 4 miles in length, east and west; its shores are bold. At its head there is a mud-flat, covered at high water; on the south is a small creek, 6 miles in length, which is passable for canoes[96]: this communicates with SARATOGA PASSAGE.[97] The marsh through which the creek runs is from 2 to 3 miles wide. There is a connection between Penguin and Hornet Harbors on the north, through LEVANT PASSAGE[98]; the water is deep and the tide runs with great velocity between the three islets and the east end of Lawrence Island, the flood setting in the direction of the arrows.

The passage through Hornet Harbor runs from 5 to 12 fathoms, except close to shore, and LAWRENCE HEAD.[99] *Beyond* SUTTON HEAD,[100] *the depth increases to 29 fathoms. Both points are high steep bluffs. The entire bay*

---

[92]CONE HILL per Wilkes' Chart, since renamed Eagle Cliff, actually 840 feet in height with Towhead Island in front.

[93]For crew member Francis Salsbury, unnamed on current charts. It is the northern point in Strawberry Bay.

[94]Presumably named for their shape.

[95]Guemes Channel, named for the *Hornet*, commanded by Captain James Lawrence during the War of 1812.

[96]Wilkes is describing the Swinomish Channel but later indicates that it "is bare at extreme low water."

[97]Named for the *Saratoga*, the flagship commanded by Thomas MacDonough during the War of 1812.

[98]Named for the British ship *Levant*, captured by the *Constitution* during the War of 1812, this short channel runs between Huckleberry, Saddlebag and Dot Islands to the east and Guemes to the west.

[99]Capsante.

[100]Southeast Point, Guemes Island.

south of the area between Lawrence Head and SACHEM POINT[101] *is very shallow particularly at* NIPPLE POINT[102] *which dries at low tide. Doubling Sutton Head, the* PORPOISE ROCKS[103] *come into view and the channel leading through Levant Passage and Penguin Harbor is clear, except for the Jacks Island, to* CLARKS POINT[104] *at the north tip of Lawrence Island. To the south of the Porpoise Rocks lies* PEACOCK ISLAND.[105] *The entire harbor to the east of the line between Point William and Sachem Point is shallow and should be avoided by all vessels. The current through Hornet Harbor runs with the channel and up to 4 knots.*

ARGUS BAY.

Argus Bay is situated on the west side of Perry Island, and protected on the west by BURROW'S[106] and ALLAN'S ISLETS.[107] The form of the bay is nearly semicircular, 3 miles long by 2 wide. Mount Erie lies due east of the anchorage. The Williamson Rocks lie off this bay, to the south of Allan's Islet, and nearly abreast of SARE'S POINT.[108] YOUNG'S ISLET[109] is between Burrow's and Allan's. All these islets are rocky, and much broken. There is deep water between them, and likewise between Burrow's and Perry Islands; this latter passage, which leads into BOXER COVE,[110] is narrow. SANFORD COVE[111] is near the entrance; it is formed by a long sandspit; the opening is on the west.

The Ringgold Channel, between Watmaugh Head, the south end of Chauncey Island, and Perry Island, is 6 miles wide; ample room for ships to beat in. Mount Erie is a good landmark for vessels intending to seek Argus Bay.

---

[101]March Point.

[102]Perhaps Weaverline Spit.

[103]This is a combination of Huckleberry, Saddlebag and Dot Islands presumably named for the *Porpoise*.

[104]Named for crew member Levin Clark.

[105]Hat Island, named for the *Peacock*.

[106]Named for Lieutenant William Burrows who served during the War of 1812.

[107]Named for Captain William Henry Allan who died during the battle between *Argus* and *Pelican* during the War of 1812.

[108]Langley Point also shown as Biz Point on some charts. Sares Head has been moved about a mile south. Named for crew member Henry Sares.

[109]Named for Ewing Young, a fur trapper who later turned to farming and cattle.

[110]The channel on the north side of Burrows Island, named for the British ship *Boxer* captured by the *Enterprise* commanded by Lieutenant William Burrows during the war of 1812.

[111]Flounder Bay, named for crew member Thomas Sanford.

Entry is possible from either direction. From the north, double RAINDEER POINT[112] into Boxer Cove; from the south, passage on either side of Williamson Rocks is possible but take caution of DENNIS SHOAL, ½ mile to the northwest. Anchorage in 5 to 6 fathoms is available between Allan Island and the shore. To the north, between Burrows and the shore, the depth increases to 15 fathoms and remains that way through Boxer Cove.

PERRY ISLAND.

Perry Island lies next to and south of Lawrence; is of an irregular shape, 10 miles in length by 6 wide. On the east, between it and the main land, there is a marsh,[113] which is bare at extreme low water. The western part of the island is a bluff shore, falling towards the east where it sinks into the marsh. Mount Erie stands isolated in the centre.

[p. 311] SARATOGA PASSAGE.

I have called Saratoga Passage, the strait leading from Deception Passage to Admiralty Inlet, at the south end of Whidby's [sic] Island on the west, and M'DONOUGH ISLAND[114] on the east. Within is Penn's Cove, HOLMES HARBOR,[115] Port Susan, and Port Gardner. Throughout Saratoga Passage the water is of sufficient depth for the largest class of vessels; it is well protected from all winds. The tides are strong, and their direction generally north and south. The southern end of this passage enlarges into Possession Sound before it joins Admiralty Inlet.

DECEPTION PASSAGE.

Deception Passage is intricate and narrow, separating Perry from Whidby's Island; its length is 3 miles; in some places it is not over 500 feet wide. KETSLUM ISLET[116] lies at the west entrance; HOPE, SKAIT,[117] and KIKET ISLETS, at the east. The three in the passage are called STAM,[118] BIG[119] and LITTLE TENIF.[120] These all have deep water close to them. This passage ought not to be attempted without a commanding breeze, which generally

---

[112]Fidalago Head.

[113]Swinomish Channel.

[114]Camano Island, named for master commandant Thomas MacDonough of the *Saratoga* during the War of 1812.

[115]Named for crew member Silas Holmes.

[116]Deception Island.

[117]Skagit Island.

[118]Pass Island.

[119]Strawberry Island.

[120]Ben Ure Island.

prevails from the westward. Small, quick-working vessels may beat out with a favorable tide, but it would not be safe for those of any burden.

While the pass is deep, entry should not be tempted more than an hour prior to or after slack as currents of 9 knots run with the channel. When entering from the west, double WATSOK ISLAND[121]; *remain well north of* MAURYS POINT[122] *as the water shoals to less than 5 fathoms. Although there are a few rocks, the water near* NAGUAMOS ISLAND[123] *is deep. Remain south of Stam Island and pass either side of Little Tenif staying mid channel between* YOKEKO POINT *on the north and* HOIPUS POINT *on the south.* SIMILK BAY *as well as most of the eastern side of the channel to* TOSI POINT[124] *is dry at low tide. Pass between* ALA SPIT[125] *and Hope Islet, behind which is* HUNOT POINT. *Further south along the eastern shore is the* TOKANO ISLETS. *Sound frequently south of Ala Spit as the channel is generally only 5 to 10 fathoms but shoals rapidly on either shore. Continuing south, the channel turns toward the west and Point Polnell but there is adequate depth off* POINT DEMOCK[126] *to pass closely. The channel between Point Demock and* WATSAK POINT[127] *is clean and from 25 fathoms, increasing to 50 further south.*

BLUNT'S ISLAND.

Blunt's Island lies north-northwest of Point Partridge, distant from it 6 miles; it is of small elevation, lies nearly east and west, and in length from its west end to the outer part of the shoal to the east, 1½ miles. There is a considerable bank at its western end, on which there is kelp. A temporary anchorage may be made near it, but it affords no shelter; elsewhere the water is deep.

WHIDBY'S ISLAND.

Whidby's Island extends from Deception Passage on the north to SCATCHET'S HEAD[128] on the south, a distance of 35 miles. On the west it is washed by Admiralty Inlet; on the east by Saratoga Passage. It [p. 312] has many indentations and small bays and coves on the eastern side; but its western side, from Deception Passage to Point Partridge, a distance of 12 miles, is a high and nearly level bluff.

---

[121] Rosario Head.

[122] West Point, presumably named after crew member William L. Maury.

[123] Reservation Head.

[124] A corruption of the Indian name meaning Single Tree Standing.

[125] Shown as Ben Ure Spit on some charts.

[126] Rocky Point, Camano Island.

[127] Snatelum Point, on the southern entry to Penn Cove, Whidbey Island.

[128] Named after the Indian tribe which inhabited the area.

3. Oregon Territory, Strait of Juan de Fuca

Point Partridge is the northern and western point of Admiralty Inlet, and can be seen a long distance down Fuca's Strait; the shore is bold and the water close to it deep.

From Point Partridge to RED BLUFF,[129] is 5 miles, southeast; thence to POINT LEAVITT,[130] is 8 miles, and ARIEL POINT[131] is 4 miles from Point Leavitt. From Ariel Point to Scatchet Head is a distance of 6½ miles; here the shore makes a sweep, forming USELESS BAY,[132] with very deep water; and with the prevailing winds it is a lee shore, affording no protection for vessels.

A mile to the north of Scatchet Head is INDIAN HEAD.[133]

NEW DUNGENESS ROADS.

New Dungeness Roads is the best temporary anchorage for vessels, as they are well protected from the prevailing winds, easy of access, and if need be, water may be filled up. It is probable that here, in future, pilots for Admiralty Inlet may be obtained, and supplies in any quantities that may be required. To vessels requiring repairs, this will be an important stopping-place, on account of its vicinity to BUDD'S HARBOR.[134]

Anchorage is available to the east of the sandspit in 5 to 10 fathoms of water. Depths increase from KULA KALO POINT *to* SAWASH POINT,[135] *but 10 to 15 fathoms was found within ½ mile of shore.*

BUDD'S HARBOR AND PORT DISCOVERY.

Budd's Harbor might be designated as an extension of New Dungeness Roads, being separated from it only by a narrow tongue of land, which lies across, and renders the harbor entirely land-locked. The narrow entrance is on the west side. Vessels drawing 12 feet can pass over the bar at low water. The rise and fall of the tide is 6 feet. The extent of this fine harbor is 3 miles north and south, by a mile wide. The water is from 4 to 20 fathoms deep. The shores are of moderate elevation, and covered with timber. There is a good watering-place at the head of the harbor. It is believed that the entrance may be deepened and improved at small expense.

---

[129]Admiralty Head, named for the reddish color of the soil on the bluff.
[130]Bush Point.
[131]Double Bluff, named for the American vessel *Ariel* during the War of 1812.
[132]Named by Wilkes for its lack of shelter.
[133]Reflected on Wilkes' table of latitudes/longitudes but not on his charts.
[134]Sequim Bay, named for crew member Thomas A. Budd.
[135]Unnamed on current charts. This represents the bluff between Kulakala Point and Port Williams.

Port Discovery lies 4 miles east of Budd's Harbor, and New Dungeness Roads; its form is serpentine, 7 miles in length by 1¼ miles wide. Protection Island is situated 1½ miles off its mouth, and covers its entrance from the northwest winds. The great depth [p. 313] of water is disadvantageous and very inconvenient for anchorage. The banks rise abruptly. The port is easily distinguished by the east and north bluffs at its entrance. Protection Island is of moderate elevation; on either side of it Port Discovery may be entered. The best anchorage is off Carr's Point, in 20 fathoms water. Wood, water, &c, may be obtained without difficulty.

Five miles east of Port Discovery lies Point Wilson, the western point of Admiralty Inlet; it is a low, sandy point. Red Bluff, on Whidby's Island, is directly opposite to it, distant 3 miles. Point Hudson is low; it bears due south from Point Wilson, 1¾ miles; near it, is a red-colored clay bluff, 80 feet high; it is the north point of Port Townshend.

Enter Budd's Harbor by doubling the tongue, KIAPOT POINT,[136] *remain close to the western shore in Budd's Harbor as it shoals to the east. A course may be set directly for* PITSHIP POINT *where anchorage is possible in 15 to 20 fathoms. Depths decrease toward the south end of the harbor: from* SAIL POINT[137] *on the western side to* SPAK POINT[138] *on the eastern side is 5 to 10 fathoms. Depths begin to increase slightly toward* TAKUP POINT,[139] *¾ mile north of Spak Point.*

When entering Port Discovery from the west, take caution near KANEM POINT, *the shoal of which projects ½ mile southwest from* DAISY BLUFF.[140] *Entry from the east of Protection Island is clear with much depth between* VIOLET POINT *and* EAST BLUFF.[141] *Passing* NORTH BLUFF,[142] *a course may be set southeast for Carr's Point, skirting* SANDY POINT[143] *on the eastern shore. Toward the south end of the bay finds* HELIX POINT[144] *on the western shore followed ½ mile by* SCORPUS POINT[145] *On the eastern side, opposite Scorpus*

---

[136] Some charts reflect this as Travis Spit with the name Kiapot Point moved eastward to the beginning of the spit. Other charts show Kiapot as the western head of the spit as Wilkes intended.

[137] Schoolhouse Point.

[138] Goose Point.

[139] Hardwick Point.

[140] Unnamed on current charts.

[141] Cape George.

[142] Diamond Point, named for crew member James North.

[143] Beckett Point.

[144] Mill Point.

[145] Unnamed on current charts.

Point is TALA POINT[146] *and to the north ½ mile,* CAMP POINT.[147] *Water is available half way to* DOUBLE POINT[148] *on the eastern side.*

PORT TOWNSHEND.

Port Townshend lies between DICKERSON[149] and CRAVEN PENINSULAS.[150] It extends to the southwest 3 miles, and then to the south and east the same distance; at its entrance it is 2 miles wide, but within increases to three. This port is capacious, and has ample depth of water for vessels of any size, and room for a large fleet; towards its head it is entirely landlocked. It is separated from Port Lawrence on the south by a very narrow isthmus of sand, joining Craven Peninsula to the main. The anchorage in Port Townshend is safe at all times; the soundings throughout are from 9 to 15 fathoms; for vessels bound up Admiralty Inlet, it affords a much better anchorage than Port Discovery. Wood and water may both be procured here in plenty.

Doubling Point Hudson, the shoreline is moderate in height until the OLUMAN BLUFF[151] *which rises 100 feet with higher hills behind. South of the bluff is* WEH-WEH POINT[152] *followed by 1½ miles to* KULA POINT.[153] *Within a cable length from shore, depths remained at 10 fathoms all the way to* SAPIP POINT[154] *at the south end. On the eastern shore of the harbor, from* MIDILLE POINT[155] *to* FLAG POINT,[156] *similar depths were encountered. The water begins to shoal towards* JACK POINT.[157] *Extensive shoaling occurs to the northwest of* POINT CARROL,[158] *however depths allow the passage of all ships. The rise and fall of the tide is up to 11 feet.*

---

[146]Unnamed on current charts.

[147]Unnamed on current charts.

[148]Unnamed on current charts.

[149]Quimper Peninsula, named for Secretary of State Mahlon Dickerson who gave the orders to Wilkes for the Expedition.

[150]Combination of Marrowstone and Indian Islands, named for crew member Thomas T. Craven.

[151]Unnamed on current charts.

[152]Unnamed on current charts but located directly south of Glen Cove.

[153]Kala Point.

[154]Unnamed on current charts, the southwest entrance to Port Townsend Canal.

[155]Crane Point.

[156]Walan Point.

[157]Unnamed on current charts but located on the northeast end of the spit in the entrance to Kilisut Harbor.

[158]Marrowstone Point. Also shown on a different Wilkes' chart as Point Ringgold.

DICKERSON AND CRAVEN PENINSULAS.

Dickerson Peninsula rises abruptly on its north and west sides, where it bounds on Port Discovery and Fuca Strait; to the south and east its elevation is less, falling in gentle declivities towards Port Townshend. Its surface is for the most part open prairie; it is 5 miles in length by 2½ wide, and separates Port Townshend from Port Discovery. The soil is a sandy loam, and easy of cultivation.

Craven Peninsula has an extensive sheet of water, called KILISUT HARBOR,[159] enclosed within its area, which communicates with Port [p. 314] Townshend by WALAN ENTRANCE.[160] The greatest depth of water within is 6 fathoms. The shores of Craven Peninsula bordering on Admiralty Inlet, from POINT RINGGOLD[161] to LIPLIP POINT,[162] is low, trending nearly due south 6 miles.

This eastern shoreline finds at least 10 fathoms of water within ½ mile of shore. Near the southeastern tip is ARIEL POINT[163] where a more fouled and rocky shore begins.

PORT LAWRENCE.

Port Lawrence lies close around Liplip Point. To enter it, haul up immediately after passing the point, when the port will be open to view, extending to the northwest 2 miles. The best place to anchor in, is to the northward of SHIP POINT,[164] on the western shore, and at the southern extremity of the port. The depth of water is 21 fathoms, with good holding-ground. It ought only to be used as a temporary stopping place.

Take caution of the shoals which extend ½ mile to the south of HEKE POINT.[165] The head of the bay along LEKU BEACH[166] is protected from all but

---

[159] Named after the Clallam Indian term meaning protected waters.

[160] This was meant to be the entrance to Kilisut Harbor and is unnamed on current charts. The name was moved southwest of the entrance as Walan Point, a replacement for Wilkes' Flag Point.

[161] Marrowstone Point, named after crew member Cadwalader Ringgold.

[162] Named by Wilkes for the Chinook word for boiling.

[163] Nodule Point, possibly named for the *Ariel*, an American ship during the War of 1812.

[164] Unnamed on current charts, but is located north of Olele Point, according to Wilkes' charts.

[165] Kinney Point.

[166] This was the name given to the sand spit which "closed" the south end of the Port Townsend Canal.

southerly winds. The western shore past SNAS POINT[167] *to Ship Point provides good holding ground in 10 to 15 fathoms.*

PORT LUDLOW.

PORT LUDLOW[168] is 4 miles due south from Port Lawrence; between them is POINT KANAWI[169] and the COLVOS ROCKS,[170] four in number, all visible: these are not dangerous and are easily avoided. KLAS ROCK lies between OLELE[171] and Kanawi Points; it is about half a mile from the shore. Port Ludlow, though of small extent, offers many facilities for vessels, particularly those wishing to make repairs; it is situated at the mouth of Hood's Canal. From its locality and the extent of agricultural land in its neighborhood, advantages are afforded to settlers, and supplies, such as the country will produce, may be raised in abundance.

The directions for entering are simple and few. Pursue a south or mid-channel course, between JONES'S BLUFF[172] and POINT TALA[173]; when within the sandspit which makes out from the western shore, drop anchor, in from 6 to 8 fathoms, off BULL'S HEAD[174]; a vessel will there find a safe and convenient berth.

South of Klas Rock and to the west of the Colvos Rocks is SNAKE ROCK. *This is close to shore and also easily avoided.*

The head of Port Ludlow, HALLETS COVE,[175] *west of Bull's Head, shoals and should be avoided. Anchorage is also possible off* SYRAL POINT,[176] *but it is more protected behind* TIT POINT.[177] *The shore here is low and flat. The northern portion of the port is more elevated.*

---

[167]Unnamed on current charts but is located north of Olele Point, due west of Kinney Point.

[168]Named for Lieutenant Augustus C. Ludlow who died aboard the *Chesapeake* in the battle with *Shannon* during the War of 1812.

[169]Basalt Point.

[170]Named for crew member George W. Colvocoresses.

[171]Named after the Chinook term meaning berries.

[172]According to Wilkes' charts, this is a bluff on the mainland north of Port Ludlow and is unnamed on current charts.

[173]The original Indian name was Tahla.

[174]Unnamed on current charts but is the peninsula on the south side of the Port Ludlow harbor and forms the northeast entrance to the inner harbor. Presumably, it was named for its shape.

[175]Unnamed on current charts but is located at the end of the harbor.

[176]Burner Point.

[177]Unnamed on current charts but is located southwest of Burner Point.

GREAT PENINSULA.

The Indian or Great Peninsula divides the waters of Admiralty Inlet and Puget Sound on the east, from those of Hood's Canal on the west. The extent of this tract is 45 miles in length by 25 in breadth; it is indented by numerous bays on the east and south, and several islands lie in close proximity to it, forming roadsteads and harbors. [p. 315] Its elevation is generally about 120 feet above tide, and composed of a sandy, light soil, and for the most part covered with timber.

SUQUAMISH HEAD,[178] its extreme northern point, is a bold bluff, and readily distinguished after passing Point Wilson.

The course from Liplip Point, in proceeding up Admiralty Inlet, is southeast: this will carry a vessel off POINT-NO-POINT,[179] after passing which, the first anchorage is at Pilot's Cove, 3 miles distant, where a vessel may stop to await a tide. Admiralty Inlet at this place is 6 miles wide.

McDONOUGH ISLAND.

McDONOUGH ISLAND[180] bounds Saratoga Passage on the east. It is 15 miles long, and at the northern part it is 3 miles wide, but diminishes in width, being little more than a narrow strip of land at its southern termination. Its eastern side forms a considerable curve. It is low land, productive, and susceptible of cultivation. There is little wood on it, but water can be obtained at TRIANGLE COVE,[181] on its east side.

POINT LOWELL[182] *is located on the southern tip of McDonough Island.*

PORT SUSAN, PENN'S COVE, HOLMES' HARBOR, PORT GARDNER, AND POSSESSION SOUND.

Port Susan is on the east side of McDonough Island, between it and the mainland. At its head is an extensive marsh and mud-flat, through which a creek passes around the north end of McDonough Island, joining Saratoga Passage, opposite POINT POLNELL.[183] The water in Port Susan is deep, except at its north end, where it decreases from 14 to 2 fathoms.

---

[178] Unnamed on current charts. This land mass is the head which terminates in Foulweather Bluff. The name was reapplied to the mainland city in Port Madison. This is an alteration of the original Indian name Suk-wa-bish.

[179] Wilkes named this for its resemblance to Point No Point on the Hudson River.

[180] Camano Island.

[181] Named for its shape.

[182] Named for crew member James Lowell.

[183] Named for crew member John Polnell.

3. Oregon Territory, Strait of Juan de Fuca 91

From POINT ALLEN,[184] the south point of McDonough Island, to the head of Port Susan, is 9 miles, north-northwest. It is completely land-locked. At its greatest width it is 3½ miles.

Penn's Cove lies on the west side of Saratoga Passage. It is formed by an indentation of the eastern side of Whidby's Island, immediately to the east of Point Partridge. In shape it is a parallelogram, 3 miles east and west, by 1 mile wide. Off the south point of its entrance is a sandspit, extending half a mile from the shore. In Penn's Cove there is good anchorage, in 8 to 15 fathoms, which is a safe and convenient harbor; and the usual supplies can be obtained.

I have named the extent of water between Penn's Cove and Point Polnell DUNCAN'S BAY[185]; it is 3½ miles wide by 1 deep. On the west [p. 316] side is KALAMUT ISLAND,[186] which is surrounded by a reef of rocks. The anchorage in the bay is from 8 to 12 fathoms in depth.

Holmes' Harbor lies in Saratoga Passage, 10 miles south of Penn's Cove, 6 miles deep by one wide, an indentation which nearly divides Whidby's Island. The water in it is deep, but anchorage may be found at its extreme south. It offers but few advantages.

Port Gardner lies at the south end of Saratoga Passage. It is 6 miles square. On the east side of it FRESH-WATER CREEK[187] empties, at the mouth of which is a broad mud-flat. The anchorage is on the southeast side. GEDNEY'S ISLAND[188] lies in the middle of Port Gardner; it is one and a quarter miles in length by one-third of a mile wide and trends northwest and southeast. There is a shoal off its southeast point.

Possession Sound joins Saratoga Passage at its southern termination. It has the south end of Whidby's Island on the west, and divides it from the mainland on the east. It leads from Admiralty Inlet into Port Gardner, a distance of four miles; it is two and a half miles wide. Vessels seeking anchorage at Port Gardner, must pass close to POINT ELLIOTT,[189] and anchor under and near to the south shore, as the bank drops off very suddenly.

---

[184]Camano Head. Some speculate that Vancouver named this to honor Sir Alan Gardner.

[185]Crescent Harbor, named for an officer who served on the *Saratoga* during the War of 1812.

[186]Forbes Point. The name originates from the Indian Cal-a-met, which means stone or rocky ground. Wilkes believed it to be separate from Whidbey Island.

[187]Snohomish River.

[188]Presumably named for Jonathan Haight Gedney, a New York inventor and friend of Wilkes. But, according to one source, the island was really named for Lt. Thomas R. Gedney. Lt. Gedney, in command of the *Washington*, captured the Spanish slave ship *Amistad*, in 1839.

[189]Named for crew member Samuel Elliott.

Between Possession Sound and Elliott Bay,[190] on the east side of Admiralty Inlet, there is no anchorage or harbor for a distance of 16 miles. The shore trends a little to the westward of south.

Five miles above Pilot's Cove, on the west side, there is another good anchorage, at Apple Cove; though small, it is very convenient for vessels passing up and down the inlet.

The northeastern portion of Port Gardner at a distance of almost 2 miles from Point Migley[191] *is dry and muddy. Northwest 2½ miles is a long sandspit fronting a high bank terminating in* Bill Point[192] *which protects* Duck Harbor[193] *behind it. Depths of from 1 to 2 fathoms of water were found in the northwest portion of the harbor but there was little water to the southeast.*

Holmes' Harbor indents the eastern side of Whidby, south of Penn Cove. North Bluff *is first passed followed by* South Bluff.[194] *Water depth of 30 fathoms were found to* Point Maury.[195] *The head of the harbor shoals slightly from* Middle Point[196] *to* Norths Landing.[197] *Depths on the eastern side of the harbor were similar to the western: 10 fathoms within a ¼ mile of shore past* Scatchel Point[198] *and* Point Williams,[199] *increasing to* Rocky Point. *Bear off Rocky Point to* East Point *because of shoaling. The channel begins to turn more southerly at* Sandy Point. *There are weak and variable current in Possession Sound; tidal range approaches 12 feet.*

South of Point Elliot 9 miles is Point Edmund[200] *followed by* Point Wells.[201] *These are the major shoreline features until reaching West Point. Within in ¼ mile of shore, water depths in excess of 50 fathoms were found. The entire shoreline is high bank. Directly across from Point Edmund is Apple*

---

[190]Presumably named for crew member Samuel Elliott. There is some controversy that this was actually named for Rev. J. L. Elliott. However, because the chaplain was in bad standing with Wilkes, the Bay is unlikely to carry his name.

[191]Priest Point, presumably named for William Migley.

[192]The north end of Mission Beach.

[193]Tulalip Bay.

[194]Unnamed on current charts but located a mile south of North Bluff.

[195]Dines Point.

[196]Unnamed on current charts.

[197]Unnamed on current charts, located east of Freeland.

[198]Unnamed on current charts but located on the eastern shore a mile north of the head of the harbor.

[199]Unnamed on current charts but located two miles beyond Scatchel Point, named for crew member Samual Williams.

[200]The name was changed to Edwards Point by the 1897 U.S. Board of Geographic Names.

[201]Named for crew member William Wells.

Cove, 3½ miles distant. Anchorage is possible anywhere inside the northern and southern points of PIPPIN and BLOSSOM.[202] *In Pilot's Cove, take caution of the rocks along the shoreline south of* POINT WASHINGTON.[203]

ELLIOTT BAY.

Elliott Bay is embraced between WEST POINT[204] and POINT ROBERTS,[205] the south bluff. From West Point the shore trends southeast 5 miles to the head of the bay, has a sweep of 2 miles to the southwest, and thence northwest the same distance to POINT RAND,[206] which is 1½ miles from Point Roberts. The anchorage is of comparatively small extent, owing to the great depth of water, as well as to the extensive mud-flats; these are bare at low water. Three small streams enter at the head of the bay, where good water may be obtained. I do not consider the bay a desirable anchorage; from the west it is exposed to the prevailing winds, and during their strength there is much sea. Admiralty Inlet at this point is 3 miles wide.

Inside the bay, at the north end, is TUBER POINT *which protects* QUARTER MASTER COVE.[207] *The shore from there to* PINERS POINT[208] *is high bank. Beyond Piners Point are the mud-flats extending nearly to* Point Rand.

[p. 317] PORT MADISON.

Port Madison is 5 miles to the southward of Apple Cove, on the west side of Admiralty Inlet; it is one of the best anchorages, capacious and safe; is 2 miles wide by 3 deep. The head of the bay communicates with Port Orchard, through AGATE'S PASSAGE,[209] a good, though narrow channel, dividing Bainbridge Island from the Great Peninsula. The north and south points of Port Madison were named JEFFERSON and MONROE[210]; under the latter a vessel may anchor, but it is better to enter the port, and there await a favorable tide to proceed up the inlet.

Agate's passage runs from the northeast to the southwest 1 mile; it is less than ¼ mile in width. AGATE POINT *lies on the eastern shore upon entering. After passing through, set a course southward for 1½ miles standing well off*

---

[202]Neither point is named on current charts.
[203]Presumably named for the president.
[204]Named because it points due west.
[205]Alki Point.
[206]Duwamish Head. However, on Wilkes' chart, this is marked as POINT MOORE.
[207]Tuber Point and Quarter Master Cove now comprise Smith Cove.
[208]Unnamed on current charts but perhaps located near the ferry terminal.
[209]Named for crew member Alfred T. Agate.
[210]Named for Presidents Thomas Jefferson and James Monroe.

the western shoreline as well as POINT BOLIN[211] *because of shoals. From there, the south portion of Port Orchard is easily accessible.*

PORT ORCHARD.

The southern entrance to Port Orchard lies to the south of Port Madison 9 miles; it has three arms, stretching to the southwest, west, and northwest; the latter communicates, as before stated, with Port Madison. The waters of Port Orchard are separated from Admiralty Inlet by Bainbridge Island, 7 miles in length, north and south, by 3 wide. Towards its southern end, on its east side, are two small coves, EAGLE HARBOR[212] and PORT BLAKELEY.[213] The main entrance to Port Orchard is through RICH'S PASSAGE[214]: this lies between the south end of Bainbridge Island and the Great Peninsula, trending in a northwest direction 2 miles in length, by half a mile wide, when it takes a sharp turn to the southwest, of one mile. Properly speaking, Rich's Passage is a part of Port Orchard, but as there were so many branches, I thought it necessary to give the arms which lead into it different names, reserving the name given by Vancouver to the largest; the others we called DYE'S,[215] SINCLAIR'S,[216] and MAY'S INLETS.[217] Port Orchard offers all that could be desired for the safety and equipment of vessels. It will be a convenient place of resort for supplies as well as repairs. It is needless to point out any particular place of anchorage; every part of it may be used, and that resorted to will depend upon future settlements that may be formed. There are several rocks at the entrance of Rich's Passage, situated near mid-channel. Vessels may pass on either side of them, but the south shore is to be preferred, offering more room and a clearer passage. If it is not the intention to enter this harbor, good anchorage may be had in BARRON'S BAY,[218] between the land and BLAKE'S ISLAND[219] at its mouth.

---

[211] Named for crew member Jacob Bolin.

[212] Possibly named for Henry Eagle of the U.S.N., the *Eagle* of 1812 fame, or the presence of eagles in the area.

[213] Named for Captain Johnston Blakeley of the *Wasp*, lost at sea during the War of 1812.

[214] Named for crew member William Rich.

[215] Named for crew member John W. W. Dyes.

[216] Named for crew member George T. Sinclair.

[217] Liberty Bay, named for crew member William May.

[218] Yukon Harbor, named for Commodore Samuel Barron who served in the Tripolitan War of 1805.

[219] Named for George Smith Blake who was in charge of the United States Coast Survey from 1837 to 1848.

Enter Eagle Harbor from the south; there is extensive shoaling off WING POINT *to the southeast. Remain mid channel to avoid shoaling off* BILL POINT[220] *as well. Once in the harbor, anchorage is possible in 5 fathoms. From Eagle Harbor, entry to Port Orchard is made by doubling* POINT GORDEN[221] *into Rich's Passage. Favor the south portion of the channel passing* POINT GLOVER[222] *on the southern shore and* POINT WHITE[223] *on the northern. Mid-channel depths range generally from 10 to 15 fathoms. Currents in Rich's Passage approach 3 knots.*

Entry to Dye's Inlet is possible for small boats only because of the narrowness of the channel and shallow water. Double POINT HERRON[224] *on the Great Peninsula remaining mid-channel with* POINT TURNER[225] *on the opposite shore. The channel winds for 3 miles into the Inlet where depths of 10 fathoms were found in the centre.* OSTRICH BAY[226] *is located on the southwest side.*

[p. 318] BLAKE'S ISLAND AND COLVO'S PASSAGE

Blake's Island is triangular in form, with deep water around it; its sides 1 mile in length, and the island elevated. It forms the protection to Barron's Bay, where good anchorage may be obtained. It lies a mile north of the entrance to COLVO'S PASSAGE,[227] which is bounded by Vashon Island on the east, and the Great Peninsula on the west: it is 12 miles in length by half to a mile in width. Throughout its length the water is very deep, with a few places where an anchor can be dropped. The shores are bold, and the largest class of vessels may approach close to them. A vessel should not drop anchor, unless from necessity, until she arrives at the southern end, where anchorage may be found in 13 to 17 fathoms, very close to the shore. Should the wind be from the west, which is generally the case, it will be very difficult to get under way on account of the eddies of wind under the bank, 300 feet high. If the tide serves through the Narrows, or the breeze be a commanding one, it would be advisable to stand on and pass through them.

Colvo's Passage is the shortest and best route to the Narrows. That on

---

[220]Unnamed on current charts but is the south entrance to Eagle Harbor.
[221]Restoration Point.
[222]Named for crew member John Glover.
[223]Named for crew member James White.
[224]Named for crew member Lewis Herron.
[225]Named for crew member Henry Turner.
[226]Presumably named for its shape.
[227]Named for crew member George Colvocoresses.

the east side of Vashon Island is broad and safe, though a much longer route; it affords better anchorages than Colvo's Passage, but it is not advisable to take it, as the wind draws through Colvo's Passage, and is more favorable than when passing round the eastern side of Vashon's Island.

VASHON'S ISLAND.

Vashon's Island divides Colvo's Passage from the eastern channel of Admiralty Inlet; it is 13 miles in length by 3 miles at its greatest breadth; it rises to the elevation of 700 feet, tapers from its middle north and south, in which direction its length lies. It is composed of rough masses of rocks, and is well covered with timber.

Depths generally in excess of 50 fathoms were found throughout Colvo's Passage; its northern extreme is formed on the west by POINT SOUTHWORTH[228] *and on the east by* VASHONS POINT, *located on the north end of the island. South of Vashons Point 2 miles is* POINT PETER. *South of Point Peter 5 miles is* POINT SANFORD[229]*; 4 miles further to the southwestern end of the island is* POINT DALCO *with* POINT NEILL[230] *to the east 1 mile. These latter points form the northern portion of* DALCO PASSAGE *and the entrance to Quarter-Master's Harbor. Along the western side of Colvo's Passage, water is available at the* KOSA RIVER, *1½ miles south of Point Southworth; south 7 miles is* POINT RICHMOND.[231]

On the eastern side of Vashon's Island, POINT BEALS[232] *is located 3 miles from Vashons Point, followed by* HEYERS POINT.[233] *On the continental shore,* POINT PULLEY[234] *is located to the south of Point Beals and* POINT WILLIAMS[235] *to the north. Depths in this eastern passage exceed 50 fathoms.*

MAURY'S ISLAND.

On the east end of Vashon's Island, and near to it, is MAURY'S ISLAND.[236] It is 4 miles in length by 1 mile wide; trends northeast and southwest. Between it and Vashon's Island is QUARTER-MASTER'S HAR-

---

[228] Named for crew member Edward Southworth.

[229] Named for crew member Joseph Perry Sanford.

[230] Named for crew member William Neill.

[231] Possibly named for crew member William Richmond.

[232] Named for crew member Artimus W. Beals.

[233] Named for crew member Henry R. Heyer.

[234] Three Tree Point, named for crew member Robert Pully.

[235] Named for crew member Samuel Williams.

[236] Named for crew member William L. Maury.

BOR,[237] which is safe, and of moderate depth. A small neck of land extends from the [p. 319] upper or northern part of Vashon's Island, where it forms a snug cove. At extreme low water, Maury's and Vashon's Islands are joined by a sandbar. Vessels wishing to pass up the inlet on the east side of Vashon's Island should steer for POINT ROBINSON,[238] the eastern point of Maury's Island. Point Robinson may be closely approached, but if the tide should be favorable, it would be advisable to keep a mid-channel course. After passing Point Robinson, Admiralty Inlet turns to the southwest and west, and again joins Colvo's Passage, at the south end of Vashon's Island, abreast of POINT DEFIANCE.[239]

COMMENCEMENT BAY.

Opposite the southwest point of Maury's Island, on the main, lies Commencement Bay, an indentation on the southeast, 3 miles deep by 2 wide. The water is too deep for anchorage, except around the borders of the bay, on its south shore. The head of the bay has an extensive mud-flat, where several small streams enter, among them the PUGALLOP,[240] which takes its rise in the CASCADE RANGE OF MOUNTAINS. The distance of this bay from Point Defiance is 5 miles.

On the south side of the bay is POINT HARMON[241]*; there is high bank behind leading to the bluff at Point Defiance. Opposite Point Harmon is* POINT HARRIS[242] *which marks the northeast entrance to the bay. The water is deep beyond Point Harris.*

THE NARROWS.

The distance through the Narrows is 4 miles; at its narrowest place it is nearly a mile wide, though from the height of the shores it appears much less. Point Defiance, on the left, is a flat bluff, 250 feet high, of yellow sandstone, and horizontal stratification. It completely commands this pass. Opposite Point Defiance is GIG HARBOR,[243] which has a sufficient depth of water for small vessels.

---

[237]Named in honor of the petty officers aboard, known in the service as Quartermasters. Nearby points named specifically for them include Piner, Neill, Sanford, Southworth, Heyer, Pully, Moody, Scott and Henderson.

[238]Named for crew member John Robinson.

[239]So named by Wilkes because he felt if properly fortified, it "would bid defiance to any attack."

[240]Puyallup, after the local Indian tribe, a combination of pough (generous) and allup (people).

[241]Named for crew member John Harmon.

[242]Named for crew member Alvin Harris.

[243]Named by Wilkes to indicate the depth was only sufficient for small vessels.

For passing the Narrows, the young flood is deemed the best time; both ebb and flood run with great velocity, the flood on the eastern shore, while the ebb generally prevails strongest on the west. With the wind from the west, it will be free until Puget Sound is opened, when it generally draws ahead, and compels a vessel to back and fill, along the east shore. The strong flood will carry a vessel through in a short time. Great care should be taken not to stand too far over towards the west shore, where an eddy current prevails with equal strength on the flood and ebb in the opposite direction; if a vessel stand to far over, and be caught within this eddy, she would be carried back from whence she came. [p. 320] There is, however, no danger to be apprehended, provided care be taken, and the vessel kept under sufficient sail to command her movements. The tide, though extremely rapid, has the line of demarcation between its currents clearly pointed out by the whirls and ripples, which an attentive eye cannot fail to notice.

When exiting the Narrows to the south, depths off POINT FOSDICK[244] *allow ships of all sizes to approach closely.*

PUGET'S SOUND.

Puget's Sound embraces the extent of waters lying within the Narrows,[245] which is the only channel by which it can be reached. The whole area comprised within its limit is about 400 square miles. Its length, northeast and southwest, is 27 miles, while its breadth extends 15 miles at right angles to the length. By an inspection of the Chart, it will be seen that this includes many islands, peninsulas, rocks, coves, passages, and inlets; forming safe harbors, and free from dangers. The land surrounding these is similar to that heretofore described, being an elevated table-land, covered sparsely with timber.

After passing the Narrows, the first island is FOX'S,[246] which lies in a southeast and northwest direction; it is 4 miles long by 1 wide, and forms the south side of Hale's Passage; which leads to VANDERFORD'S HARBOR[247] and CARR'S INLET,[248] both indenting the Great Peninsula on the south end. Vanderford's Harbor is of small extent, 1¼ miles north and south, by one-

---

[244]Named for crew member Stephen Fosdick.

[245]It must be remembered that when Vancouver named Puget Sound, it was applied to that body of water south of The Narrows, or to what we commonly refer to as "south sound." Modern charts reflect Puget Sound as that area south of the south end of Whidbey Island.

[246]Named for crew member J. L. Fox.

[247]Wollochet Bay, named for crew member Benjamin Vanderford.

[248]Named for crew member Overton Carr.

3. Oregon Territory, Strait of Juan de Fuca 99

fourth of a mile wide. Five miles to the west is Carr's Inlet, a large and fine sheet of water, 8 miles long by 2 wide. On its east side lies ALLSHOUSE'S ISLET,[249] and two small coves; at its head is a mud-flat, with a small stream entering into it. Anchorage may be obtained under 20 fathoms water, with good holding-ground, anywhere abreast of and above Allshouse's Islet. The route up Puget's Sound, for vessels, leaves Fox Island on the starboard hand, keeping well over towards the Nisqually shore, in order to avoid the TOLIVA SHOAL, which lies a mile off POINT GIBSON,[250] the southeastern point of Fox Island. This shoal is of small extent; it has 18 feet on it at low water, and requires attention only by vessels of great draft of water. The following ranges give its position, viz., the north end of Ketron Island on with NISQUALLY BLUFF,[251] the Islands of M'NIEL[252] and ANDERSON[253] just touching, and the east end of Fox Island with the bluff on the west side of the Narrows.

The east side of Puget's Sound trends from the Narrows south-by-west; it has but slight indentations in it, and the depth of water [p. 321] precludes any anchorage, except close to the shore. The bank both above and below water-line is very steep. The distance from DAY'S ISLAND,[254] at the south opening of the Narrows, to Nisqually Bluff, is 10 miles. M'Niel's Island lies above Fox's, to the southwest. It is nearly oval in form, its longest axis being east and west, 3 by 2½ miles. Between it and Fox Island is BRACKENRIDGE'S PASSAGE,[255] 1½ miles wide. This leads to the northwest, into Carr's Inlet, of which it may be said to form a part. KETRON ISLAND is high, rocky, and barren; it lies north and south; it is a mile in length and a quarter of a mile wide. Between it and the shore is a tolerable harbor; but when the wind and tide are opposed, a sharp and disagreeable sea prevails. The island affords the only protection from the westerly winds, which blow strong. The depth of water and the steepness of the bank, with the strength of tide, does not permit me to recommended [sic] it as a good anchoring-

---

[249] Raft Island, named for crew member Joseph Allhouse.

[250] Named for crew member James H. Gibson.

[251] The name derives from French explorers who called the Indians nez quarré which means square nose. It was later altered due to the natives' inability to pronounce the letter r.

[252] Named after William Henry McNeill, Hudson's Bay Company and captain of the *Beaver*.

[253] Named for Alexander Caulfield Anderson, a chief trader at Nisqually's Hudson's Bay Company.

[254] Named for crew member Stephen W. Days.

[255] On current charts, this is now considered part of Carr Inlet, named for crew member J. D. Brackenridge.

place. The sound abreast of Anderson and M'Niel's Islands is 2 miles wide. Wood and water may be easily procured. Three miles to the south of Ketron Island is the landing of Fort Nisqually. From the bank shelving very rapidly, the anchorage is of very limited extent; within a cable's length, a change of from 17 to 44 fathoms takes place. The anchorage of the *Vincennes*, at Nisqually, was directly opposite a fine stream of water; we found it very convenient for our purpose, but it is very unsafe in the winter. The steamer of the H. B. C. usually discharges her cargo here, but it is more for the convenience to Fort Nisqually, there it was chosen, than as a safe port. The bank rises abruptly 210 feet, at which height there is a plateau extending for many miles to the eastward, forming one of the prairies of Oregon. Fort Nisqually lies 1¼ miles from the sound, on the prairie. A mile beyond the anchorage to the south is the north bluff to the NISQUALLY RIVER, called KWAATZ POINT.[256] Close to it the river empties into the sound; its mouth is upwards of a mile wide, occupied by an extensive mud-flat, which is bare at low water. There is another small and tortuous channel into the river on the southwest side, near LOA POINT.[257] From the mouth of the river to POINT MOODY,[258] the shore trends northwest 6 miles; thence it turns to the south into HENDERSON INLET[259]; thence passing the south end of HARTSTENE ISLAND.[260] It divides into Budd's, ELD'S,[261] TOTTEN,[262] and HAMMERSLY INLETS,[263] all capacious, and affording every facility for vessels of any size. These inlets are separated from that of Case's by JACK'S,[264] HOPE, and Hartstene Islands; and PICKERING'S,[265] DANA'S,[266] and PEALE'S PASSAGES[267] lead into them. CASE'S INLET[268] stretches up towards the north, until it [p. 322] approaches within a short distance of the waters of Hood's Canal, where there is a portage. This is a low marshy strip, 1½ wide, forming a narrow

---

[256]Located on the eastern shore of the Nisqually Flats, unnamed on current charts.

[257]Nisqually Head, presumably named for Mouna Loa, Hawaii.

[258]Johnson Point, named for crew member William Moody.

[259]Named for crew member James Henderson.

[260]Named for crew member H. J. Hartstein, as reflected on Wilkes' muster table.

[261]Named for crew member Henry Eld.

[262]Named for crew member George M. Totten.

[263]Named for crew member George W. Hammersly. Wilkes' chart reflected it as Hammersley.

[264]Squaxin Island.

[265]Named for crew member Charles Pickering.

[266]Named for crew member James Dwight Dana.

[267]Named for crew member Titian R. Peale.

[268]Named for crew member Augustus L. Case.

isthmus, which joins the Indian or Great Peninsula to the main land. In Case's Inlet, there are two small islets, viz., HERRON[269] and STRETCH'S[270]; the former lies just within its entrance, and the latter where the waters of the southern inlets join it. From the mouth of this Inlet to its farthest point is 12 miles; its width at its entrance is 1½ miles, but it decreases gradually towards its head. There is good anchorage throughout in a moderate depth; the banks are not so high, and the shores more shelving than the other inlets.

Anderson's Island lies opposite to Nisqually, distant 1½ miles; its form is nearly oblong, 3 miles in length, north-northeast and south-southwest, and 2 miles wide. On the eastern side is the BAY OF ORO, lying opposite to the anchorage at Nisqually: it is nearly semicircular, and half a mile deep. Anderson's and M'Niel's Islands are separated from the Great Peninsula by DRAYTON'S PASSAGE.[271] The eastern branch of Drayton's Passage[272] divides Anderson's and M'Niel's Islands: in it lie also NED and TOM'S ISLETS;[273] they may be passed close on the north side, where there is sufficient water for the largest vessels, as well as ample space for manœuvring in. Puget's Sound and its inlets offer every advantage for naval or commercial purposes. The rise and fall of the tide is sufficient for dry docks of large dimensions, and there are many localities where they could be established, and built at a moderate expense.

At the north end of Anderson Island is OTSO POINT,[274] *between this and* YOMEN POINT, *and M'Niel Island forms a narrow channel of ¼ mile in width but with ample room for vessels of all sizes. At the south end of the island is* TURKU POINT[275]; *2½ miles to the northwest is* POINT TREBLE.[276] *Ten fathoms of depth was generally found within ¼ mile of shore around the island.*

Carr's Inlet.

Doubling TSIKO POINT[277] *finds 20 fathoms depth in Vanderford's Harbor at the entrance. Nearer the centre, the depth decreases to 8 to 10 fathoms. At*

---

[269]Named for crew member Lewis Herron.

[270]Named for crew member Samuel Stretch.

[271]Named for crew member Joseph Drayton.

[272]Now Balch Passage.

[273]Eagle Island, located in what is now called Balch Passage.

[274]A modification of the Puyallup Indian word "Ot-sl," a war canoe and the largest canoe that could land at the point.

[275]Lyle Point.

[276]Named for crew member George Treble.

[277]Unnamed on current charts. This is the eastern entrance to Wollochet Bay.

the northwestern head of the Harbor are mud flats. Continuing northwest through Hale's Passage, the channel off SLAVIS POINT[278] on Fox Island is less than a ¼ mile in width and narrows beyond that, rendering it unsafe for ships. At TOMOS POINT,[279] at the northwest end of Fox Island, the channel shifts to the west; between that and POINT GREEN[280] it opens into Carr's Inlet. Behind Point Green is IHIKUM COVE[281] on the east side of the inlet, 8 to 10 fathoms at the entrance, shoaling to 2 beyond the middle. There is a small sandspit extending from SCOTT POINT,[282] the west entrance; favor northeast of midchannel between Scott and NIMROD POINT.[283] The cove is shallow, well protected and surrounded by sand beach. North of Scott Point 1 mile is SILIPO ISLAND[284] which marks the extent of shoaling to the southwest off Allshouse Islet. This shoal extends almost a mile from the southwest tip of Allshouse to Silipo with very shallow water on either side. There are mud flats which dry at low tide to the south of Allshouse, entrance behind the islet is possible from the north; depths of from 10 to 5 fathoms were found at the north to east sides. Beyond Allshouse ½ mile is HASKUSE POINT[285] with some foul rocks slightly off shore. At the head of the inlet is PUKI COVE[286] which shoals gradually until mud at the very end. Anchorage is possible in 8 to 10 fathoms ¼ mile from shore but the area is unprotected from south winds. On the western side of the inlet, 4 miles from the head, is POWIE POINT[287] followed by TEKO POINT[288] 1¾ miles. There is mud flat along much of this area but depths of 20 fathoms were found within ¼ mile from shore. Currents in the inlet were weak and variable, a tidal range of up to 15 feet was observed. Continuing south along the western side is AMAH POINT located on the north side of TALIE BAY.[289] At the south end of the bay is SIKWA POINT[290] followed by NUMAN POINT.[291] Talie Bay is a short indent on the Great Peninsula, not more than ½ mile in depth

---

[278] Ketners Point.

[279] Nearns Point.

[280] Named for crew member Daniel Green.

[281] Horsehead Bay.

[282] Named for crew member Thomas Scott. Unnamed on current charts.

[283] Unnamed on current charts but is the present location of Kopachuck State Park.

[284] Cutts Island.

[285] Allen Point.

[286] Henderson Bay.

[287] The location of this point is unclear but perhaps marks the entrance to Glen Cove.

[288] Unnamed on current charts.

[289] Combination of Von Geldern and Mayo Coves with Amah Point at the entrance.

[290] Penrose Point.

[291] South Head.

and shoaling at the head to mud flats. Shoals and rocks extend to the north of Sikwa Point ½ mile as it also does around Numan Point. Carr Inlet opens to the southeast to Brackenridge's Passage on the southwestern side of Fox Island and terminates at Point Gibson. This passage between Fox and M'Niel Islands is 5 miles in length, with depths generally in excess of 50 fathoms the entire distance. Opposite Point Gibson is HYDE POINT[292] on the eastern side of M'Niel. At the north end of M'Niel is MANHAIT POINT[293] with SAMEGO POINT[294] extending to the northwest almost a mile. Passage between these two points is not possible due to shallows and rocks. Doubling Samego Point, there is a narrow channel, ¼ mile in width, between M'Niel and the peninsula. A mile into the channel is PIT ISLAND, the channel ends a mile further and opens onto Drayton's Passage. There are rocks extending ¼ mile south of Pit Island and shoals of 1 fathom on either side. There are sand beaches along M'Niel Island as well as the Great Peninsula along the channel. Currents of up to 2½ knots run through the channel.

Case Inlet.

Case Inlet runs north-south 12 miles and is generally 1½ miles in width narrowing at the end. Doubling PARK POINT[295] off Drayton's Passage, Case Inlet turns northward. Six miles to the north along the Great Peninsula and past WA WA POINT[296] is Herron Island. Near the south end of the Great Peninsula which terminates at Park Point, depths in excess of 50 fathoms were found within ¼ mile of shore, half way to Herron Island. The remainder of the eastern portion of the inlet to Herron Island was from 30 to 40 fathoms. The northeast side of Herron, at COOPERS POINT,[297] shoals toward SANDY POINT[298] on shore with depths of only 2 to 3 fathoms. At the south end of Herron is BUNG BLUFF[299] which rises 150 feet behind the water's edge. KALILA POINT[300] is 2½ miles north of Herron Island and beyond that by 2 miles is

---

[292]Named for crew member William Hyde.

[293]Unnamed on current charts.

[294]Wyckoff Shoal.

[295]Devils Head named for crew member David Park.

[296]Unnamed on current charts but is located on the peninsula ¾ mile south of Herron Island.

[297]Unnamed on current charts, presumably for crew member John Cooper.

[298]Unnamed on current charts but is located at the ferry landing on the Peninsula that runs to Herron Island.

[299]Unnamed on current charts.

[300]Unnamed on current charts. This is a nook two miles south of Vaughn Bay.

TALAPAIS POINT[301] *the south entrance to a small cove. Beyond that is* SOTA POINT[302]; *2 miles further is* PAUN COVE[303] *at the head of Case Inlet.*

On the eastern side of the inlet, TULE POINT[304] *is doubled and is followed 1½ miles by* POI POINT, *behind which is* MANE COVE.[305] *Further south is* STRETCH ISLAND[306] *which protects* YAWA ISLAND[307] *to the west.*

Hartstene Island.

At TAHALI POINT,[308] *Pickering Passage diverts to the west of Hartstene Island.* POINT DOUGAL *is located at the northern end of Hartstene, across from Tahali Point. The passage here is ½ mile in width with 18 fathoms in the centre. On the east side of Hartstene Island, 3 miles south of Point Dougal is* STUI ISLAND[309] *which is surrounded by shoals and rocks. Beyond that is* POINT WILSON[310] *2½ miles. Pickering Passage runs 3 miles to the southwest from Point Dougal, past* STOKU[311] *and* STAU POINTS[312] *on the island, and an additional 7½ miles to* BRISCO POINT[313] *at the south end of the island. Opposite Stoku on the continental shore is* POINT SQUHO;[314] *here the channel is ½ mile in width. Further south is* KOPO POINT.[315] *At* SALOM POINT,[316] *on the north end of Jack's Island, the passage separates with Peale's Passage between Hartstene and Jack's. Peale Passage is 4 miles and ranges in depth from 2 to 7 fathoms through its length. The channel on the west side of Jack's Island is similar*

---

[301] Unnamed on current charts, south entrance to Vaughn Bay.

[302] Rocky Point.

[303] Unnamed on current charts.

[304] Unnamed on current charts but is located halfway between Rocky Point and the head of the inlet, on the western shore.

[305] Wilkes' chart reflects Reach Island as a peninsula with Poi Point at the northeast tip and Mane Cove behind it.

[306] Named for crew member Samuel Stretch.

[307] This is a nonexistant island between Stretch Island and the mainland, but could have been observed as a drying area at low tide.

[308] Unnamed on current charts but marks the northern entrance to Pickering Passage.

[309] McMicken Island.

[310] Presumably named for crew member Thomas Wilson.

[311] Northwest entrance to Jarrells Cove.

[312] Unnamed on current charts but located at the northwest point of Hartstene Island at the bend in Pickering Passage.

[313] Named for crew member William Brisco.

[314] Unnamed on current charts. It is located on the north side of Pickering Passage, north of Jarrells Cove.

[315] Graham Point.

[316] On some charts, this is spelled Salmon Point, on the north end of Squaxin Island.

until reaching COOK POINT[317] *where it again divides with Hammersly inlet running 7 miles to the west where it turns 2 miles northeast. Hope Island lies in the centre of the channel on the western side of Jack's, south of Cook Point. Passage to the east of Hope is not possible for large vessels because of shoaling, the western channel is to be favored.* SANDY POINT[318] *lies west of Hope; Totten Inlet branches beyond and runs 7 miles toward the southwest. At the south end of Jack's Island is* UNSAL POINT[319] *beyond which the channel divides into Eld's Inlet running southwest, Budd's Harbor running to the south, and Dana's Passage running northeast. At the west entrance of Budd's Harbor is* POINT COOPER,[320] *opposite is* BROWNS POINT.[321] *Budd's Harbor is 5 miles in length, depths range from 5 to 7 fathoms near the centre with shoaling on either side. On the eastern shore, 2 miles from Browns Point is* WEPUSEC INLET[322]; *further into the inlet on the eastern shore is* SARINGA POINT.[323]

South Continental Shore Line

Doubling Brown's Point and running through Dana's Passage, DICKERSON POINT[324] *lies at the northwest entrance of Henderson Inlet and Point Moody at the northeast. Between the two is the* ITSAMI SHOAL *with a depth of only 1 fathom. On the far eastern shore, past Fort Nisqually, lies* TATSOLO POINT *with* QULAM POINT[325] *2¼ miles to the north; 3½ miles further is* KOSA POINT[326] *opposite Point Gibson on Fox Island.*

HOOD'S CANAL.

Hood's Canal branches off from Admiralty Inlet at Suquamish Head, where it is 2 miles wide. Its direction is south-southeast, 5 miles; it then turns to the south-southwest, 6 miles; thence to SQUALLER'S POINT,[327] southeast 6 miles, turning again to the west-southwest, 3 miles, to NUKOLOWAP POINT,[328] the south point of TOANDOS PENINSULA,[329] which divides the

---

[317] Potlatch Point named after crew member John Cook.
[318] Steamboat Island.
[319] Shown as Tucksel Point on some charts.
[320] Named for crew member John Cooper.
[321] Dofflemeyer Point, named for crew member James Brown.
[322] Gull Harbor.
[323] Unnamed on current charts but is located in East Bay of the Olympia Harbor.
[324] Named for Secretary of the Navy Mahlon Dickerson who signed Wilkes' orders.
[325] Gordon Point.
[326] Unnamed on current charts but is located near Sunset Beach.
[327] Unknown location but perhaps King Spit, south of Bangor.
[328] Oak Head.
[329] A phonetic adaptation of Twana Indian name "tu-an-hu," meaning portage.

north branch from the Canal. Continuing on this course, across the mouth of the north branch, for 4 miles, is QUATSAP POINT, passing the HARBOR AND POINT OF SCABOCK[330] on the east, thence southwest, 3 miles, to TRITON HEAD,[331] continuing to POINT CUMMINGS,[332] AYOCH'S POINT,[333] to POINT NEELIM.[334] Throughout this distance, 30 miles, the shore is elevated and well wooded. There are several small streams [p. 323] of fresh water: the one near Point Cummings is the largest[335]; at its outlet there is a mud-flat.

The eastern shore, from SANDY POINT,[336] opposite Quatsap, though not so elevated, is more precipitous. From Sandy Point to POINT MUSQUITI,[337] which lies nearly opposite to Neelim Point, the shore is of the same character, and the width of the Canal throughout the distance varies but little; the points are all low and sandy, while those on the opposite side are high. The anchorage on the west side is better than on the east, where the water is too deep in many places to admit of it. From Neelim Point, the Canal takes a sharp turn to the east-northeast. Between Neelim Point and POINT CROWLIE[338] lies ANNA'S BAY, into which empties Black Creek[339]: the distance between the points is 2 miles, the bay 1 mile deep, the eastern part of it being filled by an extensive mud-flat. From Point Crowlie to SISTER'S POINT is 3 miles. Here the northeast arm contracts to half a mile in width, whence it changes its course to the east-northeast, 8 miles, ending in LYNCH COVE,[340] which, as is usual in all these harbors, has an extensive mud-flat at its head.

The harbors in Hood's Canal are Port Ludlow, at its entrance, heretofore described, PORT GAMBLE,[341] SUQUAMISH,[342] Scabock, HOO-ET-ZEN,[343]

---

[330] Seabeck.

[331] Presumably named for Triton, the Greek god of the sea.

[332] Named for crew member W. H. Cummings.

[333] Now spelled Ayock.

[334] This point is not named on current charts. On Wilkes' chart, it is shown just short of the southwest end of the Canal on the west side near Potlatch.

[335] Hamma Hamma River.

[336] Hood Point.

[337] Now spelled Musqueti.

[338] This point is not named on current charts. On Wilkes' chart, it is shown approximately at the town of Union.

[339] Skokomish River.

[340] Named for Lieutenant William Francis Lynch who explored the Dead Sea and the Jordan River.

[341] Named for Lieutenant Robert Gamble, a War of 1812 hero.

[342] An alteration of the Indian Suk-wa-bish, now spelled Squamish.

[343] Jackson Cove.

and COL-SEE-ED HARBORS;[344] DABOP and Anna Bays; TZU-SA-TED[345] and Lynch Coves.

Port Gamble lies 6 miles within Hood's Canal from Squamish Head, on its eastern side; it is 2½ miles in length, north and south, and half a mile wide at its entrance. The channel lies through an extensive mud-flat, to the northward of its two points, TOTTEN'S[346] on the west, and POINT JULIA on the east. To enter, bring Point Julia to bear south half east, and steer due south, taking care to keep it open on the port bow. The bottom is quite soft, and a vessel cannot be injured if she grounds on either side; but those drawing less than 20 feet can find no difficulty in passing through it, even at low water, with a fair wind. Within the harbor there is from 5 to 7 fathoms water; the bottom is of mud and sand, and the holding-ground good; the shores are moderately high. At the south end, there are two or three small streams of water, but they are not at all times to be relied upon for a supply. In entering the Canal, steer for POINT HANNON, a sandy point on its western side; thence for POINT SALISBURY[347]; but to enter Suquamish Harbor, it is better to keep the western shore aboard, passing round the SISTER ROCKS, off POINT TERMINATION,[348] and anchor on the east side, avoiding the sandbank [p. 324] off the western shore. The Sister Rocks may be avoided by not shutting out the land to the south of SOUTH POINT.[349] There is no other danger to be apprehended, and these are usually visible.

The next harbor is that of Scabock. It lies on the eastern side of the Canal, directly south of Nukolowap Point, distant from it 3 miles. It is one of the most convenient anchorages in the Canal. Its shape is triangular; its shore is bordered by a sand-beach, from which the hills rise: these are well-covered with wood. The distance between the two points of the harbor (SAMUM and WIKAT),[350] is 1 mile; it is also a mile deep towards the south-west. Near its head is an extensive sand-flat, dry in places at low water. The watering-place can be approached by boats at half tide: the landing is on the south-east side, at MAKAK POINT. The best anchorage is near the centre of the harbor, Samum Point bearing northwest, with a gray sandy bottom.

---

[344] Quilcene Bay.

[345] Pleasant Harbor, spelled TZEE-SA-TED on Wilkes' chart.

[346] Named for crew member George M. Totten, this point is unnamed on current charts.

[347] Named for crew member Francis Salsbury.

[348] The point is named for its location, at the north termination of Hood's Canal.

[349] The point is named for its location.

[350] Spelled SANUM on Wilkes charts, it is the western entrance and represents the hook to the west of Misery Point; Wikat is unnamed on current charts but is located on the eastern entrance.

Opposite Scabock Point is the entrance to the north branch of Hood's Canal, which lies between the Toandos Peninsula and the western shore: it is 9 miles deep and 2 miles wide between SYLOPASH and TSKULUSCO[351] Points. It contains three harbors, but there is no anchorage in it, the water being very deep.

Hoo-et-zen Harbor is the next. It lies on the west shore of the north branch, 3 miles above Sylopash Point, and forms a segment of a circle, three-fourths of a mile in diameter; its shores are rocky and elevated, except on the northwest side, where there is a sand-beach, with the usual mud-flat. PULALI POINT lies on the east side, from which to the double heads the shore is a rocky bluff. The west side, from WEEWA[352] to NAIKA POINTS,[353] is of a similar character. At the head of the harbor is MUSAM PLACE,[354] where a small creek enters, from which good water may be obtained. The best anchorage is in 11 fathoms, about the centre of the harbor. To enter, either shore may be closely approached. After rounding Nukolowap Point, steer directly for the harbor, the course is north-northwest.

Two miles to the northward of Hoo-et-zen, you enter Col-see-ed Harbor, between BRAMBLEBLUFF[355] and ROSE POINT[356]; they are half a mile asunder. The harbor is 2 miles in length, including the extensive mud-flat at its head, which occupies nearly one-half the space, and is generally bare at low water, the upper part being a salt marsh, with creeks running through. Both shores of the southern part of the harbor are steep, hilly, and well covered with wood. The anchorage lies off POINT YAKSO,[357] half a mile above Rose Point, in 7 to 10 fathoms [p. 325] water with muddy bottom. At Point Yakso, there is an Indian village. Water may be obtained at half tide from the streams and creeks at the head of the harbor. Col-see-ed Harbor is separated from Dabop Bay by BOLTON PENINSULA,[358] which is 4 miles long by 1 mile wide. In Dabop Bay, the water to the southward of PILASH POINT,[359] is too deep for anchorage; to the north, it is necessary to anchor

---

[351] Spelled Tskutsko in Wilkes' journal.

[352] Shown as WAWA POINT on Wilkes' chart. The Indian name means to talk or speak the Chinook jargon.

[353] Located immediately north of Wawa Point, in Jackson Cove, unnamed on current charts.

[354] Located at the head of Jackson Cove, west of Camp Parsons.

[355] Frenchmans Point, the western entrance.

[356] Fishermans Point, the eastern entrance at the south tip of the Bolton Peninsula.

[357] Unnamed on current charts, however, this is located approximately ¼ of a mile north of Fishermans Point on the eastern shoreline.

[358] Named for crew member William F. Bolton.

[359] Broad Spit.

very near the shore at the head of the Bay, which terminates in a small muddy and useless cove. The land which borders this bay is high, and covered with woods; into it several small streams discharge themselves. As a harbor it is not to be compared to the others before spoken of. The shores in this arm, as well as those of the Canal, are well supplied with shell-fish.

Anna's Bay lies at the southern extremity of the Canal, where Vancouver supposed it ended. Black Creek enters into this Bay, by which the Indians make the communication with the Chekeeles and the country to the south. The anchorage in Anna's Bay is on the western side, under Point Neelim, where there is a moderate depth of water. A large Indian village is situated on Point Neelim.

A mile to the north of Quatsap Point lies Tzusated Cove. Its position may be readily known by the JUPITER HILLS,[360] which lie just above it. The best anchorage is off BOSTON POINT,[361] a rocky bluff, distant 1 mile from OLO BLUFF[362]; Between the two lies the cove: an anchorage may be obtained in any part of it. On the southwest, there is a narrow entrance between PALISI and SLIK POINTS,[363] into the basin, which is half a mile long by quarter of a mile wide, and secure from all winds. The depth of water in it is between 5 and 6 fathoms. In the entrance there is but 2¼ fathoms at low tide. It is well marked by Palisi Point, low and sandy, on the west side and the rocky bluff of Slik Point on the east. In anchoring in this cove, it is necessary to look out for the heavy flows of wind which come down from the Jupiter Hills.

Lynch Cove is situated at the farthest point of the northeast branch. The land about it is low and marshy on the east; on the west it rises, and is sparsely covered with wood. At the head of this cove is also an extensive mud-flat. There is good anchorage, in 5 and 6 fathoms, between the two small sandspits, which lie on opposite sides of and form the cove.

At the northwest end of the canal is Suquamish Harbor. West of Point Termination is YULKAT BLUFF,[364] *back from the beach and 100 feet in elevation, increasing to 400 feet progressing inland. The western beach is protected by* CASE BANK,[365] *a shoal area 1¼ miles in length and running almost north-south. Four to 6 fathoms water was found inside the bank. At the southern*

---

[360] A 1,500-foot hill located between the Duckabush and Dosewallips, it is named for the Roman god.

[361] The point east of the southern entrance to Pleasant Harbor, named for Boston, Massachusetts.

[362] Located on the Peninsula north of Pleasant Harbor, perhaps near Brinnon.

[363] The north and south entrances to Pleasant Harbor, respectively.

[364] Unnamed on current charts.

[365] Named for crew member Augustus L. Case.

end of the bank is KAKUA, a sandspit, behind which is mud that dries at low tide. South of that is POINT PETERS[366] followed by South Point. The shoreline in this area behind the spit to South Point is high bank rising to 300 feet within a ¼ mile from the beach.

On the eastern side of the Toandos Peninsula, BROWNS POINT is half way to the end. Four miles distant is SUQUALUS POINT.[367] Doubling the Toandos Peninsula and entering Dabop Bay finds ZELATCHED POINT on the eastern shoreline and 4 miles to the north, TABOOK POINT is nearly west of Brown's Point.

Four additional points on the eastern side of the canal bear mentioning. TEKIU POINT[368] is located opposite Triton Head. South of that 3 miles is TCHI-NOM POINT[369] and south a further 5 miles is DADAH POINT.[370] At the south end is AYRES POINT[371] where the canal turns towards the northeast. At the head, in Lynch Cove, KILLINAS LAKE[372] lies inland 1 mile to the southeast.

Finally, north of Quatsap Point behind Tzu-sa-ted is a high hillside bearing the name SAKALI BLUFF.[373] When heading for Tzu-sa-ted, this hillside is visible at some distance.

In closing my remarks upon the intercommunication these waters afford, it might be deemed desirable that I should point out the [p. 326] localities which afford the best positions for future settlements. These at first will be selected more from convenience for present supplies, than with a view to future trade. But the positions which must claim most attention, are those at the head of the inlets, affording facilities for trade as well as internal communication. The waters off Cape Flattery offer an extent of safe navigation unsurpassed in any country, and every facility that can be needed for carrying on the most extensive commerce. But a few years will elapse before this estuary will be overrun by the tide of emigration, which is now flowing so rapidly toward the western shores.

Our surveys did not extend to the north of Frazer's River, in the Gulf of Georgia; I omit therefore to give any particular description of it. It may be stated, however, that the tides are very strong, that there are many detached rocks, that the shores are bold and iron-bound, and that there is

---

[366] Unnamed on current charts but located near Bridgehaven.
[367] Hazel Point.
[368] Indian for elk.
[369] The "T" was apparently dropped and the point renamed to Chinom.
[370] Unnamed on current charts but is located at the entrance to Dewatto Bay.
[371] Named for crew member John Ayres.
[372] Reflected as KELLUMS LAKE on Wilkes' Chart for crew member John Kellum.
[373] Unnamed on current charts.

great difficulty in navigating through Johnson's Strait,[374] and little security to shipping against the dangers. Fogs prevail for a large portion of the year, which throw great difficulties and impediments to its ever being used as a route for navigation, even when assisted by steam.

FRAZER'S RIVER.

The mouth of Frazer's River lies 7 miles to the north of the 49th parallel. Like all the other rivers of Oregon, it is barred by an extensive mud and sand flat, extending for some 6 miles to the west; this is partially bare at low water. The channel in the river is of ample depth; its course is serpentine. From its north bluff outwards, towards the bar, the depth decreases to 12 feet, which is the greatest draft of water that can be carried in: this renders the entrance impracticable for vessels of large size. The bar bears southwest from the north bluff, and west-southwest from Cowitchen Peak. Point M'Leod, at the mouth of the north channel, now nearly filled up, is 4 miles distant. During freshets, the river discharges a part of its water through it, and then it may be passed through by boats and canoes. The south bank of the river is low and marshy. At high water the tide flows through several small inlets into the river; these once formed a delta, but they are now too much obstructed and too small to be so considered. The position [p. 327] of the north bluff, where our observations were made, is 49° 07' 05" north, longitude 123° 08' 57" west, and the variation 21° 14' 41" west. The trade of Frazer's River will be considerable when the country becomes settled; it is navigable for steamboats to its falls, 80 miles from its mouth. It has a fine salmon fishery; though the fish are not so large as those of the Columbia River, yet they abound in greater number. The principal settlement is Fort Langley, twenty-five miles from its mouth, which is one of the posts of the Hudson Bay Company.

---

[374]Wilkes meant Johnstone Strait.

4

Volume XXIII Charts

As noted previously, the second part of Volume XXIII is a two-volume atlas. Charts for Washington waters are found in Volume II as follows:

Oregon Territory (General Sheet),
Mouth of Columbia River, Sheet No. 1,
Columbia River   " No. 2,
     "   " No. 3,
     "   " No. 4,
     "   " No. 5,
     "   " No. 6,
Gray's Harbour,
Straits of Juan de Fuca,
Archipelago of Arro, Gulf of Georgia, and Ringgold's Channel,
Admiralty Inlet, Puget Sound, and Hoods Canal,
Inlets in Puget Sound (Whole Sheet),
St. Juan and Scarborough Harbours, and Port Discovery,
Dungeness Roads, and Budd's Harbour,
Ports Townsend and Lawrence,
Ports Ludlow and Gamble,
Suquamish and Colsee-ed Harbours,
Scabock and Hooetzen Harbours, and Tzu-sa-ted Cove,
Case's and Carr's Inlets,
Narrows, and Commencement Bay,
Ports Orchard and Madison,
Ports Susan, and Gardner and Apple and Pilot's Coves,
Deception Passage, Holmes' Harbour, and Penn's Cove,
Birch Bay, Drayton's Bay, and Point Roberts Anchorage,
Strawberry, and Argus Bays, Hornet Harbour, &c.

Reproducing these charts in any but a large scale format makes for difficult reading. However, many are available digitally, courtesy of NOAA. I have downloaded several and enlarged portions on the following pages. I took the liberty of removing some of the depth values in order to reduce the clutter, particularly where the numbers were close to the shoreline or interfered with names. In addition, with respect to the Discovery Bay chart, I carefully replaced all depth values and place names with a larger type size to improve readability. The charts are for reference purposes only and not intended for navagation.

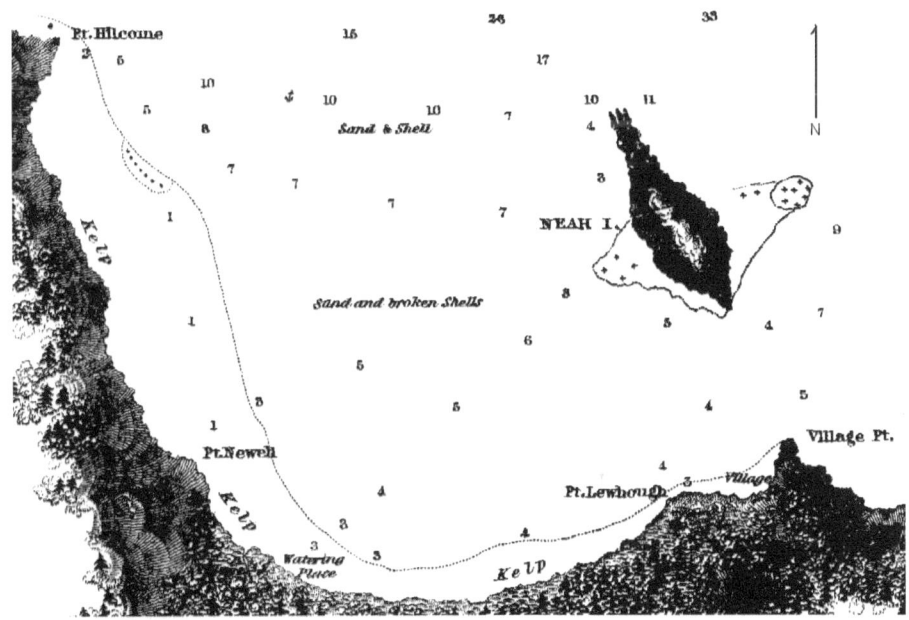

Neah Bay

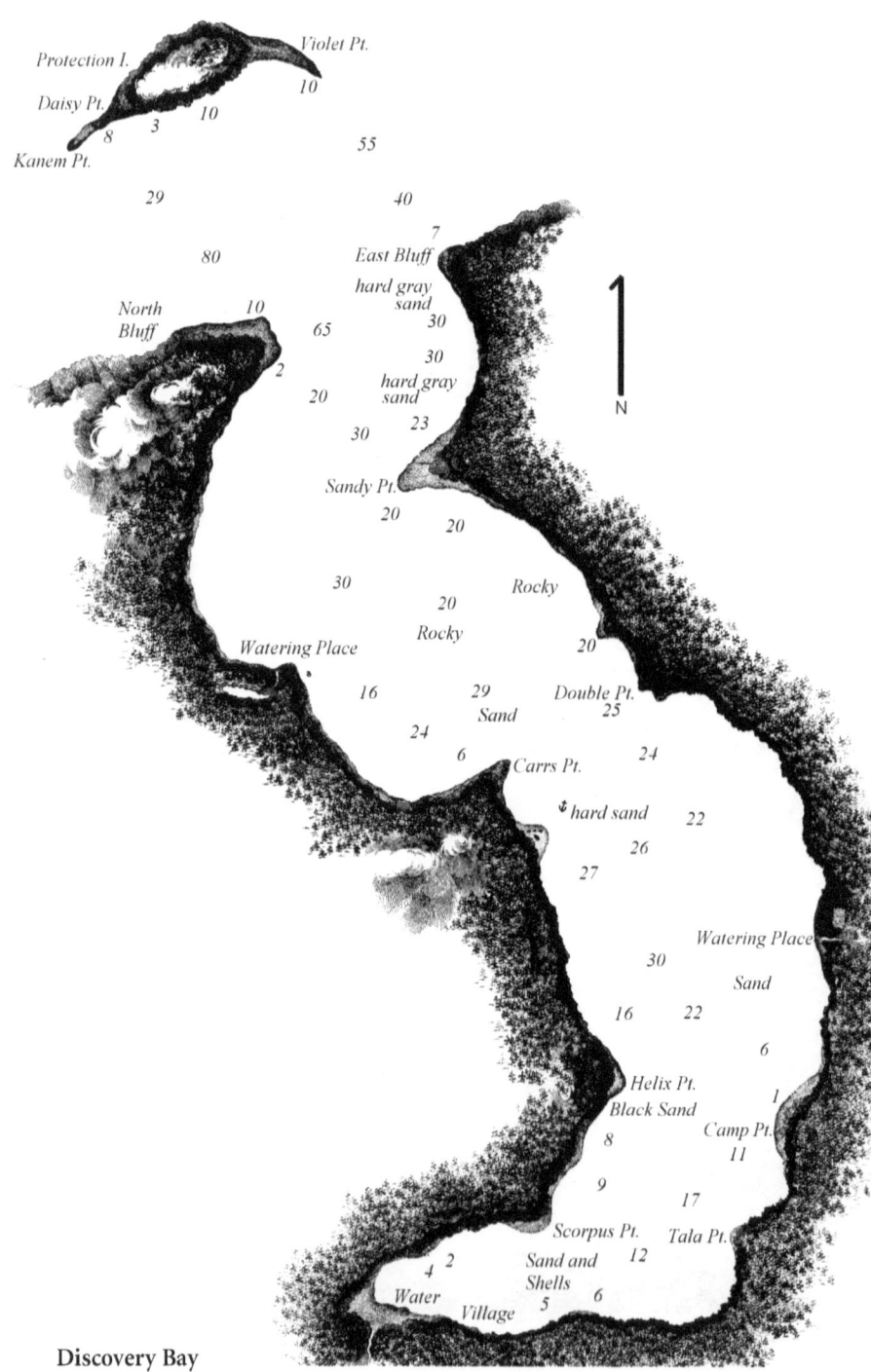

Discovery Bay

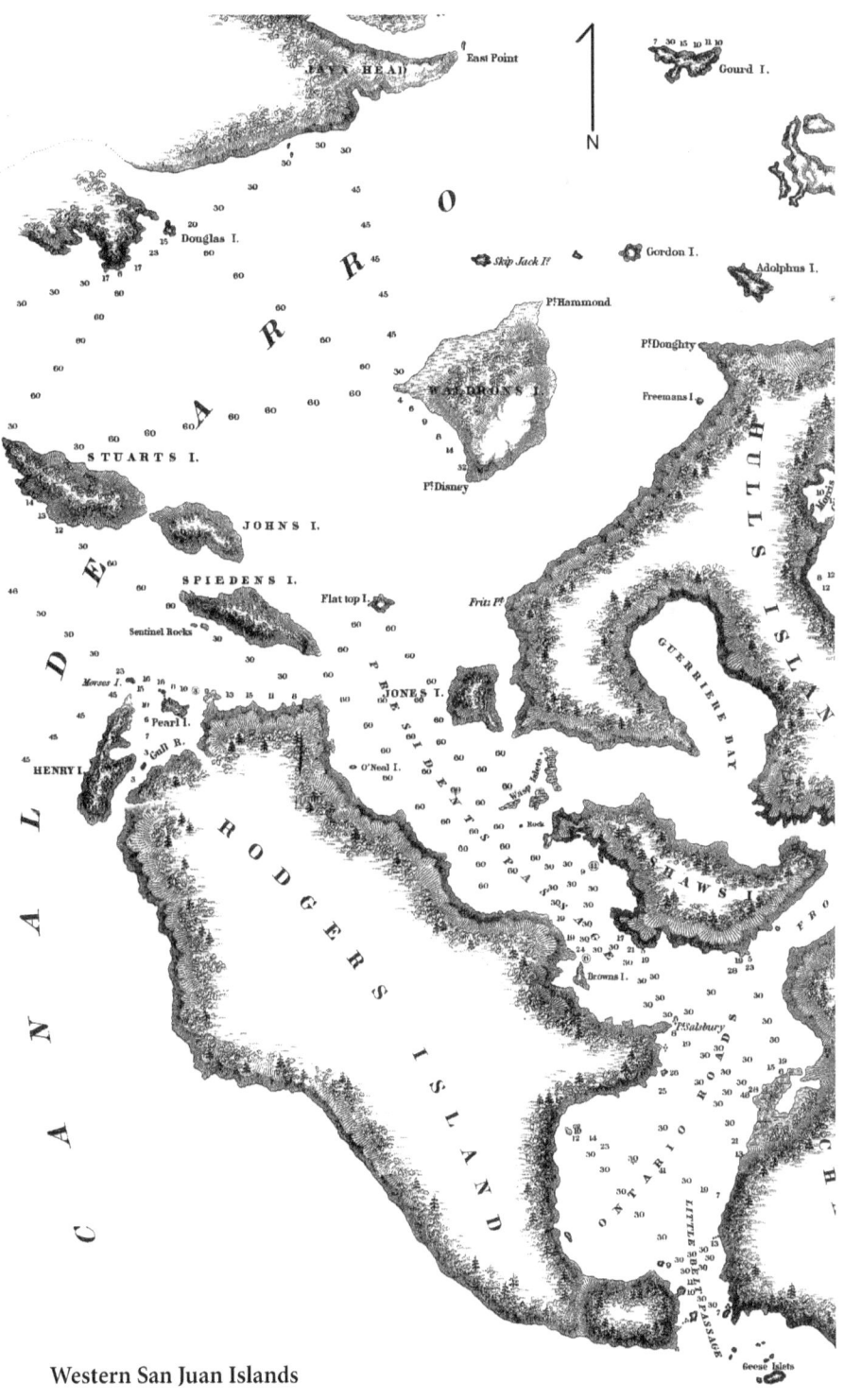

Western San Juan Islands

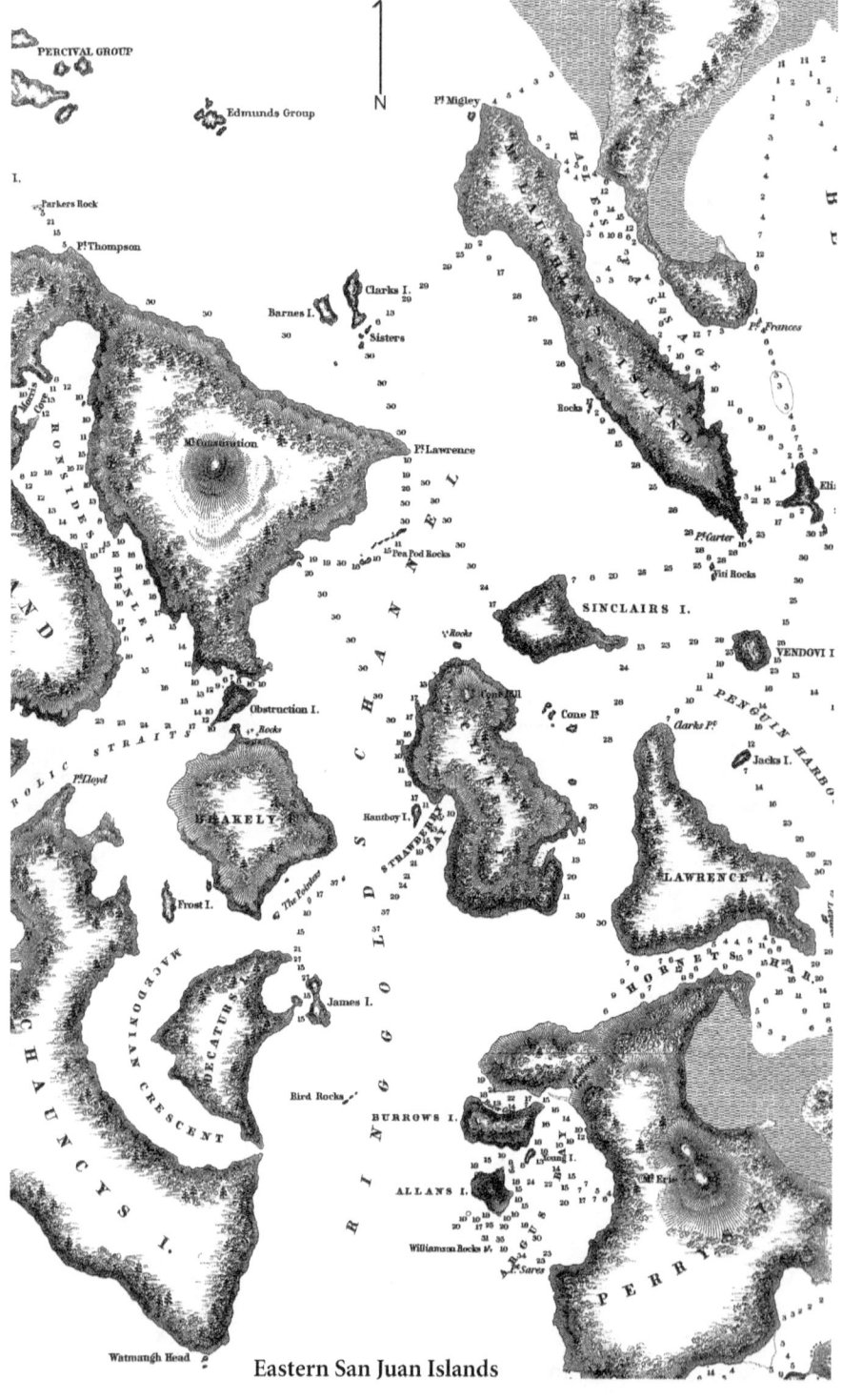

Eastern San Juan Islands

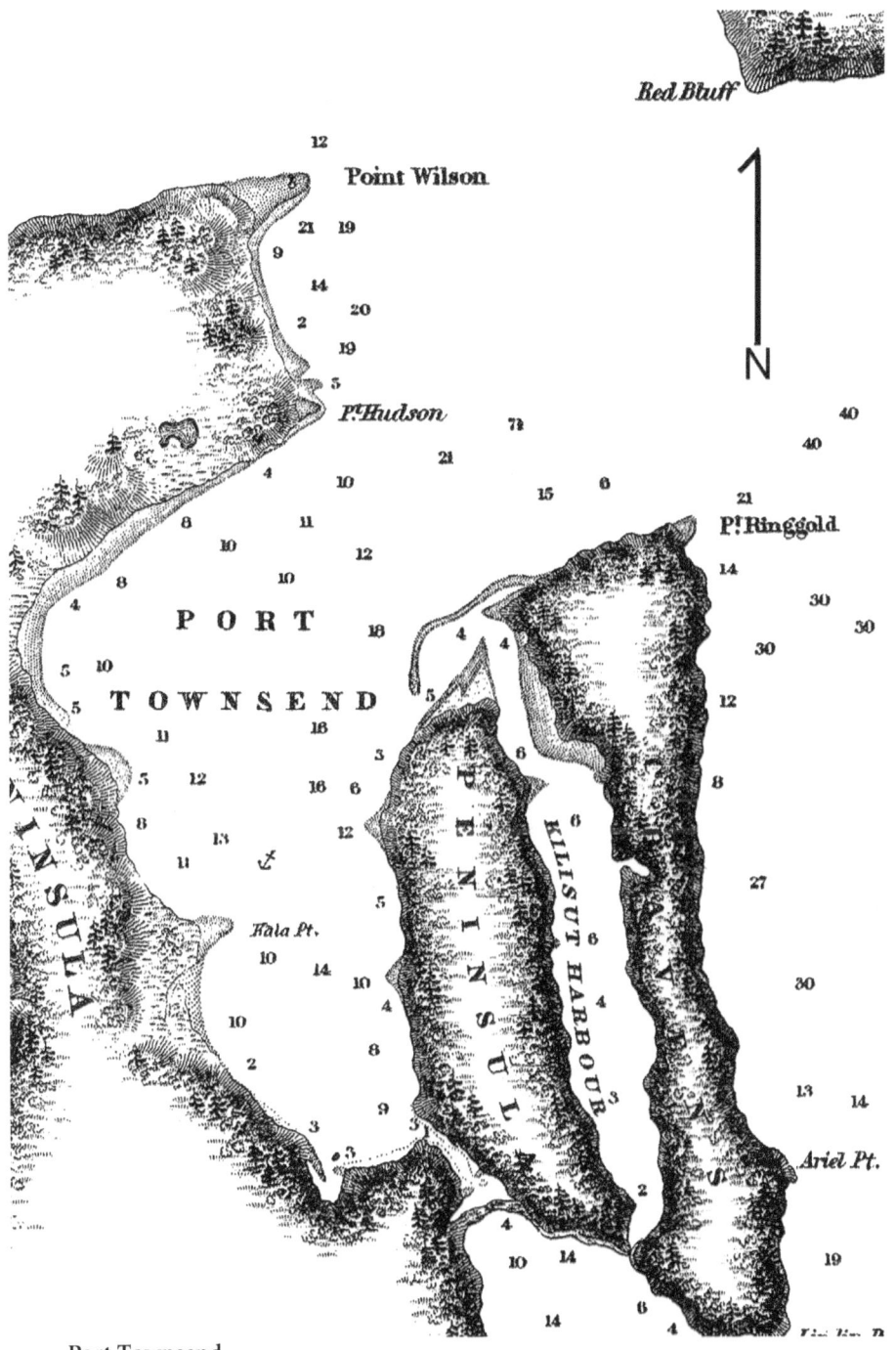

Port Townsend

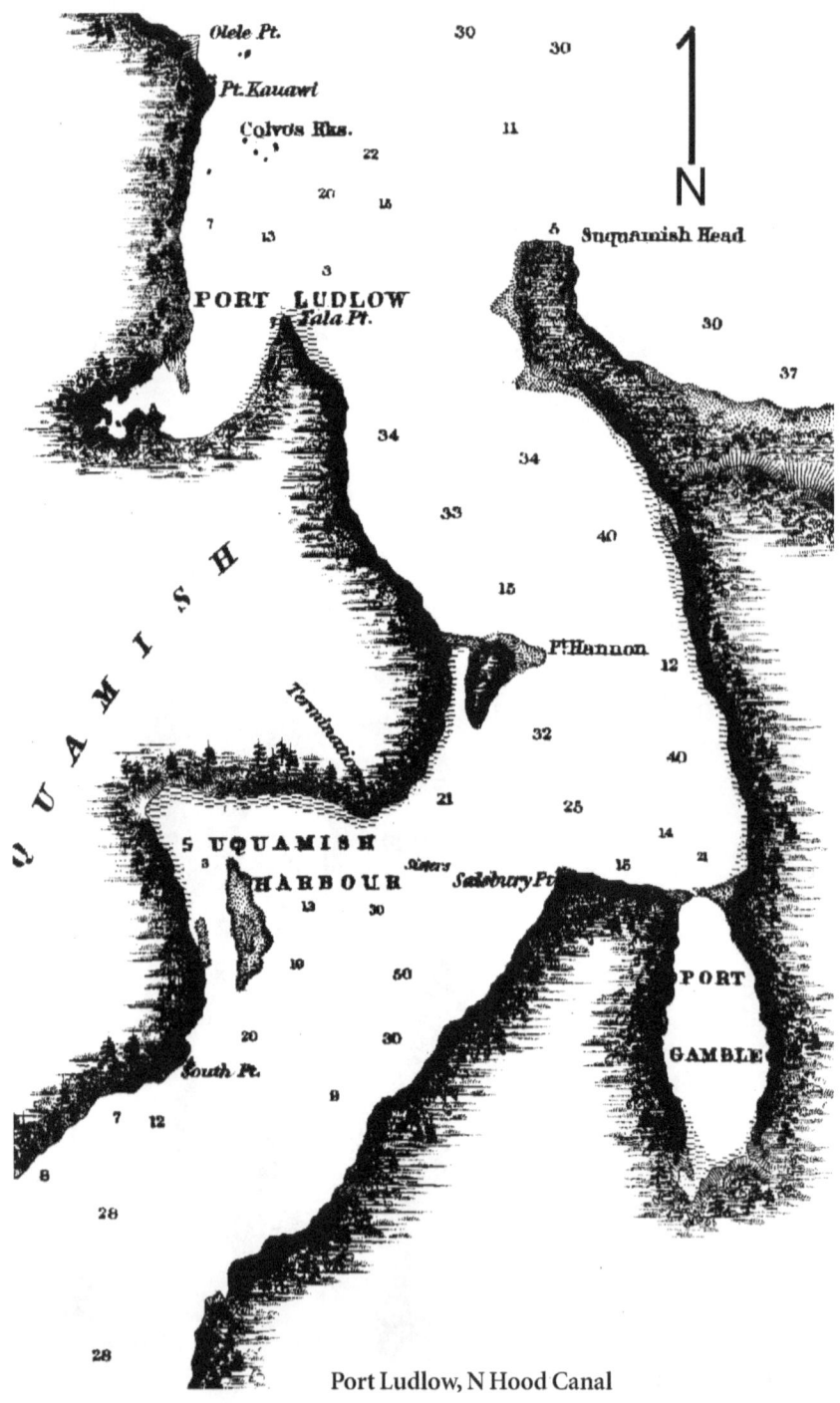

Port Ludlow, N Hood Canal

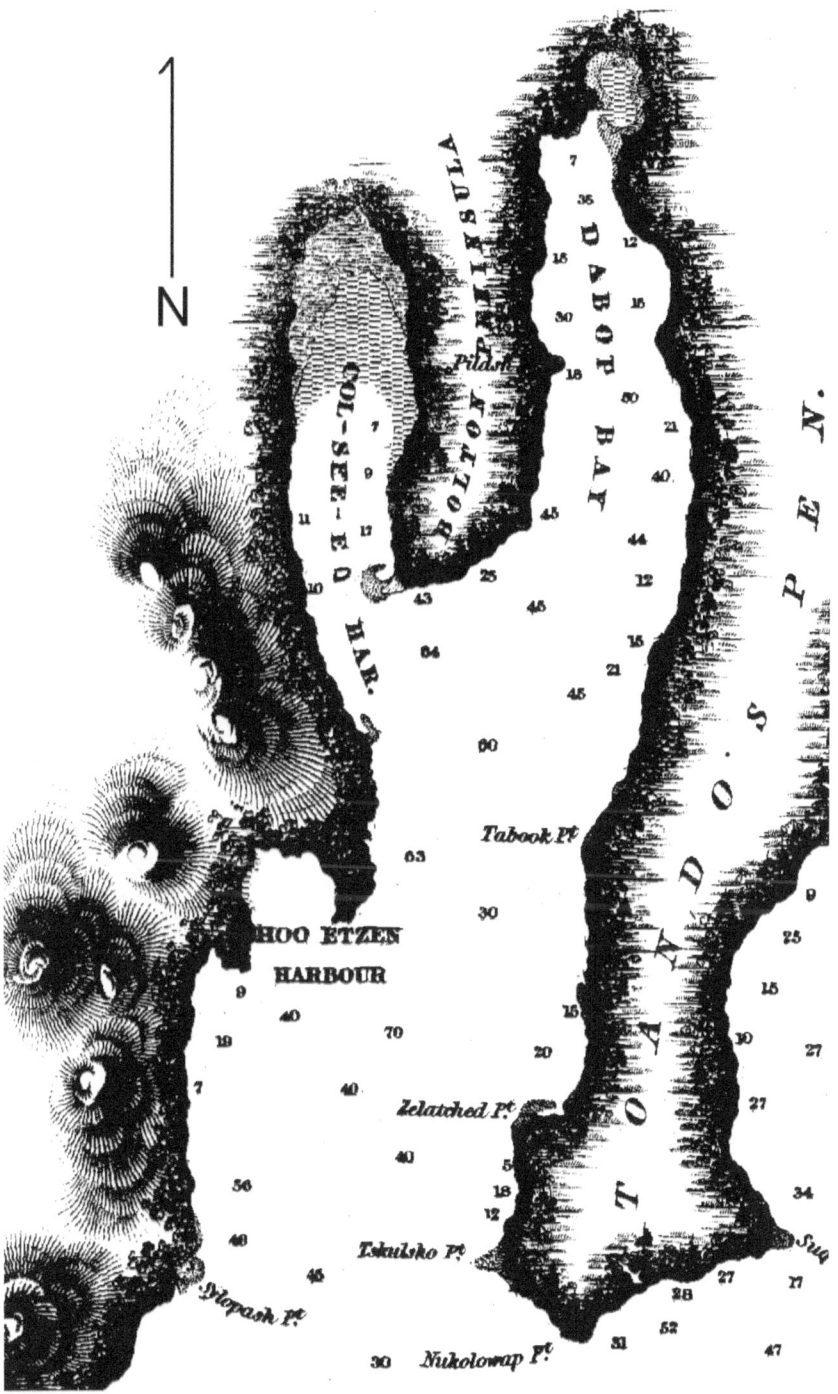

Toandos Peninsula

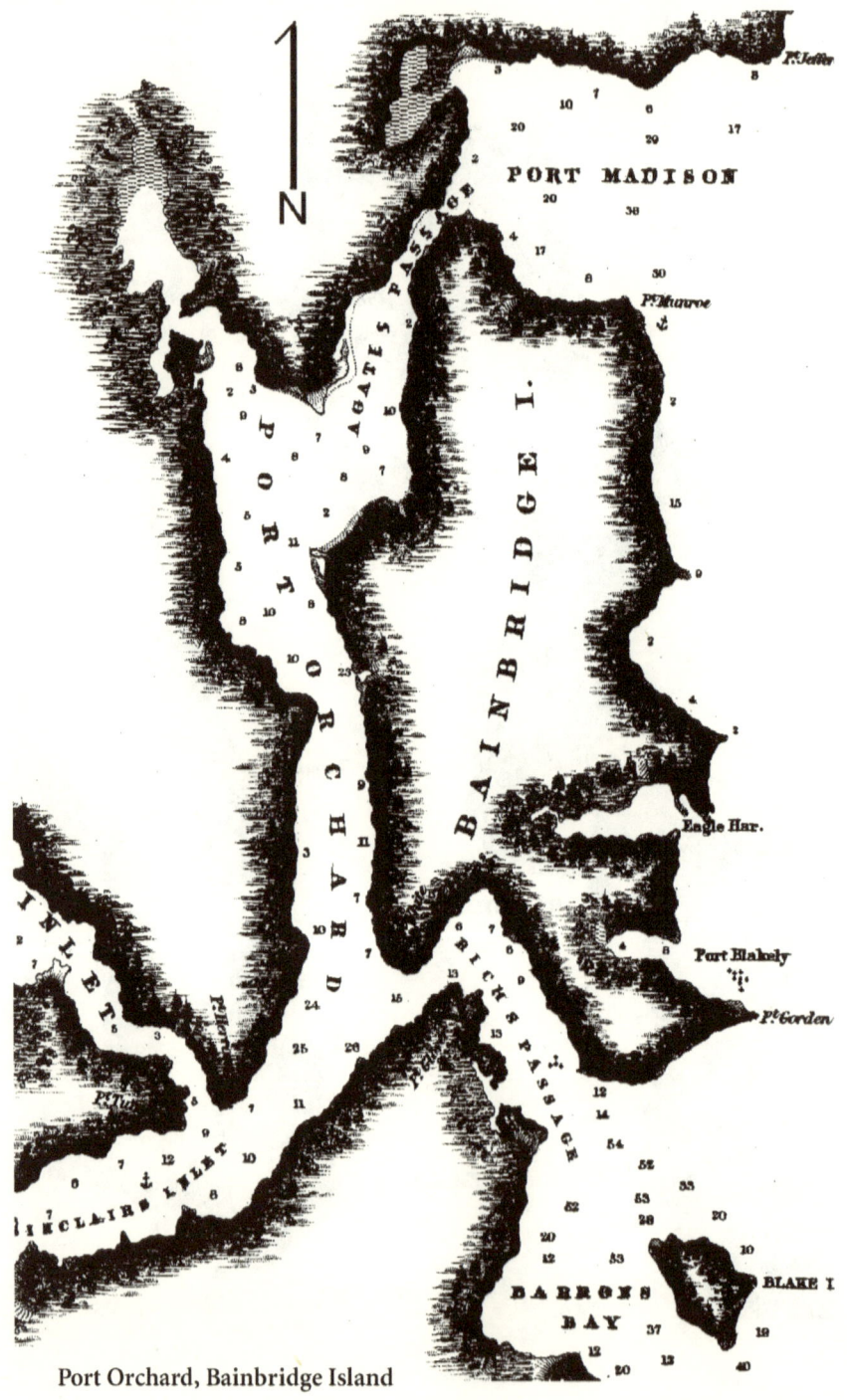

Port Orchard, Bainbridge Island

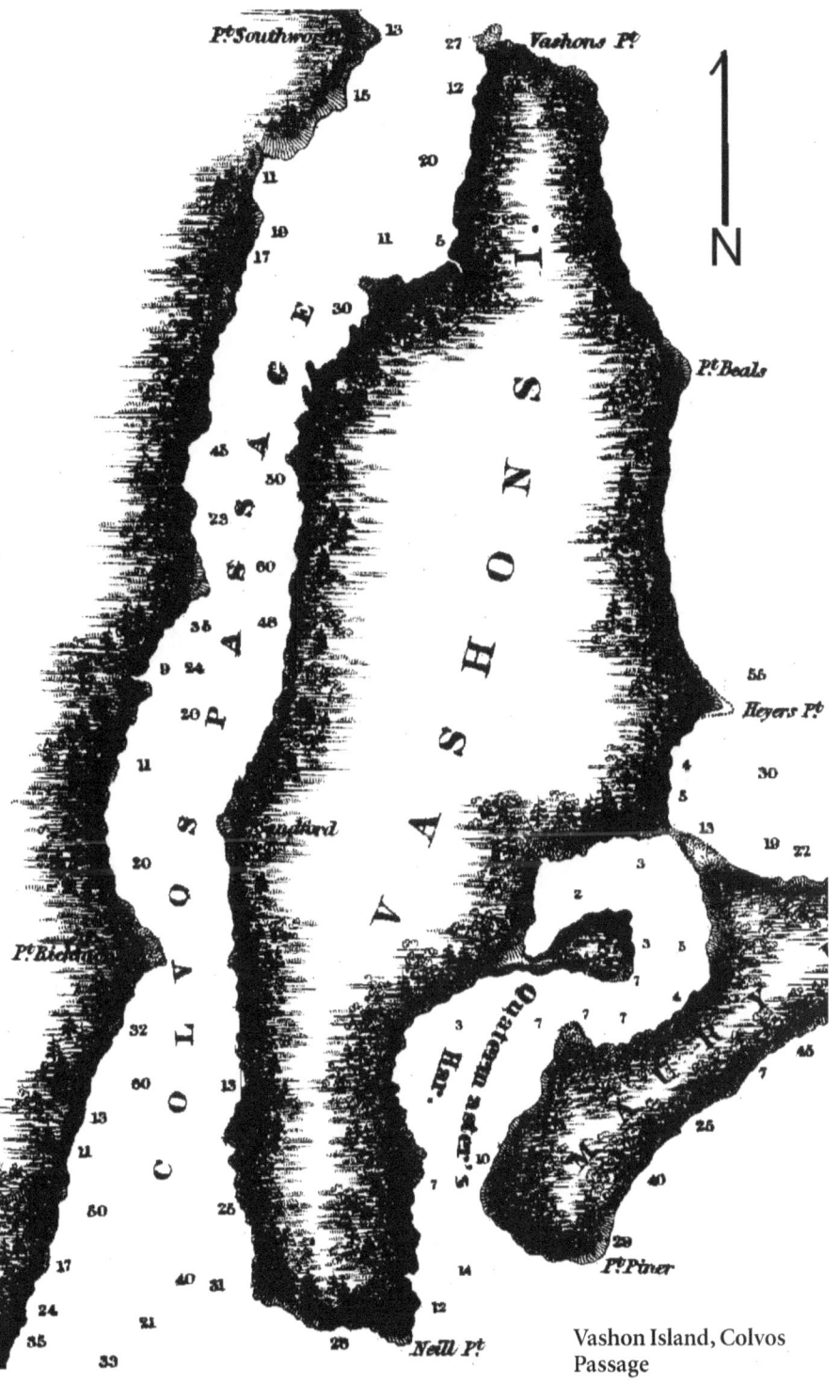

Vashon Island, Colvos Passage

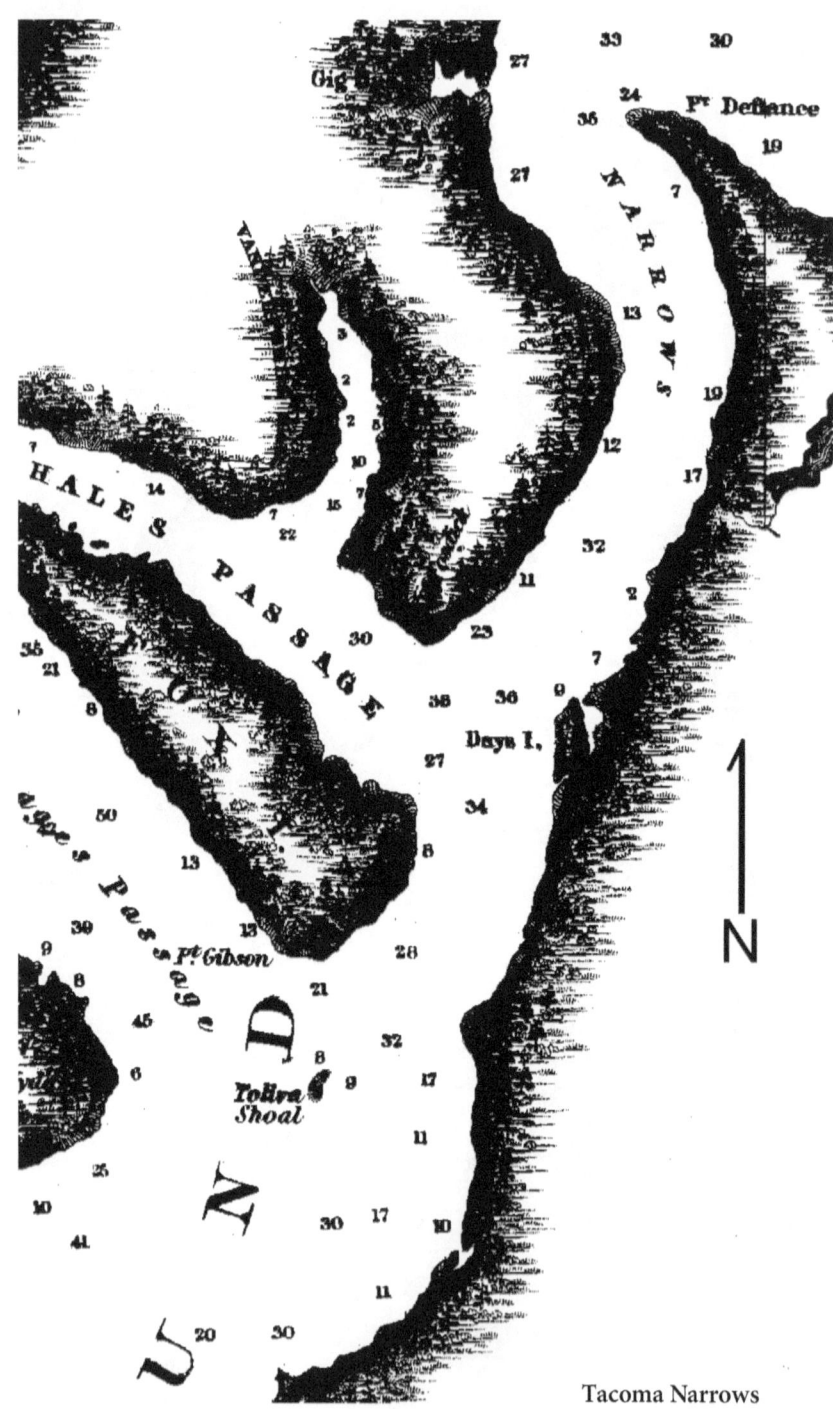

Tacoma Narrows

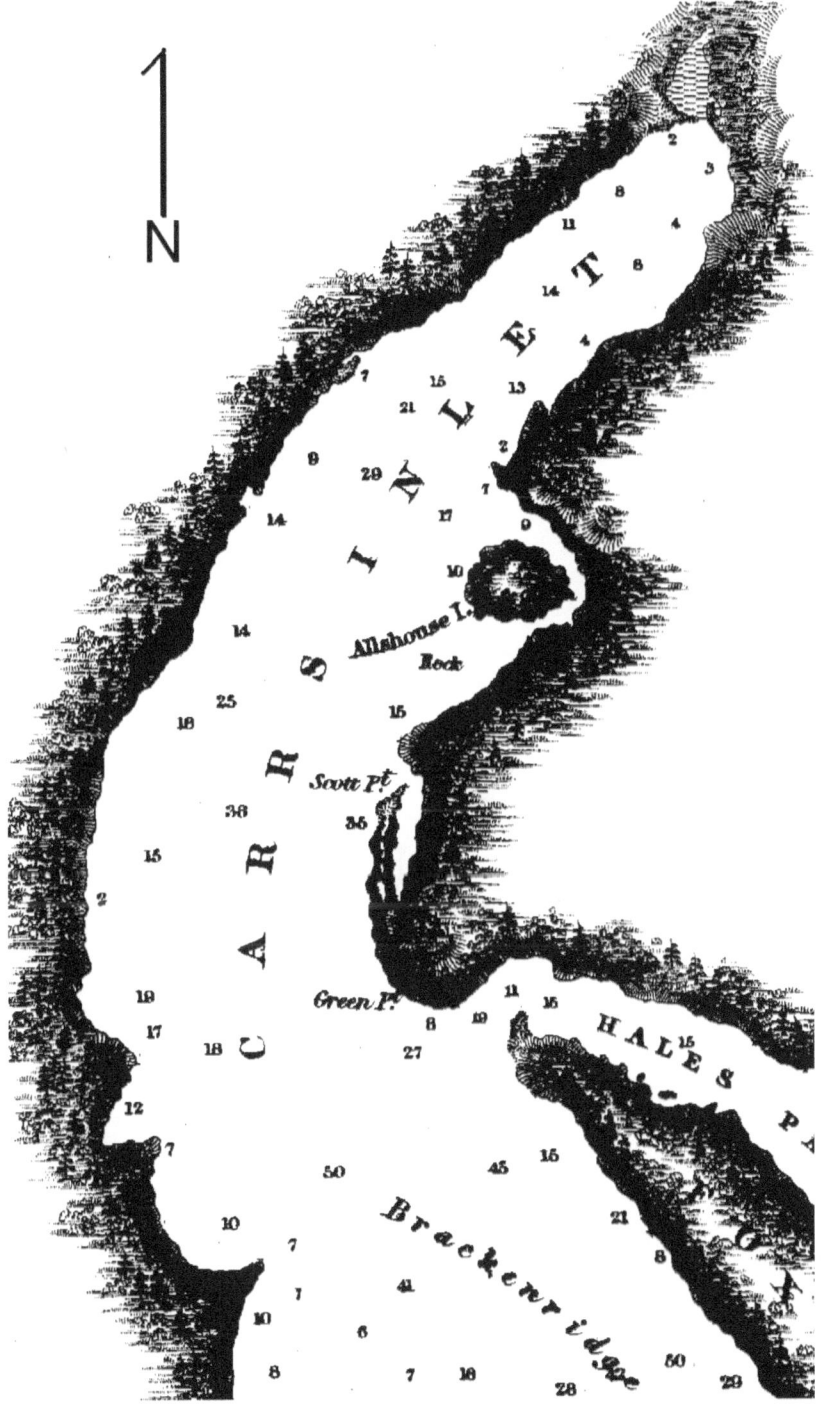

Carr Inlet

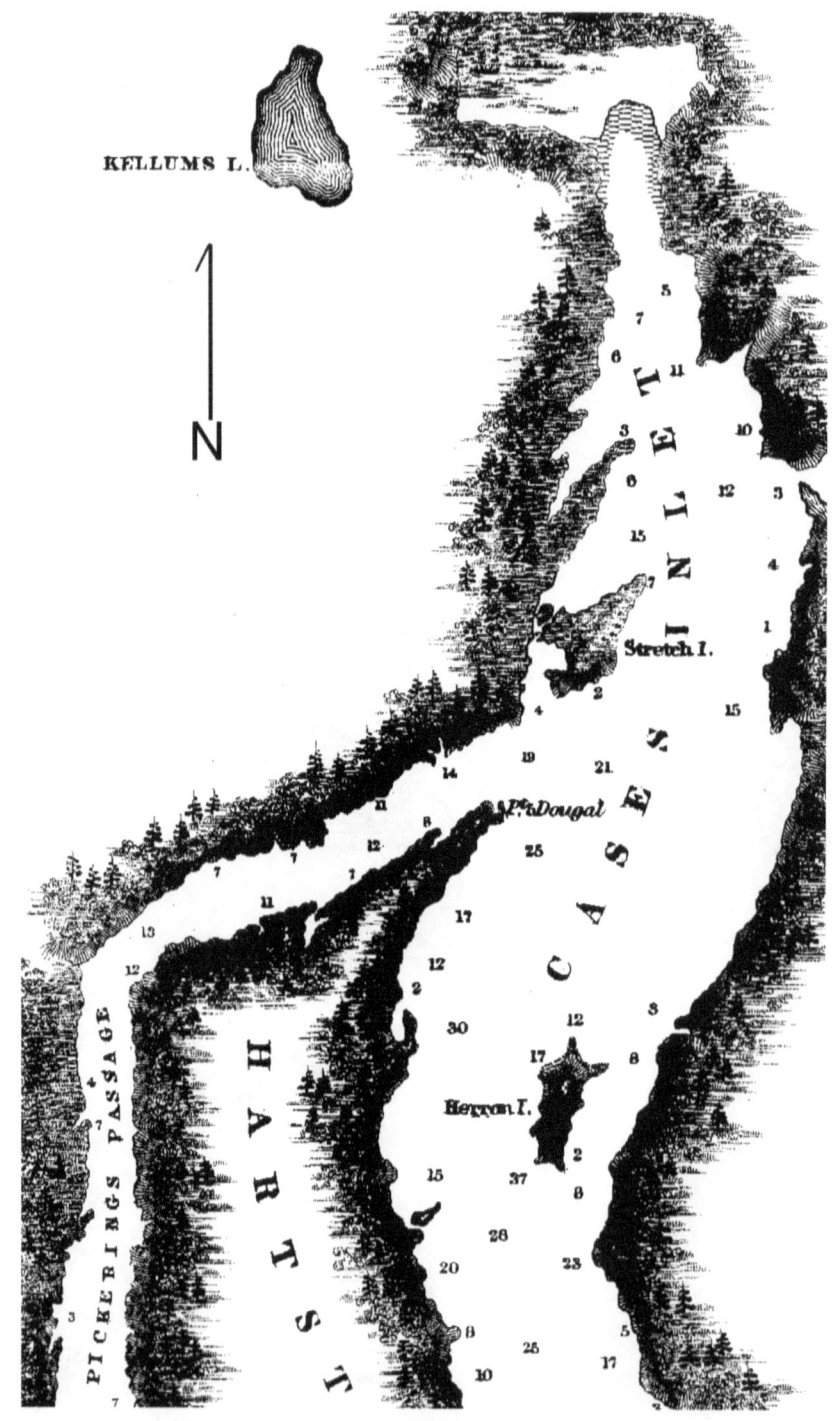

Case Inlet

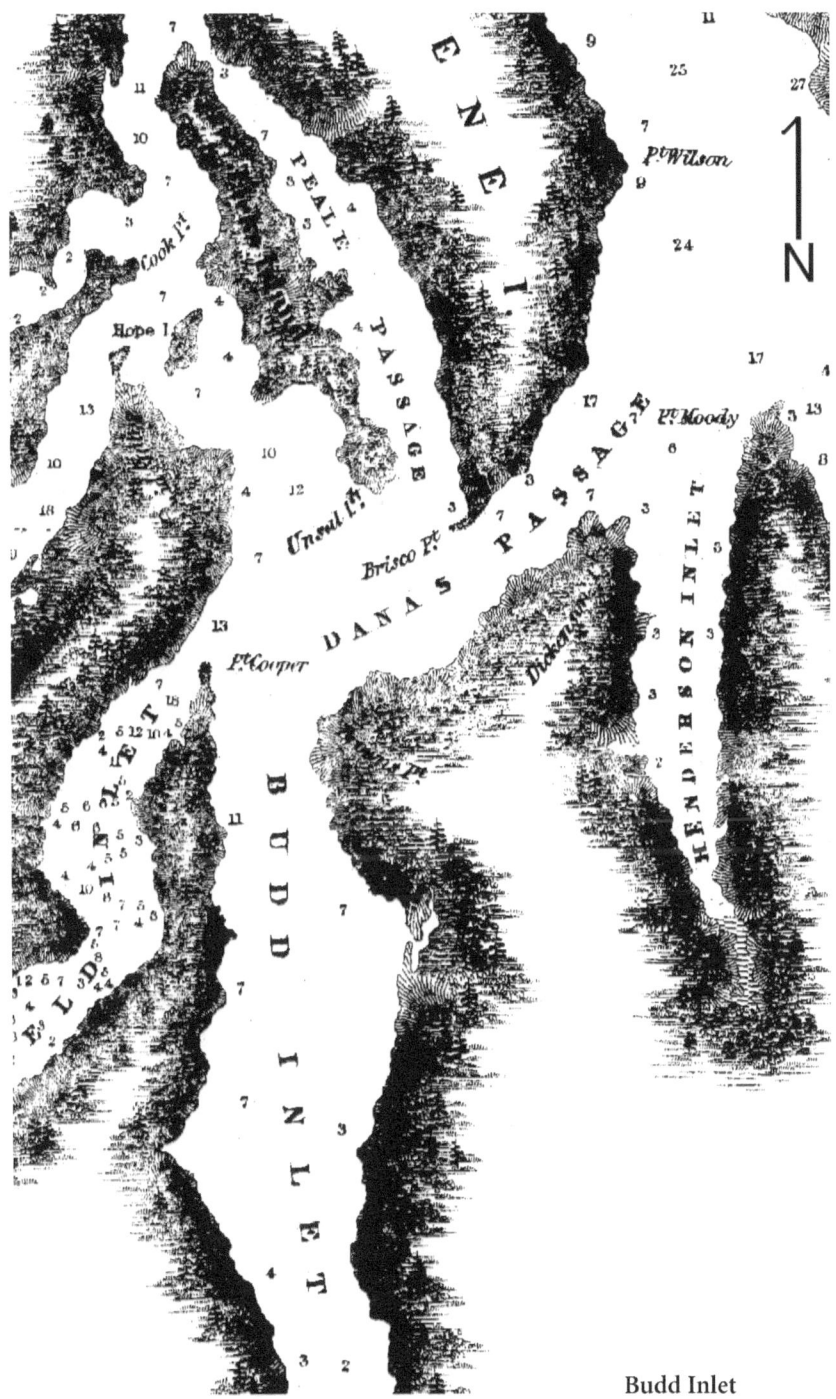

Budd Inlet

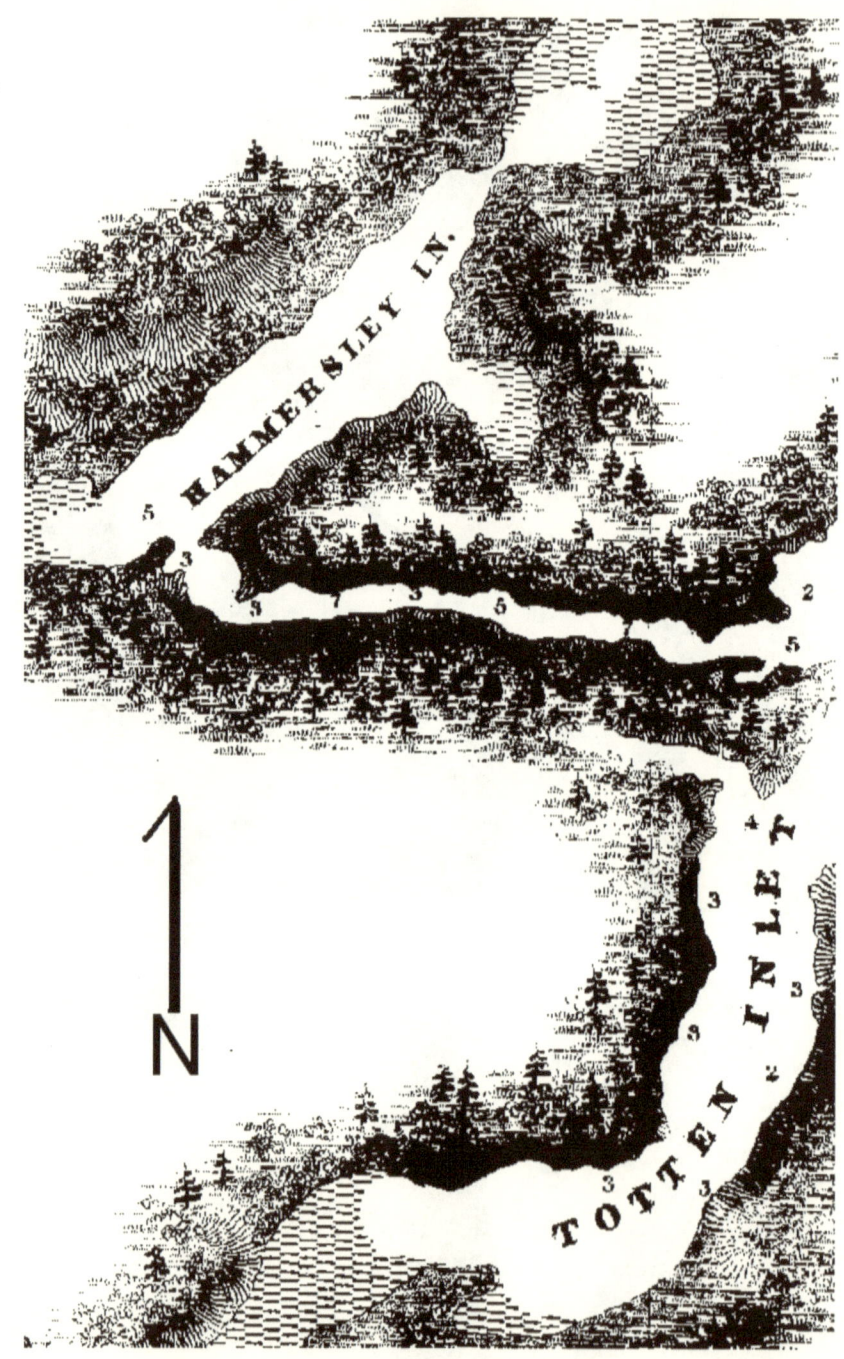

Hammersley, Totten Inlets

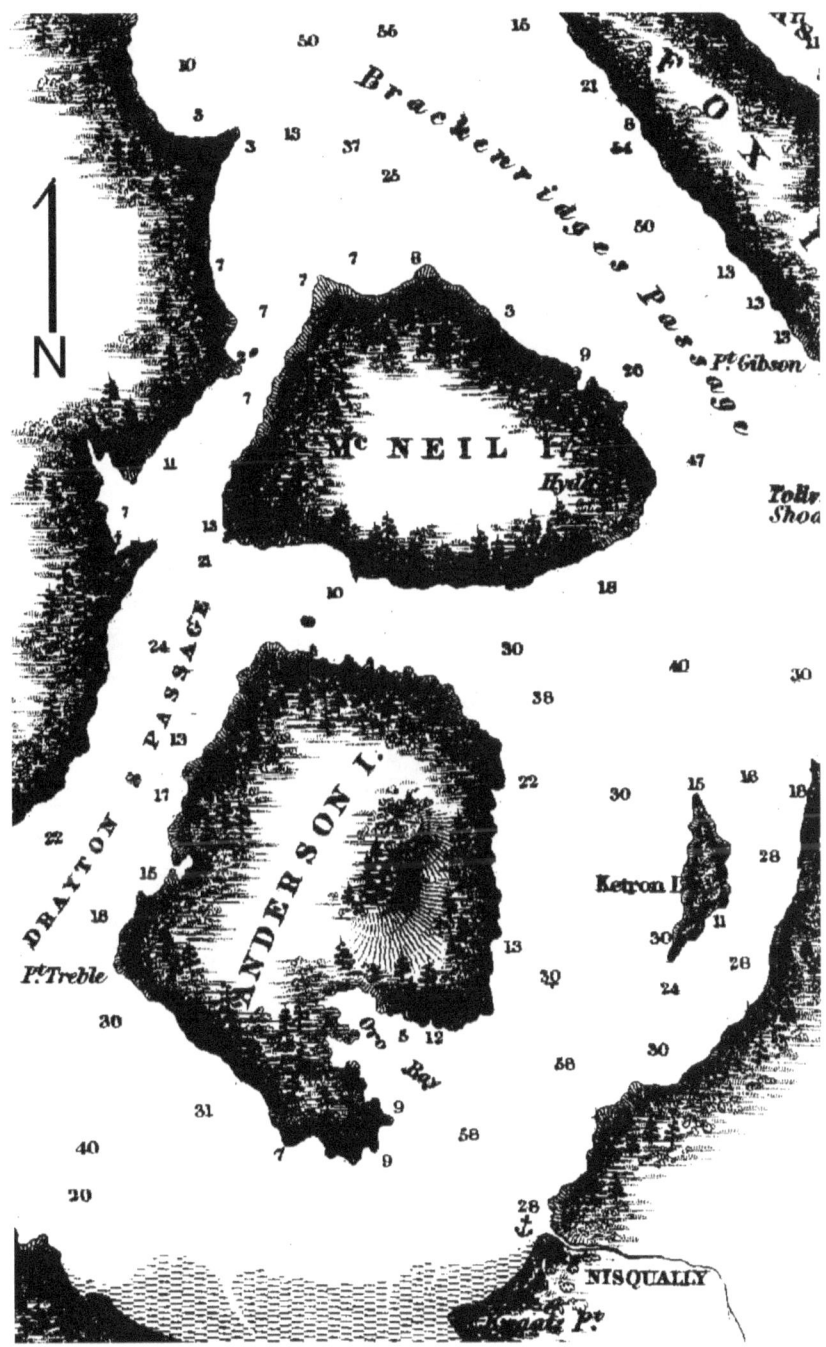

Anderson, McNeil Islands

Elliott Bay

4. Volume XXIII Charts   129

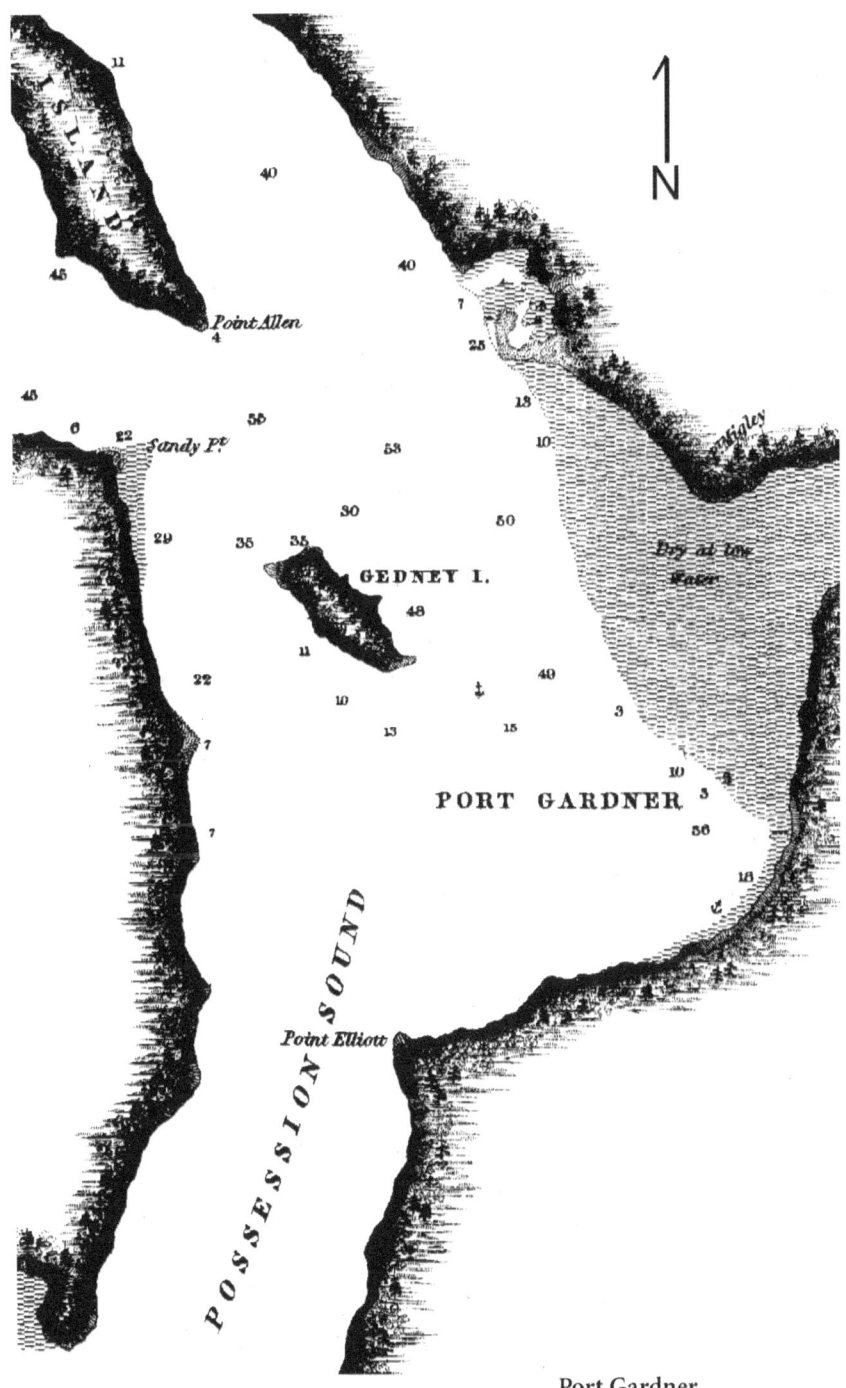

Port Gardner

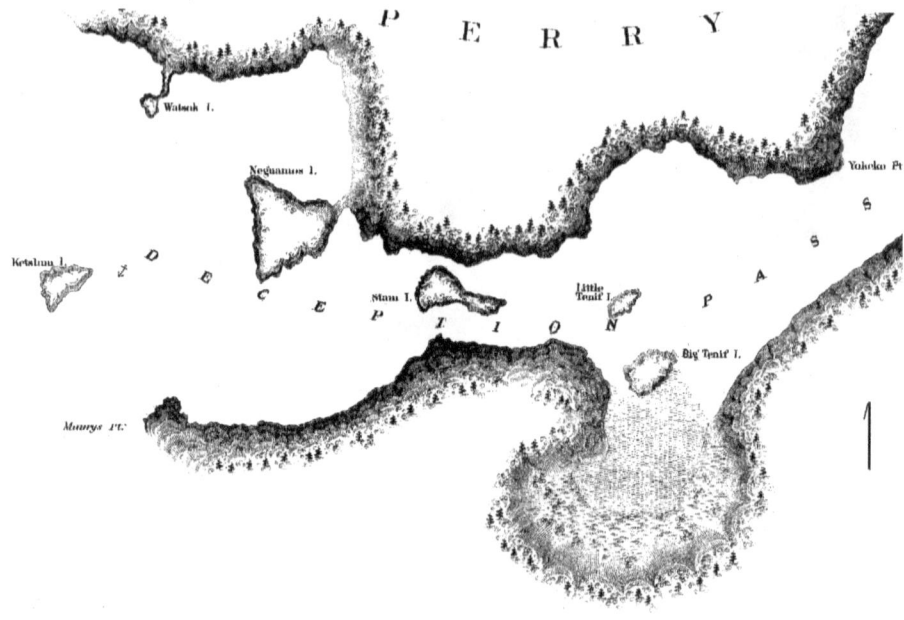

Deception Pass

5

The Journal of Augustus L. Case

Augustus Ludlow Case was born in Newburg, New York, February 3, 1812, and died February 17, 1893, in Washington, DC. He received his midshipman's appointment April 1, 1828, and reached the rank of Rear Admiral on May 24, 1872. He retired from service February 3, 1875. He married and had two sons, one of whom graduated from the Naval Academy in 1871.

Case's handwritten journal is available in the Naval Academy Museum. Even though the journal does not include a level of detail permitting the reader to determine his location during survey operations, a good sense of the inhabitants, terrain features and methods used for surveying the territory is still of interest.

Case's grammatical style is generally very good. He uses paragraph separations as appropriate; sentences are almost always ended with a period and the following sentence begins with a capital letter. It is also interesting to observe that he carefully includes a "dot" above each "i" indicating the meticulous nature in which the journal was prepared. While at times, certain sentences make little sense, in general the whole text is very understandable. His handwriting is usually good, but occasionally he runs letters together making the interpretation difficult. Spelling is excellent.

In reproducing this portion of his journal, I attempted to follow the manuscript as closely as possible, only inserting an occasional comma where the intent of a sentence was unclear without it. Brackets are used where words or groups of words are unreadable. In some cases, I include a word within brackets which is my best guess considering the context of the sentence.

1841
May 1st.

At daylight found we had made considerable progress during the night & were well advanced in the straits. At 9.30 a canoe came alongside with 5 men & a woman. One of the men was called Jack. He spoke a little English. He was a chief of the Classet Tribe & had brought a number of skins for sale. But was so much surprised by the appearance of the ship, number of men, &c., &c. that he never offered to dispose of them. He told us the H. B. C. Steamer was at the straits. Sent the master to look for our anchorage on the South Shore. When returned without finding one.

May 2nd.

The weather cleared during the night but still cold & chilly. This morning we had a visit from a party of Indians but could make little or nothing of them. The party consisted of 7 men & two women, all of the latter young & girls good looking. The oldest of the party came on board & reminded me very much of my old friends of [Fuego]. With the exception of a good blanket on his shoulders & an old cap, he was in a perfect state of nature. He brought a few fish, bows & arrows for them & showed this off.

Soon after meridian[1] a breeze made from the S W & gradually increased until the ship was passing the coast at the rate of 9 or 10 miles this hour. This soon brought us up with Dungeness point (on the South Shore) which we rounded 4½ & 5 fathoms about a ¼ of a mile dist. The point is narrow & was off from the mainland two or three miles in a N E direction, forming a good anchorage inside — we had seen of the poles spoken of by Vancouver. At 5 PM passed Protection island & came into Port Discovery. Anchored near the second point[2] on the Western Shore about 5 miles from the island in 33 fathoms water.

May 3rd.

Wind fresh from the N W until evening when it changed to the S E with rain. Canoes came along from different sides of this bay bringing fish, clams for sale. In one of these was a Chief who gave us information of an English settlement in Puget Sound. Sent a runner to it for a Pilot.

Boats employed in surveying the Harbour. Find Vancouver's survey to be generally correct. The great fault of the harbour is the depth.

---

[1]Noon.

[2]Contractors Point which Wilkes named Carr's Point, presumably for Lt. Overton Carr.

May 4.
   Wind fresh from the S. in the morning with rain. In the afternoon hauling to the N with clear weather. A number of Indians of the Clalam Tribe visited the ship bringing fish, geese & venison for sale.

May 5.
   Light N winds & pleasant. A great many Indians of the Clalam & Duquamish Tribes came alongside with venison, geese, ducks & salmon for sale. Besides this bows & arrows &c. The salmon are larger & fine but do not appear to be plenty.
   Vancouver remarks that he "found little fish provisions to eat here & had to depend almost entirely on his salt stock"—if we can judge by what is brought alongside times must have altered very much for the better since his time.
   On the E side of the bay we saw some fine patches of potatoes fenced in & well cultivated.
   This afternoon 5 men came on board who said they had come from "Squalla," the settlement of the H. B. C. & are ready to Pilot the ship there.

May 6.
   Clear N winds. At 9 got underway & stood out of the Harbour accompanied by the *Porpoise* & some twenty canoes. As we passed out we could see the mountains thickly covered with snow & every appearance of its having fallen since our arrival.
   This harbour is one of the best protected I have even been in. It extends back about 9 miles from Protection island ranging in width from ½ mile to 2 miles. Protection island lays directly in the mouth & effectually sheets out all sea from the N to which the harbour is off.
   It has our serious objection in its depth of water. You can in no place except at the head of the bay get less than 15 fathoms for yards from the shore.
   We found about 200 Clalam Indians in the bay camping in different parts of it. Generally two or three lodging together. They are rather above the middle size & look squalid, miserable compared with the South Sea Islands. The clothing was but slight consisting of a blanket knotted over the shoulder or a hunting shirt of deer skin. Some had shirts & trousers obtained from the Traders. The blankets are many [ ] of them made by themselves of dogs wool. Some neatly figured & often have down interwoven. The women wear blankets & a short petticoat made of birch bark tied over the hips & sufficiently long to cover the sexual marks. They all wear their hair long & are fond of ornaments. We saw a great many children of whom the mothers seemed very fond.

At 3 passed Protection island & hauled up around Point Wilson which separates Ports Townsend & Discovery. At 4 anchored in there from about ⅓ of a mile from the shore.

May 7.

Survey part of the Harbour & then got underway & ran round into Port Lawrence[3] near the mouth of Hoods Canal & anchored.

May 8.

Surveyed the bay this morning & then got underway for the Inlet. Winds fresh from the SW. At 5.10 PM anchored on the W shore in 15 fathoms water.[4] Mr. Heath, Mate of the H. B. C. steamer *Beaver* came on board to Pilot us to Nasqually.

May 9.

S W winds, working up the inlet on the flood tide. Keeping the W shore & surveying round our anchorage during the ebb.

May 10.

Surveyed a harbour on the W shore. Called by Capt. W. "Madison Harbour." At the head of the bay found a burying ground belonging to the Suquamish containing a number of graves. Got underway on the flood & worked up near the entrance of Pugets Sound. The tide left us [here] & we anchored on the W shore opposite Vashons island.[5]

May 11.

After surveying in the vicinity of our anchorage, got underway & stood through the Narrows into Pugets Sound. At 7.50 anchored off Fort Nasqually.

May 12.

Transferred Lt. Alden, Pass[d] Mid Sanford & Mister Elliot to the *Porpoise* for surveying duty. Lt. Johnson being detailed for the charge of the inland party.

May 14.

Sent a gang of men on shore to clear a place & erect buildings for the observatory.

---

[3]Oak Bay.

[4]Pilot's Cove.

[5]Wilkes' narrative indicates they traveled through Colvos Passage and anchored north of the Narrows on May 10.

May 15.
Porpoise after receiving two boats with their crews from us got underway & proceeded down the Sound.

May 16.
Rec^d an order to take charge of the party detailed for the Survey of Hoods Canal, Pugets Sound & &c., &c.

May 17.
The pursuance of my orders of yesterday, I this day left the ship in charge of the launch cutter. *Ariel* & *Pilot*[6] to make the surveys &c. mentioned therein. At 4 PM cleared the Narrows. Soon after met Capt. Ringgold returning to the ship from the S end of Vashons island. He informed me he should be detained for some days near his present anchorages & that I had better proceed at once without waiting for him. Made sail down the Inlet. At 6.30 landed at SW Colvos point & encamped.

May 18
At 6.30 AM commenced work. Obtained chro & circum mrn sights but did not get equal altitudes, the sun being obscured in the afternoon. At 4.30 PM landed at the *Ariel's* 2nd position on Vashons island, & finding plenty of water encamped. At 5.30 the boats returned, after our tents were pitched a couple of Suquamish indians visited us bringing fish for sale.
The shores we have worked along today are generally from twenty to fifty feet high, formed of stratified clay with a light gravelly soil & thickly covered with pines.

May 19
At 6.45 AM commenced work. At 8, landed on the N end of Vashons island. Erected two good signals for the *Porpoise* to connect with flts, L's, &c.
This end of the island on its western side is steep to 7 fathoms within a boats length, but shoals to the northward & should not be approached to close in that direction.
At 12.30 landed at Mr. Tottens station on Bainbridge island. Found he had obtained chro & circum mrn sights & was waiting for the afternoon ob for equal attitudes. Soon after I landed the winds shifted from south to S W accompanied by rain & prevented his getting them. Erected a large signal on the island as directed for the *Porpoise* to connect with.

---

[6]The ship's cutters were named *Ariel* and *Pilot*. The smaller survey boats were named *Greyhound, Lion, Fox, Turtle, Nightingale, Lizard, Leopard, Elephant, White Handkerchief, Shark, Eagle, Dolphin, Rover, Triton, Boxer,* and *Bear.*

I had now brought my work up to the points specified & although anxious to get a full set of observations—determined to take advantage of the wind & run to the northward towards Hoods Canal. At 1.15 made sail down the Inlet.

We found on the island three houses & two potato patches belonging to the Suquamish Indians. The largest house measured 45 by 70 feet built of logs & roofed with boards. About 20 men & boys of that Tribe visited us bringing salmon for sale.

At 5.30 rounded a low sand point on the W shore, landed & encamped. The land in the vicinity of our camp was much lower than usual & thickly covered with pines. Soil thin & sandy.

About ½ mile from us we found three lodges of Suquamish Indians, engaged in preparing their winter stores. They told me this was a favorite resort of the Tribe—who swim at times in great numbers.

May 20

Stormy weather. At 7.30 AM started for Port Lawrence. At 11.30 landed in a small harbour front to the S of Rock Point[7] & commenced its survey. At 2 the wind became light & variable with rain. Landed on the W shore near some lodges of Suquamish Indians & pitched our tents.

May 21

When ready for a start this morning, a heavy rain set in, with every appearance of its continuing through the day—landed & pitched the tents again. At 10.30 the weather clearing a little commenced work. At 4.00 completed the survey. This harbour (which I called A to distinguish it) is the best I have yet seen. Easy of access, & well sheltered. Soundings regular in from 2 to 16 fathoms, sand & mud. Several rocks lay off the western point bare at low water & a sand spit makes off a few hundred yards from the eastern head—as you will see by the soundings on the chart. Water can be obtained in abundance at the head of the harbour, or from either shore.

The land was low & covered with pines. The soil much the same as that at Nasqually but deeper & richer.

Some Suquamish neighbors were visited this afternoon by some fifty Clalams, making the number of the two partys near a hundred. I thought it necessary to place extra sentinels during the night. The Chiefs informed me they had met by appointment to gamble for some blankets, &c. Soon after the Clalams arrived the game commenced & continued through the night.

---

[7]From the description, this is apparently Port Ludlow.

May 22

At 6.45 AM commenced work. At 12 landed on a sand point some three miles within the heads of the canal & fired for [base] & obtained angles. At 1.20 the boats joined [ ] & we all pulled round a point near by hoping to find food, shelter & water, but were disappointed & compelled to pull some two miles further before we found both. Landed on the W shore & encamped near some lodges of Suquamish.

May 23

Employed through the day making obs for Lat, Long, &c. & inking in our work. Soil in the neighborhood of the camp thin & sandy.

May 24

At 6.40 AM commenced work. At 12.00 landed in harbour B[8] on the east shore & commenced its survey. At 4.30 landed the tents on its eastern point near a run of fresh water.[9] Pitched them. At 5.30 the boats returned.

This evening found our bread to be getting short & placed all hands on an allowance of 4 biscuits per day.

May 25

At 6.30 commenced sounding the channel which we found to be narrow but deep. At 9.30 completed the survey. This harbour would be difficult for large vessels to enter except at high water when they would find it easy with the channel buoyed. When inside the points there is plenty of room & good anchorage. Water can be obtained in abundance near the east point.

Continued the survey up the Canal. At 3 landed in harbour C[10] in the W shore & chained off a base. Encamped in our secondary station.

May 26

At 7 commenced the survey of the Harbour. At 1.15 completed it, & continued the work of the Canal.

Harbour C affords good anchorage & is well protected from the southerly winds by a reef[11] near the eastern, of considerable extent & have set low water. Water can be obtained without difficulty.

At 4.40 landed at Browns point, obtained angles &c. & encamped. At 6.45 the boats joined me. The officers of the *Ariel* & *Pilot* reporting they had not seen the signals.

---

[8] Possibly Port Gamble.
[9] Possibly Point Julia.
[10] Possibly Suquamish Harbor.
[11] Possibly Case Shoal.

Soon after our tents were pitched a party of Suquamish visited us bringing salmon &c. for sale.

May 27

At 7 sent Messrs May & Colvos to the yesterdays station to measure base &c. Mr. Totten & myself being employed the most of the day getting this for equal altitudes, tides, &c. The soil in the vicinity of the camp was much richer than any I have yet seen.

May 28

At 7 continued the survey up the Canal. At 1.30 took position on the E shore near a salmon fishery & fired for base — then crossed the Canal to the mouth of "Nu-ko-lo-wah" creek.[12] Sent Mr. May in a canoe to explore it — (the entrance being to shoal for our boats). Mr. May found deep water about 200 yards inside the mouth & was informed by some Indians he met that it runs some distance inland. I did not deem a further examination necessary (as the mouth was quite dry at low water) & crossed to the shore & encamped in D harbour.[13]

May 29

Surveyed the harbours. Found it to afford good anchorage & well protected from all winds. Excellent to the north. Water can be obtained in any quantity from the creek at the head.

A party of Seocomish Indians visited our camp bringing venison, salmon, &c. for sale.

May 30

Employed inking in our work, making obs &c. for Lat & Long — A party of Tuandos & Seocomish visited us. Reduced the allowance of bread to 3 biscuits per day.

The land in the vicinity of our camp was lower than usual & swampy & thickly wooded. The soil a rich black loam.

May 31

At 7 commenced work. Crossed to the northern shore & took positions on a point called Tskutska[14] so as to allow the boats to take second position before leaving. The Canal at this place branched into two arms,

---

[12]Fisherman Harbor on the Toandos Peninsula.

[13]Possibly Seabeck.

[14]Spelled Tskutsko in Wilkes' narrative. The point is on the SW end of the Toandos Peninsula.

one trending sharp to the northward,[15] the other continuing to the S W along the base of the Mount Olympus range of mountains.

The banks of the Canals from the entrance to this place have generally ranged from 20 to 100 high formed of stratified clay, with a light gravelly soil & thickly covered with the different species of pines. At this place the north & west shores assumed a bold & rocky appearance & the soil deeply & much richer being an alluvial deposit from the mountains. The eastern shores continuing of the same character as those below.

Worked up the northern arm. At 5 PM encamped in a small bight called Zelatched on the east shore. At 8.20 PM a very large & brilliant meteor was seen bearing from us N by W ½ W shooting in a diagonal direction nearly to the earth when it burst like a rocket. A long zig zag train was left by it, which continued of a brightness nearly equal to the moon until 8.50 when it gradually disappeared.

June 1

At 7 commenced work, continuing up the northern arm. At 10 landed in a small harbour called Hooetzen[16] on the west shore. Surveyed it & obtained observations of equal altitudes &c. Encamped on the east shore. We were now in the district of the Tuondos, a smaller Tribe by their own account mustering 100 fighting men. They generally reside among the mountains & are much the largest & best looking men we have yet met.

The land in the vicinity of our camp similar to that below the arms.

June 2

At 7 continued the work of the north arm — by meridian we had reached the head of it. The island at this place on Vancouvers chart we found to be a tongue of land[17] running out some two or three miles & forming two good harbours. The eastern called "Dabop" & the western "Col-see-ed."[18] After completing the survey of "Dabop" pulled round into "Col-see-ed" & encamped near the same lodges of Suquamish.

June 3

Rainy weather. At 8.30 it appeared to be clearing off. Started for the head of the bay to measure base, &c. but was obliged to return without

---

[15]Toward Dabob and Quilcene Bays.

[16]Jackson Cove.

[17]Although Vancouver's Narrative does not reference the island, his chart clearly shows the Bolton Peninsula as such.

[18]Quilcene Bay.

doing anything, the wind again setting in & continuing through the day, attended by heavy S E gales.

June 4

Showery. Surveyed the bay. Found it to afford every protection from the wind, & good holding ground in from 5 to 10 fathoms muddy bottom. One large & several small creeks[19] empty into the head of the bay which would answer well for milling purposes. They have formed an extensive mud flat which it would be necessary to stake or buoy in case the harbour was much used.

June 5

Run a few lines of soundings in the mouth of the harbour & then pulled for the S W arm. At meridian a heavy rain commenced. Landed on the W shore opposite Tskutska point & pitched our tents. About a mile distant from us a large creek called the "Tlobish"[20] emptied into the canal which would answer well for mills. Near it were a few lodges of Toundos containing about fifty [indians] employed fishing for salmon which they took in numbers & of a superior quality.

June 6

Easterly winds & rainy throughout the day. Employed inking in our work. A few Toundos visited our camp bringing salmon, &c. for sale.

June 7

As soon as the weather permitted this morning, commenced the survey of the S W arm.[21] Encamped on the south shore.

June 8

Commences rainy. At 10.30 the weather clearing continued the survey of the canal. Passsed a large creek on the west shore which would answer well for mills. The soil in its neighborhood an alluvial deposit from the mountains.

Encamped on the east shore which was gradually becoming lower as we approached the head of the Canal. The soil, bank is the same as that below. A small party of Clalams visited us.

---

[19]Big Quilcene River, Little Quilcene River, Donovan Creek.

[20]The log entry is unclear, thus, the proper spelling of this location is questionable. It is perhaps the Dosewallips River.

[21]The main portion of the Canal.

June 9

At 7 continued the work of the canal. Pitched our tents on the east shore.

A few Toundos & Scocomish Indians visited us bring salmon, venison, &c. for sale.

June 10

At 7 started up the Canal. At 3 PM landed at Neelim[22] point on the west shore near a Scocomish Village. On opening the theodolite at this place missed the vertical eye piece. Made a regular search for it without success & as I had [ ] been particular in seeing it in the box, was convinced one of the Indians must have picked it up. I strongly suspected a woman who sat near the box of having it but she looked so innocent & joined so readily in the search, that I did not have her blanket examined, offered two blankets for its return & dispatched the men to my last station to search for it there. At dark they returned without it.

I had been fearful for some time that it would be lost as the box was scarcely ever opened without its falling out. I had once stowed it in my calabash but afterwards replaced it on account of using it at night occasionally, trusting that as it had escaped loss nearly three years it would continue so to do.

This place was the end of the Canal according to Vancouvers survey, who had sketched it as a bay. Instead of terminating however, it took a sharp turn & continued to the N & E. On the south side of the bay empties a large creek[23] by which the Indians communicate with the Columbia. The creek is broad but shoal & has formed a large mud flat in that part of the bay.

This district is inhabited by the Scocomish — a Tribe by the arm & the Tuandos account mustering 150 fighting men. They resemble the Tuandos in appearance & appeared to be in close alliance with them.

The mountain range on the west shore land gradually sloped down into low land similar to that below the forks, thickly wooded & soil good. The last shores low & swampy & not so thickly wooded as those below.

Pitched our tents on the south shore near some Scocomish Lodges.

June 11

At 7.30 commenced work continuing up the Canal. The land very low & thickly wooded. Encamped on the west shore near a run of fresh water. Our camp was visited by a large party of Indians belonging to the different tribes we have met.

---

[22]Near Potlatch.
[23]Skokomish River.

June 12

At 7.30 continued the survey up the Canal. On this morning engaged a couple of Indians to go to Nasqually with a letter & return with a canoe load of bread. When all ready for a start they were persuaded by an old man not to go for price agreed on & I determined not to send them, trusting I should get others willing to go at [Chelauetstin] (the portage).[24] At meridian, had arrived at the head of the Canal & finished its survey. A creek[25] about 60 yards wide empties into the head of it & has formed a flat near two miles down, quite bare at low water. This creek is from 3 to 4 feet deep about ½ mile from its mouth. Land flat & wooded with here & there a clean space. The soil a mixed sand & vegetable mould.

At 1 encamped on the east shore. Walked across the portage to Pugets Sound a distance about two & a half miles over a rough & hilly road. On my return got an Indian to take Kellum (Cox of the [*Airel*]) & Jo the interpreter to Nasqually & return with a load of bread, dispatched them immediately.

On the shore opposite our camp found three board houses belonging to the Scocomish.

A large party of Indians pitched their lodges near us. Issued out the last allowance of bread.

June 13

Rainy. Employed inking in our work. At 3 PM Jo the interpreter returned having left Kellum at the landing with ten days bread for all hands. Sent the men over for it.

June 14

Immediately after breakfast this morning started down the canal on my return to the ship.

At 3 PM reached "Neelim" bay. Ran a few lines of soundings to show the flat on the east shore. Encamped at Neelim point.

June 15

Rainy weather. At 7 continued down the canal searching the different points where I have used the Theodolite for the lost eye-piece but without success. At 6 PM landed on the W shore of C harbour & pitched our tents.

June 16

Rainy. The plotting of this harbour did not come in satisfactorily & I

---

[24]The spelling is questionable, but the location is Lynch Cove where the Indians went overland into the north end of Case Inlet.

[25]Union River.

determined to reexamine it but was unable to do anything during the day on account of the rain.

June 17
Finished the reexamination of C harbour. At 2.15 started down the Canal. At 5.30 passed into Admiralty Inlet & encamped near our camp of May 19th. Found here a large party of Suquamish buildings, canoes & winter dwellings.

June 18
Showery. The ebb was unusually great this morning & the launch grounded while we were at breakfast compelling us to wait until the tide had flowed sufficiently to float her. At 10 got underway & work up to within about a mile of Madison harbour where we encamped.

June 19
Got underway on the last of the ebb tracking the launch along shore until the tide had made sufficiently strong to work her off against the wind. At 3.30 reached Bainbridge island & pitched our tents.

June 20
Rainy. Employed inking in our work &c. A party of Suquamish visited the camp bringing fish, &c. for sale.

June 21
As soon as the ebb slackened, started up the inlet. At 5.30 PM passed through the Narrows into Pugets Sound & at 9 reached the ship.

June 22
At 1 PM left the ship for the Narrows to take up the survey of Pugets Sound from points left by the ship at that place. Pitched our tents on the east shore — a few Nasquallas visited us bringing salmon &c. for sale.

June 23
Commenced the survey of Pugets Sound working through the Narrows at slack water. The tide runs through there at ebb at the rate of 4½ miles per hour. At 5.30 a canoe boarded me bringing orders from Capt. W to dispatch Mr. May in the *Pilot* to the Ship with the Theodolite & some azimuth observations made in Hoods Canal. Made signal for him to join company & on his doing so started him immediately for the ship. Employed on the W shore in harbour F.

June 23 [sic]

At 7 AM commenced the survey of harbour F. At 2.30 finished & was about leaving when I saw a boat pulling towards me from the Ship. Landed & waited for him. She proved to be the *Pilot* under charge of Lt Budd who brought orders for me to transfer the charge of the boats to him & take charge of one of the light boats & proceed to Hoods Canal in search of the lost eye piece. Encamped on the west shore plotted the days work & transferred the charge of the party to Lt Budd.

June 25

This morning started for Hoods Canal in the *Pilot*. At sunset stopped on the N point of Port Orchard & passed the night.

June 26

Immediately after breakfast continued down the Inlet. At 3 PM passed into the Canal & at sunset encamped in C harbour. Saw but few Indians & they extremely shy.

June 27

Continued up the Canal. At 2 PM landed at Quatsap point, the place I had last used the eye-piece & commenced the search going from station to station up to Neelim point without finding it. Stopped there for the night.

June 28

Started down the Canal on my return to the ship overhauling the stations again as I passed on reaching them recollected that Mr. Totten used the Theodolite at our camp near [ ] point, went back & searched the place at sunset. Stopped about 3 miles south of Quatsap point & passed the night.

June 29

A short time after sunrise went to boats to give it another overhaul before returning to the ship. While here a canoe with 3 Tuandos landed & on learning what I was looking for, they instantly said it was among the Scocomish & gave a full account of its having been picked up at Neelim station. When the Theodolite was opened by a woman who was setting near. Got one of the Indians to go with me to the Village where they had seen it & started up the Canal.

At 2 PM landed at Neelim & the men took me to the Chief here saying he could get it. The Chief was absent, on his return I took his gun & told him I should keep this until the eye-piece was brought me. After getting something to eat he started for a village a short distance inland saying it was there. While he was away a couple of Tuandos hunters landed in a canoe & I seized the gun of one & attempted to get the other but its owner was to strong for me. The chief now returned saying the woman who had the eye-piece was down the Canal. The Tuandos went to see her & about 9 PM returned saying [she] had gone up the river. Hauled off about 1–2 miles from the shore & passed the night.

June 30
At daylight the Chief started down the canal in a canoe. While getting breakfast I saw eight canoes filled with men come out of the river & pull towards us. This I did not like & directed the men — as soon as they got through pulled out into the bay when the canoes were headed for me. At this time the Tuando I had in the boat wished to be landed & on my refusing to put him on shore, gave me to understand I had better prepare my arms. I now observed several more canoes coming out of the river & I determined not to wait for this as it was evident they intended no good & my party was to small & to far from the ships to contend with them. So made sail down the canal. The canoes pulled after me a short distance until finding they were losing ground, gave up the chase & went to the village I had left. The Toando hunters followed us down & I told them at Quatsap I would give them this & the Chiefs from — about 25 miles down the Canal met the Chief returning. He said he had been to the Ylopish village learning a girl had something like the eye-piece (which proved to be a cologne bottle). I gave him his gun & was about leaving when I learned a part of his errand he had said nothing of, [this] to collect warriors. A canoe had been pulling up the centre of the Canal which now boarded us. It contained 5 of the largest & most muscular men I have seen all armed with guns & knives. After speaking with the Chief they followed us down & landed at some lodges six or eight miles below. This was a convincing proof that they had assembled [above] for no good although satisfied the eye-piece was [ ] concluded I had better return to the Chief as my party was to small to attempt anything like force. At sunset stopped on the E shore about three miles south of C harbour & passed the night.

July 1
Continued my route towards the ship.

July 2
After breakfast continued my course towards the ship. At meridian passed through the Narrows & at 2.30 PM got alongside. Made my report to the Captain. I offered to go with the launch & cutter three canoes & get the eye-piece. This Capt. Wilkes declared granting, preferring to send a

messenger to the Tribe. [ ] "if the eye piece was not returned he would come round in the ship & destroy the towns &c."

July 3

Measured a base line of 2½ miles on the plain back of the fort to ascertain the alt of Mount Rainier. The distance gave but little change of alt & of [course] was of no use.

July 6 [sic]
Sunday.

July 5

Early in the morning the din of preparation for celebrating the 4th on shore commenced. The surveying boats had returned on the 3rd & all hands except Mr. Vanderford were ordered to be out of the ship before 9 AM. Foot balls had been made for amusement & an ox roasted [ ] "nature a [ ]" on the plain near Dr Richmond's house. At daylight a salute was fired from the shore & at 9 all hands were assembled at the observatory in front of the Capts quarters ready for a start. After a short [ ] they left with charge of Passed Mid Colvo for the plain. Vendovi [ ] in full costume bringing up the rear & [ ] most conspicuously. Abreast the Fort the party halted, gave them cheers & then continued the route & then reached the scene of operations. The men immediately chose sides & commenced play. Capt Wilkes with the officers forming a [ ] of base.

To make everything completed as a 4th celebration one of the Quarter gunners (Daniel Whitehorn) in the hurry of loading a gun put the cartridge in without springing the chamber[26] & had his hand & arm nearly blown off by the cartridges exploding, thus marred the festivities a considerable.

Grog was issued in proper quantities, the ox devoured & at sunset all returned to the ship well satisfied with the days amusement. [ ] two or three hundred indians had assembled to witness the show but did not appear to know "what the devil it could all mean" & frequently asked the question why it was done? but by the lower class only, the Chiefs walking round looking dignified & knowing.

---

[26]"Springing the chamber" on a muzzle loading rifle refers to inserting the ramrod down the bore and listening to the sound as it bottoms-out. If a metallic sound is heard, the chamber is empty. If a hollow thud-like sound is heard, the chamber is loaded. I believe the reference to "cartridge" really applies to a load. That is, rather than inserting a cartridge into the chamber, a ramrod was used to push the load down the barrel. Apparently Whitehorn loaded the rifle twice. When fired, the chamber exploded, thus causing the injury.

July 6

[Dr] M'Laughlin visited the ship — received him by manning the yards & cheering when he left. At [1] PM received orders to take charge of the launch, *Ariel, Pilot* & *Triton* & take up the survey of Pugets Sound from points left by Lt Budd on the 3rd. At 3 left the ship, near sunset reached the stations of Lt Budd. In the hurry of getting off, Mr. Totten left his gear — dispatched Mr. Hammersly back in the *Pilot* for it & my bedding.

Our camp was on one of the small islands in the part of the sound, very verdant & wonderful. The soil was good & productive. This island will, when the country becomes settled be a beautiful spot for the residence of a gentleman fond of retirement & aquatic amusements.

July 7

Mr. Hammersly returned early this morning & directly after breakfast work of the survey was continued up the Sound. At my second station this sound branched into three arms trending S E, S W & N W. Worked up the latter.[27] At 5.30 encamped on the south shore. We had accomplished a distance of 11½ miles today & by 10 we had it all on paper. I saw a few Nasqually Indians going to the ship with venison. Endeavored to buy it but they asked to much & I let them [go on their] way. This shore we have worked along today was from 10 to fifty feet high & covered with verdance. The soil light & I thought well adapted for a farming country. Near my last station a small arm made to the southward.[28]

July 8

This morning continued the work up the sound. At 6 PM we had reached the Chilauetoru party & finished the survey of the arm. Pitched our tents on this N shore on a beautiful clear space covered with pines & flowers. The shores were similar to those passed yesterday lowering gradually as we neared the portage & covered with smaller pines.

July 9

After breakfast went to my last station of the 7th & took up the survey of the arm branching to the W at that place. The arm was generally about a third of a mile wide, shores bold & soundings regular in from two to twelve fathoms sandy bottom. The land was low & verdant with small pines with here & there, clean space covered with grass & flowers.

---

[27]Case Inlet.

[28]Pickering Passage.

July 10

This morning dispatched Mr. Hammersly to the ship with a tracing of our work & then continued down the arm. A few miles below our camp a small arm branched to the N — through it we had the tides in opposition to the one we were in. Continued until I found good points to leave signals on it & then continued to the north arm. Worked up it two or three miles & encamped on the north shore. Saw a few Nasquallies.

July 11

Rainy weather. After breakfast pulled down the arm to ascertain if it did not enter the Sound near any second stations of the 7th. Found it did & left a note on the signal staff for Mr. Hammersly & then returned to the camp.

July 12

[ ] meridians this weather was to bad to do anything. At that time it clearing a little. Struck the tents & started down the arm. At my 6th station discovered some boats three or four miles distant. At this place Jos Limont had his hands & face badly burned by the explosion of a charge of powder in his hands while putting it in the eprouvette.[29]

At sunset Capt Wilkes joined me in my camp with these boats & took charge of the party. Our camp was on the south side of an island we had nearly worked a round & at this place, sloping gradually to the west & covered with grass & flowers. The soil good.

July 13

All was hurry & bustle this morning to get off by 7 o'clock precisely. Start time found us in the boats & we started for a great days work.

We pulled around to points above & the work commenced by a general finding. We worked south to the signals left by me on the 10th & then took up the examination of two areas trending to the southward at that place.

At transit pitched our tents on the E shore. This part of the Sound is cut up by numerous small arms trending in different directions & forming small islands. The channels between them deep & currents rapid. The banks vary in height & are covered with pines like those at Nasqually & I suppose like them have extensive plains inland.

---

[29]An eprouvette is a pistol-like device fired by a flintlock mechanism used to test the strength of black powder. As powder improved in quality, use of the device was discontinued.

July 14
Continued up the arm we were in until afternoon when we had reached the head of it. Here we found a few lodges of Nasqually Indians. The country similar to that of yesterday but lowering as we reach the head. Encamped on the W shore of the main channel.

July 15
Directly after breakfast Lt Budd was sent back to connect the work of the 14th. Worked up the arm we were in, by noon completed it [& then] pulled down the arm making to the S E from my station of the 7th.

July 16
After breakfast went to fill up a break in the work of yesterday. Afterwards ran a few lines of soundings & then returned to the ship. This part of the sound being finished.

July 17
This morning was again dispatched in charge of 4 boats to complete the survey from the Narrows to the ship. Locate a shoal said to lay to the N W of [ ] island — was fortunate enough to strike it on the first line. By sunset had finished the survey of Pugets Sound & returned to the ship [ ] there was no more to do here.
The tides throughout the Sound [ ] very irregular & cannot [be depended on]. The currents unusually strong.

July 19
At 1 PM got underway & commenced working down the Sound.
Nisqually is situated in Lat 47°07'12" N & [left blank] W long near the head of the waters of the Sound on the east shore. The Fort stands back about a quarter of a mile from the shore on the edge of the prairie. It is picketed in the form of a square with [ ] or block houses on the corners & over [ ] gallery running all round inside for defense. The dwellings & stores inside are built of logs & so placed as to be capable of defense after the pickets have been [ ] or destroyed.
The company collect at this station beaver & other skins—what number I am unable to say. Such should suffer from the Indians I saw there at different times must be considerable although Mr. Anderson, the clerk in charge said they [ ] but from [ ]. The beaver skins are generally large & of the best quality. The company make it a point to purchase all the Indians [bring out] fixed prices never allowing them to leave with anything they are willing to part with [ ]. Mr. Anderson told me they annually [ ] hundreds of skins to that had been purchased only to induce them to bring others.

The Pugets Sound Land Company [ ] as the H.B.C. have a farm & several hundred head of cattle & sheep here under charge of Mr. A who is assisted by a former dairy man & several Canadian & half breed servants hired by the company & bound by the most rigid rules. There are a few areas laid down in wheat, oak, peas, potatoes, the latter producing well. But the [ ] (from what Mr. A told me) does not yield consistently, growing only 15 or 20 for me.

The country is well adapted for grazing being a succession of rolling prairies separated by hills of woods well watered & producing good pasture. This the company no doubt had in view when the farm was established.

The cattle & sheep all looked well & I was told increased rapidly. From the mildness of the climate they are able to find food for themselves the year round. They were generally of the California breed, the sheep mixed with the [ ] English [ ]. Mr. A told me they were now introducing the [ ] sorts among them.

Near the fort lived Dr. Richmond, an American attached to the Methodist mission — he has built himself a house & takes possession of a very large plain which he has named "Richmonds Plain" & is living very comfortably. He does little or nothing in his profession saying when asked about it: "Nothing could be done with the Indians" & having become convinced that he is correct, remains here drawing his salary for the good old women at home.

The companys steamer *Beaver* commanded by Capt McNeil (an American) makes this place his headquarters. She is kept as a dispatch vessel to carry supplies to the north forts & to collect the furs inside of Vancouvers island.

The Nasquallys are a small tribe inhabiting the plains in this vicinity & the head waters of the Sound. They are flat heads wandering in the habitation & acknowledge no Chief. They have a dialect of their own although most of them speak the Chinook or trading language. Their master residences are built of logs roofed with boards & large enough to contain several families generally situated in some sheltered spot near a spring or near of water. On the spring, these families split & wander off to different parts of the Sound or plains erecting their lodges where food is most abundant. The summer lodges are built with a few sticks & covered with mats. The whole easily transported to another place in canoes or on horse back when the game fish or clams become scarce. They own a good many horses, generally ride well always at the top of a horses [ ]. Their dress consists of a hunting shirt, trousers & moccasins made of dressed deer hide, shirts & trousers from the Fort or a blanket according to the wealth of the wearer. The woman wore frocks of deer skins or calico [ ] — some of these highly ornamented & looked very well when clean.

They were tolerably good looking, middle sized & very indolent. The woman doing all the drudgery. Our visit has been a regular harvest for them, they frequently giving a shirt for what they got [two chaws] of tobacco for at the fort. In consequence of our giving such prices the gentlemen of the Fort have gone without salmon, &c. not being willing to break the tariff.

[ ] of [herring] are found in the Sound. These the Indians take in a canoe with a species of [ ] used as a paddle front on one side & then the other — salmon follow these shoals & the Indian always has his [ ] baited with a herring for this. Flounders, rock & kelp fish are also abundant & are taken with a spear.

July 20
Working down the inlet.

July 21
At sunset anchored on the first of the flood near the village of [Chalucum]. Off this place the tide runs very strong & when it made strong we dragged nearly out to the point. Run a kedge out, hauled off & again dragged below the point into smooth water.

July 22
As soon as the ebb water got underway & stood [down] the inlet. At 9, discovered the *Porpoise* coming from Point Partridge & made signal for him to join us.

At 2 PM anchored near Dungeness point. Immediately after I received orders to take charge of the *Ariel Pilot* & *Triton* & and proceeded with Messrs Totten & Sandford to survey between the Suquamish Village & Point Partridge.

At 5 PM stopped at Point Wilson & fired for base. Put up a good signal & then [continued] up the Inlet. At 8 landed on Whidbys island for the night. Found here a few Nuhomish Indians. This tribe is the poorest of all I have visit since I entered the Straits. They occupy the shores of Possession Sound opposite the S end of Whidbys island. I have at different times met a hundred or more. Many of them are entirely naked. They are flat heads, exist on fish, clams, &c. & have the same manners & customs as the Suquamish — of which as well as the Clalams they are much afraid. [ ] I estimated from what I was told by the Indians to be about 400.

July 23
Early this morning continued [ ]. At 8.30 reached the Suquamish village & got breakfast. This was the point we were to commence work at.

After an hour I started for the village of the [ ]. Met in A harbour directly opposite on Whidbys island & took station leaving Mr. Totten to occupy a point of the *Porpoise* near the village — Mr. Sandford going to another of his on Whidbys island.

Before leaving went to [Chalacums] house to look at it & some canoes he was building. Size of the latter measured upwards of fifty feet in length, 4½ high & 4 in width — made of the large [ ] of cedar so abundant throughout this country. It was intended for a war canoe & could carry from 15 to 20 men. The canoes were hollowed by [fire] & tools made of [ ] a hard wood.

This was my fifth visit to this place & I always found a large party of Indians in the neighborhood. They were generally well behaved but required close watching as the hands were always itching to pick up any trifle in the way. (On one occasion they stole a couple [nillocks] from the *Pilot*. On complaining to the Chief of the theft he had them returned but would not point out the thief.)

This tribe occupy both shores of the Inlet from the Narrows to this place — the south end of Whidbys island & the lower parts of Hoods Canal but flat heads acknowledge Chiefs & subsist of fish, clams, &c. The head is flattened by a [couple] of cushions made for the purpose to fit the fore & hind parts of the head, they placed & kept on by a basket being passed over tightly to keep them in place. The child is then lashed to a board having a space hollowed for the head & backside & a shelf for the feet[30] & either stored up [ ] the house or suspended from a stick stuck diagonally in the ground & used as a cradle with a perpendicular motion. The mothers appeared to be as fond of the children & attentive to their wants. The fish are preserved by splitting & smoking or drying them in the [ ]. When required for use they are either cooked on a stick over [ ] fire or stewed in a basket made for the purpose water tight with stones. The clams are steamed out, strung on sticks & roasted for hours over the fire either eaten dry or stewed. All the drudgery of catching & preparing the latter as well as the smoking of the fish is done by the women.

The dress consisted of blankets obtained from the Fort made of dogs wool by themselves, shirts [ ] moccasins. The women wear blankets & a short petticoat under of birch bark of sufficient length to cover the sexual

---

[30]While this description is a bit difficult to follow, a picture from the Wilkes material provides a better image. The board contained a small shelf at the bottom for the child's feet, to prevent the child from slipping out. A second board of equal length was secured to the first at the top by a rope forming a hinge. Based upon the picture, the child was strapped firmly to the first board at the ankles and knees, and perhaps arms. The second board was lowered onto the child's forehead. A single thong near the end lashed the two boards together and provided constant compression to the forehead.

[mark]. It resembles the [ ] much. The hair is worn by both sexes [ ] is very often filled with vermin, it being a common sight to see them picking these from each others heads.

These people as well as all others about here are slaveholders. The slaves are usually obtained from the distant tribes when young. They work the land & pay but little attention to their wants, &c. From this [ ] & the account of children belonging to other Tribes, the Suquamish must number 800–1000.

Their winter quarters are built of logs fitted with [grooves] & roofed with board split out for the purpose.

As soon as I landed at my station the Chief came down. He had three buildings & was putting up [more]. They are situated on a clear space of about twenty across one half of which was planted with potatoes. The Indians have been induced by the company to cultivate potatoes, they purchasing all that are brought to the Fort. They are now becoming an article of food with the Indians themselves.

Continued the survey down the Inlet finding good anchorages all along the shores of Whidbys island in from 5 to 10 fathoms. Stopped for the night in [ ] last nights station.

July 24

Directly after breakfast continued the survey down the Inlet. The shores of Whidbys island affording good anchorages. The banks generally 50 or more feet height of stratified clay. The edges covered with pine & clear land back. Water was running out of them in different places. At 6 we crossed to Hudson point on the main shore. Here met about 31 Makah many of them as naked as they came into the world & by far the mildest set I have seen. From here went to Point Wilson got supplies & as soon as the ebb made started for the ship.

July 25

At 1 P.M. reached the ship after a long & [disagreeable] pull against a heavy head sea.

At 3 PM the *Porpoise* weighed & stood to the N^d.

At 4 Capt W left the ship with seven boats for the survey of this Canal de Arro. I went in the *Pilot*. At the [ ] of [ ] the winds were very fresh from the W & increased as we left the shore. With a heavy sea the latter making a clean breach across the boat every five or ten minutes. But before sunset finding we should not fetch the mouth of the Canal, bore up for a small bight to the E^a. This proved lucky for us to be an entrance we [ ] in to it & encamped just at dark. Had I been told that boats would have behaved so well as ours did in such a sea I should have disbelieved it & shall always hereafter have a better opinion of the capability of whale boats.

About ½ way across struck a shoal buoyed by kelp.

July 26

This morning continued the survey of the shores we were in a few miles above the entrance & found many channels in different directions cutting up the land into numerous small rocky islands. On some of them found signals left by the *Porpoise*. These islands are covered with a thick [ ], pine & oak trees the latter generally small. At sunset pitched our tents on the on the shore of [ ] running to the [ ]. Saw a few Indians of the Clalam tribe.

July 27

This morning continued the survey to the W. At my 4th station a couple of Clalams landed to see what I was about. Shortly after I saw with my glass 5 canoes crossing from the N towards us. On pointing them out to the Indians they [ ] with the utmost alarm [ ] went to their canoe & [brought] up the arms, paddles, &c. & laid them by me making signs for me to call my men & get the arms ready. As I was alone, thought this advice good & made preparations to receive the gentlemen perfectly in case they intended showing the general customs. About the time they landed the Samich came up which retired the fears of my Clalam friends much. The canoes contained 40 men, all were armed. They brought two or three carcasses of deer with them [ ] I bought for 5 charges of powder & ball each. About this time Mr. Totten found me bringing the report of Mr. May's having just arrived from the ship with the news of the loss of the *Peacock* on the Columbia cross [bar] July 18 all hands being saved.

Capt Wilkes even after came up bringing Mr. May in the cutter & the other boats with him. His party now numbered upwards of eighty apparently astonished the Indians a considerable who watched all our motions. The boats left for the station above & they soon cleared out [ ]. Worked round to the signals left last night & encamped in our old station.

July 28

This morning went to stations left yesterday & worked from them down the main channel to the Straits. Before leaving the camp Mr. Sandford was dispatched with orders for the *Porpoise* to join us at Dungeness.

At 5 PM left the entrance of the Canal for the ship & got alongside at 10 PM.

July 29
Making preparations for leaving the Straits.

July 30
The *Porpoise* arrived from Port Townsend where Mr. Sandford had met her. At 4 P.M. Mr. Waldron left in a canoe for Nasqually on his way to the Columbia with dispatches for Capt Hudson.

July 31
Wind light from the W. Got underway & commenced working down the Straits.

August 1
Light westerly winds. Working down the Straits.

August 2
Light N. W. winds. At 1.15 anchored in Claset or Scarborough harbour on the south shore just inside of Cape Flattery. Sent all boats to survey it & the coast to the eastward. Found on the east sides of the bay in larger villages of Clalam Indians & on the west villages, the Clasets & Tatooches. The two [ ] war with each other.

The *Porpoise* crossed to the south end of Vancouvers island to examine a harbour there.

August 3
This morning the ship was surrounded by hundreds of canoes filled with men, women & children bringing salmon, skins, &c. for sale. Some of the men from the southward about Grays harbour & were very [ ].

Afternoon the *Porpoise* leaving in light from the other shore. Got underway & commenced working to sea, wind light for the westward.

The following is a list of the tribes I saw while in the Straits & the numbers according to [ ] own accounts reckoning 3 women, children, &c. for each warrior. The two latter I may have overrated.

Nisqually	Pugets Sound	400
Suquamish	Admiralty Inlet	800
Tuandos	Hoods Canal	400
Scocomish	"	1500
Clalams	Hoods Canal, Straits of Juan de Fuca & islands inside of Vancouver	1800
Nuhomish	Possession Sound	300
Classets	Straits of Juan de Fuca, Cape Flattery	800
Tatooches	"	800

6

George Colvocoresses: Four Years

George Musalas Colvocoresses was born on the island of Scio in the Grecian Archipelago on October 22, 1816. In 1821 the Greeks sued for independence from Turkey. During the Turkish siege of Scio, George's father Constantine escaped and found protection at the Austrian Consulate at Scio. George, his mother, grandmother, brother, one sister and uncle were taken hostage. The Turks butchered the uncle and grandmother. Constantine, aided by the consul and friends, was able to ransom the remainder of the family. Constantine and his wife immediately put George on board the brig *Margarita* along with nine other boys, destined for Baltimore. The mate on the ship was very kind to George and upon arrival, took him home to his mother, hoping for him to remain. The Greek Relief Committee, however, took charge of the boys. Their names and histories were published in the news. Captain Alden Partridge, head of the American Literary, Military and Scientific Academy at Norwich, Vermont, took an interest in the young man and offered to educate him and raise him as his son. Sent to Norwich, George lived with the captain's brother, Aaron, and his wife, Mary, for the following nine years.

On February 12, 1832, at the age of sixteen, George entered the Navy. He was first assigned to the *United States* in the Mediterranean which provided him the opportunity to visit his parents and relatives. After serving on several other ships and a year at the naval school at Norfolk, he joined the Wilkes Expedition as a passed midshipman. After several other assignments he returned to Norwich, met and fell in love with Eliza F. Halsey. They married in May 1846.

George saw more duty at sea in the coming years and was promoted to commander during the Civil War. He married a second time to Miss Adaline M. Swasey, the younger sister of Captain Partridge's wife. In 1867 George was promoted to captain and placed on the retired list. On June 3, 1872, he was robbed in Bridgeport, Connecticut, at gunpoint and shot fatally in the back.

What I believe is his original journal, *The People's Book...*, is nearly identical to a book he published subsequent to the Expedition, *Four Years in the Government Exploring Expedition....* In the Preface of his book, he noted that it was based upon his journal or diary, maintained throughout the journey. I transcribed the following material from the book which was nearly identical to his journal.

[p. 225] On the morning of the 28th of April we made Cape Disappointment, off the mouth of the Columbia River, but, as the weather was boisterous, and the sea broke with great violence on the bar, we did not deem it prudent to attempt to enter the river. Next morning the prospects of getting in were no better; indeed, the chances seemed to be still more against us, as the wind during the night had hauled round to the southward and westward with increased strength; we therefore concluded to stand for Puget Sound, to the northward. About 10 A. M. on the 30th, the "look-outs" reported "breakers a-head"; immediately all hands were called, and the ship was brought by the wind. After standing a few minutes on this course the weather cleared, and we discovered Destruction Rocks not more than half a mile off, and exactly in the direction where the breakers had been reported to be. It was in fact a very narrow escape from shipwreck and certain destruction, for even if we had succeeded in getting ashore, we should in all probability have been murdered by the savage natives. A few years ago a Russian brig was wrecked near the same place, the vessel went to pieces, but the crew got safely on shore. They were immediately attacked by the natives and massacred. Another time they attacked the boat [p. 226] of an American vessel that was engaged in the fur-trade, and killed several of the crew. The savages pretended at first that they had come to trade. Our pilot, who has been much among them, also represents them as being a treacherous and savage set.

This circumstance goes to show that we must have been under the influence of a strong current setting to the eastward, for we had been steering all the preceding night northwest, a course which gave the rocks a berth of between thirty and forty miles.

At 3 P. M. we passed between the two outer Flattery rocks, carrying ten fathoms all the way through, and between 4 and 5 o'clock passed Cape Flattery proper.

We now sailed close along the starboard-shore, which gave us an opportunity of forming some idea of it. A chain of small islands and rocks run parallel with it some eight or ten miles after passing the Cape. It had but little beach, became high and broken in the interior, and was covered with a dense forest, apparently composed of the fir-tree.

A little before sunset several canoes put off from a small bay and pulled toward us, evidently with the intention of paying us a visit, but we had no time to wait for them to get along-side, and after following us some time they turned back. In two of the canoes we observed several women, who seemed to take as active a share in the labors of the paddle as the men. They were all dressed in skins and blankets, and their heads were covered with a green-looking straw-hat of a conical form, with a very broad base, much resembling those which the Chinese are represented in pictures as wearing.

The weather during the night was very disagreeable.

May 1st. The weather continues cold and rainy. The shore we have passed to-day has been divided into steep cliffs [p. 227] and heads, with intermediate beaches. At 9 A. M. a large canoe, paddled by nine Indians, boarded us. They were all small in stature, and far from being good-looking, having broad, flat faces, with high cheek-bones and low foreheads. They were also very dirty about their persons, so much so that it was difficult to make out the color of their skin. One of them was dressed in corduroy pantaloons, and a jacket made of scarlet cloth, and could speak a little English. Their own language was harsh and disagreeable, seeming to be made up principally of gutturals, and the sounds *cluck* and *click*. They wore as ornaments a small silver tube stuck through the partition of the nose, and small brass bells suspended around the rim of their ears. They had with them some eight or ten otter skins, but were unwilling to sell them. It seemed as though they had come merely to look at the ship, she being the largest they had ever seen. They remained on board several hours and then went along-side the *Porpoise*.

May 2d. This morning another canoe, manned by seven men and one squaw, boarded us. They brought with them some fish, which they readily exchanged for a few pipes and some tobacco. The woman was seated in the bow of the canoe, and was not permitted by the men to come on board. At 3.30 P. M. we passed Point Dungeness, a low, woody tongue of land. After passing this point, our progress was greatly impeded by a very strong ebb-tide. It run between three and four miles an hour. We observed as we sailed along this part of the coast a great number of tall poles, which our pilot informed me, were stuck up by the Indians for the purpose of suspending nets to them, in which they take geese and other wild fowl that frequent these shores at certain seasons of the year. About sunset we reached Port Discovery, and anchored for the night. Numbers of men, women and [p. 228] children came running down to the beach as soon as we made our entrance, and some of them got into their canoes and came along-side. They were no better looking nor more cleanly than those we had before seen, and we were very glad to purchase the fish they brought for sale, in order to get them out of the ship as soon as possible.

This harbor is a superb one, being easy of access, free from rocks or shoals, eight miles long, and from one and a half to two miles wide — possessing the very best kind of bottom, and with sufficient depth of water for the largest vessel to lay within two hundred yards of the shore. The country in the vicinity is not mountainous, but rises into hills of moderate elevation, covered all over with pine and spruce trees of the largest dimensions.

May 3d. The following General Order was issued this afternoon, and passed round to be read: —

> The undersigned informs the officers and crews under his command, that the duties upon which they are about to enter, will necessarily bring them at times in contact with the savage and treacherous inhabitants of this coast, and he therefore feels it is his duty, to enjoin upon them the necessity of unceasing caution, and a restrictive and mild system in all their intercourse with them.
>
> In my General Orders, of July 13th, 1839, my views are expressed fully, respecting our intercourse with savages, and I expect that the instructions therein contained, will be strictly regarded.
>
> With a knowledge that many of the misfortunes that have befallen previous voyages on this coast, have arisen from an unrestrained and unguarded intercourse with the natives, he deems it important to order officers in charge of boats, and [p. 229] those having men under their direction, to make it their especial duty to govern them so as to avoid any disputes, or maltreatment of the Indians; and that force is never to be resorted to, but in cases of self-defense.
>
> No officer or man will be allowed to visit the shore, without arms; and boats' crews upon surveying, or other duties, will be furnished with such as are necessary for their protection.
> United States ship *Vincennes*,
> CHARLES WILKES

We had a grand feast to-day, on fish and clams, which we bought from the natives along-side. The latter are not so large as those found on our own coast, but they are more tender, and much better flavored. They may be obtained in any quantities, any where along the beach. The fish were of the salmon and cod kinds. It is yet rather too early in the season for salmon, but they are very fine notwithstanding, especially when broiled.

May 5th. Several of the boats have been employed to-day in surveying the harbor.

In the forenoon I visited the shore. The beach abreast the ship was covered with Indian huts; they were constructed in the rudest manner imaginable, consisting of a few mats and rushes spread out on poles, and offering little or no protection against either the wind or rain. The fire was kindled upon the ground near the centre, and the interior of the building was filled with smoke. I was almost blinded by venturing into one of them, and was very glad to get out again into the open air. A mat or two spread on the ground near the fire, was used for sitting and sleeping upon. This was the only furniture to be seen, and the only article which could conduce [p. 230] to comfort. The owners of these wretched dwellings called themselves Clalams, and were the most singular looking people we had ever seen. The top of their heads was a flat as a board. This was caused by compression when they were very young. I was surprised to find them so poorly clad, in weather that was almost cold enough to freeze water; none had on more than one blanket, and some of them were to be seen going about in a state of perfect nudity. I never before had seen a people who seemed to have so little shame.

The children seemed to give their mothers but little trouble; the infants were tied to a piece of bark which hung to a pole, and was kept in motion by a string fastened to the toe of the mother. The little creatures were perfectly naked.

I observed the men were well supplied with muskets, fowling pieces, and knives, which they procure from the Hudson's Bay Company in exchange for furs. They had also bows and arrows, and the latter were pointed with iron.

The roofs and sides of many of the huts were hung with fish, strung on poles or sticks. There can be no want of food here, as the waters abound with excellent fish, and the forest with game of all kinds. Deer and bear-tracks are to be seen in every direction, and the natives have only to go a few yards from their huts, to kill enough to feed on for weeks together.

I spent several hours in wandering about in the neighboring woods. They were composed almost exclusively of pines, many of which were of immense diameter and height. I measured several that were twenty-five feet in circumference, and upwards of two hundred feet in height. The underbrush was not thick, and the principal impediment to clear walking was the vast number of fallen trees, over which I was obliged to climb. I saw numerous tracks of quadrupeds and one or two flocks of [p. 231] wild geese. The natives say the proper time for killing deer is early in the morning, at which time they resort to the springs to drink. Occasionally I encountered extensive thickets of rose-bushes, through which some large animal appeared but recently to have passed.

On returning to the beach I passed a burial-ground. It was surrounded with stakes to prevent the wild beasts from entering it, and the corpses instead of being interred were wrapped in mats, and placed upon the ground in a sitting posture.

May 6th. Having completed the survey of the harbor, we again spread our sails to the breeze and stood out into the Sound, followed by a great number of canoes, which had for sale fish, clams, and venison. We laid in a large supply of these; and the articles preferred in exchange were, as usual, powder, fish-hooks, clothing, and paint. The fish were the largest we had seen of the kind — some of the cod weighing between forty and fifty pounds. Towards evening the wind became so light we could not stem the tide, and so we stood into Port Townsend, and anchored in ten fathoms water. This is another excellent harbor.

A short walk from the beach here brings you to a beautiful lawn, ornamented with a great variety of pretty flowers. It extends several miles into the interior, and abounds in small lakes, around which hovered vast numbers of ducks and geese. The wood which skirts the green is composed of the same kind of trees as that about Port Discovery.

The Indians inhabiting the surrounding shores are clad in blankets and skins of wild beasts, and appear friendly. They are passionately fond of smoking, and will exchange anything they have for pipes and tobacco. The principal ornament worn by the women is a round piece of white bone, of about [p. 232] two inches in length stuck through the cartilage of their noses.

May 7th. At 1 P. M. we proceeded to get under-way, but were obliged to come-to again soon after on account of light variable winds. Mounts Reinier [sic] and Baker are visible from this point.[1] They both rise to a great altitude, and their summits are covered with perpetual snows. There were no natives to be seen at this place, nor any evidences of any ever having been here. The weather during the night was boisterous, and as the anchorage is not well protected, the ship rolled heavily, so much so that we could scarcely walk the decks.

May 8th. Early in the morning we sent the boats out to survey, although the weather was by no means favorable for such duties. Several of the boats narrowly escaped being swamped. We finished about noon, when we made sail and beat to the southward and eastward along Admiralty Sound, with a fresh breeze and a heavy head-sea till about 7 P. M., when we again let-go our anchor within a quarter of a mile of the shore. The water here was deep, and the coast on either hand bold and rugged, and apparently uninhabited. We named this place Pilot Cone, [sic] from the circumstance of our receiving there two pilots in the employ of the Hudson's Bay Company, to take the Squadron up to Nisqually.

May 10th. We have enjoyed beautiful weather all this day, and I cannot conceive a more magnificent picture than the Mountains Rainier and

---

[1]Oak Bay.

Olympus presented as the rising sun illumined their lofty peaks, and dispersed the mists that still floated in fleecy clouds over the tranquil valleys around their bases. The altitude of the latter mountain is stated to be eight thousand feet. At 2.30 P. M. we got under-way. The Sound now became quite narrow, being in some places not more than half a mile wide. Some Indians were observed [p. 233] to day, followed by their dogs, which were small, and had a head and ears strongly resembling those of the wolf. At sunset we came-to under the western shore to wait for day-light.[2] It was a rich treat to behold the sublime prospect around us through all its transitions of sunshine — purple hues, mellow twilight, and evening shades— until there was nothing else to be seen but the dark masses of Rainier and Olympus, uplifting themselves against the clear and starry skies of this region.

May 11th. At an early hour we were out surveying as usual. When finished we again spread our canvas, and made the best of our way for Nisqually, distant about twelve miles. After running about an hour we reached the narrowest part of the Sound, which, at this point was less than 400 yards wide; the shores on either side were high and precipitous, and the tide run like a sluice. Just before we arrived at the narrows, above described, we passed on our left what appeared to be a large arm of the Sound. We also passed several small conical-shaped islands. About dusk we at length reached our port, and anchored in twenty-two fathoms water. We found here a steamer belonging to the Hudson's Bay Company, and kept to run about the coast to collect furs from the Indians. The Sound is here divided into a great number of arms, some a mile or two wide, and apparently thirty or forty miles in length.

May 12th. Hauled-in close to the shore and moored ship, as we are to remain here some weeks, and perhaps months. Sent all the scientific instruments to the Observatory, except the pendulum. Lieutenant Johnson has been temporarily detached from the *Porpoise*, and ordered to take charge of a party that is to examine the interior. Received orders to hold myself in readiness to proceed with Lieutenant Case to Hood's Canal, for the purpose of surveying the same. In the afternoon a large number of natives came on board, among [p. 234] them were some women, who were very good-looking and better dressed than any we have before seen. They came to exchange some moccasins and baskets for red paint and looking glasses. The moccasins were neatly and even tastefully made, and found ready market among the officers, who wished to preserve them as specimens of Indian ingenuity and taste.

July 3d. We reported our return from the so-called Hood's Canal, hav-

---

[2]South of Gig Harbor.

ing been absent from the ship upwards of three weeks; it was found to be an arm of Puget Sound. Its shores are nowhere more than one hundred feet in height, and are formed of stratified clay, with a light gravelly soil, covered with pine and spruce. At Tskutska Point the Canal divides into two branches — one taking a direction nearly northerly, while the other pursues its course to the southwest. At the southern extremity of the canal there is an extensive inlet, called "Black Creek," by which the Indians communicate with the Columbia and Chickelees Rivers. The water in the centre of the canal is too deep for anchorage, but there are several good harbors, of all of which surveys were made.

We fell in with Indians almost every day, and had considerable intercourse with them in the way of trade — they supplying us with venison and fish, and we giving them in exchange powder, fish-hooks, red paint, and cotton handkerchiefs. The venison, in particular, was sold very cheap — five of the ordinary musket charges of powder being the price of a whole carcass.

Though these Indians seemed to understand each other, they informed us that they belonged to different tribes. One party called themselves Squamish, another Socomish, and a third party Toandos. The Squamish appeared to be the most numerous, and, according to their own account, could muster two hundred fighting men. The Toandos were the best-looking, [p. 235] and they assured us that they inhabited the mountains, and were now paying a visit to their friends the Socomish. All these tribes, in their habits and manner of living, resemble those about Nisqually. On leaving the ship we were warned to be on the watch for them, as they were arrant thieves, but I am not aware that they ever attempted to take anything from us, except one of the eye-pieces belonging to the Theodolite. This seemed to excite their attention more than anything else connected with the expedition, and they frequently asked us if it could speak, and whether it had not something to do with the "Great Spirit."* The women are not very good-looking, and the whole burden of domestic occupation is thrown upon them.

They have no permanent settlements; and there were several families who followed us wherever we went, and became familiar with some of the sailors. The men possess muskets, spears, and bows, and arrows. The bows are short and small, but have great elasticity, and when in their hands will do good execution.

---

*The eye-piece was finally recovered through the kindness of Mr. Anderson, the principal agent of the Hudson's Bay Company at Nisqually, by threatening the tribe who had it, the Socomish, with the destruction of their villages and canoes, if they did not give it up by a certain day.

The Canal does not terminate where Vancouver's charts would lead one to suppose, but extends ten miles further to the northward and eastward, and approaches within two miles of the waters of the Puget Sound, from which point we communicated with the *Vincennes*, the second week out, and obtained a fresh supply of bread and other provisions. There is plenty of fresh water along the shore, and we found several streams large enough to turn mills. Generally speaking, the soil is not rich, and the climate is similar to that experienced at this place.

[p. 236] July 5th. Yesterday was the "Glorious Fourth," but being also Sunday, it was very properly agreed that the celebration should be postponed until to-day; accordingly, at an early hour this morning, all was bustle and preparation on board the ship. By nine o'clock all the crew were mustered in clean white frocks and trowsers, and I was directed to take charge of them for the day. Soon after we landed abreast of the ship, and walked up to the Observatory. Here we formed into a procession, and marched off with drums and fifes playing, and the Star-spangled Banner waving, for Fort Nisqually, Vendovi bringing up the rear. Vendovi was dressed "a-la-Fejee," and appeared to enjoy the occasion quite as much as any one present.

On arriving abreast of the fort we halted, and gave three cheers, which were promptly returned by Mr. Anderson and people. We next marched to a piece of open ground, distant about half a mile from the fort. This was the place chosen for the dinner and amusements. There were a great many Indians gathered here, looking at us silently and with much astonishment. At the usual time, dinner was piped by the boatswain and his mates, and we all repaired to partake of the ox which had been purchased from Mr. Anderson, and barbecued for the occasion.

So far, everything had contributed to make the day a very pleasant one. But as there can be no such thing as perfect happiness in this sublunary world of ours, so now a circumstance occurred which for a time threw a gloom over the party. When the salute was fired, one of the men, named Whitehorn, had his arm seriously injured by the sudden explosion of the gun. The wound was dressed as well as it could be, and a litter was made, on which he was conveyed to the ship, under the charge of his messmates.

[p. 237] When dinner was over, the amusements of the morning were exchanged for the excitement of horse-racing — the horses having been engaged from the Indians for the purpose. Sailors like this sport better than almost any other, though very few are able to ride well; but, on this occasion, fortunately, no one was hurt, although a good many were thrown by their steeds.

All the officers, together with Captain McNeil, Dr. Richards, and Mr.

Henderson, dined at the Observatory, with Captain Wilkes. Captain McNeil and Dr. Richards are native Americans. The Captain came here a number of years since, and engaged in the fur business, and succeeded so well in it, that the Hudson's Bay Company were glad to buy him off. He is now a trader in the Company's service, owning stock, and receiving a share of the dividends. He is married to a half-breed, and resides in the fort, with Mr. Anderson.

Dr. Richards is attached to the Methodist Mission, and appears to be a kind, gentlemanly man; his residence is situated near the Observatory, and I called there, in the course of the afternoon, to pay my respects to his lady, who received me very kindly.

The doctor informed us that the Mission had but recently been established, and so far, it had not been able to accomplish much; and it was his honest opinion that it never would answer the expectations of its friends at home.

After the rejoicings were ended, I returned the men on board the ship, in the same good order as they had landed, and, I dare say, it will long be remembered by us all, as one of the most pleasant celebrations we have ever experienced.

July 6th. We received, this morning, a visit from Dr. McLaughlin. The doctor is the Chief Factor and Governor [p. 238] of the Hudson's Bay Company. He left Vancouver about a week since, and he expressed his regrets at not being able to reach Nisqually in time to be present at the celebration of the Fourth; he lost his way, when about a hundred miles from the fort. He is a tall, dignified-looking man, with a fair complexion, and I should judge his age to be nearly seventy. He is of Scotch extraction, but by birth a Canadian. He has been in the employ of the Company upwards of forty years, and is said to be pre-eminently fitted for the situation he occupies, being a man of great energy of character, and much talent.

Captain Wilkes conducted him around the ship, and he seemed much pleased.

On his leaving, to return to the shore, the yards were manned, and three cheers were given him, in a manner which showed that we appreciated his kindness towards us; they were three very hearty cheers.

July 16th. To-day, Mr. Johnson and party returned from the interior. The speak favorably of the country passed over, and of the Indians they fell in with. At a place called Chimikane, they found two missionaries, Messrs. Walker and Eel, whose labors had been attended with remarkable success. Among other duties, they had taught the Indians the art of cultivation, and many of them now subsist entirely on the produce which they raise on their lands.

As nothing has yet been heard from the *Peacock*, which, on leaving the

Sandwich Islands, was ordered to visit the King's Mill Group, and then meet the rest of the squadron at the Columbia River, fears are entertained by many, that she has met with some serious accident.

July 17th. I received orders to-day, to join Mr. Eld in an expedition, which has for its object, the exploration and survey of Chickelees River and Grey's Harbor. These orders came rather unexpectedly, and at a very late hour. The ship was already under-way, and I was at my station, when I received them. It seems, that when the expedition was first planned by Captain Wilkes, he designed having Lieutenant Johnson take charge of it, and Mr. Eld to accompany him as his assistant; but Mr. Johnson found fault with his written instructions, whereupon Captain Wilkes took the command from him, and gave it to Mr. Eld, and I am ordered to fill Mr. Eld's former place.

7

The Journal of Acting Master George T. Sinclair

For this transcription I obtained the original journal from the National Archives in Washington, D.C. In many cases, capitalization and punctuation are difficult to determine. When in doubt, I added punctuation where appropriate. Where text is unreadable, I inserted a bracket [ ] or in some cases word(s) within the bracket as my best guess based upon the context of the sentence. This journal is important because of Sinclair's candor, sense of humor, and his observation skills.

Thursday April 29th 1841
    Until 1 PM the wind fresh from the S^dW^d with the fog so thick that at times the visible horizon did not extend two hundred yards. In the morning watch the *Vincennes* hailed to know how we made Cape [Dis]. We made it S 32°E Dist 35 miles and the [ ] S 54°E Dist 40 miles. Capt Wilkes ran by his own reckoning as a matter of course, and [thinly] came within an [ ] of losing both vessels—with a thick fog [would] have been more prudent I think to have run on NE which was nearest in shore & consequently on the safe side and ultimately found to have been correct. Port Discovery was appointed a rendezvous in case of separation. Onward we drove at the rate of 8 knots steering North by which our reckoning was right in for the land and by this for the Flattery Islands, fairly cutting a passage as is wise tho the fog which was densely thick. Towards ten the water indicated that we were shoaling fast, [ ] came round us in numbers, the hand lead showed no bottom but the first cast of the heavy lead showed 4 fms and shortly after the breakers [ ] thro the fog in a most uncomfortable proximity we lost no time in bringing by the wind in [ ] which the Fore Top Mast Stg Sail Boom was broken short off. The sea was very heavy

& the Vessel plunged violently. The *Vin^s* was not long in following our Example and we were born down by a tremendous [press] of canvass. For some time it was doubtful if we would get off. Both vessels behaved well for tho a tremendous head sea we drove along at the rate of 6.4. Just as we hauled on a wind land was reported and a large Rock was plain in sight about two pts on the la^1 bow and so close did we pass to it that we had hardly got by it before it was in our wake there were many outlying rocks one of which was nearly midway between us & the large rock which was not more than a quarter of a mile off. It has a hole through it. By noon we had deepened water to 25 fms and we breathed freely once more. This was certainly a most narrow Escape and we certainly more indebted to good luck than to good management for our Escape had the *Vin^s* been as far inshore as we were she would have struck and [god knows] what would have become of us.

At 1 [ ] the wind shifted suddenly to the N^d & W^d & then fell calm & continued so for the rest of the day.

Friday April 30th

First part of the day calm — in the morning watch got a breeze from the S^d & E^d with which we stood to the N^d at 5 we made the land bearing from N & E to the NE & E. Continued standing along the land. large Flock of Geese, Ducks &c were seen, generally on the wing and we passed quantities of sea weed. About [1 PM] we passed the Flatery rock. And by 7 we had rounded Cape Flatery & commenced beating thro the Straits of Juan de Fuca. The *Vincinnes*, by mistake of the Pilot passed between two of the Flatery rocks, she carried two fathoms water, but it might have been worse. Several canoes pushed off from the shore but did not succeed in getting alongside Either of the Vessels. The land was high & well wooded principally with tall Spruce or Trees that looked as if they would make good spars— our distance was to great & the weather so thick that we could make but few observations upon the nature of the coast. Continued beating during the night with the *Vincennes*.

Wednesday [sic] May 1st

Wind light and variable with foggy wr. Beating up the Straits, barely holding our own with the Ebb but making good progress with the flood. At 11 a large & very beautiful canoe came alongside. There were six Natives in her who were stout men but rather short. they remained onboard four or five hours but it was raining on deck & they smelt rather to strong for us to tolerate them below so that we did not derive much pleasure in their

---

^{1}Larboard or port bow.

scarcity. They look very much like Russians & were of the Klasset Tribe — dressed in Skins or Blankets & had a few of the former for sale — one of them wore a Red frock coat, with Russian buttons.

Sunday May 2^d

Fine day running up the Straits, close to the South Shore which was mountainous & well wooded, the summits of these Mountains snow caped. At 6 passed a strong tide rip off New Dungeness P^t which is low & sandy running a mile or so from the Main land. At 7 we passed Protection Island & at 8 came to in Port Discovery close to the Beach in 18 fms water.

Monday May 3^d

Winds blowing fresh from the SSW and a [smart] sea running. In the afternoon the Boats started off to Survey the Harbour & some of them did not return until late at night. The [ ] and only objection to this Harbour is its great depth of water. In several places within a reasonable distance of the shore I could not get soundings with 50 fathoms, all the line I had.[2] Vancouvers chart of this Harbour can not, in my opinion, be altered for the better. The only error in his chart has been made in the topography, the projecting points being all represented as high land, whereas they are low points formed of sand and gravel with, in almost every case, a lagoon in the center. A number of the filthy flat headed beastly natives visited us today. They are the most wretched race of People I have ever fallen in with. During the night it rained.

May 4th 1841

A fresh breeze from the SSE with rain part of the time. Cut a few rough spars onshore.

I landed on one of the points to day to observe Chronometer Longitude.

Visited some of the huts of the Natives but the stench and fear of vermin forced me to make a speedy retreat. Their Hovels are formed by sticking a few sticks in the ground and partially covering it with mats and into the [ ], the Indians huddle together, men, women and children. how they manage to carry on the private affairs of life I am not prepared to say.

---

[2]Sinclair's reference to the extreme depth is confusing as the harbor is consistently 25–30 fathoms, even close to shore, except at the south end where it begins to shoal. Further, none of Wilkes' charts reflect such depths inside the harbor. He may have been located outside the entrance where the depth does exceeds 50 fathoms.

May 5th

A fine day with pleasant weather. Completed the survey of the Harbour. From the Indians we got some fine Salmon & Rock Cod.

Filled with water which is easily procured.

May 6th

Light variable breezes & pleasant wr. got underway & stood out of the harbour followed by a number of Canoes from which we got an abundance of Salmon, Rock Cod &c. Enough to supply the whole crew.

At 5 PM we came to in Port Townsend in 5¾ fms water muddy bottom. This is a much finer Harbour than Port Discovery owing to the depth of the water. Landed near a beautiful green Lawn in the Starbd Entrance. Vancouver has an accurate representation of this Point in his journal but the Indian Poles, represented in his sketch have given way to the ravages of Time. It is strange that they have not been replaced for there is a large tract of level meadow land, with a pond in the center, just in the rear of the beach, which abounds with Geese & Ducks— a few natives hovel here. I did not visit them.

May 7th

All the Boats of the two vessels were out to day under Capt Wilkes & Ringgold surveying the Harbour. In the evening got a breeze from the ESE with which we got underway and in a very short time we came to in a very good harbour[3] just to the S^d of Port Townsend and nearly communicating with the Head of that bay, only a narrow strip of land connecting an extensive Island, which forms the Eastern shore of Port Townsend[4] with the mainland. This Island itself is almost divided into two. Gap in the Island forms a beautiful & deep cove[5] communicating with the water of Port Townsend to the N° & only prevented from opening to our present anchorage by a narrow strip of land.

May 8th

During the day blowing very fresh a half gale of wind with a high sea, notwithstanding which the boats were sent out to survey. I was in perhaps the most miserable boat in the squadron I could do no work & in attempting to return to the Brig got driven to leeward, the sea broke over the boat, filled her with water, snapped two of the oars and injured my sextant. I was obliged to anchor close to the breakers & when I was on the eve of try-

---

[3]Oak Bay.
[4]Indian and Marrowstone Islands.
[5]Kilisut Harbor.

ing my luck by beaching her as an only alternative another very fine boat was sent to my assistance & the weather moderating at the same time. I shifted into the other boat & towed the old dung barge alongsides.

At 1.30 with a fresh breeze got underway in company with the *Vins* & commenced beating up the Inlet wind at SSE. At 7 we came to again under the western shore[6] in 11½ fms water. We had a strong flood in our favour.

A canoe arrived from Nasqually in Puget Sound with the mate and one of the crew of the Companys Steamer *Beaver* to act as Pilots and interpreters. Mount Rainier, so named by Vancouver presents a beautiful & majestic appearance as you approach to the S^d. We got a first view of it on the 2nd when we opened it with the land near Port Discovery. It is eight or nine thousand feet above the line of the Sea and is covered nearly to it base with eternal snow.

May 9th

Pleasant day wind from the SE. At 5 AM we got underway & beat up the Inlet until 8½ when the Ebb commencing. we anchored under the west shore[7] in 12 fms water. At 21½ we got underway again with the flood & stood up the Inlet until 7 when we anchored again.[8] Surveyed in the vicinity of both anchorages.

May 10th

Fine day. At half past three we got underway and stood to the S^d & E^d. The Inlet gets narrow as you approach Puget Sound when it branches off into several arms. It is not half a mile wide where we are now. Some Indians passed us in their canoes but did not stop alongside.

The appearance of the Country through the extent that we have passed is well wooded principally with pines and on the whole has rather a pleasing appearance. It wants variety. Every where it is the same & the eye tires in gasing on it.

May 11th

Surveyed this morning in the vicinity of our anchorage just outsides the narrows.[9] About 2 miles to the N^d of us there is an Inlet or arm several miles in depth which Vanc^r has overlooked, the entrance to it is narrow & covered by two overlapping sandy points. A casual observer would [ ] within 100 yards of & not notice it. At 3½ PM we got underway with the

---

[6]Pilots Cove.

[7]Appletree Cove.

[8]Port Madison.

[9]Just south of Gig Harbor.

flood and stood up the Narrows towards Nasqually, one of the Companys Stations. At 7½ PM we anchored in 19 fathoms under Nasqually P^t & near the Companys Steamer the *Beaver*. Puget Sound is a lovely sheet of water and I believe is deep throughout its entire extent, except where a river discharges itself into it.

May 12th

Vincennes hauled inshore of us today and moored ship, so I suppose, as usual she is going to make a stay of it, and give us the most of the work to do. She hardly does anything more than make passages. Lt Johnson & Mr Waldron left the Brig for the purpose of making an excursion into the Interior of this Oregon Territory and Lt Alden, P^d Midn Sanford, Midn Elliot joined the Brig for temporary duty. Employed wooding, watering & painting outside.

Rec^d from the Company, a present of fresh Beef for the crew. Instead of throwing impediments in our way, as we thought they would, they offer us every facility in the prosecution of our labors.

May 13th

Pleasant weather. Employed painting & [ ] the Brig off. Sent our Pocket Chronometers to the *Vincennes* to be used by the party bound into the Interior. Rec^d a visit today from the Companys [ ] onshore among them Capt McNeal an enterprising American who holds the rank of Chief Trader & commands the Steamer

Friday May 14th

A very pleasant day. Went onshore for a walk and took my gun with me but saw nothing except a few robins to shoot. The Fort is or rather stockade on which the company officers reside is not visible from the anchorage in account of the steepness of the Banks which rise abruptly from the beach several hundred feet. The present site of the stockade was never chosen by an engineer or was it calculated to stand a siege, as its inmates are compelled to go nearly a mile to get their water. It is formed of posts 8 or 10 inches in diameter and about thirty feet high, strongly & neatly put together the ends of the posts being sunk in the ground & kept upright & together by four and aft pieces bolted to them. It is square in from the whole enclosing about half an acre of land. The houses & stairs are all built inside & there is a kind of watch Tower on each corner with [ ] holes for musketry; they have no field pieces and do not need them, as there is nothing to be apprehended at present from the Natives, who are completely under subject to the Company. The Stockade is falling to decay and they are about to build another on a better site. This station formerly yielded a large revenue but for the last year they have sunk money by it. About two miles from the fort they have a farm and dairy, from which they supply their servants [ ] & a large quantity of Butter to the Russian Settlements. The soil appeared to me to be light and altho wheat was growing, I thought that Rye would have answered better, they do not average over two Bushels to the acre. The laborers here are much more [ ] & object and are not so well fed & clothed as are our slaves. They are generally either Canadians, or from the North of Scotland and the [ ] Islands and the Company exercises an unbounded Tyranny & control over them.

Saturday May 15th
    The winds variable during the day and calm at night. Two boats & their crew joined the Brig from the *Vincennes* and from the Companys Steamer we need an interpreter.
    At 1.30 got underway in obedience to a signal from Vin^s & stood out the same way we came in with the strong Ebb tide in our favour. I presume we are [ ] on surveying duty to the N^d tho is this great national enterprise no one knows where is going and what he is going for but if he has any [ ] to lay in or preparations to make he must do it at hap hazzard. At 4.40 came to in the narrows in 10½ fms water off the mouth of an excellent little Bay[10] about 2½ miles to the N^d of our anchorage of the 11th, a number of canoes came off from which we purchased an abundance of salmon &c.

Sunday May 16th 1841
    A day of rest & sport. all hands were onshore by watches and the woods resounded with reports of their guns. The Birds doubtless got a good fright but some of them were killed. About noon I took a stroll in the woods with my gun more for the exercise of a good walk than with any hopes of finding game which [ ] very scarce. I however succeeded in killing a few squirrels & a very fine pheasant. The trees increase in their size as you go back into the country. The country abounds with [ ] principally [ ] and Cedar the latter grows larger, high and straighter than I have ever seen it anywhere else. The Maple is also common. The walking difficult owing to the number of fallen trees & the [ ] of undergrowth which in many places is [ ]. The soil is in many places so soft & boggy that it gives under your weight. There are many fine springs around and about which the raspberry & gooseberry bush abound. To judge from the quantity & size of the fallen trees (many of the largest size being torn up by the roots and prostrated some twenty yards from the pit in which they formerly grow). I should say the wind must at times blow furiously here — and in the shape

---

[10]Gig Harbor.

of the whirlwinds too as the trees lay in every direction Many of them have fallen up hill.

On reaching the Beach there were several parties of Indians and their fires cooking & warming themselves, like all I have seen here they are the filthiest people I have ever seen, not even excepting the Feegians. They cooked this salmon by sticking sticks thro it and letting it hang over the fire and by way of seasoning it they would take up their blankets & scratch their [backsides] over it. At night they slept out on the beach exposed to dew and rain. The lazy brutes they have every means of making themselves comparatively comfortable.

This was the only day during the whole of my stay on the coast that I ever had an opportunity of going beyond the Points on which I landed to angle.

Monday May 17th

At 9 got underway and at 11 anchored again under the shore & sent the boats out surveying. Called this anchorage Commencement Bay. The Brig is to carry the work on from this point to the N^d keeping to the E^d of Vashon & Whidbys Island. Boats returned at Sunset having discovered a fine harbour[11] entering Vashon I^d on the SE side & two small rivers[12] emptying into Commencement Bay.

May 18th

Variable winds, fine weather for our work. two Boats examined & surveyed another Commencement Bay & the rivers emptying into it. These rivers forms a mud flat off the mouths which it is [ ] at low water but at high water boats may go in & fill with water, follow them about two or three miles up. low meadows line their Banks, covered with fine grass on which vast numbers of Ducks or geese were landing. There was an opening in the hills to the S^d as tho another small stream came in there[13] but there was not water for the boats to go up. The two boats sent to examine the harbour in Vashon Isd returned reporting the harbour to be more extensive then had been supposed—fine anchorage all thro. They had not completed their survey.

May 19th

Variable winds fine weather in the forenoon, in the afternoon blowing fresh from S^d & E^d. At noon got underway & at 1 anchored under the East

---

[11]Quartermaster Harbor.

[12]Puyallup River and perhaps the Hylebos or another branch of the Puyallup.

[13]Perhaps Delin Creek.

shore of Vashon in an excellent harbour.[14] Surveying as usual, one of the Boats in the harbour on Vashon Isd from which there is a portage communicating with our anchorage. It is a mere strip of sand so that Vashon is nearly two islands.[15]

Sent a party there & fortunately interrupted the *Shark* as she was pulling down from the head of the Bay not knowing that the Brig was so near, saved them a pull of twelve miles & a camp out.

May 20th

Fine day. Employed surveying round & in the neighborhood of our anchorage. Found but few corrections & they unimportant to make in Vancouvers chart, which is of the greatest assistance to us in cutting out our work.

May 21st

A fine stiff Breeze. Boats out as usual. At 2 the Brig got underway up & sailed round the North end of Vashon Island & anchored in Port Orchard inter harbour in 8½ fms water, in passing in shoal water was reported from the mast head & she kept off avoid it & wile she did, for when the tide fell, we found that we had just avoided a bed of rocks which were ten or twelve feet above water.

As we remained in this harbour until the 29th, I was not onboard the Brig except at night during that time I will account under one head all the observations &c made in that point.

As soon as we anchored a tide staff was put up & a regular tide table kept. The rise & fall is about 18 or 20 feet & the tides run with great velocity so that a whale boat in many places could not make way against it. In the inner harbour the tides are regular only interrupted at the entrance of the different arms of the harbour of which there are four. In the outer harbour the tides are stronger than they are inside & much more irregular — two tides frequently meeting & forming overfalls thro which it is uncomfortable & even dangerous to pass in a boat. on one occasion whilst under sail going about three knots my boat ran into a whirl pool & was turned entirely round & almost capsized.

We made a complete survey of this harbor and its environs which occupied us until the 29th. Vancouver was more incorrect here than anywhere else on the coast. The south arm is very near as we made it with a small stream emptying into the head of it. There is an immence Basin of water to the westerd then either of the other arms which he has passed over

---

[14]Tramp Harbor.
[15]In fact, Wilkes did name the outboard portion of land after Lieutenant Maury.

all together & I am not surprised at it for the entrance and passage to it, has the appearance of a small creek. whilst surveying in this arm we could distinctly hear the guns fired by Lt Case's Party in Hood's Canal & from the signs made by the natives I should think they sometimes carry their canoes across from one place to the other. Vancouver has also neglected to put down another arm[16] which heads off from the North arm to the N^d & W^d & he has terminated the north arm when it branches off again to the Nd & Ed. We found this N & E arm[17] communicating with a harbour to the N^d which we surveyed on our way to Puget Sound in Company with the *Vins* & which was named by Captain Wilkes Madison Harbour. The Island this formed by this Northern exit of Port Orchard we named Bainbridge Island.

There is not in the world nor could there be a harbour superior to Port Orchard — Good anchorage, protected from every point with many little basins about the size of a Dry Dock but hard sandy bottom, into which a ship of the line might be hauled & left dry at low water. A pair of flood gates & a foundation would make a dry dock without any other expense or trouble.

The land generally low & in many places swampy but could easily be drained & some good fields made. There are many where the land is elevated & it is densely wooded throughout a number of small streams run into the harbour which afford abundance of excellent water. Wherever we landed we found wild roses or honeysuckles growing & filling the air with the fragrance and amidst this leaves & flowers where beautiful little hummingbirds were feeding.

There were but few natives, who were as usual a filthy flatheaded race, as stupid as apes; whatever small allotment of brains nature had originally given them seems to have been [ ] into the [ ] of [ ], if there be such an organ & if there is not, the Phrenologists ought to make one for their especial benefit. They were perfectly inoffensive & seemed to be honest for we sent Provisions, trade & even Whiskey, by them to our Surveying Party & they carried it faithfully & honestly.

For the first time since we have been on this coast we found some of the Burial places of the natives which are first such as Vancouver described fifty years ago. The bodies were wrapped in several mats & in some cases with blankets, they were then laid in canoes with all their worldly goods. the canoes covered with slabs & a box built on the Top of the slabs in which were deposited some articles of household furniture &c the canoe was placed in a gallows frame elevated about four feet from the ground, in some cases Tin pots & pans were put on top of all. Many of the canoes

---

[16] Liberty Bay.

[17] Agate Pass.

were rotten & had fallen from their stands. Our Doctor robed several of these of their heads for which act they or rather their Ghosts, ought to feel under obligations to him for they will be thus immortalized.

Saturday 29th

At 1. PM got underway & anchored in a small bay in the outer harbour which we called Cumtax Bay after one of the natives to whom we had given the name.[18]

Sunday May 30th

Variable winds & cloudy with light rain. At 4 this sabbath morning I was started off in the *Shark* to survey the western arm of Port Orchard in consequence of my having expressed an opinion that the work was not complete in as much as we had not been to the back of the Bay & could not say whether there was an outlet or not. Did not return until sunset, found no outlet. During my absence a fine fawn was caught swimming across the Bay. Sent the men on liberty. We found here two Indians of the [19] Tribe who had been half converted to the Catholic religion, would never eat without saying grace, crossing themselves &c they chanted very harmoniously, one of them we named Potlatch & the other Cumtax after whom we named the bay. These Indians kept by us during the balance of our stay on the Coast & were of great service to us as couriers &c.

Monday May 31st

At half past one PM got underway & at half past four anchored out side the outer harbour of Port Orchard on the East side of Bainbridge Island near the mouths of two very fine little harbours one of which we called Eagle Harbour & the other or southern one, Blakely Harbour in honor of the memory of the brave officer of that name who was killed in the last war. Employed surveying the straits between Port Orchard & Puget Sound.

At 8 oclock PM we had a most beautiful Meteoric display: a large Ball bearing NNW½W fell from an elevation of 60 or 70° a & burst at about 20° from the horizon leaving a brilliant train behind it. The heavens, when it burst were illuminated with a brilliant light for the space of upwards of half an hour. No one onboard had ever seen any thing of this kind before.

---

[18]*Porpoise* is working its way through Rich Passage.

[19]The name is difficult to read. But it appears to be "Seatjacks" which I will adopt as it is used elsewhere in the journal. Sanford used the name Seâchêt.

Sunday June 1st

Variable winds & fair pleasant air, Boats stashed as usual. At 6 oclock working up the Inlet to the N^d 2 boats on each shore. There is a large Bay nearly opposite to Port Orchard into the head of which a small river discharges itself. I was sent to examine this Bay & found it much too extensive to pull round it in one day. I however saw enough of it to convince us that it is not of much importance, the water being very deep in the outer part & shoaling very suddenly to three miles from the back of it at which distance a mud bank commences & fills the whole back of the Bay. This bank also forms the penetration of the fresh & salt water the line being distinct by marked by a strong rif as well as by a change in the color of the water.[20]

At 1 the Brig got underway & at 5 came to in a harbour which we surveyed going up to Puget Sound in Company with the *Vins* & that Capt Wilkes called Madison Harbour. It is into the head of this Harbour that Port Orchard communicates.

June 2^d

Boats out carrying out the survey to the south P^t of Vashon Island & the entrance of Possession Sound. There is a deep Indentation in the south P^t of Vashon but the whole is filled up by a mud flat & I presume a small stream comes in there. There is much shoal water off the SW P^t of this Island & several Rocks above water off the SE P^t where there is a stockade & several of the winter residences of the Natives which are built of timbers. In the summer they live under cover of a few dirty old mats supported on sticks which does not protect them from either wind or weather. There were more natives here than I have seen any where else on the coast. They were Clallams & appeared very friendly. They were very anxious that I should land, offering their women as an inducement certainly not a very tempting one particularly when pressed for time. The women were as free in the exhibition of their persons as they were their offers. The Brig got underway in the morning & at about 1 she came to clear under the East shore near the entrance of Possession Sound. Old Cumtax & Potlatsh our couriers returned from Nasqually whither we had sent them with letters. Heard that the party for the Interior had started on the 21st & that the *Peacock* & Schooner had not yet arrived at the River.[21]

June 3rd 1841 Thursday

Cloudy with rain & squally air in the evening blowing a gale of wind, the first bad weather we have had since we commenced work. Five boats off

---

[20]Elliott Bay.

[21]Columbia River.

surveying. Lt Maury in the *Rover* carrying on the survey of West shore to the N^d of Port Madison & to connect on with Lt Case who is in Hoods Canal. About 10 the Brig got underway with a [ ] gale from the SSW & proceeded about 6 miles up the Sound where she anchored & twas well she anchored when she did for had she proceeded a quarter of a mile further a mud flat would have brought her up. Weather so stormy that Maury could not cross the Inlet & was compelled to sleep out, without a Tent.

June 4th

All the forenoon the weather was very unfavorable, in the evening however it brightened up & Six Boats went out to survey. found a river coming in at the SE P^t of the Sound, which formed the mud flat near which we were anchored. At 6 AM Maury came onboard in the *Rover*.

June 5th

Little or no work done today as it was raining & the weather otherwise unfavorable. Lt North & Mr Sanford started with three days provisions to survey Port Susan.

A number of natives of the Seatjack and Sahomish tribes came alongside with skins & fish for trade; they are better looking men than those we have hitherto fallen in with.

Brig remained at her present anchorage until the 9th & the boats were kept employed surveying in her vicinity. On the 7th North's party returned having surveyed Port Susan. They found the Back of the Bay blocked up by a mud flat with as usual Meadow land in the rear & there is little doubt but that stream discharges itself here, there was not water enough to allow the boats to go back & examine but from the fact that the ebb runs to S^d at its commencement & then to the N^d at the edge of this bank, they were lead to conclude that it communicated with the waters to the N^d thus making P^t Allen[22] the Southern P^t of an Island.

June 9

Maury, North & myself started with three days provisions to survey in advance of the Brig. Worked on as far as a large Bay[23] on the west side[24] of Whidbey Island on the western shore of which we encamped for the night. This is a fine Bay. On the NE P^t of it there is a small Islet[25] which is connected at low water with the main land both the Island & the main land

---

[22]Camano Head.

[23]Holmes Harbor.

[24]He meant east side.

[25]Rocky Point and Hackney Island.

are fortified with good strong & well built stockades & the Natives appeared more independent & inclined to be [ ]. We however had two sentinels with loaded muskets during the night.

I have noticed occasionally to the S^d on the low points long Poles, erected by the Natives, they are becoming much more numerous now & as they are on the extreme points they are good objects to angle on. I can't imagine to what use the natives put them when there is only a single one which is most generally the case, but when there are several in a line as we frequently found there, we very readily understand the purpose for which they were erected by the natives & are always in front of low meadow land to which the Ducks & geese visit in the vast numbers. The natives stretch a net from one Pole to the other, kindle a fire or fires. They then frighten the wild Foul and they fly towards the lights and are [ ] by the nets & fall to the ground where they are killed in vast numbers.

June 10th

Finished the survey of the Bay & carried the work to the N^d nearly to Penns cove. The Brig passed us, furnished us with extra provisions & anchored at the mouth of the cove. After sunset when we were pitching our Tents & our camp fire just lighted, she fired a gun to recall us altho we were ten miles from her. This was both unnecessary & annoying. We had been at work since dawn without stopping & were cheered by the prospect of a pleasant evening. Suspend dinner combined with the song & smoke round the camp fire. Besides the work was retarded by our going to the Brig for had a long pull back in the morning to resume & connect on the work. Cold supper & watch to keep—cold campfire after a hard days work.

The appearance of the country hereabouts is much more pleasing that we had hitherto found it. The land is all well wooded and has an unusual appearance of fertility. The natives are more numerous & intelligent than we have seen elsewhere. There are several strong stockades to which the natives (Seatjacks) [ ] when they apprehend an attack from the Clallams or the Naultas a Tribe to the N^d of Frasers River, of whom they stand in great dread & who they describe as cannibals. The principal chief of the Seatjacks Natluns, resides at this place. He is decidedly the most intelligent Indian we have seen & was of a vast deal of service to us during the whole time that we were at work within the range of his authority, for which we repaid him with the most unjustifiable [ ] & gratitude.

These people do not seem to be so migratory in their habits as those more to the S^d & indeed the race seemed to improve as you advanced to the N^d. There are many permanent habitations in this neighborhood. They are formed & planked with [ ] planks which they split from the log with great labour having only an axe & wedge to work with. They serve only as an indifferent protection from the weather and are as filthy as it is possible for them to be. It is dangerous to go near them as you are instantly covered with Pulgas.[26] They huddle together promiscuously, men, women & children and I have been told that incest is very common with them. The fire is kindled in the center of the house & has no other outlet than the door & chinks thro which the smoke can escape. The consequence is that diseased eyes are exceedingly common. They have no domestic animal except the dog which are very numerous. Their food consists principally of fish with which the waters abound with occasionally venison & elk which are numerous & very fat. The natives to the S^d of Frasiers River are all flat heads. When the children are a few [weeks] old they commence the operation which is a most cruel & disgusting one. A Bucket is constructed & in some cases a [ ] into which they make a soft Bed out of Moss & old rags, place the infant into it & lash it down so that it cannot move. They then put a pad upon the forehead leaving barely room for it to breath, this pad is lashed down upon the head until the childs eyes fairly start out from their sockets & in this most unnatural situation they are kept the greater part of the day. Many doubtless do not survive this operation. This Cradle is suspended to the end of a twig fixed in the ground like a snair by which means they lull the infant to sleep.

The Catholic missionarys have evidently been at work among these people. Mr Maury when absent at Port Orchard saw a large church partly constructed & there is another in a similar state here & the natives have endeavoured to show us that they were Christians by crossing, chanting, saying grace &c. I do not think that the present generations will ever be either civilized or christianised. The only plan to succeed will be to establish missions & educate the rising generation teaching them how to cultivate their lands & the useful mechanical arts.

We were employed until the 14th surveying in Penns Cove & all about in its vicinity. There is good anchorage in every direction & the cove itself is a most beautiful harbour, much deeper than Vancouver made it, there being a Portage at its back over which the natives carry their canoes into the straits.

Monday 14th June

Lt Alden, Maury & myself left the Brig with three days provisions to survey deception passage. The channel to this passage is on the Whidbey Island shore & is sufficiently wide to allow a vessel to beat through; the Eastern or Main shore must be avoided as a mud flat makes off from it in some places over a mile & there appeared to be a river coming in from the

---

[26]Fleas!

E^d. We reached Deception Passage in the evening early enough to allow the Boats to pass thro & make a few observations. Pitched our tents for the night on a rocky point on the North shore.[27]

When I landed here in the evening there 8 or 9 canoes containing about 30 natives who belonged to the Clallam Tribe & who were out upon some expedition & were waiting for the Tide to pass out of the passage. There was another canoe in which was a single Seatjack. Between these two parties there arose a dispute the cause of which I could not understand. It was near proceeding to a fatal end for the Seatjack attempted to draw his gun from the canoe to use it apparently in his defense for the other party had laid violent hands on him in the scuffle the gun was broken. I never in my life saw more savage fury than was exhibited by both parties. I interfered & separated them. I could not reconcile them to each other or induce than to take a smoke or even to accept of a present of Tobacco which I offered then simply because I gave to both parties. The Clallams got into their canoes & paddled off in a very sullen mood, the other remained behind & seemed very gratified for the assistance I had rendered him & indeed he was afterwards of great service to us, in bringing water & we afterwards sent him to the Brig for Provisions which he brought to us faithfully. When he was onboard the Brig his gun was put in better order for him than it was before the accident.

The 15th & 16th were rainy disagreeable days but notwithstanding we were out surveying & got on between the showers so as to enable us to commence on the 18th working down to the Brig joining her at sunset on that day a few miles in advance of the anchorage where we had left her. We found that the tide ran at the rate of ten miles an hour forming an [ ] during its strength but at slack water there would be no difficulty in a vessel passing through as there is good anchorage on both sides of it. The Passage is about 1000 feet through and about 500 feet wide so that a vessel can slip thro in a few moments on the slack of the tides. In the passage you have from 14 to 31 fms & there is nothing in the way, a vessel may lay alongside the rocks in any part with ten fms under her keel.

We were encamped three days at our first encampment which was the only place in the neighbourhood where a tent could be pitched. As a matter of course we put up a tide staff & found the rise & fall of 18 feet. The tides were very irregular the tides running out an hour & a half after the water had commenced rising. The eddy which extended from the north

---

[27]This and the preceding sentence imply Sinclair camped on the west side of the pass, perhaps near Lighthouse Point. However, on June 25 he noted that the *Porpoise* anchored near this camp. The June 25 entry clearly locates them on the east side of Deception Pass. My guess is Yokeko Point.

shore two or three hundred feet out was nearly as strong as the tide [ ]. On the south shore it ran near the Beach.

May [sic] 18th

Regained the Brig at sunset. Mr Sanford to day found that Ports Gardner & Susan are connected as was formerly supposed to be the case. The connection is formed by a river with two mouths, one of them emptying into the head of each Bay thro a large tract of beautiful meadow land. Mr Sanford got angles on the old stations in Port Susan & [ ] new ones in Port Gardner all of which fell to a hair in the Plotting showing the accuracy with which the plotting has been brought on.

We were employed surveying in this vicinity until the 27th when we got underway, nothing of importance transpired. we found many unimportant connections & additions to make in the charts of Vancouver.

June 22nd

At 4 AM left in company with Maury to examine what appeared to be the entrance of a River[28] on the East shore. We took with us two days provisions to survey a larger sheet of water which Maury had seen a day or so before from the top of one of the Islands. Found a communication into Bellingham Bay formed in the same manner as that between Ports Gardner & Susan by a river, emptying with a mouth in each Bay.

There is a vast deal of fine land for cultivation hereabouts & on the Banks of the river we found a number of Indians living in permanent residences with a stockade close by for retreat in case of attack. They had abundance of Salmon but showed no anxcity to trade for them.

We found the work much too extensive for us to do anything with it in two boats so after putting up a few signals, we retraced our steps and arrived onboard by 7PM.

June 23rd & 24th

Employed surveying in the vicinity of the Brig. Morning of the 24th Maury left with three boats to pass thro the mouth of the River into Bellingham Bay where he was to survey until we could reach them thru Deception Passage.

June 25th

At 9 this morning got underway & beat thru the Whidbey Island passage and at 11 anchored within the point on which we encamped when surveying here & close to the entrance of the passage. All ready for a start on the slack tide.

---

[28]Swinomish Channel which actually leads into Padilla Bay, not Bellingham Bay.

June 26th

Got underway about 8 AM & with a light wind from the SSE & on the last of the flood tide, passed thro Deception Passage without the least difficulty. By half past nine we were snug at anchor under Deception Island with broad Pacific once more open to us.

Altho Vancouver says that this passage cannot be used & we have used it, yet he is not so far out in his suppositions as would at first appear, but few vessels would venture thro for it is really frightful to look at the passage, when the Tide is at its strength, yet as I have before said, at a proper time of Tide, there is no real danger.

The country around is desolate & dreary in the extreme being composed bleak & rugged rocks with scant growth of tall Pine Trees, which seem to take root in the very rock itself, for the soil is only a few inches deep & I could not plant a signal Pole without proping and securing its heel with stones.

Sunday June 27th

Sent the boats out surveying, the sabbath to the contrary notwithstanding. Landed on one of the numerous Rocks with which the Gulf is pretty well supplied the whole face of the Rock was covered with Birds eggs & young Birds & the old Birds [hovering] overhead. Kept up such an incipient screaming as almost to deafen one. I remained on this rock for three hours waiting for the Brig to fire for Base during which time the men amused themselves collecting Eggs or feeding the young Birds with pieces of fish of which there were many laying about. The manner in which [ ] the difference between the first Eggs & those that had been set on showed a good deal of [ ] as the [ ] would sag. Every nest that contained three Eggs was left untouched whereas those that had only two in them were robed, [ ] Philosophically concluding that the Birds [ ] set until they had [ ] laying. We got about twelve dozen fine fresh eggs as large as those of the [ ] or turkey & in flavour like the latter. Whilst on the rock I shot two Birds different from any I have ever seen; They are a species of the auk but different from any that our Books described. They were of course skinned & stuffed. The Top of the rock had soil on it about six inches in depth which was riddled with burrows which must have been done by the Birds as I could find no animals altho I dug down to the solid rock.

In the evening the Brig got underway & anchored in a beautiful Bay which in commemoration of the day & of the manner in which the day was spent we called Sunday Bay. In many places in this vicinity the woods have been on fire, the undergrowth entirely destroyed having the tall & stately Pines, like so many guardians in Battle away.

Monday 28th

Maury carried the survey ahead of our present anchorage. We got underway & shortly after anchored in Strawberry Bay, so named by Vancouver. Many other places or ever the whole coast equally well deserve the name for the Berry is every where abundant.

The western shore of the gulf is formed by a Labyrinth of Islands thro which there are many fine passages to survey which properly with the straits de arro & Vancouver Island would employ the whole force of our squadron six months.

Landed to day on a rock from which Lt North only yesterday, took all the Eggs & found that the Birds had already deposited nearly eight dozzen of course [ ] fresh which afforded myself & boats crew with an excellent repast.

We remained at anchor in this Bay surveying in the vicinity & connecting with Lt Maury's work in Bellingham Bay until July 1st when we got underway & L^t M & his party having completed their work & rejoined the Brig and at 11 AM anchored in Birch Bay. Left three boats at different points to bring the work up & by sunset they had worked up to the South Point of the harbour & rejoined the Brig. A small stream, not noticed by Vancouver, comes in between Birch & Bellingham Bays & as is usual, forms an extensive mud flat making off from the East shore to the W^d of which there is a good channel into Bellingham Bay.[29]

An extensive mud flat makes off from the back of Birch Bay about half a mile. There is excellent anchorage in the Bay where wood & water is easily obtained Ash, Birch & Spruce predominate & beautiful spars may be procured here.

The Squamish Indians inhabit the shores of this Bay. They brought us off an abundance of elk & venison with some of the finest Salmon we have yet seen on the coast. Game must be very abundant & I think the natives live more by hunting than fishing. They are a much more muscular & athletic race of men than those to the S^d which I think is owing to their not setting in their canoes so much which causes them to bend the joints of the leg when standing. They, like all the tribes to the S^d of Frasers River, stand in great dread of the Ncultas, a very warlike tribe who inhabit the territory to the N^d of that river & live almost entirely by war & hunting. I saw a few of them among the Islands of the Canal & they are really an elegant looking

---

[29] According to his chart, Vancouver believed that Portage Island was connected to the Lummi Peninsula (the mainland). In fact, a sand spit actually does connect the two at low tide. Thus, Vancouver's chart is not seriously in error! Sinclair referenced Portage Channel (local name) which links Hale Passage to Portage Bay, then into Bellingham Bay. Because of shoaling, rocks and other sand bars, Sinclair stretches the truth by calling it a "good channel."

set of men, much more dignified & independent in their bearing than the Southern Indians but from all accounts it is requisite to look to your arms when they are in your vicinity for like the [ ] they are at war with all the world.

July 1st
  We remained at anchor in this Bay surveying in its vicinity until the 5th of July when we got underway & stood to the N^d for Frasers River leaving our Boats to examine the large space between Birch Bay & P^t Roberts and another on P^t Roberts. At 3 PM the Brig anchored off the mouth of the river & measured a Base with P^t Roberts.

  From Point Roberts to Desolation Inlet to the N^d an immense flat composed of sand and mud makes off to the distance of several miles thro this flat, (which is Bare in many places at low water). Frasers river swims its way into the gulf, discolouring the water nearly halfway over to Vancouver Island.

  How it was possible for Vancouver to overlook this river is more than I can imagine, the whole face of the country to the E^d indicates the passage of a river & the quantity of fresh water discharged into the Gulf & the immense Bank off its mouth shows that the river must be both an extensive & a rapid stream.

  We only surveyed the channel of this river thro the sand flat, to its [ ] open mouth. The channel is crooked but can be easily staked off and a vessel may carry three fathoms up outside the mouth at low water and I was informed by Captain Scarborough that the same depth might be carried up to Fort Langley, one of the Companys Forts, which is thirty miles from its mouth. The current is so rapid, that we could barely stem it with our fast pulling whale boats. We did not put up a Tide staff but the banks which are perpendicular indicates a rise of six or eight feet. Altho there is regular rise & fall of the tide yet the current never ceases to run out altho it stacks upon the flood tide. This river discharges as much water into the ocean as the Columbia and Doctor McLaughlin the chief Trader of the Company on the coast goes so far to say that it discharges more.

  We sent up to the fort today to try & get some vegetables [ ] for the crew but could not get any, the last years crop having been all used & that of present year being yet in the ground & not sufficiently matured.

  The Indians who inhabit the Bank of this river are called Quoitlandts; we received a visit from a number of them in a very large canoe. They all called themselves chiefs & were gaily bedecked in old coats, hats, vests & feathers a sure sign of the white man being in the vicinity. Altho once a powerful tribe they are now reduced in numbers & are under the [sway] of the Company.

On the Banks of this river I had an opportunity of seeing the natives constructing one of their canoes which are decidedly the most beautiful vessels of the kind we have seen during our cruise. They select an old log of spruce that has been seasoned on the bank of the river, hue it out roughly on the outside & burn the inside. They use the hatchet or chisel with considerable dexterity. They cut it out without sheer and after they have reduced it to two inches in thickness they put a stretch in at midships & by degrees increase the beam of the boat to nearly twice the diameter of the original log. This process gives the boat a beautiful sheer which they improve with the chisels.[30] They leave the boat there a month or so (exposed to the rise & fall of the tide being alternately afloat & ashore) before they finish them off.

The Banks of this river are overflowed in the spring but when not covered with water afford fine fields for grasing cattle & quantities of grass is cut to lay by for the winter. There are great quantities of rasberrys of a delicious flavour [growing] the river Banks. From the number & size of the trees [ ] up on the Bank, the current during Freshit months, I should think must be impossible.

July 7th
We have received letter from the *Vincennes* at Nasqually, no news as yet from the *Peacock* and schooner. Continued our surveying in this vicinity. [Found] that at the Paralax of 49° North passes thro P^t Roberts—so that Frasers River is not within the limit of our Territorial claim.

The space contained between Birch Bay and Point Roberts is nearly entirely filled up with sand & mud & into the head of this Bay a small stream emptys itself & may be considered a mouth of the River as it communicates with that stream, it is however only navigable for canoes. A Rocky shoal extends off from Point Roberts Bluff more than half a mile & needs to be looked after.

July 9th
At 9 AM we got underway with a light SE wind which died away and left us in the mid channel where we anchored in 50 fms water [vering] 90 fms chain. At 11 PM got underway again and [left blank].

July 10th
Cloudy with rain.
At 2 AM anchored again near P^t Roberts. A number of Indians visited

---

[30]Sheer is a nautical term which describes the amount of outward bulging of a boat's sides. Thus, a typical rectangular barge would have no sheer.

us here & we got a supply of fish & venison. Natives [ ] honest in their dealings than hitherto. Sent the *Rover* in charge of Mr Sanford to the *Vincennes* with letters for Capt Wilkes. At 7 PM we got underway with a light breeze from the S & SW^d and at 8.30 PM came to on the Eastern side of P^t Roberts in 5 fms water.

Sunday July 11th

In the forenoon fresh breezes from the S^d & E^d & cloudy. At 9.15 we got underway and beat round Point Roberts Bluff and at 10.20 came to in 8½ fms water [vered] 45 fms chain. The weather looking cloudy & unsettled we got underway again at 1 PM & ran over to Birch Bay for a safer anchorage when we came to at 3.45 PM in 7 fms water. Ends cloudy with rain.

July 12th

Left the Brig in the *Shark* accompanied by the *Greyhound*, to survey the space between Birch Bay & P^t Roberts. At 9.15 the Brig got underway & stood over toward P^t Roberts. At 11 she anchored off useless Bay & fired 8 or 9 guns then got underway again & anchored under P^t Roberts.

Employed all day in the *Shark* examining a Bay which may well be called useless Bay. A few Suquamish Indians reside in this Bay inside of a stockade. The chief was a very quiet civil, good looking Indian and had the only clean & pretty daughter I have seen since I have been on the Coast. about 15 years of age & realy very pretty. did not get back to the Brig until 9 at night.

July 13th

Light variable airs and calms. Kept the boats employed surveying and sent the carpenters ashore & cut some light spars. Boats did not get onboard until the first watch. Our old friend Nadlum brought us letters from Nasqually.

Wednesday 14th

Still at anchor under P^t Roberts. Employed making observations onshore and four boats out surveying. First part of the day fresh SE Breezes and squally. Ends with light airs & calms & pleasant wr. When the Brig first passed P^t Roberts on the 5th was left in the *Greyhound* & the fire with which we cooked dinner caught the grass and the logs on the Beach, of which there are vast numbers, and the whole atmosphere was filled with smoke altho we have had much rain since the fire is still burning and has had the good effect, at least of burning off the Musquitoes, with which the Point swarmed, to such an extent that it was with difficulty I could observe.

Thursday July 15th
Light variable winds. At daylight this morning we got underway & with variable baffling winds stood over towards the opposite shore. In the after noon the brig was caught with a powerful current which swept her swiftly to the S^d. Endeavoured to get under one of the Islands for anchorage when we were caught by an Eddy & at 4 PM anchored close inshore of a small Island which we called Panther Island. The shore of this Island is literally strewed with Trees & Logs thrown up by the current.

July 16th
Winds light & variable. Left this morning in the *Greyhound* in company with three other boats on surveying duty in the canal de arro & the adjacent Islands. These Islands & all these that form the Eastern shore of the Canal are high & rocky, the soil being nearly all washed off by he heavy rains during the rainy season. The currents run thru the various channels that run among these Islands with an [ ] force forming numerous overfalls among which it is dangerous for a boat to outrun. In several cases I have been running along with a fine breeze when my boat has been caught by a current & whirled round nearly capsizing by catching the sail aback. There is good anchorage under all the Islands & the whole coast is lined with excellent harbours, as is the case all along the coast. Shell fish may be taken in the greatest abundance and in nearly every case when we landed for dinner whilst the fire was being made a sufficient quantity of very fine clams was taken to make a mess for all hands.

July 17th
Wind light and variable. I went to day to examine the eastern shore of Vancouver Island to the N^d of our anchorage. A shoal skirts the shore all along with deep water between it & the beach & several entrances in, many rocks lay off the coast, but there is good anchorage all along. My own [ ] is that part of the coast laid down as Vancouver Island consists of many Islands thru which there are deep passages & I should not be at all surprized if a passage to the Pacific existed thru Vancouver Island. I found several passages into the Island but the current was rushing out so strong that I could not enter most of these but at the slack tide. I entered one of them & passed several miles along & went out at another. I passed by many channels running in various directions all broad & deep. The Indians made signs pointing up some of the passages from which I concluded that there were communications with the waters of the Pacific. The shores of these channels are rocky and steep & the whole country bleak & dreary. The stillness of death reigned round the launch was heard [ ] & even the voice in ordinary time of conversation sounded loud and harsh and I really felt

my spirits depressed by the awful stillness of the place. We all regretted that we had not time to survey there. [ ] in great abundance frequently jumping down on us from the overhanging cliffs. The small Island under which the Brig was anchored was about a mile in length with a rich meadow running thro its center & even on this spot there were [ ] but we had not time for sport.

July 18th

Fair pleasant weather. The Brig got underway & stood over towards the continental shore & at 2 PM she anchored off the Northern entrance of Bellingham Bay. I was absent during the day examining the north side of the largest & most [ ] of the Islands that form the eastern side of the canal de arro. The shores of this Island are generaly steep & one or two timbered down from a height of nearly a hundred feet. The water was clear & as cold as I am. There is a sand shoal and a rock between this Island & a small group to the N^d of us. There is good anchorage all along the north shore of this Island which may be passed any where within a cable of the beach.

July 19th Monday

The Brig got underway & anchored again at 9 near our old Birth in Strawberry Bay. on the way we passed thru a tide rip which had the appearance of Breakers & we would have avoided if we had not surveyed over this ground. Commenced to fill with water. Kept the *Greyhound* surveying & gave the men a chance to wash their clothes onshore.

As we retraced our steps to the S^d we find our signals all standing & in some cases when they have fallen & been washed away by the tides they have been picked up by the natives & stuck up along the shore and in one case when one of our ships numbers was missed & we thought it had been stolen, it was given to one of our boats several days afterwards by an old Indian who made signs that he had picked it up in the water, and another lost by us, was in like manner delivered up to the boats of the *Vincennes*. These acts speak strongly in favor of these People rude & uncivilized as they are, whither they are operated on by motives of fear or not is more than I can say, at all events I am willing to [ ] and think not. In many cases we sent to our absent parties by the natives provisions & articles of trade which were invaluable to them, yet never, in one single instance, did they appropriate anything to themselves, but delivered their charge safely into the hands of those to whom it was sent.

Many of our old acquaintances assisted visited us here & brought venison for sale.

Tuesday 20th
Slight SE winds & calms. Three Boats went off today to survey among the Islands to the W^d of us forming one side of the Canal de arro. Passed Midn Sanford found us today in the Launch of the *Vincennes* bringing with him a quantity of Provisions for the Brig & orders from Capt Wilkes. Cut a few rough spars onshore, got off a quantity of firewood.

Wednesday July 21st
[ ] wind & weather light from the S^{d}E^d— got underway at 12½ and about three anchored in 10½ fms under the Lee of Blunts Island,[31] so named by us. three boats were out surveying the Island which different from all the rest on this coast has danger extending several miles off from it. We made a good survey of it.

Toward the latter part of the day the wind freshened & the wr looked squally. [ ] 75 fms of chain.

During the night the Aurora Borealis appeared to the N^d.

July 22nd
Fine pleasant day, wind light and variable. At 7 this morning we got underway & commenced beating up for P^t Dungeness. Shortly after we made a sail in the narrows which turned out to be the Company Schooner *Cadborrow*. About half past nine made another sail in the same quarters which we took for the *Vins* & shortly after ascertained the fact by an exchange of signals.

About 1 we came to in obedience to a signal, under near Dunganess P^t in 12½ fms water, good ground. The launch and *Greyhound* with their crews were transferred to the *Vincennes*. Lt Johnson & Mr Waldron rejoined the Brig. the first named officer [ ] and P^d Midn Sanford and Midn Elliott transferred to the *Vincennes*. At 2 we got underway again and stood toward Protection Island off the entrance of Port Discovery for the purpose of surveying a shoal that makes off from the Island. [S & W] P^{ts} of that Isd are which the *Vincennes* passed this morning. At 6 PM we came to on the west side of the Isd in 7½ fms water & measured Base with the *Vincennes* & Pt Partridge. As we were laying this morning in a calm, the yards braced for the Larb^d quarters a fine breeze took us nearly ahead a little on the Larb^d bow. I directed the head yards to be braced up & the [ ] main braces manned to catch her as she fell off. The captain differed with me as to the [ ] of this evolution, he thought I ought to have braced the after yards up first. In my opinion if I had done so, I should have had to Box the head [ ] pay her off. Great men will differ.

---

[31] Smith Island.

July 23rd 1842

Very pleasant weather. Employed this morning in sounding out the shoal of Protection Isd and in the afternoon we got underway for Dungeness but the winds failing we had to drop a kedge At 5½ got a breeze with which we beat up for the *Vins* At 6½ we came to again near the *Vincennes* in 13 fms water.

Saturday July 24th

Wind light during the day from the N^d & W^d & S^d & W^d. All the boats of both vessels employed surveying about P^t Dungeness & connecting in with Port Discovery. Vancouver in his work on this coast states, that there is the appearance of a deep Bay back of P^t Dungeness that it is filled up by a white sand beach. Such would realy be the fact if one were to judge from appearances at even a short distance from the back of the Bay, but the white sand beach of which he speaks is only a long narrow strip of white sand which started nearly across a very deep Bay and which being overlaped by another sand pt from the opposite shore looks at a very short distance like one uniform sand beach.[32] The entrance to this basin of water is narrow but there is plenty of water for vessels of a large size and from the direction in which the basin trends I should think it must nearly communicate with Port Discovery. on the right hand of the entrance there is a stockade & some huts where about 20 or 30 natives are huddled together like pigs only a little more filthy. On the low sandy neck forming the Larb^d entrance there are nine of these Poles of which I have formerly spoken, standing in a straight row. The Indians made me understand in answer to my enquiries by signs that they were intended for catching wild fowl, the same as to the Northward. They also signified that a fresh water stream came into the head of the basin which was surveyed by Lt Budd from the *Vincennes*.

July 25th

Fresh Breezes from the W^d & N^{d}W^d & pleasant weather. At 3 PM we got underway in obedience to a signal from the *Vin^s* and after a beautiful run we anchored at 5½ in Port Townsend in 16 fms water.

---

[32] According to Vancouver's journal, while exploring between the Dungeness Spit and Discovery Bay: "The first opening to the SE appeared to be formed by two high bluffs; the elevated land within them seemingly at a considerable distance. It proved, however, to be a close and compact shore, the apparent vacant space being occupied by a very low sandy beach, off which extended a flat of very shallow soundings" (Blumenthal *The Early Exploration* 121). Vancouver's reference is to Sequim Bay, the entrance of which he did not discover. Sinclair's observations are very accurate—the entrance is impossible to see.

July 26th

Winds from the N^d & W^d & W^d with pleasant wr. We are furnished with Capt Wilkes chart of this harbour & have orders to complete the soundings. Three Boats have been absent all day for this purpose. Capt Wilkes had not finished the survey. A canoe passed us with letters from Nasqually for the *Vincennes*.

July 27th

Raining, the night wind from the S^d & W^d & the day from the N^d & N^d/W^d, a beautiful day. We could not make anything out of the chart furnished us, so we amused ourselves surveying the Harbour this morning and in four or five hours we had completed the work & made a beautiful chart, not very different in shape from Vancouvers. Sent a hand onshore to burn some Iron out of a piece of wood and much to our regret the fire spread and altho we sent a party onshore to put it out, they did not succeed in doing so until several canoes containing dead bodies were burned, this point having been used by the natives as a place of internment.

The canoe that passed us yesterday carried to the *Vincennes* intelligence of the loss of the *Peacock*. We did not get the news until today. She went onshore in the North breakers of the Columbia on the 18th of this month and at the date of the letters received from the River, all hands had got onshore safe not having saved an article except the charts & Instruments & what clothes they stood in. The ship a total loss but little hope entertained that anything from her would be saved. The *Flying Fish* got in safe.

Melancholy as would have been this intelligence to us, under any other circumstances, yet it is indeed glad tidings now. We had all, even the most sanguine among us, given up all hope of ever seeing either vessel again and but a faint glimmer of hope existed of our even seeing those who were in them. This loss we looked upon as a matter of course, how joyful that to us, even the tidings that they were all landed safe and in good health.

We attributed this long delay to shipwreck among the coral Islands they had been sent to survey where, if they had got onshore, they would either have been murdered by the natives or suffered a more lingering death by famine. We are not yet able to assess any reasonable cause for their delay but at all events this accident must change the present plans of the commander of the expedition. At 4.30 we got underway & commenced working out of the harbour and at 7 the wind failing we came to under P^t Hudson in 7 fms water.

July 28th

In the [ ] part of the day & to 4 PM breezes light from the N^d & W^d & wr generally foggy. the breeze then freshened from the W^d and blew a [ ] gale. At half past 7 we got underway and at 11 anchored under P^t Wilson in 15 fms water. This is the anchorage used by the Companys vessels, it is just outside of Port Townsend. Our old Friend Nadlum the Seatjack chief visited us here and was treated with a great deal of off-hand [ ]. The old man had been of vast service to us & had taken the trouble to haul his canoe over the Portage at the back of Penns Cove to visit us & was without ceremony or cause turned out of the vessel & not allowed to visit her again. True he could no longer be used.

I was ordered today to take the *Shark* & proceed to Point Partridge on Whidbey Island & get the Brigs guns from Point Wilson & observe a round of angles. Shortly after leaving P^t Wilson the fog came over so thick that I could not see the land on either side, as I could not steer a compass course under the oars, my only alternative was to make sail altho I could not quite head my course. When the fog lifted, I found myself under the influence of a current, so strong that I could not stem it. I therefore under the sail & oars, stuck her in for the eddy that I know must run close to the Whidby shore. I had but just reached this eddy & was within a mile of my station when I was recalled by the Brig. I had again to contend with this tide & reached the Brig in about two hours when another officer & crew were put into the boat & she was dispatched on the service from which I had been recalled. It is realy enough to make a man go mad with rage, to have his feelings thus publicly outraged without any cause being assigned, and I have since heard this very subject commented on by the crew and thank God I have since had an opportunity of expressing to the author of the outrage under circumstances in which he did not occupy a very enviable position, my thoughts and feelings on the subject.

July 29th

Blowing a smart gale from the W^d. P^{d}midn Sanford found us in the *Rover* & brought us orders to join the *Vins* at new Dunganess. We cannot move today as this wind is blowing entirely too fresh.

We are all delighted at the news as in all probability our cruise to the N^d thro Johnstone Straits will be knocked in the head.

Friday July 30th

Still blowing fresh from the W^d but the wr more pleasant. At 5 in the morning we got underway for Dunganess, in the first stretch we made off to the N^d the Brig plunged so heavily as to carry away her head & determine the Captain to put back. But when we closed in with the South Shore between Dunganess & Port Discovery we got into smoother water & continued to beat along close inshore [where at one] PM when we anchored close to the *Vincennes*. Mr Waldron [ ] was immediately started off in a canoe to Nasqually to carry dispatches across the land & Captain Hudson.[33] We all wrote to our friends congratulations on not having been drowned by the Kingsmile Islanders and condoling with them at the same time in their present misfortunes.

Saturday 31st July

This day wind moderate from the NW. At 1 PM we got underway in company with the *Vins* & commenced beating out the straits.

Sunday August 1st

Light winds from the N^d & W^d & fine weather. We measured Base with the *Vins* twice to day & both vessels observed angles, in no case perhaps on the same objects. What results will be obtained from these observations I cannot imagine, as there is no connection at least between the two positions occupied by the Brig. the [ ] was over for a short time — [ ] the tides —

We were close in with the shore of Quadra[34] Island today. The country is well wooded, rises gradually from the beach & is beautifully diversified with hill & valley & altogether presented a much more pleasing appearance than does any part of the Main land I have seen, there must be some firm land in the valleys & from the broken appearance of the hills near the coast & I think it very likely that six on a close survey some good harbours will be found. From the appearance of the shore I should not think the sea breaks so heavily as on the North shore. The summits of the peaks are covered with snow.

Monday August 2nd

Light airs and calms to day. From 12½ to 2½ the moon was totally eclipsed. In the morning watch this morning we went off the mouth of the Straits becalmed with a heavy swell and a strong current [ ] us out & towards some half drowned rocks off the SW Pts of the Straits and upon which the sea broke with tremendous violence. In the forenoon we communicated with the *Vincennes* and then stood over for the Port of St Juan on the NW [ ] pt of Quadra as Vancouver Island, whilst the *Vincennes* went into Classet or Scarborrow near the SW pt of the Straits. A number of canoes with a firm stout looking race of men belonging to the Classet Tribe

---

[33]Captain Hudson commanded the *Peacock*.
[34]Vancouver Island.

came off to us, whilst we were becalmed, inviting us by signs to go in and anchor where they promised to bring us skins & salmon in abundance.

At half past one we came to in 12 fms water off the mouth of Port St Juan and by half past 5 we had made a thorough survey of the harbour & were underway again standing over to rejoin the *Vincennes* at Classet. The Port of St Juan is about 2½ miles deep, the soundings decreasing gradually to the back of it. It is not a safe anchorage being entirely exposed to southerly winds, the rocks near the entrance are much worn by the beating of the sea. We saw no natives nor signs of them

At 9½ PM we anchored near the *Vincennes* in Scarborrow harbour in 16 fms water. This anchorage for [ ] is no Harbour has similar objections with St Juan being exposed to the S^d & S^d & E^d

I was suspended from duty today by Lt Commdr Ringgold for refusing obedience to a possibly illegal order. If the subject should ever be brought before any Tribunal of Justice & I shall use my endeavours to have it so, I am prepared with documents & evidence that will shift the suspension from my shoulders to his.

Tuesday August 3rd

Light and westerly winds and calms. Calm at night. We got some water off this morning.

We were surrounded today by several hundreds of natives. At one time there were over seventy canoes at a time with from ten to ten [sic] natives in each. They are vastly a superior race to any we have hitherto seen on the coast. we get from them as many salmon as we wanted for a mere trifle. They had a number of skins for sale and among them a sea otter, the first we have seen on the coast. Their canoes were well made, beautiful boats, each of the large boats was furnished with a buoy, beautifully made out of the seal skin. They are blown full of wind & are used when they catch the otter. It is attached to the upper end of the Harpoon line and prevents the animal sinking when stuck. The Buoy is made with the skin turned inside out & is fantastically painted.

At 2 PM we got underway in company with the *Vincennes* and stretched off into the broad Pacific once more. At night a heavy fog came over and we lost sight of the *Vincennes* but we were within hearing range of each others guns. No bottom with 65 fms Line.

8

The Journal of Joseph Perry Sanford

The pages are watermarked and the handwriting is difficult to read in many cases. Where the text is illegible, I inserted a bracket [ ] or in some cases, words within the bracket, as my best guess based upon the context of the sentence. There are no page numbers. Sanford was aboard *Vincennes* until the ships reached Nisqually, where he was transferred to the *Porpoise* for surveying purposes.

30th [April 1841]

A tribe of Indians inhabit this part of the coast. Wind light during the early part of the day. At Mer[1] a mod breeze with passing clouds.

At Mer, we were distant from Cape "Flattery" about 50 miles. "Destruction" Island was clear, leaving to the East^d & distant about 20 miles. "Flattery" Rocks were discernable to the N^o and E^d. We passed within a half a mile of them. There are five rocks, with a scanty soil and three rocks that are known under this denomination. The coast about here is lined with rocks but none of them are below the surface of the sea.

The Country about here is moderately elevated, but rises [ ] near the sea shore and very thickly clothed with the Cypress and a species of Pine I believe, peculiar to this Region.

At 6. 30 we passed between "Duncan's" rock and a small rocky Islet, lying immediately off Cape "Flattery": This rock can at times only be seen: but it can always be recognised by the continual break of the sea over it. On the Islet were living a few Indians: some of them came alongside; but were not permitted to come on board. Their complexion was evidently

---

[1]The meridian, i.e., noon.

much lighter than with the Polynesians, in so much, that at first, some were taken for white-men. All appeared to be suffering from opthalmia: which is caused in a great degree from smoke in which they may be said to live when not out searching for food. Their only clothing consisted of blankets; one or two had Bear skins thrown over their shoulders.

Their canoes appeared to be swift and were of a singular model: bow being very sharp and terminating in a projecting point which is notched: The stern is sharp and perpendicular. They are made of one tree and were very rickety. Paddles are short and narrow, ending in a sharp point.

During the nights, we had much rain with a fresh breeze and were employed tacking frequently, (immediately in the mouth of the straits). At daylight it cleared and we found ourselves in the [left blank]

1st May

Just within the Entrance of the Straits of "Juan de Fuca" and in view of "Neah" Harbour situated on the main coast.

The country on either side of the Straits is of a moderate elevation and woody. The shores and faults, or low cliffs, were rocky & apparently have deep water at their bases. The country as we proceeded up the straits assumed a different character: many high and naked hills covered mostly with snow [ ] formed the principle feature.

Several Canoes with the natives came alongside today from whom we obtained some fine salmon. Their continual cry was for Mânêsh tobacco—which was given to them in exchange. These people were more clad than those of yesterday. They called themselves "Clallams."

May 2nd

During the early part of the day no wind, and a strong ebb tide setting us back: By 8 A.M. we were drifted about 8 miles towards the entrance of the Straits:

Several Canoes came alongside with Salmon. The usual cry of "Mânêsh" was to be heard from young and old with an occasional varying of note and word to "Pâttâch"—give. All of them were filthy and ill clad, one or two were entirely naked, their hair hung in elf locks and strewed with vermin.

At 1 a Breeze springing up from the East^d. We were enabled to pass round "Dungess" Point and by 8 PM we were anchored in Port "Discovery." Point "Dungeness" is low and projects out from a clay bank about a mile and a half and is composed entirely of land and thickly strewed with drift timber. To the East^d of it is good anchorage which is entirely sheltered from the prevailing heavy winds. About 8 miles beyond is Port "Discovery" so named by Vancouver after his vessel, the "*Discovery.*" The best anchorage in this bay is beyond the first point on the right hand side, after entering.² Without this the depth varies from 25 to 30 fthms: and consequently is too deep for safety in the event of a heavy gale; although there can be no sea in harbour. The Entrance is of a moderate width and protected "sea-ward" by "Protection" Isl^d which stretches nearly E & West about a mile distant from it.

May 3rd

Boats employed surveying the Bay. Vancouver's survey of this bay is accurate.

May 4th

day pleasant with occasional showers.

The Country about this bay is densely clothed with trees and underbrush. The trees are mostly of the Pine and Cypress species. I measured one which was 34 feet in circumference: and this I should think couldn't be compared in point of size to many others which I got a glance of, growing on the tops of the hills about.

The Indians alongside brought "molek" & ["mouitch"] to sell. There is little or no game immediately about the shores, but the Indians say there is plenty but a short distance back. Some fine Salmon were purchased to-day. This fish here is considered inferior to the Columbia Salmon.

I was forced to take refuge from an approaching shower in an Indian hut to day. And were it not for the name of the thing, I might as well have been out doors for I was soon completely saturated with smoky water from the roof. Within a space of about 6 feet square lived a "Clallam" chief, his three wives, 4 or 4 [sic] "young" [men] and several old men and women. They all appeared perfectly happy and contented, altho: their appearance and in fact their [ ] anything but that which ought to render man contented with his lot. It proves what habit will do.

May 5th

Left the ship to obtain angles and fix position on the SE end of "Protection" Island.

This Isl^d is elevated some 70 or 80 feet above the water³ and surrounded with a beautiful green [ ] with a patch of low trees on its NE corner.

Returning to the ship saw a sea otter. It appeared to be of a greyish color and about the size of a common seal. I could not get near enough to shoot it.

---

²Contractors Point, the same as Vancouver's anchorage.

³The peak is actually 210 feet according to modern charts.

May 6th 1841

At 10. got under way with a light breeze and commenced beating out. At 12. passed through the NE passage of "Protection" Isl^d and steered to the East^d for "Admiralty" Inlet, which was distant about 5 miles. Point "Partridge" is very conspicuous from its height and steepness, and is the dividing point between Admiralty Inlet, to the East, and Straits of Juan de Fuca. About 1. passed through a strong tide rip. Rounded Point "Hudson" (so named by Vancouver)[4] and passed into Port "Townshend." This bay opens to the West^d and has its protection in that quarter by "Whidby's" Isl^d which is here the opposite shore the "Inlet." It is broader than Port Discovery, but more shallow, and affording better anchorage. Point "Hudson," which is the northern point of the Bay, is low and stretches out from a very pretty green [ ], quite elevated.

Our anchor was hardly down before several of our Indian friends of yesterday, came alongside with Salmon &c to barter.

May 7th

All the boats were dispatched early this morning to survey the harb^r which being completed by noon, we got under way and stood to the south^d up the Inlet but did not get more than six miles, when we anchored in a bight,[5] looking into Port Townshend by the small openings. "Hoods Canal" bearing a little to the East^d of South and "Possession" Sound on opposite shore visible and bearing about SE.[6]

The country on either side of us as we passed up was moderately elevated, rocky and covered with forests and brush.

May 8th

Fresh breeze from the South^d. Boats were sent out surveying before breakfast. Ten did not return until past noon.

Got under way at 1½ PM and commenced beating up Inlet. The ebb tide making after low having weathere^d [6 or 8] miles we anchored[7] near the Western shore leaving "Possession" Sound open.

The shore abreast of the ship, was very steep leaving no passage along the head at high tide.

Two natives who had been dispatched from Port Discovery to Fort

---

[4] I believe Sanford was referencing Point Wilson. Wilkes named Point Hudson.

[5] Oak Bay.

[6] Possession Sound, on the east side of Whidbey Island, is not visible from Oak Bay. Sanford was merely observing the continuation of Admiralty Inlet between Whidbey and the peninsula.

[7] Pilot's Cove.

Nassqually, one of the "Hudson's Bay" Company's posts, with letters to its commandant, returned and brought two white men as Pilots. *News* that *Peacock* and *F. Fish* both in the River.[8] Fort dist: 50 miles.

May 9th
Got under way at daylight but came to[9] at breakfast time. Got under way again about 1 PM and beat up about 11 miles and came to anchor near sunset off the low and broad sand Point forming the southern Cape of "Lawrences" Bay.[10] The entrance to a deep bay[11] on opposite shore (eastern) open. Mount "Rainier" which was distant some 60 or 70 miles, made a [fine] appearance toward sunset. Its upper part peering above the clouds and entirely covered with snow.

May 10th
Calm this morning. Got under way in the afternoon, wind fair but rather light and came to the anchor just after sunset near the narrow part of the Sound ("Puget").[12] The entrance to "Commencement" Bay open to us and shut in the back ground by Mount "Rainier."
Admiralty Inlet has its termination in what we have named "Commencement" Bay. And "Puget" Sound is the channel to the west^d of "Vashan's" Isl^d and its continuation to the south^d until it branches off into numerous small bays, sounds, inlets and canals.

May 11th
Light wind and strong tide [adverse]. got under way about 4 PM and wind and tide favoring us, reached "Nassqually" a little after sunset at 8 PM.

---

[8]The reference, although incorrect, is to the Columbia River. The *Peacock*, commanded by Captain Hudson, and the *Flying Fish* arrived off the Columbia bar in mid-July. While the *Flying Fish* waited, *Peacock* made several attempts to cross, without success. Then, from the "yards," the officers believed they sighted a passage where the breakers and surf were more calm. Heading in, *Peacock* grounded. With surf breaking around her, the ship soon began to break up. By morning, hope for saving the ship diminished; the pumps could no longer keep up with the incoming water. Hudson began sending the men ashore, starting with the scientists and public documents. The remaining crew was picked up later in the afternoon. By the next morning, *Peacock* was gone.

[9]Appletree Cove.

[10]Sanford is incorrect with the name in this and in several other references. Wilkes placed Port Lawrence at Oak Bay. Sanford's reference to Lawrences Bay or Port Lawrence is really Port Madison.

[11]Elliott Bay.

[12]The Narrows.

May 12th

Went on shore and had a fatiguing walk up to the top of plain on which the fort is situated. This plain is spacious, elevated about 300 feet above the water, and extends back until it reaches the foot of the mountains in the East. The country is chiefly open and devoid of shrubs—but scattered trees, apparently in cultivation where there is most moisture, and here too but little underbrush. The soil is very hard and generally, and hardly if any vegetable [ ] is to be found.

The "Fort" is merely a square picket enclosure with log houses ranged round, leaving a hollow square.

May 13th

Rec^d orders to join the *Porpoise*.

14th

Getting ready to sail.

15th

At 1. got underway and stood down the Sound till near 5 when we anchored near our position of the 10th with "Commencement" Bay open. Our work commences above here. Pulled into a pretty little bay that is concealed from the Sound.[13] This passage into it is about 10 or 15 yards wide and it gradually widens until it forms a circular basin. Saw no natives today.

16th

Sunday. Found some Indians had encamped during the night on beach abreast of us. They appeared to have fewer comforts and conveniences that any we have yet met with. Went into the woods but saw no game.

17th

Got under way at 9. but at 11. came to again under the Eastern shore of "Commencement" Bay and boats were dispatched to survey. This is a fine sheet of water, a flat off from its head from ½ mile. Plenty of "Ro" surrounded by range of low hills covered with splendid trees. A snow covered range in the distance to the East^d of which Mount "Rainier" is the loftiest peak.

Saw a few grey squirrels in the woods to day. Rather smaller than our common squirrel. Strawberries quite small were gathered in abundance.

---

[13]Gig Harbor.

18th

Went up the head of Bay to examine and explore a river which I saw yesterday.¹⁴ Owing to the low state of the tide could not enter. Traced the outline of the flat that stretches across its mouth and in fact across the head of bay. At the northern side of this flat, found the water deepens enough to permit the boat passing over it and entered another small river which had not been observed before and [ ] about 3 miles of it in a direction towards Mount "Rainier" when I found it branching into numerous little [ ] which completely bisects the bottom land for some distance as could be seen beyond the point reached. The face of the country in either side of this "bottom" is very much broken by hills.

19th

Boats out surveying about the head of Admiralty Inlet and South side of "Vashan's" Island. At 1 the Brig got underway and ran round to the East point of Vashan's Isl^d and it's in a deep bight which we named "Portage" Inlet.¹⁵

We found Vancouver in error as to the formation and depth of a bay which penetrates the SSE part of the Isl^d.¹⁶ It is more commodious and affords more conveniences for vessels than he describes. Its head is separated from "Portage" Inlet by a very narrow isthmus of white sand which one of our Boats that had been surveying was dragged.

Many Deer were seen on this Isl^d likewise a large black bear.

May 20th

Boats were dispatched to survey and carry it as far as the part of the Inlet immediately opposite "Port Orchard."

At 2 the brig got underweigh and sailed round the North point of "Vashan's" Isl^d, crossed the mouth of Pugets Sound¹⁷ and stood for Port Orchard through the passage¹⁸ between the East shore of the "Main" and

---

¹⁴Puyallup River.

¹⁵Tramp Harbor on the eastern side of Vashon Island.

¹⁶Puget transited Colvos Passage on the western side. Quartermaster Harbor would not have been visible. Puget returned to the ships at Restoration Point in the dead of night. Vancouver, in his journey into Puget Sound, kept to the continental or eastern shore (i.e., the Tacoma side of the channel), and returned via Colvos Passage. Although he noted the indentation on the south end of Vashon (as evidenced by his chart) he did not explore that area at all nor describe it in his journal. To state that "We found Vancouver in error" suggests Sanford thought that Vancouver actually explored the harbor, which was not the case.

¹⁷According to Sanford, Puget Sound began at the north end of Vashon Island.

¹⁸Rich Passage.

West shore of "Bainbridge" Isl^d and anchored in the head Bay at entrance to Port Orchard in 8½ fathoms.[19]

The anchorage is excellent all about here. The Country slightly elevated and well covered with forests and underbrush. A few plains are scattered about at intervals. The first Sycamore trees I observed here. Some were very large. The tide runs with great force so much so that our fastest boats could not head against it.

21st

Boats out surveying. A narrow opening[20] just to the north^d of us which can not be seen until abreast of it expands into three broad bays or arms: running North and West forms what is called at the Port.

Whilst up the North arm,[21] saw several canoes elevated on separate scaffoldings which were the graves or coffins of Indians. This appears to be the usual mode of interning among the Indians of this part of the coast.

22nd

Out surveying about passage, accompanied by Dr Holmes. On returning towards the Brig in the evening we "resurectionized" from canoes of yesterday and carried off the [casket] of an unlucky Indian.[22] The poor fellow seemed to have gone to final home, but two or three months previous. The body was enveloped in several folds of blanket and [ ] large earrings over his ears and a tin pot its head. during the operation of decapitation, a large mouse came out from among the folds of the binding sheet.

23rd

Sunday. Many Indians alongside trading Salmon, Mullet, Cat-fish, and Flounder. They encamped for the night on a beautiful green area enclosed

---

[19] Sanford's use of the name "Bainbridge Island" is interesting. The honor of place names always fell to the leader of the expedition. From May 19 through June 23, Wilkes traveled overland from Nisqually to Astoria and thus was unavailable to name the island. Sinclair in his journal indicated "...we named Bainbridge Island," thus indicating that Wilkes was not responsible for all of the place names (the same was apparently true for Eagle and Blakely Harbors). However, the explorers did not know Bainbridge was actually an island until May 25, when they discovered Agate Pass to connect Ports Orchard and Madison. Sanford's use of Bainbridge Island on May 19 indicated that he apparently maintained rough notes during survey activities and crafted his journal at a later date. This hypothesis is supported by other examples where he used a name well in advance of discovery of the event leading to the name (e.g., Perry's or Fidalgo Island).

[20] Port Washington Narrows.

[21] Dyes Inlet.

[22] According to the Sinclair journal, "Our Doctor robed several of these of their heads...."

by woods. Among these Indians opthalmia appeared to prevail. I should attribute this in a great measure to their unclean skins which is truly disgusting.

24th

Maury, North and myself started at daylight to survey the "right arm."[23] Arrangements had been made for an absence of a week. By sunset we had carried the survey some 5 or 6 miles. Encamped for the night on a low sand point,[24] around which the "arm" takes an easterly direction; it having previously pursued a northerly one. Just in the seam of our tents [ ] which had not been in use for long time, as it was fast falling to decay.

Some Indians from a remote part of the bay arrived and annoyed us much by their incessant cry for "Mânâsh." They were ill clad and filthy. Several young women and girls were among them. One or two of them had quite regular and pretty features and good figures but they were as horribly disgusting in odor and filth as the rest.

25th

Made an early start and carried on the survey. Discovered another branch of this arm which runs to the N^d and W^d, a narrow passage leading into a fine and capacious bay, forms this NW arm.[25] The original "arm" after leaving the point in which we encamped last night, pursues an Easterly direction for some 2 or 3 miles until it contracts into a narrow strait[26] which connects it with "Lawrences" Bay,[27] the bay we surveyed in the 9th.

At sunset returned to last nights place of encampment where the tents were pitched for night.

May 26th

Made an early movement. Finished the survey of yesterday's discovery.

Saw a few more Indian coffins. Rain setting in early in the afternoon, we encamped at the SW side of "arm" near the junction of the two "arms."

---

[23] Along the western side of Bainbridge Island.

[24] Perhaps Battle Point.

[25] Liberty Bay.

[26] Agate Passage.

[27] Again, this and subsequent references to Lawrences Bay were incorrect. Sanford really meant Port Madison.

27th

Completed the survey. Landed to view an Indian Temple[28] if it may be so called in the right of strait, entrance from Lawrences bay. It measured 200 ft by 100 ft. The floor is of earth and sunken. It had [ranged] on either side 20 uprights and on which were rudely carved uncouth figures with head, eyes &c. Immense timbers [ ] on these.[29] It was a matter of great [ ] how these timbers were placed on these, as their weight & size must have called into acquisition more strength than a hundred Indians could have possible used to advantage without the employing of purchasses. A large wooden cross was erected in front of it.

Encamped on the 24 and 25th encampment. Here one see^d intelligence of the Brig's have gone up left "arm." We to-day discovered in the woods near the shore a coffin which had tumbled from its resting place. Took from it a child, which was in a dried state of preservation.

May 28th

Left our place of encampment early & pulled for the Brig. Found her near head of left arm. The Boats had completed survey of this "arm" and had discovered a large bay about 60 miles in circumference. A very narrow passage [ ]. This was another oversight of Vancouver's.[30]

Two Indians named by us [Cumtax] and [Potlach] were employed to follow the Brig about and to carry letters sent Nassqually when required.

29th

Got underway but soon came to again. At 2. PM tried it again with better success. At 4 came to in ["Cumtax"] bay near SE entrance to Port Orchard.[31]

30th

Light ebb, wind with rain at intervals. Caught a deer this morning that had taken to the water in consequence of its being pursued by a dog.

The Indians from all parts of this bay are [ ] their goods and [ ] to a [ ] little spot immediately abreast of us. They suppose we intend to remain here for some time.

---

[28] "Old Man House."

[29] Totem poles.

[30] A confusing entry as Sanford referenced the exploration of Liberty Bay on May 25. "Sixty miles in circumference" is an exaggeration; perhaps he meant "six." Sanford alludes to either Vancouver's failure to discover Liberty Bay or Bainbridge Island.

[31] *Porpoise* is working its way through Rich Passage.

31st

Light winds and clear vble ensuing when a brisk NW wind sprung up.

At 8. PM saw a very large and brilliant meteor which bore NNW½W. It continued in sight [ ] seconds. Its track or tail was broad and very lumining. Its elevation when first seen was about 40°.

Boats had been dispatched in the morning to carry on survey of "Inlet": towards sunset they returned on board.

June 1st

Light vble winds and fine weather. Boats out surveying. At 1. PM got underway and stood down the Inlet until 5 when we came to on the North side of "Lawrences" Bay in 5½ fathoms water.

2nd

Boats sent out the survey to and about Mouth of Possession Sound. The Brig got underway about Mer: and sailed over and anchored in Possession S. near entrance.

A canoe arrived from Nassqually bringing letters &c, *Peacock* and *F. Fish* not yet arrived in the River.

3rd

Cloudy with rain. Five boats were dispatched to survey up sound. Mr Maury was directed to carry survey of west shore of Inlet to the North^d Lawrences bay and as far as 1st Point to the S° and E^d of Hood's Canal.[32]

At ½ past 10 the Brig got underway and sailed about [6] miles up sound and anchored. Mr Maury did not return tonight owing to the bad weather.

4th

Bad weather until evening. On its' clearing off boats sent out to survey about "Susan's Bay" and "Perry's" Isl^d.[33]

The Sound then terminates: but the sheet of water takes a sudden direction to the North and takes the name of Port "Gardiner."

Country about this region is moderately elevated and densely covered with timber. The soil of a yellow clay mould and might be with little [ ] to produce any [ ].

---

[32]I.e., from Port Madison to Foulweather Bluff.

[33]With respect to this and journal entries for the next several days, Sanford's description of their location is very confusing. I believe that substituting Gedney for Perry's Island is the only explanation that makes any sense. Perry's was the name Wilkes later used for Fidalgo. It is clear that *Porpoise* was nowhere near Fidalgo at that time.

5th

Mr North and myself started to survey "Susan's" Harbr. Owing to much rain we did not do much surveying. About lunch encamped on the Eastern side of bay immediately opposite Point "Allen."[34] Back of our tents the ground rises quickly for some 150 ft and then [ ] in a gradual escending plain for some miles when it appears to terminate by it having reached the low range of hills that runs North and South along the whole of the region.

6th

Sunday. [ ] This survey was made without the use of signals using the marks on the faces of the bluffs &c. a long mud flat extends out from the heart of this bay so that it cannot be approached nearer than ¾ mile.

7th

Finished survey and returned on board.
This Bay affords good but deep anchorage and is well protected.

8th

Employed surveying in and about the head of Possession Sound.

9th

Three boats sent to survey in advance of the vessel up Port Gardiner.
At 2 PM the Brig got underway and beat up the Sound towards Port Gardiner. At 6 anchored under the SW point of "Perry's" Isld which is situated in immediately off Point "Allen."

10th

Brig got underway and stood up Port Gardiner for "Penns" Cove. In passing up we observed many Indian Poles on either shore. Some of them I should think were 60 long and all were in an upright position having support from "props." Vancouver mentions having seen poles of this description but was at a loss to account for their use. Altho we did not see them [ ] to any particular use [ ] we understood that they were intended to spread nets-on in the meshs of which a great many ducks are caught and many are stunned by flying against it and are picked up by the Indians in water before they recover. It is only in the night that they are caught. A large fire is made near it and ducks flying towards it are intercepted by these nets.

Before reaching "Penns" Cove we passed a fine and spacious Bay[35] situated in the Western shore.

---

[34] Camano Head.
[35] Holmes Harbor.

At 12. mer the Brig anchored off the South Point of "Penns" Cove in 4 fathoms water.

The country about here and in fact the whole of "Whitby's" Isl^d is the finest and apparently the most fertile of any that we have yet seen on this "coast."

The Cove is deep and affords excellent anchorage. A sand flat extends off the South Point[36] that needs being looked out for: Its position should be approached to-within some distance, as it shoals quickly and [ ].

The "Seâchêt" Tribe inhabit the shores of this bay. [" "],[37] the chief, is the most respectable Indian we have met with. He is quick, intelligent and probably has more influence over his tribe than any other chief on this Coast. The Tribe numbers between four and five hundred souls and only inhabit this part of the Isl^d ("Whitby's"). [Descents] are frequently made on these people by [ ], a fierce and savage people inhabiting the coast to the north^d of "Frazier River." In their wars neither age nor sex is respected and only those who are reserved for slaves are spared. This system of slavery is quite [ ] among all the Indians of this Coast.

There are two pickets at the entrance of this cove enclosing quite a sizable areas. On the approach or alarm of a foe, the men retire to them while the women and children go into the woods and secret themselves.

The Villiage, or principle villiage, for there are many small ones about the bay, is on the South shore, a short walk from the outer Point. The huts are constructed of rough hewn planks. They are neither air nor water tight. The entrance and premises about are extremely filthy. There is [ ].

Fish is the principal article of food with these people, in fact with all whom we have met. Deer and Elk are in abundance but for the want of fire arms are but seldom obtained.

There is a deep but shallow bay just within the northern entrance of this cove.

June 14th

Mr Alden with the boats in charge left for the survey of Deception passage.

Mr Maury and myself [ ] surveying the "cove."[38]

19th

The Brig shifted her anchorage to the East^d near Deception Passage.

I was sent today to ascertain if there was passage connecting this part

---

[36]Snatelum Point.

[37]Sinclair indicated his name as Natluns.

[38]Oak Harbor.

of Port Gardiner with Susan's Bay. I found a [ ] which is very winding leading with the extreme depth of the Bay. At high water there is some 7 or 8 feet in the channel and at low water but 3 feet. It could be of some use for small "keel boats" and would shorten the distance were it ever necessary to pass into this deceptive passage by "Possession" Sound some 5 or 6 miles. The large Isl^d formed by this passage, and one of which "Point Allen" is the distant extreme has been named "Bainbridge" Isl^d, after the late Commodore.[39]

June 24th

Left the Brig with Mr Maury to survey "Bellingham" Bay and its adjacent Islands. We passed through passage[40] of but little width of 3 or 4 miles in length. On either hand the country was low and swampy. We reached breakfast Island about 8 AM, having previously stop^d on a low sandy point to erect a signal and measure angles. All the Islands shot here are of a uniform aspect: high, rugged, and clothed to their very summits with the pine and cypress and plants that thrive in a poor and stony soil.

Encamped for the night on "Breakfast" Island.[41]

25th

Made an early start and carried the survey as far as "Decatur's" Isl^d. Encamped on ["Dinsion"] Island. This Isl^d is the only one we have seen about here that is level.[42]

26th

Weather fair. Continued the survey. Our work brought us back to ["Dinsion"] Isl^d where we encamped.

27th

Surveying. Encamped on "Clark's" Island.[43]

28th

Employed the middle passage in to this bay. This passage is formed entirely by several Islands. The tide runs with great rapidity through here

---

[39]Sanford's reference is obviously misplaced. Wilkes named Camano Island M'Donough Island.

[40]Swinomish Channel.

[41]Perhaps Saddlebag Island from which they would have a convenient view of a signal placed on March Point, the "low sandy point" previously referenced.

[42]Dinision could be Guemes, which is relatively flat on its southern shore.

[43]This may or may not be the "true" Clark Island, which is ten miles north of Guemes.

and immediately around all points of the Islands it runs with such increased strength, that our boats were unable to make way against.

Encamped on ["Dinsion"] Island.

29th

Surveyed the passage between Sinclair's and Cypress Islands on one side and Emerson's Island on the other.[44]

Sinclair's Island is almost immediately from the water the height of 600 or 700 feet and is extremely rugged but well wooded.

Cypress Isl^d is one of the loftiest Islands about here and is also very rugged, rocky and steep. Encamped on this Isl^d.

30th

Surveyed the southern passage into Bellingham Bay[45] which finished our work. We joined the Brig at Sunset, she being at anchor in "Strawberry" bay on the north side of "Cypress" Island.

July 1st

Brig got underway and stood to the north^d for "Birch" bay. Boats were left on our way to bring the survey of the continental coast up to our anchorage. At 11 anchored in the bay in 5½ fathoms water. This is a fine deep bay with excellent anchorage in all parts of it. It is open to the West^d and N^d W^d. A small flat runs off its head and into which makes a small fresh water stream. Plenty of this article can be obtained. The land in the rear is low and in part swampy.

2nd

Light and mods vble breezes and calms. Employed surveying the bay.

3rd

Light vble winds and pleasant. Boats out surveying.

4th

Another pleasant.

---

[44]Regarding Emerson Island, Sanford used a place name that apparently did not stick. He perhaps was referencing Bellingham Channel between Cypress to the west and Lawrence (Guemes) to the east. His reference to Cypress is likely accurate as Vancouver named it! And indeed, it is very steep and rugged. However, his description of Sinclair Island is confusing. While the southern shore rises to 150–200 feet, the majority of the island is relatively low and flat.

[45]I.e., the channel between Guemes, Vendovi and Point William, named by Wilkes Penguin Harbor.

July 5th

Light winds from the SW and pleasant. At 8. AM got underway and stood to the north^d for Frazier River. About 11 passed Point "Roberts." This point from the South^d appears like an Isl^d as it runs off from a bold bluff & is elevated land. It extends to a considerable distance to the East^d. Its shores are bold. About 3. came to in 12 fathoms water, a little to the South^d of the channel which leads through a broad mud flat into the River.

6th

Boats out surveying the channel into the River.

7th

Employed surveying. Found the channel into the River narrow and winding.

8th

Out surveying. We found the tide so strong today that part of our work had to be [ ] out as the boats could not [ ] a line of soundings before they would be carried back on the tide or the channel from which they had started.

We were visited by a number of Indians deck^d out in their finery from the H. B. Company's Post about 30 miles up the River.

9th

Light vble airs and pleasant. At 9. AM the Brig got underway and anchored soon after in mid channel in 50 fathoms water. At 11. PM a moderate wind springing up got under way again and stood to the South^d.

10th

2. AM anchored again about 2 miles to the North^d of Point "Roberts."

I acc^d orders to proceed to Nassqually in the *Rover* bearing letters &c. About 3 PM reached "Cypress" Isl^d when I stopped for the night.

July 11th

Rain all night. Started about an hour before dawn. About 10 o'clock had reached Deception Isl^d where I had to remain 2 hours until the tide slacked to permit the [ ] the "Passage." The tides ran so very swift here that with all the strength of the boats crew I lost much ground and barely succeeded in reaching the Isl^d. About 12 the tide slacked sufficiently to allow my passage. Reached Port Townshend where I remained for the night.[46]

12th

Dreary rain all night. Passed a very uncomfortable and wet night. Started early in a dense fog. About 8. AM the fog rose when I found myself abreast of "Possession" Sound. I was in doubt as the direction I was taking and thought is not improbable I might find myself in "Hoods" Canal on the clearing up of the fog. The fog had hardly risen before it set into rain very hard with a high wind so that by sunset I had only reached "Lawrences" Bay where I stayed for the night.

13th

Heavy rain all night. Started early and 1 PM entered Pugets Sound.[47] At 10 PM got alongside the ship at "Nassqually." I remained here until the 17th when I was dispatched with *Vincennes* Launch being laden with bread to join the Brig in or about the entrance of the "Inlet." Not finding the Brig in Port Townshend I went to "Strawberry" bay where I met her at anchor.[48]

21st

Got underway with a light wind from the [ ] and about 3 anchored under the lea of "Blank" Isld[49] which was surveyed.

The Aurora appeared to the North[d].

July 22nd

Fine pleasant days, wind vble. At 7 the Brig got underway and commenced down the Straits for "Dungeness." Discovered the *Vincennes* near port "Discovery" underway. At 1. PM anchored near other ship under Point Dungeness in 12½ fathoms water. Rec[d] orders to join the *Vincennes*. Immediately on my joining her got orders to be prepared to go with [ ] Totten up Admiralty to survey.

---

[46]More confusing entries. Sanford indicated they waited two hours on Deception Island for slack tide "...to permit [ ] the 'Passage'" implying that they transited Deception Pass. But other entries imply they continued on the western side of Whidbey, entered Admiralty Inlet and Port Townsend and later Port Madison.

[47]From his previous definition of Puget Sound, this was likely the entrance to Colvos Passage. Regardless, it required approximately sixteen hours to cover the final forty miles from Port Madison (Lawrences Bay) to Nisqually.

[48]According to Alden's journal, *Porpoise* anchored in Strawberry Bay on July 19.

[49]Smith Island.

23rd
Commenced the survey near Hood's Canal where the Brig had left off. Connected with her signals.

24th
Finished the survey and rejoined the ship.

At this point, the leather-bound Journal ends leaving the latter half of the book entirely blank.

9

The Journal of James Alden

James Alden was born in Portland, Maine, on March 31, 1810. He received his appointment as midshipman in April 1828. He served the early years at the Naval Station in Boston, saw service on the USS *John Adams* in the Mediterranean, then returned to the Boston Navy Yard. From there, he was assigned to the U.S. Exploring Expedition. Wilkes promoted him to lieutenant in February 1841. After the Expedition, he saw continued service and was detached from duty in May 1849 for service in the United States Coast Survey. During the next two years, he surveyed the east coast and then traveled to the west coast to continue the activity aboard the USS *Active*. He was promoted to commander September 1855. During the Civil War, Alden commanded several ships on the east coast. He was promoted to captain in January 1863, commodore in July 1866 and rear admiral in June 1871. In that position, he commanded the European Fleet until relieved by Rear Admiral Augustus L. Case in June 1873, at which point he retired. Alden died in San Francisco February 6, 1877.

April 29th, 1841.

Fresh breezes from the W^d & thick rainy weather. At 11 discovered that the water was much discoloured. got a cast of the lead in 5 fath. hauled off the wind immediately, took in the studding sails & [ ] sloop up. The land was then discovered all along lee beam & close aboard. the fogg at the same time lifted a little & disclosed a huge rock about one pt on the lee bow. There was not room for wearing. As for tacking ship, it would have been folly to attempt it. The sea was so heavy & immediately on the weather bow [that] she never would have brought the wind ahead, without having [recourse] to "club hauling" but even doing that was out of the question, for our *cables were not bent* & the vessel was plunging into it so heavily that it was impossible to bend one. Several attempts were made but the men as often washed in by the sea onto the forecastle. The ship behaved well & weathered the danger. It was in every sense of the word a "hair breadth escape" for as we passed the rock I could have pitched a [ ] into the breakers they were so near. The *Porpoise* proved to be more weatherly than the *Vincinnes*. But the escape of both vessels is owing as much to their good qualities as sea boats as any thing else. The rock that was so near bringing us up is called "*Destruction* Rock." After making an offing the wind subsided & the sea went down when we kept to the N^d for the Juan de Fucca.

April 30th.

Moderate breezes from the S & E^d and foggy during the day. standing close in along the shore sometimes inside the Rocks. The *Porpoise* in Company some distance outside of us. At [6] entered the Straits of Juan de Fucca.

May 1st.

Calm & light winds. got occasionally a glimpse of the shore on both sides which were clothed with a dense vapour during the day. In the morning a canoe came along side filled with Natives. Some of them came on board. There were all about half clad, some with skins others with blankets & one of them had on a scarlet frock coat. his open countenance attracted my attention & I entered into conversation with him. His first question was— King George Ship? I said no. What ship. Boston Ship? and being ans^d in the affirmative appeared delighted. shook hands & commenced showing King George (i.e., Victoria) wonder if he knew the difference — They were all filthy & disgusting in their person & when *my friend* opened his red *frock coat* just I suppose to show his form to more advantage, such an odor filled the air that I was compelled to retreat some twenty paces & console myself for the interpretation of the conversation with "distance lands" &c. As a covering for the head they had a sort of straw hat made in the shape of an inverted cone and perfectly water tight. Their feet were entirely naked and judging from their red appearance they must be for most of the time immersed in the cold freezing water. They are in truth a miserable looking & highly [ ] race.

May 2^d.

during the day standing up the Straits. The shores in sight on both sides. The starb^d shore being the nearest of course had a better chance to examine it. It is much broken & very mountainous, thickly wood even to the summit of the highest hills where the trees appeared bending under the weight — not of fruit — but of the coldest looking *snow*. Several canoes came alongside. Their occupants were of the same miserable caste as those seen yesterday. After sundown came to anchor in Port Discovery so called by Vancouver & it is a singular coincidence that he discovered & entered it just 49 years ago today. Tis beautifully situated & its mouth is protected in a most [scientific] manner by Protection Isle. The only draw back to the harbour's being a comfortable resort for shipping is that the water is too deep. While in this harbour several Natives visited the vessels and established quite a village near us. They brought some fine large salmon alongside & several other kinds of fish. We had a tolerable opportunity of judging of the manners & customs of the tribe in this vicinity — They are called Flat Heads and I think judging from the heads of the men, they are rightly named, not that nature had any hand in *beautifying* these miserables. but tis a custom & I believe universally so, to compress the head of the males during infancy which gives them the most unsightly appearance. I had an opportunity of observing the manner that this system of torture is carried on. A small piece of board or bark is provided with a sufficient number of holes in each side. The poor little [ ] sufferer is laid upon on his back. Then a thick layer of the fiber of bark is spread over his body up to the chin. Then cord is passed through the holes in the board over the body from the feet to the shoulders. when the ugly little devil is lashed firmly down with his arms pinned to his sides, resistance of course was now out of the question but we had sufficient evidence of the strength of his lungs, for it was [ ] continued [ ] from the commencement to the end of the operation. but when the mother applied this *compress* I thought the child would go into fits. It was done too with the utmost 'sang froid' being provided with two coarse pads about 4 inches square. she placed on under its head & the other on its forehead & over all passed a cord which was drawn tight as possible. This practice is continued some 6 or 8 months & as the bones of the head are soft at that age the pressure as described above gives a permanent shape to the head. Instead of *rocking the cradle* they swing it by suspending it from the top of an elastic stick stuck into the ground which the woman kept vibrating by means of a cord made fast to the cradle & the big toe.

May 4th.
    All the Boats & officers employed surveying the harbour.

5th.
    A part of to day employed as yesterday.

May 6th.
    At 9 A.M. got underway and beat out of the harbour. At 5 came to anchor in Port Townshend which is about 10 miles from Port Discovery. I

think it a much better harbour than the last mentioned there being a less depth of water & much easier of access. it is situated just in the entrance of Admiralty Inlet on the stard[1] hand [ ].

7th.
All the boats employed surveying this harbour from daylight till 8 A.M. At Mer[2] got underway & stood to the South. anchored again after making about 9 miles.[3] *Porpoise* in Company.

8th.
All the boats employed surveying. Wind fresh from the S^d & E^d. At Mer got underway & commenced beating to wind ward. After making about 25 miles anchored[4] near the stard shore opposite to the entrance of Possession Sound. Soon after a canoe came along side with Pilots from the H.B.Co's Fort at Nasqually. they both belong to the Companys Steamer which they told us was undergoing repairs. One of them, the Mate, remained on board & the other a seaman was sent to the *Porpoise*.

May 9th.
While getting underway this morning, it being all hands I was called. turned out immediately & and as I stepped on the gun deck met Mr Eld who told me that Capt Wilkes had ordered him to tell me to consider myself suspended from duty. went immediately to my room & noticed that only *six minutes* had elapsed from the time I had been called. The ship however was got underway *without my assistance* while I was left to ruminate on the mutability of human wants. The circumstance of my suspension has annoyed me not a little & I am utterly at a loss in the [ ] after the course why — mais n'empartis pointless. I shall find out one of these days I fear although if I wait till I get a satisfactory explanation from the individual who has inflicted the punishment it will be like the *cruise, extremely protracted*.

May 11th.
At 8 P.M anchored off Fort Nasqually. *Porpoise* in Company. found the Companys Steamer here undergoing repairs

---

[1] Starboard or right hand.
[2] Noon.
[3] Oak Bay.
[4] Pilot Point.

12th.
 Received an order from the J^r Lt. to resume duty. To my question what have I been suspended for? he replied that he had not been informed by Capt Wilkes, neither did he know — that Capt W. had not even told him that I was off duty during the whole time (3 days). of my suspension I have made a note of this fact not because my commander has been singular in his treatment towards *me*, but, to show the way he has of doing things. Now for want of something little to fill this page I will speculate on the possible cause of my suspension. In the first place, I am told that all hands had been called some 30 minutes when he (Capt W) went into the Forecastle & not finding me (I of course had not been called because I had just turned in after keeping the mid watch, and be it remembered that it had been a practice during the whole cruise *to excuse the officers of the mid watch*) fell into an *awful rage* and the result of which has been told.[5]

May 15th.
 Since I joined the Brig[6] have been employed getting her ready for Surveying duty. tis said we are bound to the N^d. At 1 P.M got underway & stood out of the narrows. At 5 anchored near the mouth of quite a large inlet, with a very narrow entrance, tis situated on the west side of the sound & in such a snug corner that it would often be passed without notice.[7] several Natives visited the vessel & traded a few fish

16th.
 Sunday employed fitting out the boats for surveying duty which we shall commence tomorrow with a will

---

[5] Alden was not the first to feel the wrath of Wilkes. Throughout the voyage, the relationship between Wilkes and his officers deteriorated and is perhaps best and most eloquently summarized by a passage from Letter No. 11 from William Reynolds to his sister Lydia dated December 1st, 1839: "I cannot recount all of the atrocities he has been guilty of, but they have been of the deepest dye, deadly thrusts at the life blood of an officer — his professional conduct. There are but three individuals in the Squadron who are base and sycophantic enough to stand by Captain Wilkes and his acts. All the others who were once so ardent in his cause have now turned against him; there is the same unanimity in this as there was when the tide was in his favor, and it is this universal voice which is the strong proof of the justice of our side: the Commander and his officers are at open variance. Whatever advances he may make during the remnant of the cruise will be of no avail — his sword has cut too deep already for the scars ever to be effaced" (Cleaver & Stann).

[6] Alden was reassigned to the *Porpoise*.

[7] Gig Harbor.

17th.

Got underway & shifted our birth more to the East^d in what we called Commencement Bay just to the South of Vashon Isle. here we remained while the boats were employed surveying the Bay. Vashon Isle stands to the E^d &c &c &c over there.

19th.

At 10 A. M. got underway & stood to the East^d and anchored at 1 P.M. in Portage inlet[8] on the East side of Vashon Isle. Boats returned from surveying duty at sunrise.

May 20th.

All the boats employed surveying towards Port Orchard. At 2.30 got underway and stood to the N^d. anchored in the evening in "Port Orchard" 8½ faths water.

May 21st.

Sailed from Port Orchard while there made observations on the tide the mean rise & fall of which is about 14 feet. in the narrowest part the current runs with the velocity of about 5 & 6 Knots. We found the harbour very extensive & branching off into 4 arms which kept all the boats constantly employed while we were there. Lt Maury while surveying the N.E. arm found a narrow opening[9] leading into Madison Harbour which lies on the West side of the Sound about 8 miles to the N^d of where we entered Port Orchard. The Natives hereabouts are not very numerous. few troubled us with their visits. The day before we sailed I saw swimming across the harbour a fine large Deer with a dog in full chase. sent a boat & picked up the deer & [beat] the dog.[10] The boats employed all day surveying the shores towards Possession Sound.

June 1st.

Sent the boats at daylight on Surveying duty. Light breezes & pleasant. At Mer got underway & at 5 anchored in Madison Harbour — North side — 5 faths water.

2^d.

Boats employed as yesterday. At Mer got underway toward Possession Sound & anchored close to the East shore near the entrance. got news from Nasqually nothing from the *Peacock* or *Flying Fish*

---

[8] Tramp Harbor.

[9] Agate Pass.

[10] I think his meaning is that they got to the deer before the dog!

3^d.

Sent all the boats to survey this Sound to the N^d & the entrance of Possession Sound. At 10 got underway, stood into the Sound & anchored near the East shore.

4th.

Early this morning Lt Maury returned on board having been kept out all night by stress of weather. Started all the boats on surveying duty. This Sound takes its name from the circumstances or rather it received its appelation from Vancouver who took possession of the country near this pt.

June 5th.

Sent two boats under charge of Lt North to Survey Susan Bay & 2 others towards Port Gardner.

7th.

The boats returned.

8th.

All boats out surveying.

9th.

Sent 3 boats under charge of Lt Maury to survey ahead of the Brig. At 2 got underway & commenced working to windward toward Port Gardner. in the evening anchored under the South end of [ ] Island.[11]

10th.

got underway & stood to the N^d. At [left blank] communicated with the boat. Lt Maury came along side furnish his party with more provisions. filled away & stood on. At Mer anchored off the South Pt of Penns Cove. This is one of the most delightful places my eye has rested upon during our sojourn on the coast. The cove is beautiful in the extreme. good anchorage all about. undulating country, hills & valleys interspersed just right to make it agreeable &c &c &c. The Natives appear to be in rather an unsettled state during our stay in the Cove. They [are too] quite an excitement. a canoe came alongside with 5 or 6 Natives men, woman & children. They appeared to be much alarmed & begged for permission to remain on board till morning. they stated that the [Waleta's] a tribe from the North who were at war with them & who frequently make descents upon them & tak-

---

[11]Likely Gedney Island.

ing away their women — were in the vicinity & would no doubt use them up before morning. We consoled them as well as we could & pursuaded them to leave the vessel after which we heard no more of troubles from the North.

June 14th.

Started this morning with three boats—for the Survey of Deception Passage, an inlet opening a communication into Possession Sound at the North end of Whidby Island — arrived there in time to pass through & examine the passage before dark. decided that it would be practicable to take the Brig through. informed the Commander that such was the first — next day, although it rained, done some work between the showers— we were employed on this survey & in connecting on with the Brig to the South^d until the 21st.

during most of the time however the weather was so bad that the boats could not be employed. today passed through Deception Passage in the Brig without any difficulty. on the 24th Lt Maury left in charge of 3 boats with orders to pass through a passage that we had discovered a few days previous leading into Bellingham Bay[12] carrying on the Survey as he proceeded & to join the Brig outside.

July 1st.

Anchored in Birch Bay having brought the Survey up to this point on both sides of the Gulf of Georgia. Lt Maury returned yesterday from the Survey of Bellingham Bay. The shores of the Gulf of Georgia possess an entirely different character from those of Possession Sound. They are bold & rocky for the most part, but thickly wooded, pine, cypress & birch I believe abound in this vicinity.

9th.

At Frasiers River since the 1st. have been employed Surveying between this & Birch Bay. also 6 miles of the River, The bread getting low Cap^n Ringgold determined to retrace our steps in order to obtain a further supply from the *Vincennes*, having previously dispatched Passed Mid^n Sanford in the *Rover* to [inform] the Com^{dr} of the Ex. Ex. of our wants. At 9 called all hands. got underway & commenced working to the E^d towards Pt Roberts. at [ ] anchored. Pt R. bearing E.S.E.

July 10th.

Shifted our Birth to the East side of Pt Roberts. I would have [remark] that this Pt resembles an Island [ ] is from the South.

---

[12]Swinomish Channel.

11th.
Anchored again in Birch Bay.

15th.
Shifted our birth over on the North side of the Gulf of Georgia and anchored on the North side. a small Island near the Northern entrance of the Straits of d'Arro. All the boats constantly employed on Surveying duty. This portion of the coast is most dreary I've seen in comparison with those we just left, few trees, perpendicular shores, rocky & almost inaccessible to us [ ].

19th.
Anchored once more in Strawberry Bay Cypress Island. All boats employed surveying.

20th.
The *Vincennes* Launch arrived and brought us Whiskey, Bread & butter & orders for us to proceed to [ ] the Dungeness & join the *Vins.* completing some Surveys on our route there.

21st.
At 9 got underway. stood to the S^d & anchored under Blunts Island.[13] boats employed Surveying [ ].

22^d.
got underway & soon after discovered the *Vincennes* standing out of Admiralty Inlet. joined company. stood for Dungeness & anchored in 12½ faths water.

25th.
At 3 P.M. got underway & stood to the E^d. While we lay Dungeness [ ] by the *Vincennes* & done some Surveying. This a most singular place. a very low long sandy neck extending out in a curve from the main land some 2 or 3 miles in the light of which on the East side there is very good anchorage. Vancouver gave it the name from its resemblance to Dungeness in England. At [five] anchored in Pt. Townsend.

July 26th.
All boats employed Surveying Port Townsend. It will be recollected that our squadron (i.e., the *Vincennes* & this vessel) on their way to Puget's

---

[13]Smith Island.

Sound surveyed this harbor, or rather, commenced it. so we have been sent here to do the work over again. 27th all boats employed on the survey. ditto 28th. heard today of the loss of the *Peacock* on Columbia River Bar.

29th.
At 9 A.M. Passed Mid^n Sanford arrived with orders from the Commander of the Expedition to join him at Dungeness.

30th.
Fresh gales & cloudy. At 8 moderate. got underway & stood out of the Harbour. experienced a heavy sea in the channel pitched away the head [ ] & stood towards Pt Hudson where we found the water much smoother. worked up to Dungeness & at 10 came to near the *Vincennes*.

31st.
At 1 P.M. got underway in company with the *Vincennes* & commenced working to the West^d.

August 2^d.
Standing towards the mouth of the Straits of Juan de Fucca. Sent a boat to the *Vincennes* which returned. brought orders to us to proceed to Port St Juan & Survey the harbour. kept away as it stood over towards the N^d side of the Straits— At 1.30 came to in 12 faths water in the mouth of the harbour. Surveyed it & at 6 got underway again & stood towards the South side of the Strait. At 9.30 anchored in Classet Harbour near the *Vincennes*. While we lay becalmed off Port St Juan several canoes came along side containing natives from Vancouver Island. They are a fierce looking but a much more savage race than those we met with in the Straits.

3^d.
At 2 the *Vincennes* made signal where we both got underway & commenced working out of the Straits— Nothing farther of note occurred till we arrived of the Columbia River on the 6th.

10

The Journal of Samuel B. Elliott

Although Wilkes spells his name "Elliot" in the muster table (one "t"), and Elliot Point was likely named for the man, Elliott himself spells it with two "t's" in his journal, which is what I shall use. Samuel Elliott used a columnar format while the ship is at sea, based upon an astronomical calendar which begins at noon of the previous day to that listed at the top of the table and ends at noon of the day listed. When the ship is in harbor, he used a paragraph form. Punctuation and spelling is good, and the handwritten text is generally very legible. Where the text is illegible, I insert a bracket [ ] or word(s) within the bracket as my best guess. The journal does not contain page numbers.

The column headed "H" refers to the hour. The "K" and "F" columns require some additional explanation. The explorers used a "ship's log" or "chip log" to determine speed. Early on, the log was just that, a piece of wood tied to a long line. During Vancouver's time and later with Wilkes, it evolved to the shape of a quarter circle, approximately twelve inches in diameter and weighted with lead on the arc portion. The shape acted as an efficient drogue. The line tied to the log was wound around a small drum with handles so that it would pay out with little friction. It was knotted at intervals. In Wilkes' case, I believe that the interval was seven fathoms. The log was lowered over the taffrail. After a sufficient amount of line was released so that the log cleared the ship's wake (perhaps ten fathoms), an "egg timer" was turned over. When the sand ran out, the line was stopped and the number of knots counted. In addition, the length from the final knot to the taffrail was also determined, as measured in fathoms. Thus, the "K" column reflected the physical number of knots passing over the rail, not the ship's actual speed. The "F" column reflected the length of the "partial knot," measured in fathoms. Elliott's second entry, 2K and 4F, represents 108 feet of line (2 knots ×

7 fathoms per knot × 6 feet per fathom + 4 fathoms × 6 feet per fathom). The egg timers were typically twenty-eight or thirty seconds. With this information, the ship's actual speed was calculated. "A" is air temperature, "W" is water temperature. One final note. Elliott used an astronomical calendar for the columnar format of his journal. The entries run from noon of one day to noon of the next. Thus, the first line below represents 1:00 PM on May 1st. The paragraph form of the journal simply reports events that occurred on the day shown.

Journal of a Cruise of the U. S. Ship Vincennes
Charles Wilkes Esqr., Commander

May 1st, 1841

H	K	F	Course	Winds	A	W	Remarks
1	3	-	S.E. by S.		44	46	Commences with moderate breezes and rainy
2	2	4	NE by N	44	46		weather. Working up the Straits of Juan de
2	2	2	SE by E½E				Fuca. At 9 Inspected the crew at quarters. A
3	2		E by S ½ S	44	46		Canoe with Several Indians from the south side
3	4		NE				of the Straits came along side. Found the
4	3	-	N.E. by E.	44	46		current running W.N.W. 5/8 mile per hour.
5	5		N.E. by N.	44	46		Made and reduced sail as occasions required,
5	1	4	SSE				hoisted out the light Boats and sent them ahead
6	7	4	S by E ½ E	45	46		to tow ship.
7	1	4	N.N.E ¼ E	45	46		Day ends with light airs and variable.
7	5	4					
8	6	-	N by E ¼ E	45	46		
9	5	-	S by E	E^d	45	46	
10	3	-	South	"	46	46	
11	2	4	East	W^d	46	46	
12	3	4	"	S^d	46	46	
1	1		E ½ N	variable	46	46	
2	1		"	"	47	47	
3	1		"	"	50	47	
4	1		"	"	49	49	
5	1	6	E by N	N by W	47	47	
6	3		"	"	45	47	
7	2	2	"	"	45	47	
8	1	4	"	"	45	46	
9	1	-	"	N	44	46	
10	1	4	"	"	44	46	

H	K	F	Course	Winds	A	W	Remarks
11	1	4	"	"	43	46	
12	2	4	"	"	40	46	

May 2nd, 1841

H	K	F	Course	Winds	A	W	Remarks
1	2	-	E by N	S & E^d	43	46	Commences with light airs and clear over head.
2	1	-	"	"	43	46	Brig *Porpoise* in Company. Made and reduced
3	-	4	"	"	43	46	sails as occasions required. A Canoe came
4	1	-	E ½ N	"	43	46	alongside manned by seven natives.
5	1	2	drift up tide	"	43	46	
6	2	6	"	"	43	46	
7	2	6	"	"	44	46	
8	3	6	"	"	44	46	At 8.15 took in all studding sails. at 8.45
9	4	-	"	"	49	47	clewed up Topsails and came to in 27 fathoms
10	4		SE by S	S	49	47	water with starboard anchor having reached
11	1	4	N.N.E	"	49	47	Discovery harbour. Vered out to 75 fms chain.
12	2	4	S.E	"	49	47	Furled sails, Brig anchored in shore of us.
1	48	47					Day ends with light airs and pleasant.
2	48	47					
3	6	2	E by N¾ N	West	46	46	
4	6	-	E.N.E	"	46	46	
5	6	4	E by N ½N	47	47		
6	8	4	E.N.E	45	47		
7	47	48					
8	46	51					
9	46	48					
10	46	48					
11	46	48					
12	46	48					

May 3^d, 1841

H	K	F	Course	Winds	A	W	Remarks
							Commences with light variable airs and
							pleasant. At 9 Inspected the crew at quarters.
							Several Indian canoes came alongside trading
							fish clams &c. 8 boats Employed surveying.
							At 4.00 fired four guns for base. Day ends
							light airs and pleasant with fine rains.

Discovery Harbour May 4th, 1841

Commences with moderate breezes and cloudy. Sent Carpenters on shore to work. Received a load of water by the 1st Cutter. Day was light variable airs and cloudy.

Discovery Harbour May 5th/41

Commences with light airs and variable weather. At 9 00 loosed sails. Cutter Employed watering and three Boats surveying. Day was light airs and cloudy.

May 6th/41

Commences with light airs from the S & E^d, & pleasant. Hoisted up the launch and 1st cutter. At 8 got underway and made all sail by the wind and commenced beating out. At 2 00 kept away and set starboard studding sails. At 5 00 worked into a bay and came to anchor in 15 fathoms water.[1] *Porpoise* came to at the same time on our starb^d Bow. Day ends moderate breezes and pleasant.

May 7th 1841

Commences with light variable airs and pleasant. Got underway and stood up the sound. At 7 00 came to in [left blank][2] bay in 21 fathoms water with larb^d anchor. Day ends fresh breezes from the S^o & E^d and cloudy.

May 8th 1841

Commences with fresh breezes from S^o & W^d and cloudy. Called away all Boats and sent them surveying. Fired 4 guns to measure base. At 1 00 got underway. Single reefed the Topsails. Commenced beating up Admiralty Inlet. *Porpoise* in company. At 5 00 anchored in 15 fathoms water.[3] Mr Heath came on board as Pilot from Nasqually. Inspected crew at quarters. Day was light airs from S^d and E^d and cloudy.

May 9th 1841

Commences with fresh breezes from N^d and E^d and thick weather. At 4.15 call all hands and got underway and beat up sound until 8 00 AM where we came to anchor[4] 4 miles to windward of where we anchored last

---

[1] Port Townsend.

[2] Elliott left the entry blank. Wilkes named this Port Lawrence. Vancouver previously named it Oak Bay.

[3] Pilot's Cove.

[4] Appletree Cove.

night. At 1 00 the Gig and 3 Boats left on Surveying duty. Called all hands and got underway and commenced beating up the inlet. At 6.50 came to under the weather shore, vered 35 fathoms chain. Day ends moderate breezes from S^d & E^d and pleasant.

May 10th 1841
Commences with light baffling airs and pleasant. Inspected the crew at quarters. At 1 00 called all hands and got under way.

May 11th 1841
Commences calm and cloudy. At 6 called all hands and hove up the starboard anchor hauled nearer in shore and moored letting go the starb^d anchor in 29 fms and larb^d one 12 fms. Veered to 60 fms on starb^d chains and 45 on the larb^d. Hoisted out all Boats. Sent two boats sounding. Lt Alden left the ship to join the *Porpoise*, also Pass^d Mid Sandford, & Mid Elliott.[5]

U.S. Brig *Porpoise*
Nasqually, May 12th
Pass^d Mid Sandford & Mid Elliott reported for duty.

May 13th
Painted ship. Wind light from the S° & E^d & S° & W^d.

May 14th
Commences with light winds from S^d & E^d & cloudy. Day ends with occasional puffs form S^d & E^d.

May 15th
Commences with fresh winds from S^d & W^d. received two boats with their crews from the *Vincennes*. Also Thomas Wade, as Pilot and Interpreter. At 1.15 got underway standing to the N^d. At 4.40 came to anchor in the Narrows in 10½ fathoms water. Unbent mainsail for repairs.

May 16th 1841
Commences calm, cold and clear. Crew went on shore. Ends calm and cloudy.

---

[5] At this point, Elliott was reassigned to the *Porpoise*, tasked with the survey of Admiralty Inlet.

May 17th 1841

Commences calm and pleasant. At 8.45 a breeze sprung up and we got underway. At 10.45 came to anchor. Five boats surveying—fired 4 guns for Base. 4 of the *Vincennes* boats passed.

May 18th

Commences calm and pleasant. Boats surveying. Day ends calm and pleasant.

May 19th

Commences calm and pleasant. At 6 00 A.M. got underway. At 1 came to anchor[6] under the East side Vashon Isld. Day was light breezes from S^d & E^d.

May 20th

Commences with strong breezes from the S^d & E^d & cloudy. Five boats surveying the passage East side Vashon Isld. At 10 fired 4 guns for base. At 2 15 got underway and stood for Port Orchard Harbour. At 4.15 came to anchor in Port Orchard. Wind S^d & E^d.

May 21st

Commences calm & cloudy. Five boats surveying.

May 22nd 1841

Commences calm and pleasant — three Boats surveying.

May 23rd

Commences calm and pleasant, the *Eagle* capsizes alongside. Sent a boat to pick up the things. Crew went on shore to wash clothes. Day ends pleasant. Winds from S^d & E^d.

May 24th

Commences calm and pleasant. Sent these three boats under Lt Maury on surveying examination of Northern Arm of Port Orchard. the Boats employed on surveying duty.

May 25th

Commences calm and cloudy with light passing showers. *Shark* and *Eagle* on surveying duty. Day ends light breezes from E ½ S and pleasant.

---

[6]Tramp Harbor.

May 26th
Commences with light breezes from the S^d & E^d and cloudy. One boat surveying. At 3.30 got underway and stood up through the narrows. At 5.30 came to anchor in Southern arm of Port Orchard in 7½ fathoms water.

May 27th 1841
Commences calm and pleasant. *Shark* and *Eagle* employed surveying. Sent provisions for Boats under charge of Lieut Maury having completed the survey of the Southern arm P. Orchard.

May 28th
Commences calm and pleasant. Boats surveying. Day ends with light breezes and pleasant.

May 29th
Commences with moderate breezes from N^d & E^d and cloudy. From 4 to 8 A.M. saw a deer swimming across the passage. Sent a boat and picked it up. Crew went on shore to wash clothes. Wooding and watering. Winds N^d & E^d.

May 30th
Commences calm and pleasant. At 4 00 AM got underway and sent the Boats ahead to tow. 7 tide turned against us. Let go the stream anchor. At 2 00 PM got underway. At 4 30 came to in [Comas] Bay South^n arm Port Orchard. Day ends light breezes from S^d & E^d.

May 31st
Four Boats under Lt Maury were dispatched to survey that portion of the straits contained between this inlet and Possession Islands.[7] At 1.30 PM got underway and towed out and made sail. Standing to west^d. Sent Lieut Alden on shore to obtain angles with Theodolite. At Tree point saw the party surveying. Boats returned from surveying. At 8.00 P.M. a bright Meteor made its appearance bearing N.N.W ½ W. At first it assumed all the appearance of a common Meteor, but the light continued for some minutes [contracting] but widening and assumed a zigzag shape. Winds N & W & N & E.

---

[7]The other journals indicated that Maury was dispatched June 3 to survey from Port Madison to Foulweather Bluff.

June 1st 1841
　　Commences with light breezes from S^d & E^d & pleasant. All Boats employed surveying. At 1 got underway and stood to N^d. At 4.30 came to in Port Townsend.[8] Winds S^d & E^d.

June 2nd
　　Commences with light airs from S^d & E^d and pleasant. Surveying toward Possession Sound. Came to with the stream anchor near the Eastern shore of this Strait. Day ends light airs from the S^d & E^d.

June 3rd
　　Commences calm and cloudy with light rain. At intervals five Boats surveying about Possession Sound. At 10 fired 4 guns for base. At 10.30 A.M. got underway and stood into the sound with fresh squalls and rain. At 12.30 P.M. came near the Eastern shore of Possession. Day ends with moderate breezes from S^d & E^d.

June 4th
　　Commences calm and cloudy. At 2 [ ]. At 4 fired the small guns for the *Rover* which boat was away all night. At 6. AM the *Rover* returned having been kept out by the badness of the weather. Wooding and watering. Boats surveying. Day ends light winds from S^d & E^d.

June 5th
　　Calm and pleasant, wooding and watering. Boats surveying.

June 6th
　　Commences calm with occasional thick mist. Men on shore to wash. Day ends with light variable breezes with heavy rains.

June 7th
　　Commences calm and pleasant. Boats surveying. Day ends light winds from N^d & W^d.

June 8th
　　Commences with light breezes from the N^d & W^d with showers of rain. Day ends calm.

June 9th
　　Commences light and variable airs and pleasant. Sent 3 Boats in charge of Lt Maury for surveying Port Gardiner & Penn Cove. At 1 40 PM

---

[8] Port Madison according to the other journals.

hove up and stood over toward the western shore. Wind failing sent the boats ahead to tow. At 7 00 came to anchor off the Southern Point of Perry's Island.[9]

June 10th 1841

Commences with light variable breezes and overcast. At 7 30 A.M. got underway and made sail up the sound. Saw the Launch in Port Gardiner. Called her alongside and supplied her with another days provisions when she shoved off. At 12.30 came to near the S^n pt of Penns Cove. Boats employed surveying. 4.30 P.M. hove up and shifted our birth, fired 4 guns for base. All the boats returned.

June 11th

Commences light variable breezes. Boats surveying. Day ends clear and pleasant.

June 12th

Commences calm and pleasant. At 9.30 hove up the anchor and made sail and worked up into Penns Cove and came to anchor. Boats surveying. Day ends pleasant.

June 13th

Commences calm and cloudy with rains. Sent the men on shore to wash clothes. Day ends rainy.

June 14th

Commences calm and cloudy with fine rain. 3 Boats surveying. Day was light winds from SW and pleasant.

June 15th

Calm and cloudy with rain. Carpenters repairing Boats. Day was light winds from SW and pleasant.

June 16th

Commences light breezes from S^{d}W^d and cloudy with rain. 3 Boats surveying.

June 17th

Commences cloudy with rain, light breezes from the SW. Boats surveying. At 5 00 got underway and stood over for Deception Passage. At 6.30 came to anchor.

---

[9]Perry's was Wilkes' name for Fidalgo Island. However, *Porpoise* was really in the neighborhood of Gedney Island.

June 18th
Commences with light breezes and rainy. Sent the Boats surveying. At 2 00 P.M. got underway and stood to the N^d. At 4.30 came to anchor. Day was light winds from S^d & E^d and pleasant.

June 19th
Commences with strong breezes from the S^d & E^d and pleasant.

June 20th
Commences calm & pleasant. Sent crew on shore to scrub Hammocks, clothes & bedding. Boats surveying.

June 21st 1841
Commences with fresh breezes from the S^d & E^d & cloudy. Boats surveying. At 4 got underway and stood to the W^d. At 5 30 the wind hauled ahead. Let go the starb^d anchor and furled sails. All Boats surveying. Day ends moderate breezes from the S^d and pleasant.

June 22nd
Commences light breezes and pleasant. 3 Boats left in charge of Lieut Maury to survey Bellingham Bay. Day ends light winds from S^d & E^d.

June 23rd
Commences light breezes from S^d & W^d and pleasant. Boats returned.

June 24th
Commences and ends with strong breezes from the S^d & W^d and pleasant.

June 25th
Commences with fresh flows of wind from the S^d & W^d with calms at intervals. At 8.45 got underway working up for Deception Passage. At 11 00 came to anchor on south side of passage. 11 30 shifted birth to opposite shore. Sent the Launch for water. Hauled the *Eagle* up for repairs. Received wood and water. Day ends pleasant breezes from SW.

June 26th
Commences pleasant. At 7 30 got underway and stood through Deception passage and came to anchor under Deception Island at 9.15 A.M.

June 27th
Commences with light breezes from S^d & E^d and cloudy. Boats surveying. At 2.20 P.M. got underway and stood to N^d. At 4.40 came to in Sunday Bay. Day ends light winds from S & E^d.

June 28th
Commences with light airs from the W^d. Scrubbed and washed clothes. *Dolphin* and *Eagle* surveying. got off a Launch load of water. At 5 PM got underway & stood to the N^d. Came to anchor in Strawberry Bay. Day ends with light breezes from the SW.

June 29th
Commences calm and cloudy. Sent 3 Boats on surveying duty. fired four guns for base.

June 30th
Commences calm and pleasant, received a load of water per Launch. Boats employed surveying. Day ends light winds from S.E. and pleasant.

July 1st
Light breezes from the S^d & E^d & pleasant. At 4.40 got underway and stood to Nd. Boats left for surveying. At 1.30 hove to off the south point of Birches Bay and fired for the Boats. At 1 P.M. came to anchor in Birch Bay. Sent wooding and watering parties on shore. Shifted our birth nearer in shore, hauled up the *Rover* and *Greyhound* received a launch load of water. Light airs from the SW.

July 2nd
Commences with pleasant weather and light winds from the S^d. Boats surveying. Launch employed watering. Day ends moderate breezes and pleasant.

July 3rd
Commences calm and clear weather. Launch wooding. Carpenters cutting spars. Boats surveying. Day was light winds from the S.E.

July 4th
Commences with light airs and pleasant, men on shore. Carpenters cutting spars. Day was light winds from the N° & W^d.

July 5th
Commences calm and pleasant. Launched the boats brought them alongside. At 8 30 A.M. hove up anchor and made sail to W^d. At 2.30 P.M. shortened sail and hove to off Pt Roberts. sent *Greyhound* to pr-filled away for Frazers river. At 2 15 anchored off the mouth of Frazers river. Fired 4 guns for base. Sent *Shark* to sound out anchorage. Fitted two Bouys for the bar of river. At 10 burnt blue light for *Rover* and fired gun to windward,

burnt a port fire at 11 20 the *Rover* came alongside. Day ends moderate breezes from S^w & E^d and pleasant.

July 6th

Commences with mod breezes from S^d & E^d and pleasant. 4 boats surveying the mouth of the river. planted the two buoys. Day ends moderate breezes and pleasant.

July 7th

Commences with fresh breezes from the S^d & E^d and pleasant. Sent the Boats into the river sounding. Sent the Launch to the buoys.

July 8th

Commences with moderate E^{ly} breezes. Sent Boats sounding the river. Day ends moderate breezes from the S^o & E^d.

July 9th

Commences with light airs and pleasant. At 9. A.M. got underway. Made all sail. Sent the boats to tow endeavouring to work toward point Roberts. fired a gun for the absent boats. At 5.30 came to with stream anchor. Wind light Eastl^y. At 11 00 P.M. got underway standing for Pt Roberts.

July 10th 1841

At 3 20 came to anchor. the *Rover* Mr. Sandford left with dispatches for *Vincennes*. Boats on Surveying duty.

July 11th

Commences with moderate breezes and cloudy with rain at intervals. At 9.15 A.M. got underway and beat round the bluff of point Roberts and came to at 10 20. At 1 P.M. got underway and stood over for Birch Bay. at 3.45 came to. Day ends light wind from S.E. and pleasant.

July 12th

Commences with fresh breezes from S^o & E^d & constantly rains. Boats surveying between Birch Bay & point Roberts. At 9.25 A.M. got underway and stood toward Point Roberts. 11 20 anchored with the Kedge. fired for base. Day ends moderate breezes from S.E. and pleasant.

July 13th

Commences with light breezes from the SE. and cloudy. Boats surveying. fired for base. Day ends light winds from S^d & E^d.

July 14th
Commences with fresh breezes and squally, afterwards moderate. Boats surveying. Day ends pleasant.

July 15th
Light breezes from N^d & E^d and pleasant. At 4 30 A.M. got underway and stood to the S^d & E^d working up for the land on Western shore of the Gulf. Boats surveying. At 4 P.M. came to. Day ends light winds from S^d & E^d.

July 16th
Commences with light breezes from the S^d & E^d. Boats surveying. Wind light from the S^d.

July 17th
Commences calm & pleasant. Boats surveying. Day ends light winds from E.N.E. and pleasant.

July 18th
Commences with light breezes from the S.S.W and pleas^t. At 8.45 A.M. got underway beating up for strawberry Bay. At 5 P.M. came to anchor. Day ends light winds from the S^d & E^d and clear.

July 19th
At 5 00 got underway. At 9 20 came to. Light winds from the S.E.

July 20th
Commences calm and pleasant — wooding and watering. At 2 P.M. the *Vincennes* Launch arrived alongside under charge of Pass^d Mid Sandford brought provisions &c. Day ends light winds from S.E.^{ly} and pleasant.

July 21st 1841
Commences calm and cloudy. At 8 30 got underway sent Boats to tow. At 9 00 a breeze sprung up from the S^d & E^d. Fired a gun shotted. At 2.45 P.M. came to under Blunt Island.[10] 3 Boats employed surveying. Day ends pleasant.

July 22nd
Commences with light breezes. At 4 A.M. fired a gun. At 6 40 got underway and commenced beating up for Duneiness. At 7 30 discovered a

---

[10] Smith Island.

sail in the narrows. fired a gun to attract her attention. At 9 30 discovered the *Vincennes* shortly after fired a gun. standing for her. Transferred the *Grey hound* & Launch with their crews to the *Vincennes*. Pass^d Mid Sandford and Mid Elliott left the Brig—

U.S. Ship *Vincennes* July 23rd

Commences with fresh puffs of wind from the S^d & W^d and clear. Sent the 1st Cutter with the Carpenters to bring off a piece of wood for the anchor stock. At 7 sent the boats surveying. At 1 the *Porpoise* got underway and commenced beating up. At 6 30 she came to anchor near to us. Day ends light breezes and pleasant.

July 24th

Commences with light breezes from the S.E. and clear. Hoisted up the starbd bower anchor into the Fore Castle. At 7 dispatched the Boats surveying. Compared [ ] with the *Porpoise*. Got the starbd anchor on the bows. At 7 Capt Wilkes returned on board. At 9 fired a gun which was continued every half hour. At 8.30 [sic] three boats returned from surveying. Day ends with moderate breezes and clear.

Sunday July 25th

Commences with fresh winds from the W^d and pleasant. The *Ariel*, *Pilot* and *Triton* returned to the ship. Made signal 4 15 preparatory and 4 30 to the Brig. At 3 the *Porpoise* got underway and stood out to the N^d & E^d. At 4 Capt Wilkes left the ship with seven Boats on a surveying Expedition. Day ends fresh breezes from the west^d and clear.

Monday July 26th

Light breezes from the W and cloudy. Sent the cutter to dredge and the *White handkerchief* on shore with the tide staff. Received intelligence of the *Peacock* being ashore on the bar of Columbia River. Fired two guns in quick succession as signal to Capt Wilkes and dispatched the 1st Cutter to communicate with him. Day ended squally and cloudy.

July 27th

Commences with fresh breezes from W.S.W and cloudy. Day ends moderate breezes from the W^d and thick foggy weather.

July 8th

Commences with light breezes from the S^d & W^d and cloudy. The gig and 1st Cutter from surveying. All boats returned from surveying. Day ends moderate breezes from the SW and pleasant.

July 29th

Commences with light breezes from the west^d & pleasant. Hoisted in the Launch and 1st Cutter. Sent 3 Boats surveying. Sent down the Top gall^t and Royal Yards and veered to 80 fms of the chain. Day ends strong westerly gales and pleasant.

July 30th

Commences with strong breezes from W.S.W. and cloudy. At 3.40 the Brig *Porpoise* hove in sight beating down. At 1 the *Porpoise* anchored on the larb^d quarter. Compared chronometers with the Brig. Day ends fresh breezes and pleasant.

H	K	F	Course	Winds	A	W	Remarks July 31st 1841
1							Commences with moderate westerly winds and
2							cloudy. Hove in to 30 fms chain. Sent aloft
3							Top gallant & royal yards. Made signals to
4							Brig. Got the swinging booms alongside, at
5							1 30 got underway and made all sail by the
6							Winds and stood across the Straits.
7							
8							
9							
10							
11							
12							Dungeness Beacon varying with extreme pt
1							E^n shore N 8 W with extreme pt W^n side
2							S 70 W with Indian pole 7.20 Black pt or
3							False Dungeness & Beacon ranging S 68 W.
4							Visit Indians pole 7.38
5							
6							
7							
8	6	4	NW½W	N^d&W^d			
9	2	6	S by E	"			
9	2	"	NWbyN½W	"			
10	5		WNW	"			
11	4	6	S½E	"			
11	2	4	S by W	"			
12	2	"	N by W¼W	"			

H	K	F	Course	Winds	A	W	Remarks August 1st 1841
1	4	4	NW	S^d&W^d	53	53	Commences with light breezes and pleasant.
2	3	6	S½E	"	53	53	*Porpoise* in company.
3	3	2	"		53	53	Standing down the Straits.
4	2	4	WNW		52	52	Made & reduced sail as occasion required.
5	2	2	"		52	52	fired 4 guns for base.
6	1		W by N		53	52	Day ends light breezes & pleasant.
7					53	52	
8				Calm	53	53	
9	1	4	West		53	53	
10	1	4	"		60	54	
11	1	"			61	54	
12		6	W½S	57	54		
1		6	West	Est^d	61	57	
2				Calm	61	56	
3					61	55	
4	1	6	NW		60	55	
5	3	"			60	55	
6	2		SSW		56	53	
7	3	2	NN½N		55	53	
8	3	4	NW½W		55	53	
8	2		SW		55	53	
9	2	2	South		55	54	
10	1		W½S		54	54	
11					55	53	
12				Calm	53	53	

H	K	F	Course	Winds	A	W	Remarks August 2nd 1841
1		4	W by N		53	53	Commences with airs & pleasant. At 8 Cape
2		2	W½N		52	53	Flattery bore south about 3 miles distant.
3	1		West		52	53	At 9 30 wore ship and stood in for Scarborough
4				Calm	52	53	Harbour. Made signal 90 to *Porpoise*. she sent
5				"	52	53	a boat on board of us. Several canoes came
6				"	54	54	Alongside. at 1 45 came to in Scarborough
7				"	57	54	Harbour in 10½ fms water and veered 45
8				"	57	54	fms on starboard chains. Sent the boats
9				"	59	54	Surveying. Inspected the crew at quarters.
10				"	59	55	Day ends light southerly winds and pleasant.
11	2		ESE		60	55	
12					60	55	
1					59	55	

					60	55	
2					60	55	
3					61	55	
4					61	55	
5					62	54	
6					59	54	
7					58	54	
8					57	54	
9					56	53	
10					56	55	
11					56	55	
12					52	50	

H	K	F	Course	Winds	A	W	Remarks August 3rd 1841
1							Commences calm and pleasant. Sent two
2							boats for water & a third to dredging. Canoes
3							of the tribes Chitichat & Classet around the
4							ship. Watering ship and surveying. At 2 got
5							underway under all sail by the wind &
6							commenced beating out of the Straits.
7							At 4 30 took the departure *Porpoise* to
8							Windward. Day ends light breezes and cloudy.
9							
10							
11							
12							

11

The Narrative of Joseph B. Clark

While not intimately involved with survey duties, Joseph Clark's shoreside observations are of great interest. Several years following the return of the Exploring Expedition, Clark, a seaman, published a book on "sailors life."

[p. 212] On the following day, April 29th, we squared away for Puget Sound, distant 120 miles north-east from Columbia River. We proceeded on our course with a fine breeze, but had thick weather until 11 o'clock, when we were suddenly arrested by the cry of "breakers on the lee bow!" It was reported to Capt. Wilkes, who lost no time in getting upon deck, at which time all the studding sails were taken in, and the ship hauled "close on a wind;" shortly after, we sounded, and found that we were in five fathoms of water. At this time we passed the points of rocks not more than a stone's throw distant. Had we continued our course for five minutes longer, we must have been dashed in pieces against the rocks, and as the result of such a circumstance, inevitable death must have been the consequence.

On the morning of the 30th, the weather was still foggy, so much so indeed, that we could not venture to run in for the land. We saw an abundance of geese and ducks flying in every direction. At 10 [p. 213] o'clock, the weather clearing up a little, we made sail and stood in for Puget Sound. At 4 o'clock we passed Cape Flattery and entered the Straits of Juan de Fuca. The shores are composed of low sandy cliffs, overhanging beaches of sand or stones; from them the land ascends gradually to the foot of the mountain, which rises abruptly to a great height within a few miles. The country here is thickly wooded, but affords but little variety in its growth, being principally cedar and spruce, some of which are very lofty.

During the evening several canoes passed near us with indians in them, who seemed very anxious that we should heave to for them; several attempted to catch hold of the ship, but were unsuccessful. Their dress consisted of a skin, thrown over the shoulders and fastened round the neck, leaving the lower extremities bare.

We continued to beat in this sound with a head wind until the 2d of May, when we were favored with a fine wind; we made sail and at 8 o'clock passed Protection Island, and in about an hour afterward, came to anchor in thirty fathoms of water in the harbor of Port Discovery. This is the only harbor immediately on the Straits of Juan de Fuca, and is situated near the south-east angle. It is safe for ships of any size, it runs southward from the straits into the land and is defended from the violence of the waves by Protection Island, which stretches partly across its entrance on the north. Vancouver says in his book, "when he was engaged in surveying these straits, that he never had occasion to anchor, but [p. 214] always hauled close in to the banks and made fast to a tree."[1]

Soon after coming to anchor we were visited by a canoe having in it two indians; one of them came up the gangway and asked, in broken English, if we were from Boston. This led us to believe that the first American vessel trading here, was from that place, as the indians seemed to know of no other place in the United States. They called all of us Bostonians, while they called the English King George.

On the morning of May 3d, at daylight, several boats were sent on surveying duty. The land everywhere in the neighborhood is moderately high, very broken and thickly covered with wood. The mountains in the interior are very high, and present quite a variety in their shape and appearance; the tops of some are seen above the clouds, which are covered with everlasting snow, and afford a striking contrast to the valleys near the sea, which are covered with verdure, and trees in full bloom.

We were at this time on our native continent, although more than three thousand miles from the place of our birth, yet I could not resist the sensations kindled by the remembrance of "dear home;" all the emotions incident to natural attachment and early prejudices played around my heart.

We had been literally surrounded with canoes all the morning; most of them were loaded with a variety of fish, venison and bears' meat, all of which they bartered at very moderate prices, in exchange for knives, fishhooks, old clothes and files, the principal articles for which they

---

[1]In my research of the journals of Vancouver and his men while in inland Washington waters, there is no reference to tying to a tree. The first such reference occurred in Canadian waters on the east side of Calvert Island.

seemed anxious. They particularly [p. 215] valued our files; for one we could purchase a salmon weighing upwards of forty pounds.

These natives are a meager, dirty race of savages; they have no fixed habitations, but, like a snail, carry their houses with them, and seldom stop more than two days in a place. They all have their heads flattened by compression in infancy, which disfigures them to such a degree that they look more like monsters than human beings. They have small eyes, flat noses and wear their hair long, both men and women.

Our stay at this place was not of long continuance. At dawn, May 6th, we made necessary preparations, and sailed, beating out of the harbor. After clearing the point which forms the harbor, we changed our course and ran down the coast to the eastward, a distance of about twelve miles from Protection Island, from which point we entered Admiralty Inlet, which penetrates the continent southward from the straits more than ninety miles, terminating near the forty-seventh degree of latitude, in a bay named by Vancouver, Puget Sound. Hood's canal is a branch of this inlet, nearly opposite which we came to anchor, the wind and tide being against us.

The country surrounding Admiralty Inlet is beautiful, fertile, and in every respect agreeable; and the bay, with its numerous arms stretching into the interior, must offer great advantages for commercial intercourse hereafter. The country here is extensively covered with trees of a gigantic growth, and from their appearance, I think some are well adapted to ship and house building. We anchored opposite a piece of table land about two miles in circumference, [p. 216] the most beautiful spot I ever beheld. It was perfectly level, as if made so by artificial workmanship, covered with green grass about two feet high, and variegated with different kinds of shrubbery, and fringed with a variety of vegetation. It affords a delightful prospect, especially in this high latitude, and would make a neat location for a village or city, and probably, at some future period, will become a flourishing settlement.

We got underway the next day, and commenced beating up the bay for Nasqually, and on the 11th of May, came to anchor off Nasqually, at the head of Puget Sound. Soon after coming to anchor, we were visited by Mr. Anderson, agent for the "Hudson's Bay Company," at this station. Capt. McNeal, commander of the company's steam boat *Beaver*; Mr. Wilson of the American Mission to the Oregon Territory, and Doct. Richmond, physician to the mission, comprised the whole number of residents here, except some of the half-breed race, and a few Canadians, servants of the "Hudson's Bay Company."

On the 17th, the expedition of boats under Lieut. Case, left the ship on a surveying cruise. Also an expedition to the interior of Oregon Territory was projected,—composed of the following gentlemen, viz. Lieut. Johnson, Doct. Pickering, Naturalist, Mr. Breckenridge, Horticulturist, Mr. Waldron, and T. A. Stearns, Q. M. G. The most satisfactory results were anticipated from these competent gentlemen, in every department of science. On the following day, Capt. Wilkes, accompanied by Mr. Drayton and purser Waldron, left the ship for the Columbia River.

[p. 217] At ten minutes past 8 o'clock, on the 31st, a meteor of immense magnitude and brilliancy shot across the heavens in a north-west direction, illuminating the heavens to such an extent that there was a resemblance to a sheet of fire, till it nearly reached the horizon, when it exploded, sending off myriads of corruscations in every direction. When it first commenced its flight, it was exceeding slow in its descent, but as it increased its distance towards the horizon, it increased its velocity considerably, until it burst. Many old seamen on board never witnessed a meteor half so large, nor one whose light remained so long visible. From the time it was first seen until it entirely disappeared, was *one hour and twenty-five minutes.*

On our arrival at this place we were expecting to join the *Peacock* and Schooner, but in this we were disappointed; they parted from us some time before, and were to be at the Columbia River two months previous to that time. Fears were entertained in reference to their safety. From the importance of this position it was decided to make critical surveys of the harbor and its vicinity. Accordingly, temporary houses were erected for that purpose, and other necessary arrangements made. The carpenter deposited a sealed bottle under the corner of one of the houses, containing a piece of paper with the following inscription: —

> Though far from our homes, yet still in our land
> True yankee enterprise will ever expand,
> And publish to all each side of the main,
> We triumphed once and can do it again.
> A problem, a problem, oh! hear great and small,
> The true owners of the country are still on the soil,
> [p. 218] While Jonathan and John Bull are growling together
> For land which by right belongs not to either.
> Let philosophers listen, and solve the question
> Which has troubled the statesmen of each nation,
> By what right the "Big Bull" claims sustenance here,
> While he has plenty of pasturage elsewhere.
> Lines written by R. P. R.[2]

---

[2]R. P. Robinson, the purser's steward.

Observatory of the U.S. Ship Vincennes, *Charles Wilkes, Esq., Commander in Chief of the U.S.S.S. and Exploring Expedition, by Amos Chick, of Portland, Maine, Carpenter of the U.S.S.* Vincennes, *June, 1841.*

Mr. Dyes, assistant to the scientific corps, deposited in the same bottle two pieces of American coin, — one a cent coined in 1817, and the other a dime coined in 1838. The paper was enclosed in parchment and well secured in the bottle.

On the 12th of June, Thomas Harden, officers' cook, and John McKean, ship's cook, having been three days lost in the woods, were found by a white and some indians who were sent in search of them. When found they were so exhausted as not to be able to walk to the ship; — horses were procured for them. They had eaten nothing since leaving the ship.

July 4th coming on Sunday, we celebrated the 5th, commencing in the morning with a national salute of twenty-six guns, which were fired at the observatory on shore. Capt. Wilkes gave a dinner and invited the officers to it. An ox was roasted whole for the crew, on a plain about one mile from the ship. At 9 o'clock, every man and officer was ordered on shore, except Mr. Vanderford, who was left in charge of the ship. On landing, the men proceeded up the hill to the observatory, [p. 219] where Capt. Wilkes was residing, there to await his orders. At 10 o'clock the procession was formed and marched in order, the starboard watch in advance, the marines in the center, and the larboard watch bringing up the rear. We proceeded through a narrow strip of wood about half a mile, when we came to the company's fort; there we halted and formed in front of it, and gave three cheers, which were returned by the people in the fort, and answered by us. The procession was again formed and marched as before, about one mile further, when we came to a deep valley, — crossing which we came to a plain several miles in circumference, in which Doct. Richmond's house is situated.

Here was the place intended for the exhibitions of the day; various kinds of amusements were proposed, in which Capt. Wilkes took an active part. Every thing went on well for a time, and bade fair for a day of recreation and pleasure, but soon an accident occurred, which could not but disturb the feelings of all. At 12 o'clock, when firing a salute, Daniel Whitehorn Jr., gunner, while loading one of the guns, it accidently discharged, and lacerated his forearm very seriously. All the integuments, from midway of the forearm to the wrist, were blown off — the carpal extremity of the ulna exposed for about two inches upon the outer face. All the tendons for about three inches from the carpus were much torn. The surgeon having thoroughly examined the wound, decided that it was his duty to recommend the removal of the limb. At the time the accident happened, the weather was quite warm, and tetanus was to be apprehended. All the large blood vessels were either carried [p. 220] away entirely, or much injured, and the consequences of an attempt to save the arm were much to be dreaded. Dr. Richmond, physician to the mission family, was called upon, who agreed in opinion with our surgeon, that amputation was the only means to insure life. The doctors then stated to the patient their views of the case, and recommended an operation. He declined for the present, and chose to risk an attempt to save the limb.

The amusements proceeded, but not with that spirit with which they were commenced; a deep melancholy seemed to mark the countenance of many. Whitehorn was much esteemed by all his shipmates.

Such events, the sailor is often called upon to witness. Perils and death often surround him. Disease may make a stealthy approach, when far away from the comforts and endearments of home, and the last throes of expiring nature are witnessed by tearful shipmates, and the departed is consigned to his deep, coral bed, unhonored by the respects of sympathizing survivors in the land of his nativity, and the last tokens of affection, by kindred hearts. A boom may strike, a yard break, and a struggling victim is hurled into the foaming waves, to sink beneath its restless waters, with no solacing word of comfort or hope, in the hour of conflict. By the frequent occurrence of such painful incidents, his sympathies are ever awakened, and his better nature constantly developed. He almost instinctively is taught to "Rejoice with those that rejoice, and weep with those that weep."

[p. 221] Situated about half a mile from the sound is a fort or trading post, belonging to the Hudson's Bay Company, composed of upright posts eight or ten feet high, secured with trunnels at top and bottom. At the corner, is a sentry-box or house, large enough to hold fifteen or twenty persons, perforated with holes large enough to admit the muzzle of a musket.

Within this stockade is a number of wooden houses, serving as dwellings, store-houses, magazines and workshops, and also one or two small buildings occupied by the laborers and servants. The nature of the country in this region of the Oregon Territory, will not admit of extensive cultivation, and seems to be best adapted to a pastoral life, especially in the immediate [p. 222] vicinity of the streams and mountains; irrigation must be resorted to, if a large population is to be supported in it. This country, which affords little prospect for the tiller of the soil, is, perhaps, one of the best in the world for grazing.

Every where, in this part of the country, the prairies open wide, covered with a low grass of a most nutritious kind, which remains good throughout the year. In September there are slight rains, at which time the grass commences a luxuriant growth, and in October and November, there is an abundance of green grass, which remains until the ensuing summer;

about June, it is ripe in the lower plains, and, drying without being wet, is like our hay in New England; in this state, it remains until the Autumn rains begin to revive it.

The Hudson's Bay Company has here about one thousand sheep, six or eight hundreds of cattle — all of which are in a thriving condition. Wolves are very numerous in this region of the Oregon Territory, and are very destructive to the sheep when they get among them, but the shepherd uses great caution in protecting the sheep from the ravages of these ferocious animals. Upwards of one hundred have been killed by them within the last three years. These animals when pressed with hunger, often attack horses, and I was told that seven were eaten by them in a single night, in this immediate neighborhood. Foxes, deer, and bears are common, but not so numerous as they are in Upper California.

On the evening of the 17th of July, having completed the survey of Puget Sound, and its multifarious arms and bays, and completed the series of observations, [p. 223] we got underway and left our anchorage off Nasqually, and commenced beating down the bay for Columbia River. A surveying party was sent over land to meet us at the mouth of the river, composed of the following persons. Passed Midshipman Eld, in charge of the party, passed Midshipman Colvocoressis, Mr. Breckenridge, Horticulturist, Simeon A. Stearns, Q. M. S., to assist in the surveys, with two marines and two seamen. At 9 o'clock on the same evening we came to anchor, the wind and tide being against us. On the following morning we got underway and proceeded on our voyage.

At 2 o'clock, P. M. of the 22d, we came to anchor of Point Dungeness, in 12 fathoms of water. Immediately on coming to anchor, three boats were got ready, and were sent on surveying duty for three days. Here we met with the Brig *Porpoise*. She had been engaged in surveying this part of the sound, and Hood's Canal, for two months.

Another accident happened at this time with powder. Samuel Williams, gunner's mate, was firing a four pounder, for the purpose of measuring a base line by sound; a spark had remained in the gun after its discharge, which communicated with the horn containing about four pounds of powder, while in the act of priming. A terrific explosion followed, but, as if by some miraculous interposition, no very serious injury was done. His hands and arms were burned, though not badly, as the cuticle only was destroyed.

At this anchorage our anchor was scarcely gone, before we were literally surrounded with canoes, bringing salmon, codfish, and venison to sell, which are taken here in great abundance.

[p. 224] On Point Dungeness, is one of the most remarkable settlements of indians seen any where on the sound. They have a stockade of considerable size, in which they retreat when driven to extremities in time of war. Such a retreat is rendered necessary from the frequency of their wars; and since the most of them have obtained guns and ammunition, they are very destructive to each belligerent party. Their prisoners taken in war, they do not murder as many savages do, but keep them as slaves, and make them perform all the more laborious work.

At each corner of this stockade is erected a bust of some of their most distinguished chiefs, roughly carved and constructed of wood; these are venerated and worshiped by the indians. In this place they also deposited their dead, the chiefs always having a separate place allotted to them. Their *Bouri*, or spirit house, is also here.

We remained at this anchorage for six days, during which time we were plentifully supplied with salmon, venison, &c., by the indians.

On the 28th of July, we got underway and proceeded down the Straits of Juan de Fuca, bound to Columbia River. On the 2nd of August we were off Cape Flattery. After beating with light and head winds for four days, we succeeded in reaching the outer extremity of the straits, opening into the North Pacific, and were nearly opposite Clausette Harbor, so named after a tribe of indians inhabiting this part of the coast. At 9 o'clock, a canoe came off to us, bringing fish, &c., for trade. In this party was a chief of some distinction, who stood erect in the canoe, no doubt to render himself more conspicuous. When he [p. 225] came alongside, Capt. Wilkes asked him if he wished to come on board, to which he replied in broken English in the affirmative; and accordingly he was permitted to come on board. Afterwards several others were permitted to come on board. One or two of them spoke a little English; the chief in particular, spoke many words quiet distinctly. The chief informed Capt. Wilkes that opposite to us there was a good harbor, and invited him to go in and anchor.

The stature of these people, like most on this coast, is much below the general standard. The height of an old man who came on board, and who was rather bent with age, was about four feet ten inches, and that of the others was about five feet. Their faces are flat and broad, but quite plump in the young individuals; their skin is smooth,—complexion not very dark, except in some who were smeared with charcoal; their teeth were very white, nose flat and broad, hair black, straight and glossy, and their hands and feet extremely diminutive. The adult females are quite as tall as the men, being from four feet eleven inches to five feet. The features of the children were regular, their complexion clear and by no means dark, their eyes small, and although the form of their faces is flat, their countenances might perhaps be considered pleasing, according to the ideas of beauty which habit has taught us to entertain.

12

The Journal of Purser R. P. Robinson

Thursday Ap 29th 1841

Stood on the starboard tack, standing for Cape Flattery. at the entrance to the straits of St Juan de Fuca, which lead to Peugets Sound, which we bore away for at 6 AM this morning — While the watch below about 10 AM were stowed away asleep, and no danger apprehended although the weather was foggy & misty a Qr master report to the officer of the deck that the water was discloured, as if we were in shoal water, it was immediately reported to the Captn who ordered a cast of the deep sea lead which resulted in finding ourselves in only 15 fathoms water — at the moment breakers ahead on the lee bow were reported and almost in a moment after they were reported, we were amongst them. All hands were called instantly & stud^n sails & Royals taken in & the ship hauled clear by the wind, the *Porpoise* signalized "Breakers under the Lee" while thus situated waiting with breathless interest, expecting every moment to feel her strike, and our ship diving bows completely under, a man aloft reported "Land on the lee bow and breakers." The Captain would not believe it at first, as his reckoning placed him some distance from the land. we were going at a tremendous rate through the water, and in less than a minute I saw it myself (from the weather gangway) about one point on the lee bow, it loomed very high in shape like a sugar loaf, and looked really dismal, through the mist & spray. the sea was breaking tremendously heavy against it and over some smaller ones just showing their heads out of the water alongsides of it we lay well up however & weathered it by about a third of a mile. as we passed abreast of it we [ ] through the center of it of considerable size and leeward was still highest layer Rock or Island as we weathered it looming through the mist we also passed clear of the breakers & left as we thought all danger astern but just as we were congratulating ourselves on our narrow escape, "breakers ahead & to leeward" once more brought all hands to their stations with but faint hopes of eventually saving the old bark. we got a cast of the lead in five & a half fathoms water. the breakers making a clean breach over our bows & almost drowned the armorers who were shackling the chains. as we were just passing out of this dangerous situation, a large rock was discovered about pistol shot from the ship to leeward, but it was passed almost as soon as discovered & we passed out of this labyrinth of danger triumphantly, and grateful for our miraculous deliverance. we now stood off again to get an offing.

Had this occurred at night instead of daylight, not a soul of our whole crew would have lived to reach the land — these Rocks are exactly half way between Columbia River & Cape Flattery, five miles from [ ] and all called by some Grenville Rock & others Queens Isle Rocks — after weathering the rocks the main land was plainly visible to leeward but dimly seen.

Friday Ap 30th 1841

Steering to the Nor^d with light winds. Land in sight, passed a rock, shaped like a sail. land in sight on the starboard beam & bow. with small Islands every few miles along the coast — the hills appeared covered with stupendous Pine trees & rich vegetation. at 4 PM called "all hands work ship" & entered the Straits of Juan de Fuca which leads to Peugets Sound, passed a number of large rocks & Islands which were (some of them) covered with seal. Rainy, misty & disagreeable weather — as we entered the straits (which are [ ] miles wide) a canoe just off to us containing Indians but we could not heave to for them, another canoe afterwards attempted to board us but failed — the view of the Land is much obscured by the rain & fog. Towards night it commenced raining heavily & blowing in squalls — all hands kept on deck the best part of the first watch — wind blowing [ ] right in our teeth — at 2 Bells mid watch in tacking ship nearly ran the *Porpoise* aboard — squally all night

Saturday May 1st 1841

Weather as bad as ever, rainy, foggy & squally — a canoe with five Indians came alongside at 10 AM one could talk broken English — at noon fell calm & every few minutes would clear up & cloud over again. when the sun shone we had a fine view of the shore. the Pine covering every rock & hill, to the summits, which were shrouded in fleecy clouds & mist — lowered seven boats at 2 PM & sent six ahead to tow the Ship, a bay on our starb^d hand — after towing Ship about half an hour, a slight breeze sprang up, which did not last, however, more than half an hour. It would clear up sometimes & the sun come out beautifully. When whilst congratulating ourselves on the change of temperature, it suddenly became overcast & formed a deluge of rain & so it was all day.

Sunday May 2^d 1841

Last night cold & dry, wind ahead & fell calm towards morning. during fore part of day, light, head winds. afterwards fell calm & a strong current against us. about noon a stiff breze sprang up in our favor & we made all sail to it — the men did not make sail to please the Com^d & he ordered them to set all Stud^n Sails ten times, until they should set them smartly — in setting the Starb^d Lower Mainsail they tore it nearly in half & then they knocked off. comment is unnecessary. The Land to day appears the same as usual, with the exception of the summits & sides of the mountains & hills, being covered with snow, which fell during the past night — we continued our way through the most intricate passages imaginable, with bold water close in shore the whole distance except once we found only 3½ fathoms water. we had a bright moon after night & ran along finely & at 8 PM rounded a beautiful Island called Protection Island & ran into a beautiful basin or bay, completely land locked & protected from the sea by the above Island (which is very properly named. we came to, about ½ past 8 in 34 fathoms water 49 years precisely from the date of Vancouvers arrival at the same place.

Monday May 3^d 1841

Clear & cold. The bay in which we are is called Port Discovery, & is a clear basin of water, capable of holding the largest fleet in the world & thickly wooded in every direction with Pine Spruce & Cedar. upwards of twenty different canoes visited during the day & furnished us with a fine supply of Salmon, Clam, Codfish & Herring — they appear to be a most miserable race, filthy in the extreme, long hair & wrapped in filthy blankets & skins. Some of the large canoes contained a whole family perhaps fifteen or twenty, with their whole stock of moveables with them — they appear cunning & treacherous like all savage nations and cannot be trusted — Fort Nesqually is situated about 100 miles from this place & the Steam Boat belonging to the Hudson Bay Company under the command of Capt McNeil is also there. We hired an Indian Chief to carry a letter to the above person & requesting him to forward up a Pilot to there place. an answer is expected tomorrow or day after. our boats were away surveying the harbor all afternoon. the carpenters crew have been engaged all day selecting timber for spars & cutting a mast for the Launch.

Tuesday May 4th 1841

Raining & disagreeable, carpenters ashore cutting spars. the first Cutter watering & the boats surveying — numerous canoes alongside with fish

& clams to trade — the Indians have assembled & raised quite a village abreast of the ship, their huts are merely from cross pieces at a few feet distant. & hard rain again the weather side, to keep the rain & wind off

Wednesday May 5th 1841
A fine day. hove up anchor and beat out of the bay. an Indian Chief of the Nesqually tribe having offered to pilot us to that place — the scenery was the same as usual. the land wooded down to the waters edge & the snow clad summits of the mountains, peeping out through the clouds — at 3 PM came to anchor again in a fine harbor for the night.[1] abreast of our anchorage was a piece of land containing perhaps twenty acres without a tree & covered with vegetation. while just to the left was a fine piece of meadow land. there is an Indian village of some fifteen or twenty huts on the opposite side of the bay & a small river makes in near by — the days are very long here & are increasing in length.

Thursday, May 6th 1841
Called away "all boats" at daylight & surveyed the harbor. at 1 PM hove up & made sail, several canoes keeping way with us — venison is brought off by some of the canoes but very badly butchered & very dirty — at 4 PM came to anchor again in a fine large bay,[2] the wind having headed us off — Fort Nesqually is like Peter [ ] who was always [ ] the road to Boston. We are continually enjoying the road to Nesqually & when we shall make the fort, for we think of course, that the sooner we arrive there and commence operations, the sooner we shall arrive home. The weather very cool & rainy.

Saturday May 8th / 41
At daylight blowing nearly a gale. sent off six boats to survey the harbor. they all returned about nine A.M. except the *Rover*. Mr Colvo which was several miles to seeward was forced to bear up for a harbor until the wind should lull and after a very fatiguing pull they arrived on board at 1 PM nearly done out — although still blowing very hard we hove up anchor in company with *Porpoise*, and made sail to beat to windward. we reefed Topsails & set Top Gall^t Sails over them — the Ship worked very well & did not miss [ ] once, but she careened so much that the lee guns were muzzles under. we at length ran close under the land on the starb^d hand & came to anchor in 15 fathoms water.[3] Just as we came to, a large canoe came along-

---

[1] Port Townsend.
[2] Oak Bay.
[3] Pilots Cove.

side with our messenger to Nesqually & two whites one of which was our pilot Mr Heath the mate of the Steamboat at the Fort — we learn from him that the *Peacock* & [ ] are in the Columbia River — that we are forty five miles from the Fort

Sunday May 9th / 41

Blowing fresh in forepart of the day. at 5 bells in afternoon watch after surveying our anchorage we hove up & made sail. wind ahead as usual — we beat up well today & made 15 miles. at 6 PM came to in 10 fathoms water under another point of Land[4] for the night. on our larb^d hand is the summit of a very lofty mountain overreaching the clouds & looking on us with a rather chilly conntenance. it is completely covered with snow. a single solitary canoe came off to us — the same scenery as usual along the shore thick impenetrable forests & bold shores. *Porpoise* in company.

Monday May 10th / 41

Commenced with a dead calm. sent boats away surveying & a party ashore on an excursion — at noon although the boats are away hove up our bower & dropped a kedge in lieu of it & made sail to be ready against the return of the boats but drifted ashore before we could get another kedge out by mistake, the starb^d anchor was again let go just as we had succeeded in clearing the shore & we had to heave that up again & so were humbugging for near two hours. before we got clear of the shore one of the shore party shot a very large bald headed eagle & red squirrel, Blue Jay, Raven & several other animals & birds — we made sail with a fair wind & entered a narrow inlet about half a mile wide, with beautiful scenery all around. at ½ past 7 PM anchored[5] at the mouth of the Inlet which leads to the settlement.

Tuesday May 11th 1841

Light winds & ahead — sent boats away surveying at ½ past 3 PM hove up & made sail with the tide in our favor. we had a little difficulty in beating up the Inlet in account of the water being bold, however, we lay up well & at 8 PM came to anchor in 35 fathoms water. The Company's Steam Boat lies at anchor on the shore of us. it appears to be a fine vessel. abreast of our anchorage is a cleared bluff about 100 feet high, with a road cut up it. as yet I can perceive no town, village or settlement. as we came to anchor Capt McNeill & a Rev^d Mr Wilson came aboard. Mr Wilson is a missionary from Boston

---

[4]Port Madison.
[5]South of Gig Harbor.

12. The Journal of Purser R. P. Robinson

Wednesday 12th / 41
 Unbending sails & mooring ship — weather mild

Thursday 13th / 41
 Went gunning, had a very fatigueing walk to a small river, which runs very swift & very deep & on the opposite side of which is a large flat covered with Geese & Duck. I shot two & in returning got into the muddy bottom of a small stream & had difficulty in getting out. Got two Squaws to show me the road to Nesqually Got stuck through the woods in a direct line & after a fatiguing walk arrived at the fort. it is a stockade enclosure, with look outs at each corner & reasonably defended against the Indians should they attack it. the land is excellently cultivated & is well stocked with cattle & horses. we had some good fresh Beef killed yesterday. I saw several half breed children, beautiful & rosy as any I ever saw.

Friday 14 / 41
 Busy fitting out *Porpoise* & all our boats for surveying duty.

Saturday May 15th / 41
 Erecting an observatory on Shore. the *Porpoise* sailed taking two of our boats crews with her weather rather cold & disagreeable. at 7 PM an Indian arrived from Columbia River. he reported the [ ] & an English vessel there, besides one man of war. which one he could not say.

Sunday 16 / 41
 Had muster, & then hauled the Launch alongside & commenced rigging & fitting her out for surveying. taking in Provisions & also fitting out a party to explore the interior under Lt Johnson.

Monday 17th / 41
 Boats busy fitting out & the land expedition also. at ½ past 2 PM the Launch 1st Cutter, *Ariel* & *Pilot* shoved off with colors flying & looking remarkably well. just as they got clear of the ship the square topsail was set on the Launch & carried away almost instantly the Topmast. at 4 PM the land party consisting of Lieut Johnson, Mr Pickering, Breckenridge & [ ] Stearns—[ ] left the ship.

Tuesday 18th / 41
 Erecting an observatory on shore etc, building house etc.

Wednesday 19th 1841
 Capt Wilkes, Messrs Drayton & Waldron with 3 cabin Boys started for Columbia River. blew fresh & rained slightly during the day.

Thursday 20th 1841

Cold, rainy & disagreeable. went gunning in Company with the [ ]. had a disagreeable tramp over the Flats. had no great luck

The Hudson's Bay Co Schooner *Cadborough* Capt [ ] Scarborough arrived May 22nd from Columbia River & sailed again for the Nor^d taking Mr Newell (an American from Boston) 2^d mate & an extra crew from the Steamer *Beaver*— and now for a little sketch of the natives, country &c — the natives in the 1st place are treated like slaves by the Companys Agents & tyranised over so much as to cause me to expect them to retaliate woefully on some proper opportunity. They universally dislike King George's people, as they call the English, and like the Boston men as they call all Americans in proportion as they dislike the English. the word Boston ship operates as a [ ] on them & draws them from all quarters to trade. The principal features in the character of these people are their treachery and cunning which they pride themselves upon. They are filthy in the extreme, and universally wear their hair long which of course [ ] more filth. They are good hunters but not as good marksmen as our Indians. They use the [ ] or common musket & have not yet a single cut rifle amongst them

I visited a salmon Fishery on Squally River about 15 miles from here in Company with Mr Newell, the other day. we descended a bluff covered with Pine about 200 feet deep & almost immediately came to the river which ran very swift. it is about 30 yards wide & close to the banks were several huts just erected & a basket work dam just finished. The stakes for the dam were about 3 inches apart & there was a double line of them about four feet apart & cross pieces to support them both & on which the Indians stand & spear the Salmon as they leap the barrier. between the two rows of stakes are nets spread to catch those who fall between the two lines in the fishing season.

They catch a great quantity of Salmon which they dispose of to the Company Agents who sell & send them to Fort Vancouver — Land otter, Beaver, Mink, Wild Cat, Wolf, Raccoon & Deer skins appear plenty. Clothes are the greatest trade for anything.

There is a Scotch Sheppard living here by the name of McLean who has charge of about 1000 sheep belonging to the Company. Horned cattle are in great abundance & the Company supplies the Russians to the Nor^d by contract with considerable Butter, Wheat etc yearly, which they raise on their farms. I am astonished that our country should let them get such a secure footing as they have already got on the land.

What is a rather singular circumstance is that every short distance there are different tribes & every tribe speaks a different language. They are at war with each other very often & to the Nor^d they are inveterate cannibals. The farther you go North, apparently the more savage the natives become. but they universally (if they have been committing some rascality) dread the name of Boston Ships ever since the *Lydya* Brig, several other vessels from Boston at different times punished their villany by sacrificing great numbers of them for attempting to take the vessels by surprise — the Squally tribe are no ways deficient in treachery & the will to act as their neighbors to the Nor^d do on every occasion viz cutting off vessels & massacuring all hands, but they are well convinced of the white mans prowess & are fearful (as they may well be) of [ ] themselves — They have the common traits of all Indians although getting from us ten pieces to what they would get from the HB Co yet they want more still & are never satisfied.

June 11th
  Jno McKeen Ships Cook & L Harden Officers Cook went on shore on liberty & having procured guns & a few charges of Power & Shot strayed away into the woods & were lost, no traces of them were found until sending out a young Chief Patty Wa Wa & his father. on the 13th in the evening they were brought back nearly worn out.

June 13th
  Kellim [ ] at daylight arrived from Lt Case's Party with a request for a further supply of Bread & they were laying at Hoods Canal about 190 miles distant by water, but only 15 or 20 in a direct line, so close in fact as to enable them to hear our daylight & 9 oclock PM Gun — an isthmus two miles wide separates them from this sound, across which Kellim travelled & then took a canoe for the ship.
  Gambling appears to be a fashionable business amongst these people. I have seen them gamble away every thing belonging to them, even to their slaves, wives & children & go away without even a skin to cover them — their games are not easily understood & are still were difficult to describe on paper — slaves, male & female are an article of commerce among them & are procured in their wars from the adverse tribes — every now & then we come across a native who has been converted by the French Catholic missionaries sent out here, & whose first movement to attract your attention is to cross themselves and show that he is a Christian.

Monday June 21st
  No news from the Com^r & his party. the weather for some time past has been very cool wet & disagreeable for this season, raining almost continually. The tides here rise & fall the enormous height of 18 to 19 feet — at sundown one surveying squadron of four boats hove in sight & came alongside shortly, being out of Provisions all well, they have made a thor-

ough survey of the part they were ordered to, & met with no material difficulty — all well, we fitted them out again & started them.

June 22^d
    at 10 AM we [ ] their orders from the Com^r.

Wednesday June 23rd
    At noon precisely Capt Wilkes arrived from Columbia River six days since — the *Peacock* & Schooner have not yet arrived and by a letter I rec^d from Mr Waldron he advising me that he shall stay there until the arrival there of this Ship about the 15th of next month — what can be the reason of the delay of the *Peacock* I cannot conceive but am much afraid that some disaster has occurred. the skipper has kicked up a terrible breeze all around the board keeping every body on the [ ] and making every body uncomfortable as he always does

Friday July 2^d 1841
    Lieut Case returned to the ship in one of the six oared boats having been ordered to leave the surveying squadron & return to a place in Hoods Canal where he has lost part of the Theodolite. he had made the attempt to recover it (it having been taken by some of the Tribes there) by seizing two [ ] from the Chief, but still could not recover it & while they were delaying, the Indians to the number of several hundred assembled, well armed with fire arms & knives two feet long & placed the boat in an alarming situation. they were forced to return the muskets & come to the Ship without recovering the article they were in search of.

Saturday July 3^d
    The Boats returned from surveying, by order of the Capt to spend the 4th July. We are to have a bullock roasted whole & the whole crew are to have a run ashore — we shall of course keep it on Monday

Sunday July 4th
    A beautiful day. a party of men went ashore in afternoon to kill & prepare the Bullock & commence operations.

Monday, July 5th / 41
    at sunrise a salute of twenty six guns was fired from shore by the Gunner and at 9 AM every man & officer except Mr Vanderford left the Ship & assembled at the observatory & from thence marched out to the ground (about one mile) Stab^d watch ahead, Marines in center & Larb^d watch behind. Drums beating & colors flying, as they passed the Fort they

cheered which was returned — they arrived on the ground & planted five stands of colors & commenced enjoying themselves in every possible manner. some riding like wild men to and fro over the plain which is six miles long, others playing corner ball, others football & the liveliest set to work dancing like mad, having a good fiddler & a portable door to foot it on —

The morning passed very well, but at Meridian we fired another salute of 26 guns & ten rounds from the Marines & I am sorry to say that Dan[l] Whitehorn, Sr Gunner, had his left hand nearly blown off, by a cartridge exploding as he was ramming it home, occasioned by the chamber not being properly [ ], and part of the former cartridge (which was of paper) being on fire. The Surgeon and Dr Richmond a missionary Doctor expressed their opinion that he would be compelled to lose his arm, but still entertain hopes of saving it — he stood the pain remarkably well & only expressed sorrow at the prospect of losing his hand —

The main brace was spliced & all hands had an extra allowance of old Rye, and the Bullock eaten with great relish by all hands, & considering that it was roasted by [Luck] it was done well. I made a hearty meal off of it.

Tuesday 6th
    Dr McLaughlin, Governor of Fort Vancouver etc arrived from the River. the *Peacock* had not arrived. Four boats under command of Lt Case started on surveying duty, up the Sound.

Friday 9th
    Capt Wilkes with the Gig, 1st Cutter & [ ] left the Ship on a surveying Expedition.

Sunday 11th
    Weather cold, wet disagreeable —

Thursday 15th
    Lt Johnson & party returned, after having traveled upwards of 120 miles. they experienced many hardships in crossing Mt Rainier and the range in the immediate vicinity of it & visited Fort Vancouver, Fort Colville & several other stations of the HB Co. they report favorably of the land in its general features, as susceptible of high cultivation in some parts, but in others, it is boggy [ ] or else a dry arid plain covered with pebbly & small stones. they crossed the upper branch of the Columbia several times — at one time they were very near starvation & they killed a number of horses by fatigue & hard riding & when those they rode gave out they would exchange the broken down horses for good fresh ones, giving 2 or 3

Blankets to boot between the two—The party themselves made several narrow escapes from breaking their necks down the numerous precipices & Lt J actually fell & rolled, horse & self over & over down a precipice 150 feet without injury—the different tribes were found friendly disposed and at several American Missionaries farming on settlements, they were treated remarkably well. Mount Rainier was measured from the plain below by Capt W & Lt Case & found to be 12434 feet above the level of the plain, which plain is about 300 feet above the level of the sea

Sunday July 18th

unmoored Ship yesterday & got ready for sea today. I visited Mr Newell & Mr Cailess of the Steamer this afternoon & while setting very easily in the cabin was roused by the Signal gun & going on deck, saw the [ ] flying at the fore, a signal for all Officers & boats to return on board. I bade them all good by & came on board, fired several guns for our boats, which were away with the crews washing their clothes, not having had an opportunity while absent in the boats surveying. they all joined when we made sail & hove up, & came about 15 miles, when we came to for the night in 34 fathoms water.[6]

Tuesday 20th

At 8 AM hove up & made sail, wind ahead still breeze light but freshened in latter part to a 6 knot breeze but still head. looked squally at sunset. several canoes around us today, one of which had a [puffing] jig in it, being the first I have seen on this coast—this sound is dotted with large Islands, covered with vegetation & lofty trees & such as Vancouver has not named, we have. we passed to day a large Island called Bainbridge Island on which was a large low house built of logs, by the Indians to dry Salmon in.

Wednesday 21st

Kept underway until 3 AM this morning when we came to on [ ] of the wind falling calm—at 8 AM hove up & made sail again, wind light—in afternoon towed ship for an hour or more—and at 9 PM finding the current drifting us off shore, we let go an anchor in 5 fathoms water & then ran out a kedge & hauled her into deeper water. she then dragged her anchor for ½ mile & we payed out 90 fathoms chain before she brought up—

---

[6]Wilkes indicated they "anchored under Vashon's Island for the night."

12. The Journal of Purser R. P. Robinson

Thursday 22^d

At 5 AM hove up & made sail, wind favoring us. a sail reported, supposed to be Schooner *Cadborough*. at 8 AM the *Porpoise* hove in sight to leeward. we ran down the land towards Protection Island & Port Discovery with a fair wind & tide, and came to anchor 1 PM to the Nor^d of Protection Island, & to the Southw^d of a long low point of land. The *Porpoise* & our Launch came to about the same time — after dinner every boat in the Ship was sent away on surveying or other duty while the *Porpoise* made sail & took her station to leeward to measure base by sound. blew in squalls towards night & weather looked threatening.

Friday 23^d July

A warm day. All boats away surveying & the carpenters away cutting an anchor stock for the starb or best Bower, which broke two days since in heaving up — *Porpoise* 15 miles off measuring base. anchored close to, at dusk

Saturday 24th

Boats absent surveying etc. returned at midnight.

Sunday 25th

A fine day. *Porpoise* sailed for Port Townsend on surveying duty. sent all boats away surveying for 4 days. Capt Wilkes accompanied. blew heavy during early part of the night in squalls—

Monday 26th

At 1 PM a canoe arrived from Nisqually with dispatches for Capt Wilkes & Lt Carr, from [RRW] & Capt Hudson, by which we heard the disastrous news of the loss of the *Peacock* on the Bar at the mouth of the Columbia River yesterday week. her masts were cut away, but I understand she went to pieces in two days. officers & crew all got safe ashore saving almost all their [ ], all Papers, Charts, letters & were saved, nothing further is known, but we have sent our 1st Cutter with the dispatches to the Com^d. expect to see him tonight or in the morning as he is only 31 miles distant

Wednesday 28th 1841

Capt W & the boat Expedition arrived in a heavy blow. Got ready for sea.

Friday 30th

Porpoise arrived. took a small supply of Bread from her & secured boats etc for sea.

Saturday 31st
 at 1 PM hove up & made sail. *Porpoise* in company. wind light. Lt W started for Nisqually in a canoe bound to Columbia River. wind freshened in after part of afternoon. wind dead ahead.

Sunday Aug 1st
 light winds ahead, beating out of the straits.

Monday 2nd August 1841
 Very little wind & ahead, nearly out of the straits. several canoes came alongside from Classet on the main land, the chief of that tribe came off to us. he spoke broken English & [ ] to anchor. No Natives of Vancouvers Island have come off to us. at 3 PM we ran into Classet Harbor & came to anchor in 11 fathoms. This is only an open roadstead but affords good anchorage in case of a gale, there being excellent holding ground, on the Starb^d hand is a ledge of rocks, & on the lab^d a small Island with a small passage between it & the main land & a singular shaped rock seen between them in the distance. The head chief of this tribe came alongside & on being refused permission to stay on board as long as he pleased, he said that the land was his & if he could not come on board, we should go away ourselves for we had no right here at all. his arguments had no effect at all & he left us very sulky. in the afternoon sent boats away & surveyed the harbor. a number of canoes alongside trading. This tribe is one of the strongest this part of the coast & can muster a large number of fighting men. they are very fierce & warlike & are dreaded by their neighbors. they paint themselves with black & red paint in every shape & have pieces of shell strung through the nose. they wear hats like an [inverted] fishnet, without the tube. their canoes are large & well made & capable of carrying thirty persons—

Tuesday 3rd Aug 1841
 Sent boats away to water ship. An immense concourse of canoes came alongside with fish venison etc. took on board 2000 gallons water. at 1 PM hove up & made sail wind ahead. *Porpoise* arrived last night from Vancouvers Island. a harbor in which she had been ordered to visit. beating out all afternoon.

Wednesday Aug 4th / 41
 almost calm, & foggy. parted company with the *Porpoise* in early part of last night, fired several guns & could hear hers in return. a school of Fin Back Whales close aboard.

13

Private Notes of J. W. W. Dyes

John Dyes was an assistant taxidermist. The Journal is very difficult to read. Sentences tend to "run on" with no punctuation indicating the end of one or a capital letter beginning the next. I transcribed it without modification except to add periods to separate the run-on sentences. Pages are not numbered. Spelling is phonetic. Paragraphs are not indented, entries by date are not always separated. Dyes was not a part of any surveys in that he stayed on board at Nisqually the entire time. I include the text of some random days simply to provide a sense of his literary style as well as a bit more information on the "lot" of a crew member.

May 1st 1841

All this day standing up the sound with Light Wind — scasley[1] to stem the current. at 10.30 a canoe caim along side with Natives, tow caim on Bord — one had on a long Sutute[2] coat — maid up of Scarlet blouth with [ ] Button on it. he spoke a few Words of English & told us that a Ship had Been Here. [ ] at the Head of the Sound there was a Steam Boat. the wind continued Light throw out the day. at one time were compled to get the Boats a head & tow the ship, the Gigg was sent at the same time with Mr totten to survey & sound a Round a promanny a head. while absent two [guns] were fire to measure Base by [sound]. the Gigg soon Returnd. finding no [ ] at a Boats [ ] with in 40 fathoms line. Every part of the Land is thickly Wooded with trees of an amense size as thick as they can grow. from their Emense size [ ] appear to never have the sound of the Woodmans axe.

---

[1]Scarcely
[2]Suit

May 2ᵈ 1841

all this fornoon [ ] up the Strates of Juan de fuca. at 12 the Wind Became fair & we maid all sail. a canooe in the fornoon Borded us & one of the Nativs caim on Bord. he was Entirely Naked — except a Blanket around his shoulders — one of the Captains Regulations is that no more work shall be done on Sunday than is actually — but instead of that Rule being observed to day [ ] sails because that did not Happen to set the [ ] sails to suit Him & then set them to trimming Ship Because [ ]³

May 11

got under way after [ ] & with a fair Wind. made sail for the Settlement. at [ ] place we caim to Anchor at 830 pm. Brig in company near us. [ ] stream [ ]. this day the Captain got into one of tantomes about tobacco spittle upon the Deck & took away some of the mans tobacco from them as well as stopped some of their grog

May 15

this Day the Brig *Porpus* with tow Boats & their crew on Bord. up Anchor & left for the North to [ ] — this is a Wild and interesting country. this Sound is one of the nearest majestic sheets of Water I Ever saw in all my life. the forest trees of the largest size grow to the very Waters Edge. Where you may cut a mast a solid stick for a [ ] of Battle Ship — I never saw such large forest trees in any part of the World Befor. they it principally Pint⁴ tho there is considerable oak maple & [ ]

May 17 1841

this Day the Launch the first Cutter & two whale boats left the Ship in charge of Lt Case sailing master totten Pasd mid shipman May & Colvolocesses on a surveying party — in the afternoon with the his party — left the ship for an Exploring Voyage to the Rocky Mountains

June 1st

this day two Indians caim with a Letter from the Brig *Porpus* —

June 3rd

this Day it blew a gail of Wind — from the South with Rain Barometer down to R8 — during the Day Dr Richmond Mr Wilson Captain McNeal with their Ladies & children paid a Visit to the Ship — and [ ] took of Refreshments — the written Navy code of Shilley — no natives vidited the Ship to day —

---

³A better description of these events may be found in Robinson's journal.
⁴Pine.

13. Private Notes of J. W. W. Dyes

June 11
 this morning John Mc Kein & Thomas Harding went on shore —

June 21 1841
 this Evening the Launch & first cutter & two whale Boats Returned from their surveying Excurtion Having partly completed — as wanted a fresh suply of stores. there were some exchange in the men man the Kanakos were all kept on Bord [ ] good for nothing Some sick (Deserted) Remain on Bod

June 22
 at 1030 the Launch first cutter & two whale boats left restored & with the saim officers, mr Case totten may & Colvocoresses—

June 23rd 1841
 this Day Captain Wilkes Returned Leaving Mr Waldron & Drayton Behind, he left ponte Gerge on the 17 [ ]

June 24
 this day Captain Wilkes took up his Residence at the observatory. two new log Cabins Built during his absense. at 430 he caim on Bord & all Hands were called to witness punishment of Owne Roberts (six cat of nine tales) for Refusing to do double duty by the orders of Mr Carr.

July 5
 this day at sunrise a sallute of 26 guns were fird in Honor of the Day — the Crew were all drest and went on shore to Enjoy them selves. fresh Bread were Baked at our oven Erected on shore for that purpas— they had previously been provided with foot and hard Balls for the occasion then grogg — was carried out to them. the marines were in uniforme and under arms— as soon as they had all got out there having all marched out two & two— then Capt Wilkes & officers joined in the Play at a [game] of soft & foot Ball. two small Brass cannon Had Been Carried out to fire a Salluet and at 12 oclock a salute of 26 [ ] were fired — during which in charging one of the cannon, the cartrages were paper one of them exploded — blowing to [ ] the Left Hand & part of the Rist of Daniel Whitehorn [master] gunner who was in the [ ] of Raming Home the Cartrage the man who had his thumb over the Vent taking it off when the [ ] and the gun went off. the marines fired several Rounds By Stations. the Indians appeared to be very much astonished — at the Various Sports of the men, and perticular at their Dancing to the music & the fiddle. this was something new & [ ] their conception how it was possible for the Little Box

as they called the fiddle to make so manney strange sounds—and the different attitudes that the men put them selves in they thought they were possest with a Devil & that he must Be in the Little Box & they actually Examined it to see, But when they found it was Hollow, they were still more surprise & said he was invissable to Indians, at 3 Capt Wilkes & officer & the gentlemen who were out there Returned to partake of a [ ] intertainment—prepared by Him for the occasion. When they all set down at 4 PM & did not leave until 1—AM the governer of the Hudson Bay Company arrived [ ]

July 9—
    this morning Capt Wilkes things were Brought on Bord & the first Cutter Gigg & one of the whale Boats were got Redy for to go surveying and at 3,30 PM the party started. Capt Wilkes in the Gigg with Mr Anderson the first cutter with Pass Midshipman Eld in the *White* [*handkerchief*] with Lt Budd—with [ ] Chief from this place this party was fitted out for a week. at 450 all the Sails Were Bent, the greater part of the instruments were Brought off & stowed away—Whitehorn in greate misery with his shattered Arme, tho the Doctor Reports as yet faivorable of it.

July 16
    this day the launch & gigg & two of the Whale Boats Returnd from Surveying. the Launch was got Redy to take provisions for the *Porpus* at frazers River. at 5 PM the English N West Companys Schooner *Cadburough* Capt Scasborough arived—

July 18 (Sunday) 1841
    this morning five Boats with their crewes who had Been surveying were sent in charge of the gunner to wash & scrub their close about 3 miles Below the ship. at 10 the gigg with Mr totten were sent to the larg flates at the upper end of this Anchora to finish some undone surveying—at 1230 the [ ] wer Hoisted and a gun [ ] tha Returned at Dusk without having doon much. the canooe from Squally was sent to the Brig with a Letter. the Wind increasing. Sent down the Royal & topgalen yards & give the ship moor chain. It Blew hard during the Night—

August 1st (Sunday)
    all this day working over the Strates. fired 8 guns during the day to measure base By sound with the *Porpus* she one side of the Strates & We the other side. made But little progress

August 2, 1841

this Day light Breezes. Beating drifting down the Strates. at 10 we were abrest of Cape Flattery — stood Back about 2 miles & Anchored in Classet Harbour. the Brig Anchoring on the opposite side on Vancouvers [ ] — at 1 PM caim to Anchor in 16 fathoms Water. as soon as the Anchor was down 7 Boats were dispatch to sound & survey the Harbour. We Were soon surrounded By a great many very Large canoes containing from ten to twelve Natives— of the maust Warlike that I seen around this part of the World. the Boats Returned at Sundown. the Brig caim over & anchored in company and at 12 AM this morning there was a total Eclips of the moon

14

The Journal of Charles Erskine

Charles Erskine was an ordinary seaman aboard *Vincennes*. He published his recollections in 1890 (Morning Star Press, Boston) and reprinted the volume in 1896. The original was photocopied and reprinted in 1985 by the Smithsonian Institution Press.

[p. 230] Early in the morning of the 28th [April 1841] we heard the cheerful cry of "Land-ho!" It proved to be Cape Disappointment, Columbia River, our own native land. At about nine o-clock we entered a strong tide-rip and soon after came within sight of the Columbia River. It was blowing pretty fresh, with a considerable sea on, and heavy breakers extended from Cape Disappointment to Point Adams, in one unbroken line. Nothing could exceed the grandeur of this scene when viewed from aloft. The Columbia is a thousand miles long, and has its source eight hundred feet above the level of the sea.

To view its powerful floods of light, milky water rushing down and contending with the tides of the blue water of old ocean and see the marked line of separation between the sea and the river water, and a line of breakers nearly seven miles long dashing its silvery spray high in the air, is a wild sight. All who have seen it have [p. 231] spoken of the incessant roar of the waters, representing it as one of the most awful sights that can possibly meet the eye of the sailor.

On heaving the lead we found only five, eight, and nine fathoms of water, where on the chart it was laid down twenty-eight fathoms. The two quarter boats were lowered to sound for the channel, at six bells, three o'clock; but the wind beginning to freshen and the weather to thicken, they were recalled, and we hauled off with the tide, which was running with great rapidity and soon carried us back into the blue waters of the ocean.

During the night the weather was very boisterous. The following morning it was quite foggy. We bore away for the Straits of Juan de Fuca, and at eleven o'clock the man at the mast-head cried out, "Breakers on the lee bow!" The ship was at once brought by the wind, the studding-sails taken in, and a cast of the lead taken, when we found ourselves in five fathoms of water. The fog soon lifted and we saw, not half a mile off, a high point of rocks. Had we continued on our course fifteen minutes longer the ship must have been dashed to pieces and all hands sent to Davy Jones' locker.

This place proved to be Point Grenville, off Vancouver and Destruction Isle. This is one of the hair-breadth escapes from a wreck incident to this cruise.

A canoe soon came alongside with two old Indians, who kept singing out, "*Squik quak manash, squik quak manash. Nusk quall, nusk quall. Miso Wilszon Misoly, Miso Wilszon Misoly, Bosson, Bosson.*" Then they [p. 232] would turn one hand over the other with great rapidity. Some time after we found the meaning of the first three words to be, "Give us some tobacco"; the next was "Nisqually"; the other words meant a Mr. Wilson, a missionary from Boston. The motion of the hands was to describe a small stern-wheel boat at Nisqually, belonging to the Hudson Bay Company. After giving the Indians some tobacco we put to sea.

The morning of the 30th was still foggy. We saw a great abundance of wild geese and ducks flying in almost every direction and appearing very tame, probably having never heard the report of a gun. We captured many of them with little trouble.

During the night, which was very dark and rainy, the ship was hove to, a cast of the lead being taken every fifteen minutes. The morning of the first of May proved to be fair and beautiful. With a light sea-breeze we doubled Cape Flattery and entered the Straits of Juan de Fuca. While beating up the straits we were boarded by many canoes. At nine o'clock on the 2d we made Port Discovery. We came to anchor close in shore, in twenty fathoms of water. While surveying this place we came in contact with many of the Indians, who, in their broken language, would ask if we were Boston or King George ships. There was a great difference between the islanders of the Pacific and these Indians, both in language and appearance. They seemed to have scarcely any idea of decency or cleanliness, and seemed to be almost as low in the scale of humanity as the Terra del Fuegians.

It was indeed amusing to observe the contempt that [p. 233] our prisoner, the Fiji chief Vendovi, entertained for these Indians. He would hardly deign to look at them. While here we were plentifully supplied with venison, ducks, geese, pork, salmon, cod, flounders, herring, clams, quahaugs, mussels, long oysters, and small crabs.

Our general orders at this time were as follows:

The undersigned informs the officers and crews under his command that the duties on which they are about to enter will necessarily bring them in contact at times with the savage and treacherous inhabitants of this coast, and he therefore feels it his duty to enjoin upon them the necessity of unceasing caution and a restrictive and mild system in all their intercourse with them.

In my general order of July 13, 1839, my views are expressed fully respecting our intercourse with savages, and I expect that the injunctions therein contained will be strictly regarded.

No officer or man will be allowed to visit the shore without arms, and boat's crews when surveying or on other duty will be furnished with such as are necessary for their protection.

CHARLES Wilkes,
Commanding U.S. Ex. Ex.

At daylight on the morning of the 6th we got under way and proceeded to Puget Sound. After having finished our work here, we commenced beating up the bay for Nisqually Bay. We arrived on the 11th, at eight P.M., dropping anchor close in shore in seven fathoms of water. The *Flying Fish*[1] and *Porpoise* were also here, safely moored, and with the boats hoisted out. We were now on our native soil, and, though more than three thousand miles away from the place of our birth, could not resist the sensations kindled by the remembrance of "home, sweet, sweet home."

On May 15th surveying parties were sent out from the [p. 234] various ships. The *Porpoise* was to survey Hood's Canal; the boats of the *Vincennes* were to survey the rivers and bays in the vicinity; a land party was sent to explore the interior, and another was assigned to the Cascade Mountains.

Your humble servant was left, with others, to establish the observatory. This was done near a brook, abreast [p.235] of the ship, and within hail of it. We built a log-cabin for a pendulum house, to take the place of the old one which was scattered to the four winds of heaven from the summit of Mount Loa. It was soon finished, the instruments set up, and everything complete.

The Indians at this place belonged to the flat-headed tribes. When infants their heads are compressed by a sort of clamp, which gives them a wedge-shape. The females, commonly called squaws, were very scantily

---

[1]Erskine is incorrect here. Only the *Vincennes* and *Porpoise* traveled to Nisqually. In his preface Erskine indicated, "I have refreshed my memory by reading the history of our cruise in the United States exploring expedition, under the command of the late Admiral Charles Wilkes, and wish to acknowledge my indebtedness to the same for dates and a few facts and illustrations." Either his memory failed, or he confused the facts.

attired, and were very fond of ornaments. A small, dirty bone, two or three inches long, was stuck through the cartilage of the nose. All the unmarried squaws wore small brass bells suspended around the rims of the ears. Most of the women were bow-legged. The men were rather short and thick-set, with high cheek-bones, fine eyes, set wide apart, and black hair, which was worn long and flowing. The countenances of both sexes wore an expression of wildness.

On the banks of the river is dug a kind of ochre, both yellow and red, with which these Indians paint their faces. Their language was the strangest we had yet heard. Such words as *klick, kluck, tsk, sustiki,* and *squassus,* we did not understand; but *saantylku* and *selamp* both meant hot, gathering brooms, and August; *skelues* meant exhausted salmon, and September; *skaai* meant dry moon, and October; *kinni-etylyutin* meant house-making, and November; and *kumakwala* meant snow-moon, and December.

Independence Day fell on Sunday, so we celebrated on Monday. We commenced at daybreak by firing a national salute of twenty-six guns, one for each State in [p. 236] the Union, two brass howitzers having been brought on shore to the observatory for the purpose. The reports of the guns not only astonished the natives, but waked up the red-coats in the fort, who came running up to the observatory with the Indians, nearly out of breath, to inquire the cause of the racket. We pointed them to our country's flag, which was so proudly waving in the breeze over our observatory. They looked thunderstruck, and wanted to know what we meant. We told them that it was Brother Jonathan's birthday. They then called us a crew of crazy Americans.

At two bells, nine o'clock, all hands, including the officers, with the exception of Mr. Vanderford, our master's mate, who remained as shipkeeper, went on shore. At the observatory the commodore formed us into a procession. The starboard watch took the lead, then came the *Vincennes'* band, fife and drum, then the master-at-arms with Chief Vendovi dressed in the Fiji fashion, and leading our ship's pet, the dog Sydney, by two fathoms of marling; then the larboard watch, and finally the marines. We were all dressed in span-clean white frocks and trousers. The commodore led the procession, followed by the other officers, and we all marched off, with colors flying and music playing. In passing Fort Nisqually we gave three tremendous cheers, which were returned very faintly from the ramparts by several red-coats.

We soon arrived at a clearing near the edge of the prairie, a spot which the commodore had chosen for the Fourth of July exhibition. Here we found an ox which had been slaughtered and dressed on the preceding [p. 237] Saturday. We ran a pole through the ox from end to end, and then placed the ends of this pole upon two forked tree-trunks which had been securely planted in the earth. A trench was dug under him in which a fire was built, and a windlass arranged with which to turn him at intervals, while a committee detailed from the crew dredged him with flour and basted him every hour.

At ten o'clock all hands were called to "splice the mainbrace." Not a man being sick, all indulged. After this the commodore ordered the starboard watch on the right and the larboard on the left, and then he produced a foot-ball, gave it a tremendous kick which sent it high [p. 238] into the air, and sang out, "Sail in, my shipmates!" We did sail in. With others I got my shins barked from my ankles to my knees, but never got so much as a kick at the ball.

At eight bells, noon, the grog was rolled and all hands piped to dinner. When we repaired to the barbecue the Indians had gathered in large numbers, looking silently but wistfully at the novel sight before them. The ox proved to be as tender as a lamb.

In firing the salute at midday, Daniel Whitehorn, one of our quartergunners, ramming home a charge, had his arm dreadfully lacerated by the unexpected discharge of the gun. This accident put a momentary stop to our hilarity. His messmates took him in charge and soothed his wounds. Jack before the mast is familiar with such scenes as this. A shipmate falling from aloft, thrown from a yard, getting washed overboard in a gale, getting tied up in the rigging or his back lacerated with the cats, getting knocked down with a hand-spike by the captain or one of his mates, — witnessing such scenes it becomes his nature to weep with them that weep and to rejoice with them that rejoice.

After dinner the amusements proceeded, but not with the mirth of the of the morning, for the accident threw a gloom over all hands. Some ball and card playing, chatting with the Indians, and taking a cruise into the woods wound up the day. At night all hands returned on board excepting two, who had become lost in the woods. They were found three days afterward by the Indians, more dead than alive. They were nicknamed the "Babes in the Wood."

[p. 239] The next day the surveying parties were sent to survey Puget Sound. The scenery from the observatory was grand. In the distance, far beyond the prairie, might be seen the snow-capped summits of Mount Hood, Mount St. Helen's, and Mount Ranier. They are beautiful to view at sunrise and at sunset. The woods were very thick, the trees large and close. Wolves were very numerous, and also foxes. Deer and bears were common, but not so much so as the treacherous wolves. Birds of all kinds were plenty, especially wild ducks and geese, which appeared very tame. While here we saw many of the Crows, Shoshones, Apaches, and Blackfeet Indians.

The survey of Puget Sound having been completed, the observatory was broken up, the instruments taken down, packed, and sent aboard ship.

On the morning of the 17th we weighed anchor and took our departure for Point Dungeness, arriving there on the 22d. The boats were immediately sent away on surveying duty. Here another accident happened. Samuel Williams, gunner's mate, was firing a four-pounder for the purpose of measuring base by sound, when, as he was priming from a well-filled powder-horn, a terrific explosion took place, sending him with much force to the other side of the deck. His hand, arms, and face were much burned, but no bones were broken. On coming to, he wanted to know "if the powder-horn had busted." He was soon taken below and cared for.

We had scarcely dropped our anchor ere we were surrounded by many canoes bringing salmon, codfish, venison, and bear meat for sale.

[p. 240] On the 28th we got under way again and stood down the straits. When off Cape Flattery, the wind being ahead, we put into Neah Harbor. It is the first in the straits after rounding the cape, and is sheltered on the northeast by Neah Island. While surveying this harbor the ship was fairly surrounded by canoes. A vigilant watch was kept on them, and only a few Indians were allowed on board at a time.

There were two tribes, the Classet and Patouche. They brought many fine furs, seal and sea-otter skins, to trade, and were taken all aback when they found that we were not eager to make a bargain. The furs were cheap enough, but we did not want them. They offered us two or three fine fur-seal skins for a pound of tobacco, a pound of powder, or fifteen leaden bullets. A bottle of New England rum would fetch half a dozen of the finest furs. This showed what sort of trade was carried on when the Boston ships traded on this coast for furs and salmon. They would keep asking, "What for so big ship? What for so many mans? and no trade for furs for a lite rummie?"

This would be a good field for a missionary, for these Indians appear to be quite ignorant of any religious notions.

On the 1st of August we witnessed a beautiful eclipse of the moon. We found the Indians very numerous in the woods, wearing nothing but old dirty blankets. The men were very short and had extremely broad faces, which were besmeared with salmon oil, soot, and red ochre. The inside of their wigwams was very filthy. The squaws of the Classet tribe were much better looking [p. 241] and more lady-like than those of other tribes. Their hair, which was jet black and very long, hung loosely about their shoulders, and most of them had fair complexions and rosy cheeks.

On the 3d a carrier arrived from Nisqually, bringing news of the loss of the *Peacock* on the bar of the Columbia.

We soon weighed anchor and put to sea.

Appendix: List of Officers and Men Attached to the United States Exploring Expedition

United States Ship Vincennes

CHARLES WILKES, ESQ	Commanding	
JAMES ALDEN	Lieutenant	Joined brig *Porpoise* at San Francisco, October, 1841.
OVERTON CARR	Lieutenant	Took command of brig *Oregon*, at San Francisco; October, 1841.
THOMAS T. CRAVEN	Lieutenant	Left at Valparaiso June 6th, 1839, to take command of the *Sea-Gull*.
ROBERT E. JOHNSON	Lieutenant	Commanded *Sea-Gull* on her Southern Cruise, detached at Honolulu, November, 1841.
WILLIAM L. MAURY	Lieutenant	Joined *Peacock* at Orange Bay, and *Porpoise* at Callao.
JAMES H. NORTH	Acting Master	Joined *Porpoise* at Callao.
EDWARD GILCHRIST	Acting Surgeon	Detached at Sydney, March, 1840.
R. R. WALDRON	Purser	
J. L. ELLIOTT	Chaplain	Detached at San Francisco, October, 1841.
J. L. FOX	Assistant Surg.	Joined *Porpoise* at San Francisco, October, 1841.
J. S. WHITTLE	Assistant Surg.	Joined *Peacock* at Honolulu, and *Vincennes* again at San Francisco.
WILLIAM MAY	Passed Mid.	Joined *Flying-Fish* on a cruise south, 1839–40, and *Vincennes* again, May, 1840.

276   Appendix

WILLIAM REYNOLDS	Passed Mid.	Joined *Peacock*, 1839, and *Flying-Fish* at Honolulu, 1840, and *Porpoise* at Singapore.
GEORGE M. TOTTEN	Passed Mid.	Joined *Porpoise* at Callao, and *Vincennes* at Honolulu.
JOSEPH P. SANDFORD	Passed Mid.	Joined *Porpoise* at Tahiti, schooner *Flying-Fish* at San Francisco, and *Porpoise* at Singapore.
GEORGE W. CLARK	Midshipman	Joined *Peacock* at Tahiti, and *Vincennes* again at San Francisco.
SAMUEL ELLIOT	Midshipman	
WILLIAM SMITH	Boatswain	
WASHINGTON BRIGHT	Gunner	Joined *Relief* at Callao.
WILLIAM M. LAIGHTON	Carpenter	Joined *Relief* at Callao.
SAMUEL N. HAWKINS	Sailmaker	
BENJ. VANDERFORD	Pilot	Died April 1842.
R. P. ROBINSON	Purser's Steward	
JOHN G. WILLIAMSON	Gunner	

Scientific Corps

CHARLES PICKERING	Naturalist	
JOSEPH DRAYTON	Artist	
J. D. BRACKENRIDGE	Assistant Botanist	
JOHN G. BROWN	Mathematical Instrument Maker	
JOHN W. W. DYES	Assistant Taxidermist	
JOSEPH P. COUTHOUY	Naturalist	Left at Sydney, and detached at Honolulu, November, 1840.

United States Ship Peacock (wrecked July 18, 1841)

WILLIAM L. HUDSON, ESQ	Commanding	Joined *Vincennes* at San Francisco
GEORGE F. EMMONS	Lieutenant	Joined *Vincennes* at San Francisco.
SAMUEL P. LEE	Lieutenant	Detached at Orange Bay, Feb. 1839.
O. H. PERRY	Lieutenant	Joined *Vincennes* at San Francisco.
W. M. WALKER	Lieutenant	Command *Flying-Fish* first cruise, joined *Porpoise* at Columbia River, and *Vincennes* at San Francisco.
THOMAS A. BUDD	Acting Master	Joined *Vincennes* at Feejee.
J. F. SICKLES	Surgeon	Joined *Relief* at Callao.

List of Officers and Men Attached to the U.S. Exploring Expedition   277

WILLIAM SPIEDEN	Purser	Joined *Oregon* at Columbia River.
SILAS HOLMES	Assistant Surg.	Joined *Porpoise* at Sydney, and *Oregon* at San Francisco.
HENRY ELD	Passed Mid.	Joined *Vincennes* at Feejee.
HENRY GANSEVOORT	Passed Mid.	Detached at Callao, 1839.
GEORGE W. HARRISON	Passed Mid.	Joined *Flying-Fish* on a cruise south, *Peacock* at Feejee, and *Oregon* at Columbia River.
JAMES B. LEWIS	Passed Mid.	Joined *Flying-Fish* at Feejee, returned home from Oahu sick.
WILKES HENRY	Midshipman	Joined *Vincennes* at Callao, killed, July 24th, 1840, at Malolo.
WILLIAM H. HUDSON	Midshipman	Joined *Vincennes* at Columbia River.
FREDERICK D. STUART	Captain's Clerk	Joined *Porpoise* at Columbia River, and *Vincennes* at San Francisco.
THOMAS G. BELL	Boatswain	Joined *Porpoise* at Columbia River, and *Oregon* at San Francisco.
JOHN D. ANDERSON	Gunner	Detached at Callao.
JONAS DIBBLE	Carpenter	Joined *Oregon* at Columbia River.
J. D. FREEMAN	Sailmaker	Joined *Porpoise* at Columbia River.
WILLIAM H. INSLEY	Purser's Steward	Detached at Callao.

Scientific Corps

JAMES D. DANA	Mineralogist	Joined *Vincennes* at San Francisco.
T. R. PEALE	Naturalist	Joined *Vincennes* at San Francisco.
HORATIO HALE	Philologist	Joined *Vincennes* at New Zealand, *Peacock* at Honolulu, and was left at Oregon to cross the country.
F. L. DAVENPORT	Interpreter	Detached at Rio.

United States Ship Relief (sent home from Callao by way of Sandwich Islands and Sydney)

A. K. LONG	Lieutenant-Commandant	
A. L. CASE	Lieutenant	Joined *Vincennes* at Callao.
R. F. PINKNEY	Lieutenant	Joined *Peacock* at Orange Bay, *Flying-Fish* at Callao, and detached at Honolulu, 1840.
JOSEPH A. UNDERWOOD	Lieutenant	Joined *Vincennes* at Callao, and killed at Malolo, July 24th, 1840
GEORGE T. SINCLAIR	Acting Master	Joined *Porpoise* at Callao; Commander *Flying-Fish* at Feejee; joined *Porpoise* again at Honolulu, November, 1840.

J. C. Palmer	Acting Surgeon	Joined *Peacock* at Callao, and *Oregon* at Columbia River, and *Vincennes* at San Francisco.
Thomas W. Cummings	Passed Mid.	Left sick at Rio.
Alonzo B. Davis	Passed Mid.	Joined *Peacock* at Callao, and *Vincennes* at Columbia River, and *Oregon* at San Francisco.
James L. Blair	Midshipman	Joined *Peacock* at Rio, schooner *Flying-Fish* at Columbia River, and *Vincennes* at Honolulu.
James R. Howison	Captain's Clerk	Joined *Vincennes* at Callao.
J. Black	Boatswain	
Thomas Lewis	Gunner	Joined *Peacock* at Callao, and *Oregon* at Columbia River.

Scientific Corps

William Rich	Botanist	Joined *Peacock* at Callao, and *Vincennes* at San Francisco.
Alfred T. Agate	Artist	Joined *Peacock* at Callao, and *Vincennes* at San Francisco.

United States Brig Porpoise

Cadwalader Ringgold	Lieutenant-Commandant	
M. G. L. Claiborne	Lieutenant	Joined *Relief* at Orange Bay.
John B. Dale	Lieutenant	Joined *Relief* at Callao.
H. J. Hartstein	Lieutenant	Joined *Relief* at Callao.
A. S. Balswin	Acting Master	Joined *Peacock* at Callao, and *Oregon* at Columbia River.
C. F. B. Guillou	Assistant Surg.	Joined *Peacock* at Sydney, *Flying-Fish* at Columbia River, and detached at Honolulu, November, 1841.
Simon F. Blunt	Passed Mid.	Joined *Vincennes* at Orange Bay, and left sick at Honolulu, in April, 1841.
Geo. W. Colvocoressie	Passed Mid.	Joined *Peacock* at Rio, *Vincennes* at Feejee, and *Oregon* at San Francisco.
Thomas W. Waldron	Captain's Clerk	
John Frost	Boatswain	
O. Nelson	Boatswain	Detached at Rio
Amos Chick	Carpenter	Joined *Vincennes* at Callao.
John Joines	Sailmaker	Detach at Callao; joined *Relief*.
William H. Morse	Purser's Steward	

List of Officers and Men Attached to the U.S. Exploring Expedition   279

Tender Sea-Gull   (lost about May 1, 1839)

James W. E. Reid	Passed Midshipman, Commandant	
Frederick A. Bacon	Passed Mid.	
Isaac Percival	Pilot	Joined *Relief* at Callao.

Tender Flying-Fish   (sold at Singapore)

Samuel R. Knox	Commandant	Commanding schooner most of the cruise; joined *Vincennes* at Singapore.
H. A. Clemson	Midshipman	Joined the *Vincennes* at Rio; detached at Callao.
George W. Hammersly	Midshipman	Joined *Peacock* at Callao, and *Vincennes* at Feejee.
Egbert Thompson	Midshipman	Joined *Vincennes* at Rio, *Peacock* at Feejee, and *Vincennes* again at Columbia River.
E. H. De Haven	Acting Master	Joined *Vincennes* at Callao, *Peacock* at Feejee, and *Oregon* at Columbia River.
Richard Ellice	Ac. Master's Mate	Detached; joined *Relief* at Rio.
A. M. Cesney	Master's Mate	Detached at Honolulu.
James S. Power	Purser's Steward	Joined *Peacock* at Callao, and *Oregon* at Columbia River.
Peter Ackerman	Seaman	Joined in the United States; served the cruise.
Charles Adams	Cooper	Joined at Oahu; served the cruise.
Charles Allen	Ord'y Seaman	Joined at Oahu; served to the end of the cruise.
James Allman	Private	Joined in the united States; served the cruise.
Joseph Allshouse	Private	Joined in the United States; died October 30th, 1841.
James Anderson	Ord'y Seaman	Joined at Callao; served the cruise.
John Anderson	Seaman	Joined in the United States; returned expiration of cruise.
John Anderson	Seaman	Joined at Callao; killed by the natives at Drummond Island.
Jean Antonia	Ord'y Seaman	Joined at Cape Town; served to the end of the cruise.
Joseph R. Atkins	Ord'y Seaman	Joined at Sydney; served to end of cruise.
Silas Atkins	Seaman	Joined in the United States; returned in the *Relief*.
John Ayres	Landsman	Joined at Callao; run at Sydney.

Philip Babb	Private	Joined in the United States; served the cruise.
Francis Baker	Ord'y Seaman	Joined in the United States; served the cruise.
David Banks	Ord'y Seaman	Joined in the United States; discharged at Rio, Dec. 31st, 1838.
Ebenezer Bartholomew	Ord'y Seaman	Joined at Maui; served the cruise.
John Bartholomew	Ord'y Seaman	Joined at Maui; served the cruise.
John Baptiste	Seaman	Joined at Valparaiso; served the cruise.
Alexander Barron	Ord'y Seaman	Joined in the United States; discharged at Oahu, Nov. 2d, 1840.
David Bartlett	Seaman	Joined at Rio; served the cruise.
Joseph Bass	Ord'y Seaman	Joined in the United States; served the cruise.
Derby Batchelor	Ord'y Seaman	Joined at Maui; run at Oahu, Nov. 26th, 1841.
Henry Batchelor	Seaman	Joined in the United States; served the cruise.
David Bateman	Private	Joined in the United States; died at Feejee Islands, June 30th, 1840.
Davy Beal	Landsman	Joined at Callao; left sick in charge of Consul at Sydney.
Frederick Beale	Ord'y Seaman	Joined at Sydney; run at New Zealand.
Artimeus W. Beals	Capt. Hold	Joined at Upolu; served the cruise.
Shelden Benedict	Qr. Gunner	Joined at New Zealand; served the cruise.
Robert C. Bernard	Quarter Master	Joined at Valparaiso; served the cruise.
Charles Berry	Mast. Arms	Joined in the United States; returned in *Relief*.
James Berry	Seaman	Joined at Rio; served the cruise.
Theodore Beton	Ord'y Seaman	Joined at Rio; served the cruise.
Henry Bingham	Ord'y Seaman	Joined at Oahu; served the cruise.
John Black	Boatsn's Mate	Joined in the united States; discharged at Oahu, Oct. 31st, 1840.
Henry Blackstone	Seaman	Joined in the United States; discharged at Oahu, Oct. 31st, 1840.
John L. Blake	Ord'y Seaman	Joined at Rio; discharged June 30th, 1840.
David Blodget	Officers' Cook	Joined in the United States, died at Navigator's Islands, Nov. 6th, 1839.
Jacob Bolin	Capt. Forecastle	Joined in the United States; served the cruise.
William Bostwick	Capt. Cook	Joined in the United States; served the cruise.

List of Officers and Men Attached to the U.S. Exploring Expedition   281

PETER BOWEN	Seaman	Joined at Rio; run at Valparaiso.
ALEXANDER BOWMAN	Seaman	Joined at Oahu; run at Singapore.
PATRICK BOYLE	1st Class Boy	Joined in the United states; run at Rio.
ROBERT BOYLE	Seaman	Joined in the United States; run at Sydney.
JOHN W. BOYSON	1st Class Boy	Joined at the Feejee Islands; run at Oahu.
WALSTON BRADLEY	Ord'y Seaman	Joined at Valparaiso; run at Callao.
JOHN BREMOT	Ord'y Seaman	Joined at Rio; run at Callao, July 13th, 1839.
JOSEPH BRIMBLECOMB	Seaman	Joined in the United States; returned in *Relief*.
WILLIAM BRISCO	Armourer	Joined in the United States; served the cruise.
JOHN BROOKINS	Ord'y Seaman	Joined at Upolu; served the cruise.
JOHN BROOKS	Seaman	Joined in the United States; served the cruise.
RICHARD BROTHERS	Seaman	Joined in the United States, sent home from Rio, sick.
ANDREW A. BROWN	Ord'y Seaman	Joined at New Zealand; served the cruise
FRANKLIN BROWN	Ord'y Seaman	Joined in the United States; served the cruise.
JAMES BROWN	Carpenter's Mate	Joined in the United States; served the cruise.
JOHN BROWN, 1ST	Seaman	Joined in the United States; served the cruise.
JOHN BROWN, 2D	1st Class Boy	Joined at Rio; run at Sydney, Dec. 31st, 1839.
JOHN A. BROWN	Landsman	Joined at Oahu; served the cruise.
JOHN B. BROWN	Seaman	Joined in the United States; returned in *Relief*.
JOHN F. BROWN	Seaman	Joined at Oahu; served the cruise.
PETER BROWN	Ord'y Seaman	Joined at Rio; run at Upolu, Nov. 10th, 1839.
ROBERT BROWN	Boatsn's Mate	Joined in the United States, served the cruise.
SAMUEL BROWN	Capt. Forecastle	Joined in the United States; discharged at Oahu, Nov. 2d, 1840.
WILLIAM BROWN, 2D	Ord'y Seaman	Joined in the United States; run at Rio.
WILLIAM BRUCE	Ord'y Seaman	Joined at Valparaiso; run at Sydney.
HENRY BUCKETT	Quarter Master	Joined in the United States; discharged at Sydney.
JOHN BUCKLEY	Officers' Steward	Joined at Valparaiso; discharged at Callao, June, 1839.

Thomas Burke	Private	Joined in the United States; served the cruise.
David Burns	Officers' Cook	Joined in the United States; returned in *Relief*.
George Butter	Officers' Cook	Joined in the United States; served the cruise.
Paul Camell	Officers' Steward	Joined at Valparaiso; run at Sydney.
Robert Campbell	Private	Joined in the United States; served the cruise.
Roswell Cann	1st Class Boy	Joined in the United States; lost in the *Sea-Gull*.
Isaac Carmey	1st Class Boy	Joined in the United States; served the cruise.
William Carter	Capt. Top	Joined in the United States; served the cruise.
Joshua Cary	Private	Joined in the United States; run at Rio.
George Case	Seaman	Joined at Oahu; served the cruise.
Alfred Cassedy	Ord'y Seaman	Joined in the United States; run at Callao.
Lawrence Cavenaugh	Private	Joined in the United States; served the cruise.
Charles Chancy	Ord'y Seaman	Joined at Callao; run at Sydney.
Charles Chapman	Capt. Top	Joined at Callao; served the cruise.
Gaylord P. Churchill	Ord'y Seaman	Joined at Oahu, served the cruise.
Joseph Clark	Corp'l Marines	Joined in the United States; served the cruise.
Joseph Clark	Seaman	Joined in the United States; served the cruise.
Levin Clark	Capt. Top	Joined in the United States; served the cruise.
William Clarke	Ord'y Seaman	Joined at Sydney; served out the cruise.
William Clegg	Ord'y Seaman	Joined in the United States; returned in *Relief*.
Charles Clifford	Capt. Top	Joined in the United States; discharged at Oahu, 2d November, 1840.
Daniel Clute	Quarter-Master	Joined in the United States; lost in the *Sea-Gull*.
James Coburn	Ord'y Seaman	Joined at New Zealand; served the cruise.
Ephraim Coffin	Ord'y Seaman	Joined at Oahu; discharged at California.
Tom Coffin	Seaman	Joined at Oahu; run at Hawaii.
Garret Cole	Ord'y Seaman	Joined in the United States; served the cruise.

List of Officers and Men Attached to the U.S. Exploring Expedition

JOHN H. COLE	Capt. Top	Joined in the united States; discharged at Oahu, 2nd November, 1840.
CHARLES J. COLSON	Hosp. Steward	Joined in the United States; discharged at Oahu, Oct. 31st 1840.
GEORGE COOK	2d Class Boy	Joined at Oahu; discharged same place, November 19th, 1841.
ISAAC COOK	Ord'y Seaman	Joined in the United States; served the cruise.
JOHN COOK	Boatsn's Mate	Joined in the United States; served the cruise.
JOHN COOK	Seaman	Joined in the United States; returned in *Relief*.
EZEKIEL COOPER	Ord'y Seaman	Joined at Oahu; run, same place.
JOHN COOPER	Armourer	Joined in the United States; served the cruise.
RICHARD COOPER	Ord'y Seaman	Joined at Upolu; run at Sydney.
JAMES CORSE	Seaman	Joined at Rio; sent home in *Relief*.
GEORGE CROKER	Ord'y Seaman	Joined at Hawaii; run at Oahu.
JAMES CRONTU	Ord'y Seaman	Joned in the United States; run at Sydney.
DAVID CROPSEY	Ord'y Seaman	Joined at Maui; served the cruise.
JASPER CROPSEY	Ord'y Seaman	Joined at Oahu; served the cruise
JOSEPH CROSBY	Carpenter's Mate	Joined in the United States; return in *Relief*.
MASON CROWELL	Landsman	Joined in the United States; served the cruise.
JAMES CUMMINGS	Seaman	Joined in the United States; discharged at Oahu, Oct. 31st, 1840.
W. H. CUMMINGS	Boatsn's Mate	Joined in the United States; served the cruise.
JAMES CUNNINGHAM	Ord'y Seaman	Joined at Callao; run at Tahiti.
GEORGE DAILY	Ord'y Seaman	Joined at Oahu; served the cruise.
WILLIAM DAILY	Ord'y Seaman	Joined at Oahu; served the cruise.
DAVID DALTON	Officers' Steward	Joined in the United States; served the cruise.
WILLIAM DAMMON	Ord'y Seaman	Joined at Callao; served the cruise.
JAMES DANIELS	Ord'y Seaman	Joined at Sydney; run at New Zealand.
JEROME DAVIS	Ord'y Seaman	Joined in the United States; served the cruise.
JOHN DAVIS, 1ST	1st Class Boy	Joined at New Zealand; run at Oahu.
JOHN DAVIS, 2D	Seaman	Joined at Oahu; run at Hawaii.
JOHN E. DAY	Landsman	Joined at New Zealand; served out the cruise.

Stephen W. Days	Hosp. Steward	Joined in the United States; served the cruise.
Harvey Dean	Ord'y Seaman	Joined at Oahu; run at Singapore.
John N. Dean	Ord'y Seaman	Joined at Sydney; served the cruise.
John Demock	Capt. Top	Joined in the United States; served the cruise.
James Derley	Seaman	Joined at Oahu; served the cruise.
Thomas Derling	Ord'y Seaman	Joined at Valparaiso; run at Oahu.
Joseph De Silva	1st Class Boy	Joined at Rio; transferred to Falmouth at Callao.
Thomas Dewees	Corporal	Joined in the United States; served the cruise.
Thomas Dickenson	Carpenter's Mate	Joined in the United States; served the cruise.
William Dillon	Ord'y Seaman	Joined at Sydney; run at Oahu.
Samuel Dinsman	Corp'l Marines	Joined in the United States; served the cruise.
Samuel Dinsman	Seaman	Joined in the United States; returned in the *Relief*.
John Disbrow	Private	Joined in the United States; served the cruise.
John Dismond	Seaman	Joined in the United States; served the cruise.
Solomon Disney	Sailmaker's Mate	Joined in the United States; served the cruise.
Valentine Dister	Ord'y Seaman	Joined in the United States; transferred to Independence, at Rio.
John W. Divin	Ord'y Seaman	Joined at Rio; run at Sydney.
Christian Dobleman	Master-at-Arms	Joined in the United States; served the cruise.
Joseph Dolevar	Seaman	Joined at Valparaiso; served the cruise.
John Doughty	Capt. Top	Joined in the United States; served the cruise.
James Dowling, 1st	Seaman	Joined at Sydney; run at New Zealand.
James Dowling, 2d	Landsman	Joined at Oahu; served the cruise.
Charles Duegen	Seaman	Joined at Rio; returned in *Relief*.
Addison Dunbar	Private	Joined in the United States; served the cruise.
Alexander Dunn	Cockswain	Joined in the United States; discharged at Rio, November 30th, 1838.
James Dunn	Officers' Steward	Joined in the United States; served the cruise.

List of Officers and Men Attached to the U.S. Exploring Expedition   285

SAMUEL EASTMAN	Quarter-Master	Joined in the United States' discharged at Oahu, October 31st, 1840.
WILLIAM EASTWOOD	Ord'y Seaman	Joined in the United States; served the cruise.
W. H. ELDRIDGE	Ord'y Seaman	Joined at Cape Town; served the cruise.
GEORGE ELLIOTT	1st Class Boy	Joined at Valparaiso; served the cruise.
JAMES ELLIOTTE	Gunner's Mate	Joined in the United States; sent home in the *Relief*.
CHARLES ERSKIN	Ord'y Seaman	Joined in the United States; served the cruise.
HENRY EVANS	Officers' Cook	Joined in the United States; run at Fort George, Columbia River.
HENRY A. FELSON	Ord'y Seaman	Joined in the United States; served the cruise.
JOHN FENNO	Seaman	Joined in the United States; served the cruise.
WILLIAM FINNEY	Landsman	Joined at Callao; run at Oahu.
JOHN FISK	Ord'y Seaman	Joined at Rio; served out the cruise.
ROBERT FLETCHER	Ord'y Seaman	Joined in the United States' discharged at Oahu, Oct. 31st, 1840.
THOMAS FORD	Ord'y Seaman	Joined at Rio; served out the cruise.
KINNARD FOREMAN	Sailmaker's Mate	Joined at Callao; returned to United States in the *Relief*.
WILLIAM FORSDICK	Ord'y Seaman	Joined in the United States; run at Oahu, Oct. 31st, 1840.
STEPHEN FOSDICK	Gunner's Mate	Joined in the United States; served the cruise.
ALEXANDER C. FOWLER	Seaman	Joined in the United States; served the cruise.
EDWARD FOX	Officer's Steward	Joined at Sydney; discharged at Oahu.
JOHN FRANCIS	Ord'y Seaman	Joined in the United States; run at Rio.
JOSEPH FRANCIS	Seaman	Joined at Oahu; discharged at same place.
MATTHEW FRANCISCO	Ord'y Seaman	Joined at Oahu; discharged same place.
WILLIAM FRAZIER	Seaman	Joined in the United States' run at Sydney.
WILLIAM FRAZIER, 2D	Ord'y Seaman	Joined at Rio; lost in the *Sea-Gull*.
THEODORE FRENCH	Ship's Cook	Joined in the United States; discharged 5th August, 1839.
FREDERICK FRIENDS	Ord'y Seaman	Joined at Oahu; served out the cruise.
ISAAC FRIETUS	Ord'y Seaman	Joined at Madeira; discharged March 31st, 1840.
VINCENT FRIETUS	2d Class Boy	Joined at Rio; run at Valparaiso.

James Fritz	Qr. Gunner	Joined at Rio; served the cruise.
Robert Furman	Ord'y Seaman	Joined in the United States; discharged at Oahu, 31st Oct. 1840.
Moses Galchell	Seaman	Joined at Callao; run at Tahiti.
Fergus Gallagher	Cooper	Joined in the United States' returned in the *Relief*.
John A. Gardner	Ord'y Seaman	Joined at Callao; run at Oahu.
Matthey Garrigan	Landsman	Joined in the United States; sent home in the *Relief*.
Francis Garrison	Seaman	Joined at Rio; run, April 9th, 1840.
John Gaunt	Seaman	Joined in the United States'; sent home sick from Madeira.
Lyman Gaylard	Carpenter's Mate	Joined in the United States; discharged at Sydney.
Barney Gibbons	Landsman	Joined at Rio; run at Valparaiso.
James H. Gibson	Cockswain	Joined in the United States; served the cruise.
John Gillin	Ord'y Seaman	Joined in the United States; served the cruise.
William Gillan	Seaman	Joined in the United States; served the cruise.
John Glover	Capt. Top	Joined at Callao; served the cruise.
Omingo Golzalez	Seaman	Joined at Rio; returned in the *Relief*.
Nathaniel Goodhue	Capt. Fore-top	Joined in the United States; served the cruise.
William Goodman	Ord'y Seaman	Joined in the United States; run at Rio.
Robert Goodwin	Ord'y Seaman	Joined at Callao; served the cruise.
John Gorden	Quarter-Master	Joined in the United States; served the cruise.
Thomas Gorden	Ord'y Seaman	Joined at Oahu; served the cruise.
James Graham	Ord'y Seaman	Joined in the United States; served the cruise.
Ludwig Graves	Seaman	Joined at Rio; served the cruise.
Daniel Green	Gunner's Mate	Joined in the United States; served the cruise.
Ezra Green	Yeoman	Joined in the United States; served the cruise.
James Green	Capt. Top	Joined in the United States; served the cruise.
John Green	Boatsn's Mate	Joined in the United States' discharged at Oahu, Oct. 31st 1840.

List of Officers and Men Attached to the U.S. Exploring Expedition

Madison Green	Ord'y Seaman	Joined at Rio; served the cruise.
Thomas Green	Quarter-Master	Joined in the United States; served the cruise.
Henry Greenfield	Boatsn's Mate	Joined in the United States; served the cruise.
James Grey	Pilot	Joined at Tongataboo; discharged at Oahu, Oct. 31st 1840.
James H. Grey	Ord'y Seaman	Joined in the United States; run at Oahu.
John Griem	Seaman	Joined in the United States; transferred to the Independence.
John P. Griffen	Seaman	Joined in the United States; served the cruise.
Griffith Griffith	Capt. Top	Joined in the United States; run at Sydney.
Henry Gross	Officers' Cook	Joined in the United States; run at Oahu.
Manuel Guido	2d Class Boy	Joined at Madeira; returned to United States in the *Relief*.
Joseph Gundy	Ord'y Seaman	Joined in the United States; discharged at Rio, Dec. 31st, 1838.
James Haggerty	Ord'y Seaman	Joined in the United States; sent home in the *Relief*.
John Haggerty	Ord'y Seaman	Joined at Upolu; run at Sydney.
Thomas Harden	Officers' Cook	Joined in the United States; served the cruise.
David Haining	Ord'y Seaman	Joined at Rio; lost in the *Sea-Gull*.
John Hall	Ord'y Seaman	Joined at Cape Town; served the cruise.
Henry Hammond	Quarter-Master	Joined in the United States; served the cruise.
James G. Hanbury	Hosp. Steward	Joined in the United States; served the cruise.
Lewis Hanson	Ord'y Seaman	Joined at Callao; discharged at Sydney, Dec. 16th, 1839.
Join Harman	Private	Joined in the United States; served the cruise.
Jon Harmon	Seaman	Joined in the United States; served the cruise.
Jacob Harrid	Seaman	Joined in the United States; run at Callao.
Alvin Harris	Sailmaker's Mate	Joined in the United States; served the cruise.
John Harris	Landsman	Joined at Rio; run at Sydney.
Nathaniel Harris	Ord'y Seaman	Joined in the United States; discharged at New Zealand, 31st March, 1840.

JAMES HARRISON	Officers' Steward	Joined in the United States; served the cruise.
JOHN HARRISON	Seaman	Joined at Oahu; run at Singapore.
ASA HART	Ord'y Seaman	Joined in the United States; served the cruise.
JAMES HASKINS	1st Class Boy	Joined in the United States; served the cruise.
LYRANUS HATCH	Seaman	Joined in the United States; discharged at New Zealand.
JAMES HAYES	Ord'y Seaman	Joined in the United States; served the cruise.
WILLIAM HAYES	Seaman	Joined in the United States; served the cruise.
JOHN C. HEAD	Capt. Top	Joined in the United States; served the cruise.
WM. P. HEFFERMAN	Capt. Top	Joined in the United States; discharged at Oahu, Oct 31st, 1840.
JOHN HELLENDER	Seaman	Joined at Rio; served the cruise.
JAMES HENDERSON	Quarter-Master	Joined in the United States; served the cruise.
SANTO HERCULES	Seaman	Joined in the United States; discharged in New Zealand.
ANTONIO HERNANDEZ	Officers' Steward	Joined at Callao; discharged at California.
LEWIS HERRON	Cooper	Joined in the United States; served the cruise.
HENRY R. HEYER	Quarter-Master	Joined in the United States; served the cruise.
ROBINSON HICKS	Ord'y Seaman	Joined in the United States; run at Sydney.
WILLIAM H. HICKS	Ord'y Seaman	Joined in the United States; sent home in the *Relief*.
WINSLOW F. HIGGINS	Ord'y Seaman	Joined at Maui; served the cruise.
EDWARD HILL	Seaman	Joined in the United States; discharged at Oahu, Nov. 2d, 1840.
THOMAS HINES	Ord'y Seaman	Joined at Oahu; served the cruise.
SAMUEL HOBSEN	Armourer	Joined in the United States; returned in the *Relief*.
BENJAMIN HOLDEN	Private	Joined in the United States; died at Callao, July 8th, 1839.
SAMUEL B. HOLT	Capt. Hold	Joined in the United States; discharged at Oahu, October 31st, 1840.
ROYAL HOPE	Landsman	Joined at Rio; run at Oahu.
CHAS. E. HORNISTON	Seaman	Joined at Rio; run at Valparaiso.

List of Officers and Men Attached to the U.S. Exploring Expedition

EMANUEL HOWARD	Ord'y Seaman	Joined in the United States; served the cruise.
AMOS HOWELL	Capt. Hold	Joined in the United States; sent home from Rio, sick.
EDWIN HUBBARD	Seaman	Joined in the United States; served the cruise.
HENRY HUDSON	Seaman	Joined in the United States; served the cruise.
LAWRENCE HUFFORD	Seaman	Joined in the United States, sent home in the *Relief*.
FRANCIS G. HUGGINS	Seaman	Joined at Sandwich Islands; served the cruise.
ARTHUR HUGHES	Private	Joined in the United States; served the cruise.
HENRY HUGHES	Ord'y Seaman	Joined in the United States, discharged at Oahu, Oct. 31st, 1840.
JOHN HUGHES	2nd Class Boy	Joined at Callao; run at Oahu.
JAMES HUNT	Private	Joined in the United States; served the cruise.
GEORGE HUSTED	Quarter-Master	Joined in the United States; discharged at Oahu, Nov. 2d, 1840.
WM. HUTCHINSON	Ord'y Seaman	Joined at Hawaii; served the cruise.
WILLIAM HYDE	Carpenter's Mate	Joined in the United States; served the cruise.
ARCHIBALD JACKSON	1st Class Boy	Joined in the United States; discharged at Oahu, Oct. 31st, 1840.
A. JACQUINOT	Ass't Sc. Corps	Joined at Rio; run at Callao.
WILLIAM JARRETT	Master-at-Arms	Joined in the Unit3ed States; discharged at Oahu, October 31st, 1840.
DANIEL JEFFERSON	Ord'y Seaman	Joined in the United States; returned in the *Relief*.
THOMAS JEFFERSON	Seaman	Joined in the United States; returned in the *Relief*.
WILLIAM JEFFRIES	Ord'y Seaman	Joined in the United States; run at Rio.
WILLIAM JEWELL	Seaman	Joined in the United States; discharged at Oahu, Nov. 2d, 1840.
FRANCIS JOHNSON	Ord'y Seaman	Joined at Rio; sent home in the *Relief*.
HENRY JOHNSON	Ord'y Seaman	Joined at Oahu; served the cruise.
ROBERT JOHNSON	Seaman	Joined at Rio; lost in the *Sea-Gull*.
WARREN JOHNSON	Officers' Steward	Joined at Oahu; run at Fort George, Oregon.
WILLIAM JOHNSON	Seaman	Joined in the United States; sent home in the *Relief*.

DAVID JONES	Seaman	Joined at Oahu; served the cruise.
JOHN JONES	Ord'y Seaman	Joined at Sydney; served the cruise.
THOMAS JONES	Seaman	Joined in the United States; sent home in the *Relief*.
WILLIAM JONES	Seaman	Joined at Rio; served the cruise.
WILLIAM JONES, 1ST	Seaman	Joined at Rio; run at the same place.
SAMUEL J. JORDON	Ord'y Seaman	Joined at Sydney; run at the same place.
CHARLES JORFF	Ord'y Seaman	Joined at Valparaiso; served the cruise.
FRANCIS JOSEPH	Seaman	Joined in the United States; served the cruise.
JOHN JOSEPH	Capt.'s Steward	Joined at Valparaiso; served the cruise.
JOHN KEDD	Seaman	Joined in the United States' run at Sydney.
SAMUEL KEENAN	Seaman	Joined in the United States; discharged at Oahu, Oct. 31st, 1840.
JOHN KELLUM	Quarter-Master	Joined in the United States; served the cruise.
THOMAS KENNEDY	Seaman	Joined at Rio; run at the same place.
ELIJAH KING	Ord'y Seaman	Joined in the United States; served the cruise.
JOHN KING	Seaman	Joined in the United States; discharged at Oahu, Oct 31st, 1840.
RICHARD KING	Ord'y Seaman	Joined at Maui; served the cruise.
WM. H. KING	Corp. Marines	Joined in the United States; served the cruise.
CHARLES KINGSLAND	Ord'y Seaman	Joined at Upolu; served the cruise.
ALLEN W. KIRBY	Capt. Hold	Joined in the United States; discharged at Oahu, Nov. 2d, 1840.
STEPHEN KNIGHT	Ship's Cook	Joined in the United States; discharged at Oahu, Oct. 31st, 1840.
CHARLES KNOWLES	Ord'y Seaman	Joined in the United States; served the cruise.
HORACE LAMSON	Ord'y Seaman	Joined at Valparaiso; sent to United States in *Relief*.
JOHN LATTY	1st Class Boy	Joined at Rio; served out the cruise.
WM. LAWRENCE	Ord'y seaman	Joined at Valparaiso; run at Sydney.
CHARLES LEAR	Ord'y Seaman	Joined at Maui; served the cruise.
JAMES LEAVETT	Capt. Top	Joined in the United States; served the cruise.
DAVID LEAVITT	Ord'y Seaman	Joined at Maui; served the cruise.
WILLIAM LEE	Seaman	Joined at Callao; run at Sydney.

List of Officers and Men Attached to the U.S. Exploring Expedition 291

JOHN LENNARD	Seaman	Joined at Rio; sent to the United States in *Relief*.
WM. J. LESTER	Seaman	Joined at Rio; served out the cruise.
GODFREY LETOURNO	Seaman	Joined in the United States; served the cruise.
JOHN LEWIS	Seaman	Joined in the United States; run at Rio.
PETER LEWIS	Ord'y Seaman	Joined at Rio; served out the cruise.
JOSEPH LIMONT	Seaman	Joined in the United States; served the cruise.
PETER LINES	Ord'y Seaman	Joined in the United States; served the cruise.
FRANCIS LINTHICUM	Cockswain	Joined in the United States; discharged at Oahu, October 31st, 1840.
LAWRENCE LITTLEYEAR	Private	Joined in the United States; sent home in the *Relief*.
WILLLIAM LLOYD	Capt. Top	Joined in the United States; served the cruise.
BERNARD LOGAN	Ord'y Seaman	Joined in the United States; returned in the *Relief*.
WM. S. LONGLEY	Seaman	Joined in the United States; served the cruise.
CHARLES LOWE	Seaman	Joined in the United States; served the cruise.
WILLIAM LOWE	Seaman	Joined in the United States; served the cruise.
JAMES LOWELL	Capt. Forecastle	Joined in the United States; served the cruise.
JOHN LOYD	Ord'y Seaman	Joined in the United States; run at Sydney.
WILIAM LOYD	Landsman	Joined in the United States; sent home in the *Relief*.
HENRY LUTHER	Seaman	Joined at Rio; run at Valparaiso.
WASHINGTON LYNER	Ord'y Seaman	Joined in the United States; run at Rio.
HENRY MABEE	Seaman	Joined in the United States; run at Sydney.
FRANK MACKEY	Seaman	Joined at Rio; served the cruise.
JUSTIN MANDON	Captain's Cook	Joined at Rio; served the cruise.
JOHN C. MARCH	Private	Joined in the United States; served the cruise.
JAMES MARSHALL	Seaman	Joined in the United States; served the cruise.
THOMAS MARTIN	Landsman	Joined in the United States; discharged at Rio, Dec 31st, 1838.

THEODORE MATHER	Ord'y Seaman	Joined at Oahu; served the cruise.
JOHN MATTOX	Seaman	Joined at Rio; served the cruise.
HUGH M'BRIDE	Ord'y Seaman	Joined at Upolu; served the cruise.
DANIEL M'CARTY	Ouarter-Gunner	Joined in the United States; discharged at Rio, Dec. 31st, 1838.
JAMES M'CORMICK	Seaman	Joined in the United States; served the cruise.
ALEXANDER M'DONALD	Landsman	Joined in the United States; served the cruise.
WM. M'DONALD	Seaman	Joined in the United States; served the cruise.
LEWIS MEAKER	Ord'y Seaman	Joined at Sydney; discharged at Oahu, 25th Nov. 1840.
JOSEPH MEDLEY	Seaman	Joined at New Zealand; served the cruise.
JOHN MEINEY	Master-at-Arms	Joined in the United States; served the cruise.
PETER M'FEE	Ord'y Seaman	Joined at Callao; served the cruise.
BERNARD M'GEE	Seaman	Joined at Callao; run at Sydney.
ARTHUR M'GILL	Seaman	Joined at Upolu; discharged at Oahu, Nov. 20th 1841.
LAURENCE M'GILL	Ord'y Seaman	Joined in the United States; run at Manilla.
WILLIAM MIGLEY	Quarter-Gunner	Joined in the United States; served the cruise.
JOSEPH M'GOMEY	Ord'y Seaman	Joined at Callao; discharged at Oahu, Oct. 31st, 1840.
DAVID MILLER	Ord'y Seaman	Joined in the United States; returned in the *Relief*.
JACK MILLER	Seaman	Joined at Sandwich Islands; served the cruise.
MICHAEL MILLER	Ord'y Seaman	Joined in the United States' died at sea, 15th August, 1839.
WILLIAM MILLER, 1ST	Ord'y Seaman	Joined in the United States; lost in the *Sea-Gull*.
WM. MILLER, 2D	Ord'y Seaman	Joined at Rio; run at Callao.
EARL MILLIKIN	Quarter-Gunner	Joined at Oahu; served the cruise.
EDWARD M'INTIRE	Ord'y Seaman	Joined at Cape Town; served the cruise.
GEORGE MITCHELL	Quarter-Master	Joined at Valparaiso; served the cruise.
JOHN MITCHELL	Ord'y Seaman	Joined at Rio, served the cruise.
THOMAS MIZIR	1st Class Boy	Joined at Tahiti; served the cruise.
JOHN M'KEEN	Ship's Cook	Joined in the United States; served the cruise.

List of Officers and Men Attached to the U.S. Exploring Expedition 293

JAMES M'KENZIE	Private	Joined in the United States' served the cruise.
THOMAS M'MANUS	Ord'y Seaman	Joined in the United States; served the cruise.
FRANCIS MONTSERAT	Officers' Steward	Joined in the United States; served the cruise.
WILLIAM MOODY	Quarter-Master	Joined in the United States; served the cruise.
SAMUEL MOORE	Capt. Top	Joined in the United States; discharged at Oahu, Nov. 20th 1841.
JAMES MORAN	1st Class Boy	Joined in the united States; returned in the *Relief.*
STEPHEN MORANT	Seaman	Joined at Sydney; run at Oahu.
JOHN MORE	Seaman	Joined in the United States; discharged at Oahu, Oct. 31st, 1838.
EDWARD MOTT	Ord'y Seaman	Joined at Oahu; served the cruise.
JOHN MUNROE	Seaman	Joined at Valparaiso; run at Sydney.
ROBERT MUNROE	Ord'y Seaman	Joined at Valparaiso; run at Sydney.
ANDREW MURRAY	Seaman	Joined at Sydney; run at Oahu.
JOHN MYRES	Seaman	Joined in the United States; served the cruise.
JOHN H. MYRES	2nd Class Boy	Joined at Callao; served the cruise.
JOSEPH NEALE	Officers' Cook	Joined at Callao; run at Sydney.
JOHN NEBHUT	Private	Joined in the United States; served the cruise.
WILLIAM NEILL	Quarter-Master	Joined in the United States; served the cruise.
HORATIO NELSON	Seaman	Joined in the United States; discharged at Oahu, Oct. 31st, 1840.
EDWARD NICHOLS	Ord'y Seaman	Joined at Cape Town; served the cruise.
GEORGE NICHOLS	Ord'y Seaman	Joined at Varparaiso; run at Sydney.
CHAS. H. NICHOLSON	Seaman	Joined in the United States; discharged at Oahu, Nov. 25th 1841.
THOMAS NISBET	Ord'y Seaman	Joined at Singapore; served the cruise.
THOMAS NOBLE	Seaman	Joined at Rio; sent home in the *Relief.*
WILLIAM NOBLE	Seaman	Joined in the United States; run at Valparaiso.
ANDREW NORDSTON	Ord'y Seaman	Joined in the United States; served the cruise.
BENJAMIN NORTON	Ord'y Seaman	Joined in the United States; served the cruise.

Nelson Norton	Capt. Top	Joined in the United States; discharged at Oahu, Nov. 2d, 1840.
William Norton	Seaman	Joined in the United States; discharged at Rio, Dec. 31st, 1838.
James Nowland	Capt. Top	Joined in the United States; run at Sydney.
James Nurse	Officers' Steward	Joined in the United States; discharged at Rio, Dec. 3rd 1838.
Alexander Ogle	Corp. Marines	Joined in the United States; died at sea, Aug. 12th 1839.
Ambrose W. Olivar	Ord'y Seaman	Joined in the United States; served the cruise.
John Orr	Ord'y Seaman	Joined in the United States; served the cruise.
William Orr	Ord'y Seaman	Joined in the United States; served the cruise.
Daniel Osmand	Seaman	Joined in the United States; run at Valparaiso.
David B. Park	Sailmaker's Mate	Joined in the United States; served the cruise.
George Parker	Capt. Top	Joined in the United States; run at Sydney.
Thomas Parker	Seaman	Joined at Rio; run at Sydney.
George Parmilla	Ord'y Seaman	Joined at New Zealand; run at Oahu.
James Patterson	Landsman	Joined in the United States; returned in the *Relief.*
William Pearson	Ord'y Seaman	Joined at Oahu; served the cruise.
Thomas Penny	Ord'y Seaman	Joined in the United States; run at Oahu.
Samuel Pensyl	Private	Joined in the United States; served the cruise.
James Perry	Ord'y Seaman	Joined at Oahu; served the cruise.
Thomas Piner	Quarter-Master	Joined in the United States; served the cruise.
John Polnell	Quarter-Gunner	Joined in the United States; served the cruise.
George Porter	Seaman	Joined in the United States; died at sea, March 3d, 1842.
James Potter	Ord'y Seaman	Joined in the United States; run at Rio.
James M. Pottle	Private	Joined in the United States; run at Valparaiso.
Calvin Proctor	Seaman	Joined at Oahu; served the cruise.
Robert Pully	Quarter-Master	Joined in the United States; served the cruise.

List of Officers and Men Attached to the U.S. Exploring Expedition 295

BENJAMIN PULMAR	Ord'y Seaman	Joined in the United States' run at Sydney.
JAMES QUIN	Ord'y Seaman	Joined in the United States; discharged at Oahu, Nov. 2d, 1840.
JOHN RADLEY	Ord'y Seaman	Joined at Oahu; served the cruise.
THEODORE RAMERIS	Ord'y Seaman	Joined in the United States; run at Sydney.
NELSON RANSOM	Seaman	Joined at Sandwich Islands; served the cruise.
CHARLES RAY	Ord'y Seaman	Joined in the United States; served the cruise.
JOSEPH REBO	2nd Class Boy	Joined at Rio; served the cruise.
RAYMOND REED	Seaman	Joined at Oahu; served the cruise.
GEORGE REYNOLDS	Ord'y Seaman	Joined in the United States; died at sea, Aug. 22d, 1839.
EDGAR A. RICHARDSON	Private	Joined in the United States; served the cruise.
JOHN D. RICHARDSON	Cooper	Joined in the United States; served the cruise.
WM. RICHMOND	Boatsn's Mate	Joined in the United States; served the cruise.
JOHN RILEY	Private	Joined in the United States; served the cruise.
JOHN RIVERS	Ord'y Seaman	Joined at Rio; lost in the *Sea-Gull*.
JOHN ROACH	Landsman	Joined at Sydney; served the cruise.
MATTHIAS ROACH	Ord'y Seaman	Joined in the United States; run at Rio.
WILLIAM ROBB	1st Class Boy	Joined at Rio; served the cruise.
WILLIAM ROBBIN	Quarter-Master	Joined in the United States; returned in the *Relief*.
ABRAHAM ROBERTS	Ord'y Seaman	Joined at New Zealand; served the cruise.
HUMPHREY ROBERTS	Armourer	Joined at Sydney; served the cruise.
OWEN ROBERTS	Private	Joined in the United States; served the cruise.
WM. ROBERTS	1st Class Boy	Joined in the United States; served the cruise.
GEORGE ROBINSON	Ord'y Seaman	Joined at Maui; served the cruise.
JOHN ROBINSON	Capt. Forecastle	Joined in the United States; served the cruise.
WILLIAM ROBINSON	Seaman	Joined in the United States; served the cruise.
JAMES ROCK	Ord'y Seaman	Joined at Oahu; run at California.
GEORGE ROCKET	Landsman	Joined at New Zealand; discharged at Oahu, Oct. 31st, 1840.

Goerge Rodgers	Private	Joined in the United States; served the cruise.
James G. Rowe	Seaman	Joined in the United States; served the cruise.
Elias Russel	Ship's Cook	Joined in the United States; run at Callao.
Morris Russel	Landsman	Joined in the United States; run at Rio.
Michael Ryan	1st Class Boy	Joined at Rio; run at Sydney.
John Rye	Seaman	Joined in the United States; served the cruise.
John Sac	Seaman	Joined in the United States; discharged at Oahu, Oct. 31st, 1840.
Francis Salsbury	Capt. Top	Joined in the United States; served the cruise.
Thomas Sandford	Quarter-Master	Joined in the United States; served the cruise.
Henry Sares	Capt. Top	Joined at Callao; served the cruise.
James De Sauls	Ship's Cook	Joined at Callao; run at Astoria.
Thomas Scarpa	Officers' Steward	Joined at Rio; discharged at same place.
Wm. Schenk	Carpenter's Mate	Joined in the United States; served the cruise.
James Scott	Seaman	Joined at New Zealand; run at Oahu.
Thomas Scott	Quarter-Master	Joined in the United States; served the cruise.
George Seabold	Seaman	Joined at Rio; run at Aurora Island.
Frederick Seymore	Ord'y Seaman	Joined at Rio; run at Sydney.
George Sharrock	Carpenter's Mate	Joined at Valparaiso; served the cruise.
Peter Shaw	Seaman	Joined at Valparaiso; served the cruise.
James Sheaf	Ord'y Seaman	Joined in the United States; served the cruise.
Simon Shepherd	Ord'y Seaman	Joined in the United States; served the cruise.
Charles C. Sherwood	Seaman	Joined at Rio; served the cruise.
Thomas Shor	Seaman	Joined at the Sandwich Islands; served the cruise.
Joseph Silvery	1st Class Boy	Joined at Oahu; discharged at the same place.
Thomas Sinclair	Seaman	Joined in the United States; served the cruise.
Thomas Simmons	Ord'y Seaman	Joined at Hawaii; run at same place.
Allen Simons	Ord'y Seaman	Joined in the United States; run at Valparaiso.

List of Officers and Men Attached to the U.S. Exploring Expedition

William Slater	Ord'y Seaman	Joined at Oahu; served the cruise.
John Small	Baker	Joined at Rio; discharged at New Zealand.
David Smith	Ord'y Seaman	Joined in the United States; served the cruise.
David M. Smith	Armourer	Joined in the United States; served the cruise.
Frank Smith	Officers' Steward	Joined in the United States; served the cruise.
George Smith	Private	Joined in the United States; served the cruise.
George Smith	Seaman	Joined in the United States; discharged at Rio, Nov. 28th, 1838.
Hendrick Smith	Ord'y Seaman	Joined in the United States; discharged at Oahu, Nov. 2d, 1840.
James Smith, 1st	Seaman	Joined in the United States; run at Sydney.
John Smith	Seaman	Joined at Rio; run at Sydney.
John Smith	Ord'y Seaman	Joined at Feejee Islands; discharged at same place.
John Smith	Private	Joined in the United States; served the cruise.
John Smith, 1sdt	Ord'y Seaman	Joined in the United States; run at Rio.
John Smith, 2d	Ord'y Seaman	Joined in the United States; lost in the *Sea-Gull*.
James Smith, 2d	Ord'y Seaman	Joined in the United States; lost in the *Sea-Gull*.
John W. Smith	Seaman	Joined in the United States; discharged at Rio, Dec. 31st, 1838.
Moses J. Smith	Ord'y Seaman	Joined at Rio; run at Sydney.
William Smith	Seaman	Joined at Rio; drowned at Feejee.
William Smith	Yeoman	Joined in the United States; served the cruise.
William J. Smith	Quarter-Master	Joined in the United States; discharged at Sydney, 19th March, 1840.
Benj. Somerndyke	Carpenter's Mate	Joined in the United States; served the cruise.
William Soule	Landsman	Joined at Rio; served the cruise.
Edward Southworth	Quarter-Master	Joined in the United States; served the cruise.
James Spear	Armourer	Joined at Valparaiso; run at Sydney.
Robert Spears	Capt. Top	Joined in the United States; discharged at Oahu, Oct. 31st, 1840.

Wm. H. Spencer	Seaman	Joined at Rio; run at Sydney.
James Stark	Ord'y Seaman	Joined at Callao; discharged at Sydney, Dec. 15th, 1839.
George Stauton	Ord'y Seaman	Joined at Sydney; run at Oahu.
Henry Stephens	1st Class Boy	Joined at Sydney; run at New Zealand.
Simeon Sterns	Orderly Sergeant	Joined in the United States; served the cruise.
Benjamin Stevens	Seaman	Joined in the United States; returned in the *Relief*.
John H. Stevens	Ord'y Seaman	Joined at Tahiti; run at Sydney.
John Steward	Ship's Cook	Joined in the United States; served the cruise.
Robert Steward	Ord'y Seaman	Joined at Rio; run at Aurora Island.
Samuel Steward	Landsman	Joined in the United States; run at Rio.
William Steward	Capt. Top	Joined in the United States; died at sea, 11th March, 1839.
James Stover	Ord'y Seaman	Joined at Oahu; served the cruise.
John Strafford	Seaman	Joined at Valparaiso; served the cruise.
James Straham	Seaman	Joined in the United States; discharged at Oahu, Oct. 31st, 1840.
Samuel Stretch	Gunner's Mate	Joined in the United States; served the cruise.
George Sudor	Quarter-Master	Joined in the United States; sent home in the *Relief*.
Samuel Sutton	Seaman	Joined in the United States; served the cruise.
James Sweeney	Seaman	Joined at Sydney; run at Oahu.
Peter Sweeny	Seaman	Joined at New Zealand; discharged at Oahu, Oct. 31st, 1840.
Antonio Sylvester	Ord'y Seaman	Joined at Oahu; run at the same place.
Samuel Taber	1st Class Boy	Joined at Oahu; served the cruise.
Ashton Taylor	Private	Joined in the United States; served the cruise.
William Teneycke	Seaman	Joined in the United States' sent home in the *Relief*.
Richard Terry	Seaman	Joined in the United States; lost in the *Sea-Gull*.
Edwin Thene	Seaman	Joined in the United States; served the cruise.
Charles Thomas	Seaman	Joined in the United States; run at Sydney.
David Thomas	Officers' Cook	Joined at Feejee Islands, served the cruise.

List of Officers and Men Attached to the U.S. Exploring Expedition 299

HUMPHREY THOMAS	Ord'y Seaman	Joined at Upolu; run at Sydney.
HENRY THOMPSON	Landsman	Joined in the United States; run at Callao.
JOHN THOMPSON, 1ST	Seaman	Joined in the United States; run at Sydney.
JOHN THOMPSON, 2D	Capt. Forecastle	Joined in the United States; served the cruise.
JOHN THOMPSON, 3D	1st Class Boy	Joined at Sydney; run at same place.
MATTHEW THOMPSON	Capt. Top	Joined in the United States; sent home in the *Relief*.
WILLIAM THOMPSON	Seaman	Joined in the United States; served the cruise.
EDWARD TOWNSEND	Ord'y Seaman	Joined at Oahu; served the cruise.
JAMES TOWNSEND	Seaman	Joined in the United States; discharged at Oahu, Oct 31st, 1840.
JOHN TRACK	Seaman	Joined at Oahu; discharged same place.
ABIJAH TRAVERSE	Ord'y Seaman	Joined at Oahu; served the cruise.
GEORGE TREBLE	Seaman	Joined in the United States; served the cruise.
CHARLES TRUELARE	Ord'y Seaman	Joined in the United States; served the cruise.
HENRY TUBOR	Seaman	Joined in the United States; served the cruise.
HENRY TURNER	Capt. Forecastle	Joined in the United States; served the cruise.
WM. W. TURNER	Quartermaster-Gunner	Joined in the United States; discharged at Oahu, Oct. 31st, 1840.
JOHN UNDIETCH	Ord'y Seaman	Joined in the United States; served the cruise.
JOHN VANCLECK	Seaman	Joined in the United States; served the cruise.
JOHN VANDERVEER	Seaman	Joined at Varparaiso; sent home in the *Relief*.
EDWARD VERRY	Ord'y Seaman	Joined in the United States; served the cruise.
ANTONIA VINES	Officers' Steward	Joined at Callao; sent home in the *Relief*.
JAMES C. WALFE	Quarter-Gunner	Joined in the United States; discharged at Oahu, Oct. 31st, 1840.
THOMAS WALLACE	1st Class Boy	Joined in the United States; served the cruise.
AARON WALMSLEY	Sergeant Marines	Joined in the United States; served the cruise.
HENRY WALTHAM	Ord'y Seaman	Joined in the United States; served the cruise.

Michael Ward	Private	Joined in the United States; served the cruise.
John A. Weaver	Seaman	Joined at Valparaiso; served the cruise.
Josiah Weaver	1st Class Boy	Joined at New Zealand; run at Oahu.
Benjamin Webb	Ord'y Seaman	Joined in the United States; discharged at Oahu, Oct. 31st, 1840.
John Weller	Ord'y Seaman	Joined at Cape Town; served the cruise.
William Wells	Yeoman	Joined at Valparaiso; served the cruise.
Peter Welsh	Seaman	Joined in the United States; sent home in the *Relief*.
George Wesson	Seaman	Joined in the United States; served the cruise.
Zaccheus Wheeler	Ord'y Seaman	Joined at Oahu; served the cruise.
James White	Capt. Forecastle	Joined in the United States; served the cruise.
John White, 2d	Ord'y Seaman	Joined in the United States; run at Rio.
William White	Ord'y Seaman	Joined at Callao; served the cruise.
Daniel Whitehorn	Quarter-Gunner	Joined in the United States; served the cruise.
Nicholas Whiteston	Ord'y Seaman	Joined at Rio; lost in the *Sea-Gull*.
Kembal Whitney	Ord'y Seaman	Joined in the United States; served the cruise.
Mark Widden	Landsman	Joined in the United States; returned in the *Relief*.
Edward Widdows	Seaman	Joined in the United States; discharged at Oahu, Oct 31st, 1840.
Jedediah Wilber	Ord'y Seaman	Joined at Callao; served the cruise.
Thomas Wilkins	Ord'y Seaman	Joined at Oahu, served the cruise.
James Wilkinson	Seaman	Joined in the United States; served the cruise.
Francis Williams	Boatsn's Mate	Joined in the United States; served the cruise.
George Williams	Boatsn's Mate	Joined in the United States; served the cruise.
Henry C. Williams	Landsman	Joined in the United States; served the cruise.
Jack Williams	Ord'y Seaman	Joined in the United States; served the cruise.
James Williams	Landsman	Joined in the United States; sent home in the *Relief*.
John Williams	2nd Class Boy	Joined at Sydney; served the cruise.

Michael Williams	Seaman	Joined in the United States; served the cruise.
Philip Williams	Ord'y Seaman	Joined in the United States; returned in the *Relief*.
Samuel Williams	Gunner's Mate	Joined in the United States; served the cruise.
Thomas L. Williams	Seaman	Joined at Upolu; served the cruise.
Charles Willis	Ord'y Seaman	Joined at Oahu; run at Hawaii.
Robert Willis	Seaman	Joined in the United States; discharged at Rio, Dec. 31st, 1838.
John Wilson	Ord'y Seaman	Joined in the United States; run at California.
Joseph Wilson	Ord'y Seaman	Joined in the United States; run at Rio.
Thomas Wilson	Sailmaker's Mate	Joined in the United States; served the cruise.
William Wilson	Quarter-Master	Joined in the United States; sent home in the *Relief*.
Stephen Winks	Ord'y Seaman	Joined in the United States; run at Rio.
Horace Wister	Ord'y Seaman	Joined in the United States; discharged at Oahu, March 31st, 1841.
Daniel Wright	Cockswain	Joined in the United States; returned in the *Relief*.
Noah Wyeth	Quarter-Master	Joined in the United States; discharged at Rio, Dec. 31st, 1838.
William York	Ord'y Seaman	Joined in the United States; sent home in the *Relief*.
Henry Young, 1st	Ord'y Seaman	Joined at Hawaii; served the cruise.
Henry Young, 2d	Ord'y Seaman	Joined in the United States; discharged at New Zealand.

Bibliography

Alden, James. *Journal*. Handwritten journal. Newport News, VA: The Mariners Museum Library.
Barkan, Frances B., ed. *The Wilkes Expedition Puget Sound and the Oregon Country*. Olympia: Washington State Capital Museum, 1987.
Blumenthal, Richard W., ed. *The Early Exploration of Inland Washington Waters. Journals and Logs from Six Expeditions, 1786–1792*. Jefferson, NC: McFarland, 2004.
_____. *With Vancouver in Inland Washington Waters. Journals of 12 Crewmen, April–June 1792*. Jefferson, NC: McFarland, 2006.
Brunjes, Robert A. *Hat Island History*. http://www.hatisland.org/library/HAT_ISLAND_HISTORY.pdf.
Case, Augustus Ludlow. (Untitled.) Case Journal. Annapolis: U.S. Naval Academy.
Clark, Joseph G. *Lights and Shadows of Sailor Life, as Exemplified in Fifteen Years' Experience, Including the More Thrilling Events of the U.S. Exploring Expedition, and Reminiscences of an Eventful Life on the "Mountain Wave."* Boston: Benjamin B. Mussey, 1848.
Cleaver, Anne Hoffman, E. Jeffrey Stann, eds. *Voyage to the Southern Ocean: The Letters of Lieutenant William Reynolds from the U.S. Exploring Expedition, 1838–1842*. Annapolis, MD: Naval Institute Press, 1988.
Cogar, William B. *Dictionary of Admirals of the U.S. Navy Volume 1 1862–1900*. Annapolis, MD: Naval Institute Press, 1989.
Colvocoresses, Lieut. George M. *Four Years in the Government Exploring Expedition; Commanded by Captain Charles Wilkes, to the Island of Maderia — Cape Verd Island — Brazil — Coast of Patagonia — Chili — Peru — Paumato Group — Society Islands — Navigator Group — Australia — Antarctic Continent — New Zealand — Friendly Islands — Fejee Group — Sandwich Islands — Northwest Coast of America — Oregon — California — East Indies — St. Helena, Etc., Etc. In One Volume*. Fifth Edition. New York: J. M. Fairchild, 1855.
_____. *The People's Book Or, a Narrative of a Cruise on a Government Expedition to the Island of Madeira, Cape Verd Islands, Brazil, Coast of Patagonia, Chili, Peru, Paumato Group Society Islands, Navigator Group, Australia, Antarctic Ocean, Friendly Islands, Fejee Group, Sandwich Islands, Northwest Coast of America, Oregon, California, East Indies, St. Helena, &c &c. In One Volume By an Officer of the Expedition*. Yale Collection of Western Americana, Beineke Rare Book and Manuscript Library.
Colvocoresses, Harold. "Captain George Musulas Colvocoresses, U.S.N." *Washington Historical Quarterly*. Vol. XXV, No. 3. July, 1934.

Dyes, J.W. *Private Notes of J.W.W. Dyes, at Different Times & Places*. Handwritten journal. U.S. National Archives.
Elliott, Samuel B. *Journal of the Cruise of the U.S. Sloop Vincennes Flagship of the Ex. Expedition During the Years 1838, 39, 40, 41 & 42 Charles Wilkes Esqr., Commander*. Microfilm U.S. National Archives (Seattle) Box 91, Records Group 39, M-75, roll 17.
Erskine, Charles. *Twenty Years Before the Mast*. Washington, D.C.: Smithsonian Institution, 1985.
Haskett, Patrick J. *The Wilkes Expedition in Puget Sound — 1841*. Sponsored by the Resources Development Internship Program of the Western Interstate Commission for Higher Education and the State Capitol Museum, Olympia, WA. 1974.
Hitchman, Robert. *Place Names of Washington*. Washington State Historical Society, 1985.
Meany, Edmond S. *Diary of Wilkes in the Northwest*. Seattle: University of Washington Press, 1926.
Morgan, Murray. *Puget's Sound: A Narrative of Early Tacoma and the Southern Sound*. Seattle & London: University of Washington Press, 1979.
Phillips, James. *Washington State Place Names*. Seattle: University of Washington Press, 1976.
Sanford, Joseph Perry. (Untitled.) Sanford Journal. Microfilm U.S. National Archives (Seattle), Box 91, Records Group 39, M-75, roll 19.
Sinclair, George T. *The Journal of George T. Sinclair*. Microfilm U.S. National Archives (Seattle), Box 91, Records Group 39, M-75, roll 21.
Taylor, E.G.R., and M.W. Richey. *The Geometrical Seaman: A Book of Early Nautical Instruments*. Hollis & Carter for the Institute of Navigation, University Press, Cambridge, 1962.
Vancouver, George. *A Voyage of Discovery to the North Pacific Ocean, and Round the World in Which the Coast of North-West America Has Been Carefully Examined and Accurately Surveyed*. London: Printed for G.G. and J. Robinson, Paternoster-Row and J. Edwards, Pall-Mall, 1798.
Viola, Herman J., and Carolyn Margolis, editors; with the assistance of Jan S. Danis and Sharon D. Galperin. *Magnificent Voyagers, The U.S. Exploring Expedition, 1838–1842*. Washington, D.C.: Smithsonian Institution Press, 1985.
Wilkes, Charles. *Diary*. Microfilm U.S. National Archives (Seattle) Box 91, Records Group 39, M-75, roll 9.
_____. *Journal Kept by Charles Wilkes Commanding the Exploring Expedition*. Handwritten between 1838–1842.
_____. *United States Exploring Expedition During the years 1838, 1839, 1840, 1841, 1842*. Vol. 4. Philadelphia: Lea & Blanchard, 1845.
_____. *United States Exploring Expedition During the years 1838, 1839, 1840, 1841, 1842*. Vol. 23, Ch. 16. Philadelphia: Lea & Blanchard, 1845.
Wilkes charts, available electronically at *http://www.chartmaker.ncd.noaa.gov/csdl/mapcoll.htm*, courtesy of the NOAA.

Index

Active 215
Adie 55
Admiralty Head 85
Admiralty Inlet 15–18, 24, 35, 39, 45, 47, 72, 73, 83–88, 90–94, 96, 97, 105, 112, 143, 155, 200, 201, 203, 213, 218, 223, 228, 229, 244
Admiralty Sound 35, 161
Adolphus Island 74, 78
Agate, Alfred T. 93, 278
Agate Pass 36, 93, 176, 204, 205, 220
Agate Point 93
Ala Spit 84
Alden, James 2, 134, 172, 181, 209, 213–215, 219, 229, 231, 275
Alki Point 93
Allan, William Henry 82
Allan's Islet 82, 83
Allen, Charles 279
Allen Point 102
Allhouse, Joseph 279
Allshouse's Islet 99, 102
Amah Point 102
Anderson, Alexander Caufield 17, 19, 21, 23, 25, 27–30, 32, 34, 99, 100, 149, 163, 164, 165, 244, 266
Anderson Island 99, 101
Anna's Bay 106, 107, 109
Appletree Cove 171, 201, 228
Argus 74, 82
Argus Bay 73, 82, 112
Ariel 47, 85, 88, 135, 137, 147, 151, 238, 255
Ariel Point 85, 88
Armitage Island 76
Astoria 8, 18, 19, 23, 32, 41, 204
Ayoch's Point 106
Ayock Point 106
Ayres, John 110, 279
Ayres Point 110

Baadah Point 73
Bainbridge, William 3, 47

Bainbridge Island 47, 93, 94, 135, 143, 176, 177, 204–206, 210, 260
Balch Passage 101
Bare Island 78
Barkley, Charles W. 7
Barlow, Mr. 54, 64
Barnes Island 77
Barron, Samuel 94
Barron's Bay 94, 95
Basalt Point 89
Battle of Lake Erie 73, 77
Battleship Island 75
Beals, Artimus W. 96, 280
Bear 135
Beaver 16, 22, 99, 134, 150, 171, 172, 244, 256
Beckett Point 86
Bellingham, William 80
Bellingham Bay 39, 45, 79–81, 183, 185, 190, 210, 211, 222, 234
Bellingham Channel 211
Bells Chain 78
Ben Ure Island 83
Ben Ure Spit 84
Big Quilcene River 140
Big Teniff 83
Bill Point 92, 95
Birch Bay 39, 45, 78, 79, 112, 185–188, 211, 222, 223, 235, 236
Birch Point 79
Bird Rocks 63, 77
Biz Point 82
Black Creek 26, 106, 109, 163
Blake, George Smith 94
Blakeley Island 74–76
Blakely, Johnston 74, 94
Blakely Harbor 177, 204
Blake's Island 94, 95
Blossom Point 93
Blunden Island 78
Blunt, Simon F. 73, 278
Blunts Island 73, 84, 191, 223, 237

305

Bolin, Jacob 94, 280
Bolton, Mary Lynch 5
Bolton, William F. 108
Bolton Peninsula 108, 139
Bond, George 61
Bond, W.C. 61
Bond, Wm. Cranch 62
Boston 3
Boston Point 109
Bowditch, Nathaniel 3
Boxer 82, 135
Boxer Cove 82, 83
Brackenridge, J. D. 13, 18, 33, 99, 276
Brackenridge's Passage 99, 103
Bramblebluff Point 108
Bridgehaven 110
Brisco, William 104, 281
Brisco Point 104
Broad Spit 108
Brown, James 105, 282
Brown, John G. 76, 276
Browns Island 76
Browns Point 105, 110, 137
Buck Island 76
Budd, Thomas A. 22, 24, 29, 85, 144, 147, 149, 192, 266, 276
Budd Inlet 100
Budd's Harbor 29, 85, 86, 105, 112
Bull, John 245
Bull's Head 89
Bung Bluff 103
Burner Point 89
Burnie, Mr. 8
Burrard Inlet 22
Burrows, William 82
Burrows Bay 73
Burrow's Island 82
Bush Point 85
Bute Prairie 29

Cadborough 43, 256, 261, 266
Cadborrow 191
Cailess, Mr. 260
Cal-a-met 91
Camano Head 90, 179, 208
Camano Island 83, 84, 90, 210
Camp Point 87
Canal de Arro 40, 41, 72, 74, 77, 78, 112, 153, 185, 189–191, 223
Cape Disappointment 157, 268
Cape Flattery 5, 7, 8, 41, 43, 44, 70, 71, 110, 155, 157, 197, 240, 242, 249–251, 267, 269, 273
Cape Flattery Point 43
Cape George 86
Capsante 81
Carr, Overton 14, 22, 33, 98, 132, 261, 265, 275
Carr's Inlet 98, 99, 101–103, 112
Carr's Point 14, 86, 132

Carter, William 79, 282
Cascade Range of Mountains 18, 97, 270
Case, Augustus Ludlow 18, 22, 24–26, 28–30, 40, 45, 47, 50, 100, 109, 112, 131, 162, 176, 179, 215, 244, 257–260, 264, 265, 277
Case Bank 109
Case Inlet 100, 101, 103, 104, 142, 147
Case Shoal 137
Cerantes Rocks 72
Chauncey, Isaac 74
Chauncey Island 74–76, 82
Chesapeake 74, 77, 89
Chevalier, Mr. 52
Chick, Amos 246, 278
Chickeelees River 26, 33, 163, 166
Chinom Point 110
Clalam Indians 10, 25, 39, 133, 136, 140, 151, 154, 155, 160
Clark, John 77
Clark, Joseph 242, 282
Clark, Levin 82, 282
Clark Island 77, 210
Clarks Point 82
Classet 195, 196, 224, 241, 262, 267
Classet Indians 42, 43, 132, 155, 195, 273
Cole, Humphry 54
Col-see-ed Harbor 107, 108, 139
Columbia River 4–6, 18, 19, 22, 23, 26, 34, 36, 40, 41, 60, 111, 112, 141, 154, 155, 157, 163, 166, 178, 186, 193, 199, 221, 224, 238, 242, 245, 248, 249, 251, 254–256, 258, 259, 261, 262, 268, 273, 276–279, 285
Colvocoresses, Constantine 156
Colvocoresses, George W. 22, 34, 47, 89, 95, 138, 156, 248, 265, 278
Colvo's Passage 134, 203, 213
Colvos Point 135
Colvos Rocks 89
Commencement Bay 35, 97, 112, 174, 201, 202, 220
Cone Hill 81
Cone Islets 81
Constitution 47, 74, 81
Cook, John 105
Cook Point 105
Cooper, John 103, 105, 283
Coopers Point 103
Cowlitz Farms 23, 28
Cowlitz River 23, 41
Crane Point 87
Craven, Thomas T. 87, 275
Craven Peninsula 87, 88
Crescent Harbor 91
Cummings, W.H. 106, 283
Cutts Island 102

Dabob Bay 139
Dabop Bay 107, 108, 110, 139
Dadah Point 110
Daisy Bluff 86

Index

Dalco Passage 96
Dana, James Dwight 100, 277
Dana's Passage 100, 105
Daniell, John 55
Days, Stephen W. 99, 284
Day's Island 99
de Borda, Chevalier 52
Decatur Island 74–76, 210
Decatur, Stephen 74–76
Deception Island 83, 212, 213, 234
Deception Pass 38, 45, 83, 84, 112, 181–184, 209, 222, 233, 234
de Eliza, Juan Francisco 80
de Fuca, Strait of Juan 6, 8, 17, 40, 42, 45, 70, 72, 75–77, 112, 155, 168, 198, 200, 216, 224, 242, 243, 249–251, 264, 269
de Fuca's Pillar 45
Dennis Shoal 83
Dents, Mr. 52
Destruction Isle 7, 197, 269
Destruction River 7
Destruction Rocks 157, 216
Devils Head 103
Dewatto Bay 110
Diamond Point 86
Dickerson, Mahlon 4, 87, 105
Dickerson Peninsula 4, 87, 88
Dickerson Point 4, 105
Dines Point 93
Disney, Solomon 78
Dofflemeyer Point 105
Dolphin 135, 235
Dosewallips 109
Dosewallips River 140
Dot Island 81, 82
Double Bluff 85
Double Point 87
Doughty, John 75, 284
Douglas Island 78
Drayton, Joseph 18, 23, 78, 101, 245, 255, 265, 276
Drayton Bay 78, 79, 112
Drayton Harbor 78
Drayton's Passage 101, 103
Duck Harbor 92
Duckabush 109
Duncan Rock 63, 71, 72, 197
Duncan's Bay 91
Dungeness 10, 35, 39–41, 45, 72, 73, 85, 86, 112, 154, 192, 198, 213, 223, 224, 239
Duntze Rock 71
Duquamish Indians 133
Duwamish Head 93
Dyes, John W.W. 94, 246, 263, 276
Dye's Inlet 94, 95, 204

Eagle 94, 135, 230, 231, 234, 235
Eagle, Henry 94
Eagle Cliff 81
Eagle Harbor 94, 95, 177, 204

Eagle Island 101
East Bluff 86
East Point 77, 78, 92, 203
Edmund Group 78
Edwards Point 92
Eel, Mr. 165
Eld, Henry 22, 29, 33, 34, 47, 100, 166, 218, 248, 266, 277
Eld's Inlet 100, 105
Elephant 135
Eliza Island 80
Elliott, Rev. J.L. 92
Elliott, Samuel B. 91, 92, 191, 225, 276
Elliott Bay 92, 93, 178, 201
Emerson Island 211
Enterprise 82
Ertel, Mr. 52, 53

Fairfield 3
Farmer, Moses G. 62
Fidalgo Island 73, 205, 207, 233
Fisherman Harbor 138
Fishermans Point 109
Fishing Bay 77
Flag Point 87, 88
Flat Top Island 78
Flattery Islands 167
Flattery Rocks 157, 197
Flounder Bay 82
Flying Fish 4, 18, 34, 40, 193, 201, 220, 270
Forbes Point 91
Fort Erie 73
Fort Langley 39, 40, 111, 186
Fort Nisqually 14, 16, 18, 27, 100, 105, 163, 271
Fort Vancouver 18, 20, 256, 259
Fosdick, Stephen 98, 285
Fox 135
Fox, Dr. 27
Fox, J.L. 98, 275
Fox's Island 98, 99, 102, 103, 105
Franklin 3
Fraser River 39, 40, 45, 180, 185–187
Fraunhofer, Mr. 52, 53
Freeman, J.D. 75, 277
Freemans Island 75
Frenchmans Point 108
Fresh-water Creek 91
Fritz Point 75
Frodsham, Charles 52, 56
Frolic 74
Frolic Straits 75, 76
Frost, John 76, 278
Frost Island 76

Gambey, Mr. 52–55
Gamble, Robert 106
Gardner, Alan 90
Gedney, Jonathan Haight 91
Gedney, Thomas R. 91
Gedney's Island 91, 207, 221, 233

Index

Geese Islets 76
General Pike 74
Gibson, James H. 99, 286
Gig Harbor 63, 97, 162, 171, 173, 202, 219, 254
Gillis, James M. 62
Glen Cove 87, 102
Glover, John 95
Gonzales Point 77
Gooch Island 77
Goose Point 101
Gordon Island 74, 78
Gordon Point 105
Gourd Island 77
Graham Point 104
Gray's Harbour 33, 112, 155
Great Peninsula 90, 93–95, 98, 101–103
Green, Daniel 102, 286
Gregory, Captain 4
Grenville Rock 251
Greyhound 135, 188, 189–191, 235
Griffin Bay 75
Guemes Channel 81
Guemes Island 74, 80, 81, 210, 211
Guerriere 3, 74
Guerriere Bay 74
Gull Harbor 105
Gull Rock 74
Gunter, Edmund 55

Hale, Horatio 79, 277
Hale's Passage 79, 98, 102, 185
Hallets Cove 89
Halsey, Eliza F. 156
Hamma Hamma River 106
Hammersly, George W. 101, 147, 148, 279
Hammersly Inlet 101, 105
Hammond, Henry 78, 287
Harbor of Scabock 106, 107, 112
Harden, Thomas 246, 257, 287
Hardwick Point 87
Harmon, John 97, 287
Harney Channel 75
Harris, Alvin 97, 287
Hartstein, H.J. 100, 278
Hartstene Island 100, 104
Haskuse Point 102
Hat Island 82
Hautboy Islet 80, 81
Hazel Point 110
Heath, Mr. 134, 228, 254
Heke Point 88
Helix Point 86
Henderson, James 97, 100, 165, 288
Henderson Bay 102
Henderson Inlet 100, 105
Henry, Wilkes 77, 277
Henry Island 75, 77
Herron, Lewis 95, 101, 288
Herron Island 101, 103
Heyer, Henry R. 96, 97, 288

Heyers Point 96
Hogun-maru 7
Hoh River 7
Hoipus Point 84
Holmes, Dr. 36, 38, 204
Holmes, Silas 83, 277
Holmes Harbor 83, 90–92, 112, 179, 208
Hood Point 106
Hood's Canal 16–18, 24–26, 29, 35, 40, 45, 47, 48, 89, 90, 100, 105–108, 112, 134–136, 143, 144, 152, 155, 162, 176, 179, 200, 207, 213, 214, 244, 248, 257, 258, 270
Hoo-et-zen Harbor 106, 108
Hope Island 100, 105
Hope Islet 83, 84
Hornet 80, 81
Hornet Harbor 81, 82, 112
Horsehead Bay 102
Huckleberry Island 81, 82
Hudson, Captain 18, 34, 68, 155, 195, 201, 261, 276
Hudson, William L. 15, 277
Hudson Bay Company 7–9, 11, 13, 16, 20–22, 31, 39, 41, 43, 45, 71, 99, 111, 160–163, 165, 201, 244, 247, 248, 252, 256, 266, 269
Hudson River 16, 90
Hull, Isaac 74
Hull Island 74–77
Hunot Point 84
Hyde, William 103, 289
Hyde Point 103

Ihikum Cove 102
Imperial Eagle 7
Independence 3
Indian Head 85
Indian Island 87
Ironsides Bay 74, 75
Ironsides Inlet 76
Isla de Dolores 7
Itsami Shoal 105

Jack Point 87
Jack's Island 80, 82, 100, 104, 105
Jackson Cove 106, 108, 139
James, Reuben 76
James's Island 76
Java 47
Java Head 77
Je-ach-tac Indians 36
Jefferson, President Thomas 93
John Adams 215
John's Island 77
Johnson, Robert E. 18, 23, 31, 33, 35, 134, 162, 165, 166, 172, 191, 245, 255, 259, 275
Johnson Point 100
Johnson's Straits 40, 111
Johnstone Strait 40, 111, 194
Jones, Jacob 74, 76
Jones, Mr. 52, 55, 56

Jones, Thomas Ap Catesby 4, 51
Jones, William 53
Jones Island 74, 75
Jones's Bluff 89
Jupiter Hills 109

Kakua 110
Kala Point 87
Kalamut Island 91
Kalila Point 103
Kanem Point 10, 86
Kaset Rock 72
Kater, Mr. 64
Kearney, Captain 4
Kellett, Henry 2, 42
Kellum, John 110, 142, 290
Kellums Lake 110
Ketners Point 102
Ketron Island 31, 99, 100
Ketslum Islet 83
Kiapot Point 86
Kiket Islet 83
Kilisut Harbor 87, 88, 170
Killinas Lake 110
King Spit 105
Kinney Point 88, 89
Kitron's Island 31
Kittson, William 31
Klachopis Point 71
Klas Rock 89
Klasset 169
Koitlah Point 42
Kopo Point 104
Kosa Point 105
Kosa River 96
Kula Kalo Point 85
Kula Point 87
Kuwo Point 79
Kwaatz Point 100

Lake Erie 73, 77
Lake Ontario 75
Langley Point 82
Lawrence, James 16, 74, 77, 80, 81
Lawrence Head 81, 82
Lawrence Island 74, 80–83, 211
Lawrences Bay 201, 205–207, 213
Leku Beach 88
Leopard 135
Levant 81
Levant Passage 81, 82
Liberty Bay 94, 176, 205, 206
Lighthouse Point 182
Lincoln, President Abraham 5
Lion 135
Liplip Point 88, 90
Little Belt 74, 75
Little Belt Passage 75
Little Tenif Islet 83, 84
Lizard 135

Llama 7
Lloyd, Mr. 52
Loa Point 100
Long Island 76
Lopez Island 74
Lopez Sound 75
Lowell, James 90
Ludlow, Augustus C. 89
Lummi Island 76
Lummi Peninsula 185
Lyle Point 101
Lynch, William Francis 106
Lynch Cove 106, 107, 109, 110, 142

MacDonough, Thomas 81, 83
Macedonian 75
Macedonian Crescent 75
Makah Indians 42, 153
Makak Point 107
Makomek Point 71
Mane Cove 104
Manhait Point 103
March Point 82, 210
Margarita 156
Marrowstone Island 87, 170
Marrowstone Point 87, 88
Massey, Edward 54
Matia Island 78
Maury, William L. 36, 84, 96, 175, 179, 181, 183, 185, 205, 207, 209, 210, 220–222, 230–232, 234, 275
Maury's Island 96, 97
Maurys Point 84
May, William 40, 47, 74, 94, 138, 143, 154, 264, 265, 275
Mayer, Johann Tobias 52
Mayo Cove 102
May's Inlet 94
McDonough Island 90
McKean, John 246
McLaughlin, Dr. John 77
McLaughlin Island 77
McLean, Mr. 256
McMicken Passage 104
McNeal, Captain 172, 244, 264
McNeill, William Henry 99, 254
M'Donough Island 83, 210
Meares, John 1
Meyer, Mr. 52, 53
Middle Channel 75
Middle Point 92
Midille Point 87
Migley, William 79, 92, 292
Mill Point 86
Misery Point 107
Mission Beach 92
Mission Prairie 26
M'Laughlin, Dr. John 20, 28, 147
M'Laughlin Island 79, 80
M'Niel, Captain 7, 16, 17, 19, 21, 22, 27, 34

Index

M'Niel Island 99–101, 103
Monroe, President James 93
Moody, William 97, 100, 293
Moolyneux, Mr. 52
Morse, William H. 75, 278
Morses Cove 76
Morses Island 75
Mount Baker 15, 161
Mount Constitution 74, 75
Mount Erie 73, 82, 83
Mount Hood 21, 28, 272
Mount Olympus 8, 18, 25, 26, 72, 139, 162
Mummy Rocks 76
Murray, James 56
Musam Place 108
Mush Rock 72
Musqueti 106

Nadlum 288, 194
Naguamos Island 84
Naika Point 108
Nanitch Indians 39
The Narrows 17, 34, 35, 45, 47, 95, 97–99, 112, 134, 135, 143, 145, 149, 152, 172, 201, 229, 231, 238
Nasqually 134, 136, 142, 148, 155, 171, 172, 178, 187, 188, 193, 195, 218, 220, 228, 229, 244, 248
Nasqually Indians 143, 147–150
Navy Archipelago 74, 75
Neah Bay 42, 71
Neah Harbour 8, 41, 198, 273
Neah Island 42, 44, 71, 273
Nearns Point 102
Ned Islet 101
Neelim Bay 142
Neill, William 96, 97, 293
Newell, Mr. 256, 260
Nightingale 135
Nimrod Point 102
Nipple Point 82
Nisqually 13, 17, 18, 20, 21, 24, 26, 28, 30–32, 35, 40, 41, 48, 99–101, 149, 155, 161–163, 165, 197, 204, 213, 261–263, 269, 270, 273
Nisqually Bay 270
Nisqually Bluff 99
Nisqually Falls 35
Nisqually Flats 100
Nisqually Harbour 45, 47
Nisqually Head 100
Nisqually River 17, 100
Nodule Point 88
Noon Island 77
Nootka Sound 40
North, James 86
North Bluff 86, 92
Norths Landing 92
Northwest Company 43
Nuhomish Indians 151, 155
Nu-ko-lo-wah creek 138

Nukolowap Point 105, 107, 108
Numan Point 102, 103

Oak Head 105
Obstruction Island 75
O'Cain 3
Old Ironsides 74
Old Man House 36, 206
Olele Point 88, 89
Olo Bluff 109
Oluman Bluff 87
O'Neal Island 76
Ontario Roads 75
Orcas Island 74, 75, 78
Oregon 4
Oro, Bay of 101
Ostrich Bay 95
Ot-sl (war canoe) 101
Otso Point 101
Owen Point 71

Palisi Point 109
Park, David 103, 294
Park Point 103
Parker, George 75, 294
Parker Reef 78
Parkers Rock 75
Parkinson, Mr. 52, 56
Partridge, Aaron 151
Partridge, Alden 151
Partridge, Mary 151
Pass Island 83
Patos Island 77
Paulding, J.K. 4
Paun Cove 104
Peacock 4, 18, 19, 21, 27, 28, 34, 40, 41, 63, 67, 82, 154, 165, 178, 187, 193, 195, 201, 207, 220, 224, 238, 245, 254, 258, 259, 261, 273
Peacock Island 82
Peale, Titian R. 100
Peale's Passage 100
Peapod Rocks 77
Pearl Island 75
Pelican 82
Penguin 80
Penguin Harbor 80–82, 211
Penns Cove 36, 37, 83, 84, 90–92, 112, 180, 181, 194, 208, 209, 221, 232, 233
Penrose Point 102
Percival, John 74
Percival Island 74, 78
Perry, Oliver Hazard 73
Perry's Island 73, 74, 76, 81–83, 204, 207, 208, 233
Pickering, Charles 18, 100, 245, 255, 276
Pickering Passage 100, 104, 147
Pilash Point 108
Pilot 47, 135, 137, 143, 144, 147, 151–153, 238, 255
Pilot Point 16, 218

Pilot's Cove 16, 90, 92, 93, 112, 134, 161, 171, 200, 228, 253
Piner, Thomas 97, 294
Piners Point 93
Pippin Point 93
Pit Island 103
Pitship Point 14, 86
Pleasant Harbor 107, 109
Poi Point 104
Poinsett, Joel R. 4
Point Allen 90, 179, 208, 210
Point Angeles 72
Point Beals 96
Point Bolin 94
Point Carrol 87
Point Carter 79, 80
Point Cooper 105
Point Crowlie 106
Point Cummings 106
Point Dalco 96
Point Defiance 97
Point Demock 84
Point Disney 78
Point Dougal 104
Point Doughty 75
Point Dungeness 72, 132, 151, 158, 169, 191, 192, 213, 248, 273
Point Edmund 92
Point Elliott 91
Point Fosdick 98
Point Francis 80
Point Gibson 99, 103, 105
Point Glover 95
Point Gonzalo 77
Point Gorden 95
Point Green 63, 102
Point Grenville 7, 269
Point Hammond 78
Point Hannon 107
Point Harmon 97
Point Harris 97
Point Herron 95
Point Hilcome 42
Point Hudson 15, 86, 87, 153, 193, 200, 224
Point Jefferson 93
Point Julia 107, 137
Point Kanawi 89
Point Kilcome 42
Point Lawrence 77
Point Leavitt 85
Point Lewhough 73
Point Lloyd 76
Point Lowell 90
Point Maury 92
Point M'Leod 111
Point Migley 79, 92
Point Migly 79
Point Monroe 93
Point Moody 100, 105
Point Moore 93

Point Musquiti 106
Point Neelim 106, 109, 141, 142, 144
Point Neill 96
Point Newell 72, 73
Point-No-Point 90
Point Partridge 84, 85, 91, 151, 191, 194, 200
Point Peter 96
Point Peters 110
Point Polnell 84, 90, 91
Point Pulley 96
Point Rand 93
Point Richmond 96
Point Ringgold 87, 88
Point Roberts 39, 78, 79, 93, 112, 186–188, 212, 222, 235, 236, 265
Point Robinson 97
Point Salisbury 107
Point Salsbury 76
Point Sanford 96
Point Southworth 64, 96
Point Squho 104
Point Tala 89
Point Termination 107, 109
Point Thompson 75
Point Treble 101
Point Turner 95
Point Washington 93
Point Watmaugh 76
Point Wells 92
Point White 223
Point Whitehorn 79
Point William 80, 82, 211
Point Williams 92, 96
Point Wilson 15, 45, 64, 76, 86, 90, 104, 134, 151, 153, 194, 200
Point Yakso 108
The Pointers 76
Pole Island 75
Polnell, John 90, 294
Porpoise 4–6, 14, 17, 18, 34, 35, 38–41, 44, 47, 48, 82, 133, 135, 151–155, 158, 162, 177, 182, 197, 202, 206, 207, 213, 216, 218, 219, 227–229, 233, 238–241, 248, 250, 251, 253–255, 261, 262, 270
Porpoise Rocks 82
Port Blakely 94
Port Gamble 106, 107, 112, 137
Port Gardner 37, 83, 90–92, 112, 183, 221
Port Lawrence 16, 35, 47, 87–89, 112, 134, 136, 201, 228
Port Ludlow 89, 106, 112, 136
Port Madison 16, 36, 90, 93, 94, 112, 134, 143, 171, 176, 178, 179, 201, 204, 205, 207, 213, 220, 231, 232, 254
Port Nunez Gaona 42
Port San Juan 41
Port Scarborough 41, 42, 71
Port Susan 83, 90, 91, 112, 179, 183, 207, 208, 210, 221
Port Townsend 15, 40, 45, 86–88, 112, 134, 155,

161, 170, 192, 194, 200, 213, 217, 223, 228, 232, 253, 261
Port Townsend Canal 87, 88
Port Townshend 86–88, 200, 213, 217
Port Washington Narrows 204
Port Williams 85
Portage 100, 105, 142, 147, 175, 181, 194, 203, 220
Portage Bay 185
Portage Channel 185
Portage Island 185
Potlatch Point 105, 106, 141
Powie Point 102
President 74
President Channel 74, 78
President's Passage 74, 76
Priest Point 92
Protection Island 10, 40, 86, 132–134, 169, 191, 192, 199, 200, 217, 243, 244, 252, 261
Puffin Island 78
Pugallop 35, 97
Puget, Peter 203
Puget Sound 1, 5, 13, 17, 24, 26, 28, 29, 33, 47, 90, 98, 99, 101, 112, 132, 134, 135, 142, 143, 147, 149, 150, 155, 157, 163, 164, 171, 172, 176–178, 201, 203, 213, 223, 242, 244, 248, 270, 272, 273
Puget Sound Company 20
Puki Cove 102
Pulali Point 108
Pulley, Robert 96, 294
Puyallup 35, 97, 101, 174
Puyallup River 174, 203

Quadra and Vancouver Island 45, 46, 195
Quadra Point 71
Quadra, Juan Francisco de la Bodega y 7
Quarter Master Cove 93
Quarter-Master's Harbor 96
Quatsap Point 106, 109, 110, 144, 145
Quilcene Bay 107, 139
Quimper Peninsula 87
Qulam Point 105
Quo-eet-la 42
Quoitlandt Indians 186

Raft Island 99
Raindeer Point 83
Reach Island 104
Red Bluff 79, 85, 86
Reservation Head 84
Restoration Point 95, 203
Reynolds, Lydia 219, 276
Reynolds, William 219, 276
Rich, William 94, 278
Richmond, Dr. 19, 28, 146, 150, 244, 246, 247, 249, 264
Richmond, William 96, 295
Rich's Passage 94, 95
Ringgold, Cadwalader 18, 24, 34, 35, 38, 39, 45, 47, 48, 73, 88, 135, 170, 196, 222, 278
Ringgold's Channel 73–76, 79–82, 112
Robinson, John 97, 295
Robinson, Mr. 55
Robinson, R.P. 245, 250, 276
Rocky Point 84, 92, 104, 179
Rodgers, John 74
Rodgers Island 74–76
Rosario Head 84
Rosario Strait 73
Rose Point 108
Rover 135, 179, 188, 194, 212, 222, 232, 235, 236, 253

Sachem Point 82
Sachet Indians 36–39
Saddlebag Island 81, 82, 210
Sahomish Indians 179
Sail Point 86
Sail Rock 43, 73
Sail Rock Point 71, 73
Sakali Bluff 110
Salmon Point 104
Salom Point 104
Salsbury, Frances 76, 81, 296
Salsbury Point 81
Samego Point 103
Samum Point 107
San Jacinto 5
San Juan Channel 74, 75
San Juan Island 74
San Juan Islands 1, 2, 74
San Juan River 72
San Juan Point 71
Sandy Point 79, 86, 92, 103, 105, 106
Sanford, Joseph Perry 96, 97, 134, 172, 177, 179, 183, 188, 191, 194, 197, 200, 201, 203–207, 210, 211, 213, 222, 224
Sanford, Thomas 82
Sanford Cove 82
Sanum 107
Sapip Point 87
Saratoga 81, 83, 91
Saratoga Passage 81, 83, 84, 90, 91
Sares, Henry 82, 296
Sares Head 82
Sare's Point 82
Saringa Point 105
Sawash Point 185
Scabock Point 106, 108
Scarborough, Captain James 71, 186, 256
Scarborough Harbor 71–73, 112, 155, 195, 196, 240
Scatchel Point 92
Scatchet's Head 84, 85
Schoolhouse Point 86
Scocomish Indians 24, 25, 39, 141–143, 155
Scorpus Point 86
Scott, Thomas 97, 102, 296
Scott Point 102

Sea Gull 4
Seabeck 106, 138
Seal Rock 73
Seatjack Indians 177, 179, 180, 182, 194
Seattle, Chief 36
Seaver, Benjamin 61
Semiahmoo Bay 78
Sentinel Rocks 64, 75
Seocomish Indians 138
Sequim Bay 14, 85, 192
Seton, Elizabeth 3
Seton, Mary 3
Shannon 74, 89
Shark 135, 175, 177, 188, 194, 230, 231, 235
Shaw, Captain John D. 74
Shaw Island 74
Ship Point 88, 89
Shubrick, Commodore 4
Shute's River Falls 29
Siki Point 72
Sikwa Point 102, 103
Silipo Island 102
Similk Bay 84
Sinclair, Arthur 74
Sinclair, George T. 94, 167, 169, 182, 185, 192, 204, 209, 277
Sinclair Island 74, 76, 77, 80, 81, 209, 211
Sinclair's Inlet 94
Sister Rocks 107
Sisters 77
Sister's Point 106
Skagit Island 97
Skait Islet 83
Skip Jack Island 64, 78
Skokomish River 106, 142
Slavis Point 102
Slik Point 109
Smith Cove 93
Smith Island 73, 191, 213, 223, 237
Snake Rock 89
Snas Point 89
Snatelum Point 84, 209
Snohomish River 37, 91
Sonora 7
Sota Point 104
South Bluff 92
South Head 102
South Point 107, 110
Southworth, Edward 96, 97, 297
Spak Point 86
Spieden, William 77, 277
Spieden Island 75, 77
Squaller's Point 105
Squamish Head 107
Squamish Indians 106, 163, 185
Squaxin Island 100, 104
Stam Islet 83, 84
Stau Point 104
Steamboat Island 105
Stearns, T.A. 33, 245, 255

Stearns, Simon A. 248
Sterns, Simon 298
Stoku Point 104
Strawberry Bay 80, 81, 112, 185, 190, 211, 213, 223, 235, 237
Strawberry Island 80, 83
Stretch, Samuel 101, 104, 298
Stretch Island 101, 104
Stuart, Frederick D. 77, 277
Stuart Island 77
Stui Island 104
Suk-wa-bish 90, 106
Sunset Beach 105
Suqualus Point 110
Suquamish Harbor 37, 106, 107, 109, 112, 137
Suquamish Head 90, 105
Suquamish Indians 25, 39, 134, 135–139, 143, 151, 153, 155, 188
Sutton Head 81, 82
Swasey, Adaline M. 156
Swinomish Channel 39, 81, 83, 210, 222
Sylopash Point 108
Syral Point 89

Tabook Point 110
Tahali Point 104
Takup Point 86
Tala Point 64, 87
Talapais Point 104
Talie Bay 102
Tatouche Indians 43, 44
Tatsolo Point 105
Tchinom Point 110
Tekiu Point 110
Teko Point 102
Thatcher Pass 75
Thompson, Matthew 75, 299
Three Tree Point 96
Tit Point 89
Tlobish 140
Toandos Indians 24, 25, 145, 163
Toandos Peninsula 25, 105, 108, 110, 138
Tokano Islets 84
Toliva Shoal 99
Tomos Point 102
Tom's Islet 101
Tongue Point 79
Torricelli, Mr. 55
Tosi Point 84
Totten, George 22, 47, 100, 107, 135, 138, 144, 147, 151, 152, 154, 213, 263–266, 276
Totten Inlet 100, 105
Totten's Point 107
Towhead Island 81
Travis Spit 86
Tremble, George 101, 299
Trent 5
Triangle Cove 90
Triton 135, 147, 151, 238
Triton Head 106, 110

Troughton, Edward 52–55
Tsiko Point 101
Tskulusco Point 108
Tskutska Point 25, 138, 140, 163
Tskutsko Point 25, 108, 138
Tuber Point 93
Tucksel Point 105
Tulalip Bay 92
Tule Point 104
Tumbo Island 78
Turku Point 101
Turn Island 76
Turner, Henry 95, 299
Turtle 135
Tzee-sa-ted 107
Tzu-sa-ted Cove 107, 110, 112

United States 156
Unsal Point 105
Upright Channel 75
Upright Head 76
Useless Bay 85, 188

Van Buren, President 4
Vancouver, George 1, 7, 8, 10, 15, 16, 26, 35, 38, 40, 42, 80, 94, 98, 109, 132, 133, 139, 141, 164, 169–171, 175, 176, 181, 183–186, 192, 193, 198–200, 203, 206, 208, 211, 217, 221, 223, 225, 228, 243, 244, 252, 260
Vancouver Island 40, 41, 45, 46, 53, 70, 72, 77, 150, 155, 185, 186, 189, 195, 224, 262, 267, 269
Vanderford, Benjamin 98, 146, 246, 258, 271, 276
Vanderford's Harbor 98, 101
Vashon Island 17, 34, 35, 45, 47, 95–97, 134, 135, 174, 175, 178, 203, 220, 230, 260
Vashons Point 96
Vendovi 9, 26, 80, 146, 164, 269, 271
Vendovi Island 80, 211
Village Point 73
Vincennes 4, 5, 13, 17, 18, 27, 33, 34, 39, 41, 45, 47, 50, 64, 67, 71, 100, 159, 164, 167, 168, 172, 173, 187, 188, 190–193, 195–197, 213, 222–224, 226, 229, 230, 236–238, 246, 268, 270, 271
Violet Point 86
Viti Rocks 64, 79, 80
Von Geldern Cove 102

Wa Wa, Chief Patty 257
Wa wa Point 103
Waadah Island 42, 71

Wade, Thomas 229
Walan Entrance 88
Walan Point 87, 88
Waldron, Thomas W. 18, 23, 41, 77, 155, 172, 191, 195, 245, 255, 258, 265, 278
Waldron Island 77, 78
Walker, Mr. 165
War of 1812 47, 73–77, 80–83, 85, 88, 89, 91, 94, 106
Washington 74
Wasp 74, 76, 94
Wasp Islets 76
Waterwitch 3
Watmough, John Goddard 73
Watmaugh Head 73, 82
Watsak Point 84
Watsok Island 84
Weaverline Spit 95
Weewa Point 108
Weh-Weh Point 87
Wells, William 92, 300
Wepusec Inlet 105
West Point 84, 92, 93
Westsound 74
Whale Rocks 76
Whidbey Island 84, 85, 92, 98, 179, 181, 183, 194, 200, 213
White, James 223, 300
White Handkerchief 135, 238, 266
Whitehorn, Daniel 27, 79, 146, 164, 246, 247, 259, 265, 266, 272, 300
Wikat Point 107
Wilkes, John Deponthieu 3
Williams, Samuel 96, 248, 273, 301
Williamson, John G. 71, 276
Williamson Rocks 71, 82, 83
Wilson, Mr. & Mrs. 19, 244, 254, 264, 269
Wilson, Thomas 104, 301
Wing Point 95
Wollochet Bay 98, 101
Work, John 17
Wyckoff Shoal 103

Yawa Island 104
Yokeko Point 84, 182
Yomen Point 101
Young, Ewing 82
Young's Islet 82
Yukon Harbor 94
Yulkat Bluff 109

Zelatched Point 110, 139

www.ingramcontent.com/pod-product-compliance
Lightning Source LLC
Chambersburg PA
CBHW051209300426
44116CB00006B/487